WHEN
I SURVEY....

WHEN
I SURVEY....

A Lenten Anthology

by

Herman Hoeksema

REFORMED FREE PUBLISHING ASSOCIATION
Grand Rapids, Michigan

Library of Congress Catalog Card No. 76-57122
ISBN 0-916206-15-7

Printed in the United States of America

FOREWORD

This volume is a collection of six smaller works of the author. All of the latter were devoted to a specific aspect of the suffering and death of our Lord Jesus Christ, and they had originally been radio messages delivered during Lent. The author always followed the custom in the church which he served of devoting one sermon a Sunday during Lent to special contemplation of Christ's passion and death. In his radio messages on his church's broadcast, the Reformed Witness Hour, he followed the same custom. And although this was not mandatory, the author welcomed the opportunity which this season afforded to "survey the wondrous cross" in a special way.

The original six volumes, published between 1943 and 1956, have long been out of print; and some of them have been virtually unavailable for many years. Since these books enjoyed a rather wide reception when they were first published, and since their content is as fresh today as when they first appeared, it was decided to make them available in one large volume.

The title of this anthology, taken from Isaac Watts' hymn, is not of the author's choosing; and yet it' is. For on numerous occasions, both in the pulpit and in his radio messages, he would quote the stanzas of what was probably his favorite hymn in connection with his sermons. What could be more appropriate, therefore, than to include all of these Lenten meditations under the title, *When I Survey . . . . ?*

—Homer C. Hoeksema

CONTENTS

BOOK ONE

THE

AMAZING CROSS

Part I:
Amazing Judgment

CHAPTER 1

The Judgment of the World

Now is the judgment of this world. — JOHN 12:31.

"Now is the judgment of this world; now shall the prince of this world be cast out." These words were spoken by our Lord only a few days before His final suffering and death on the cross. In fact, they were spoken specifically with a view to that death. It was the first day of that final week of Jesus' public ministry, the day on which He had made His royal entry into Jerusalem in fulfillment of Zechariah's well known prophecy: "Fear not, daughter of Sion: behold thy king cometh, sitting on an ass's colt." In those last days, more crowded with events than any other part of Jesus' ministry, all things clearly pointed to the Saviour's death. The day before, at the supper they had prepared for Him at Bethany, in the home of Lazarus, Mary had prophesied of His approaching end, when she anointed Jesus' feet with the precious spikenard which she had kept "against the day of His burying." John 12:7. Spurred on in their evil designs by the apparent popularity of the Saviour which seemed to have reached a new climax through the raising of Lazarus from the dead, and which revealed itself in the enthusiastic acclamations with which the multitude accompanied Him on His royal entry into the holy city, the chief priests consulted to kill, not only Him, but also Lazarus. In the request of the Greeks that had come to worship at the feast to see Jesus, the

1

Lord evidently beholds a sign of the fulfillment of the promise
that He would see His seed, when His soul should have been
made an offering for sin, Isa. 53:10; for in connection with this
incident the Lord says: "The hour is come that the Son of man
should be glorified. Verily, verily, I say unto you, Except a corn
of wheat fall into the ground and die, it abideth alone: but if it
die, it bringeth forth much fruit." Indeed, the Lord was that corn
of wheat that must needs fall into the ground and die, before
it could bring forth fruit at all. And being conscious of this, and
the shadow of the cross creeping over His soul that moment, He
cries out: "Now is my soul troubled; and what shall I say?
Father, save me from this hour; but for this cause came I unto
this hour. Father, glorify thy name." John 12:20-29. O, indeed,
it was "the hour," the hour in which God would be glorified
through the death of His Son. And with a view to that hour the
Lord solemnly declares: "Now is the judgment of this world;
now shall the prince of this world be cast out." vs. 31.

Strangely unreal and contrary to fact these words sound from
the lips of our Lord at this moment. "Now is the judgment of
this world!" But how could He speak thus, and that, too, at this
time, and with direct reference to that moment? Did not the day of
the judgment of this world appear far off, farther, in fact, than
ever before? Did not the prince of this world seem more firmly
established on his throne than ever before? Was not the truth
of the matter rather the exact opposite from that which Jesus
here so solemnly and confidently declared? Would not the whole
world, presided over by its wicked prince, sit in judgment over
the Son of man, and would they not have the complete and final
victory over Him? Or did not our Saviour know what awaited
Him in this hour? Already the leaders of the Jews took counsel
together, how they might kill Him. Another day or two, and one
of His own disciples would covenant with the enemy for thirty
pieces of silver to betray Him. The night was not far off, when
they would come against Him with swords and staves, and would
take Him captive, forsaken even by the offended disciples. He
was to be brought before the Jewish council, not, indeed, as the
judge, but as the judged, accused, maltreated, blindfolded, buffeted,
spit upon, the helpless and powerless object of their furious hatred.

Before the Roman governor He was to appear, indicted as a malefactor, a common rebel, who incited the people to insurrection
against Caesar. He was to be subjected to Herod's cruel and cowardly mockery; to the contempt and reproach of the Roman soldiers: the purple robe, the crown of thorns, the mock sceptre;
to the shame of being rejected in favor of a common criminal.
And He was to be condemned to the shameful death of the cross,
nailed to the accursed tree as a public spectacle, exposed to the
reproach of the whole world. Did not the Lord know? O, but He
did! He saw the way that stretched itself before Him in all its
horror! And yet, quite contrary to all external appearances, He
solemnly declares: "Now is the judgment of this world; now shall
the prince of this world be cast out!"

Thus, then, it must be. What was historically, as men view
the events of this world, the trial by the world of Jesus, was in
reality the trial of the world by God. What was to all appearances
the condemnation of the Son of man by the tribunal of the world,
was in deepest reality the condemnation of the world before the
tribunal of the Judge of heaven and earth. Nineteen hundred years
ago, more definitely speaking in "the hour" of Jesus, in that brief
period when the Christ of God was tried, condemned, crucified
by the rulers of this world, the world stood very really in judgment
before God, was tried and condemned. True, there will come a
final day, a day of the revelation of the righteous judgment of God,
when all that is implied in the judgment of the cross shall be publicly verified and exposed; but that does not alter the fact that in
a very real sense of the word the judgment of the world has already
become a fact through the death and resurrection of the Lord
Jesus Christ from the dead. And we must understand and believe
this truth. The world is already, and irrevocably condemned. The
prince of this world has already been utterly cast out. And in the
midst of this condemned world with its deposed prince, we must
take shelter by faith in the shadow of the cross, and take hold
of the justifying power of the resurrection, that we may be saved!
And for a few Sundays of this Lenten season we will, the Lord
willing, stand by and watch some of the chief episodes in this
judgment of the world.

In this judgment, then, God appears as Judge, and the world

is summoned before the bar of His justice as the defendant. But what is this world of which the Lord speaks here? The word "world" does not always denote the same thing in Scripture. You cannot quote the Bible at random on this point, as many do, and explain as if "world" simply means the same as "all men." In the main, we may say that the Word of God speaks of two quite distinct and totally different worlds. The one is God's world, the other is fallen man's world. A glance at some of the passages in which the word occurs will at once verify this statement. On the one hand, we read in John 3:16 the well known words: "For God so loved the world, that he gave his only begotten Son, that whosoever believeth in him should not perish but have everlasting life." That is God's world, the world of His everlasting good pleasure, the world of His love, the world He purposes to save in Christ, and that will be revealed in all its perfection of beauty in the new heavens and the new earth in which righteousness shall dwell, and of which Christ is the Prince and Head for ever. On the other hand, we read in I John 2:15-17: "Love not the world, neither the things that are in the world. If any man love the world, the love of the Father is not in him. For all that is in the world, the lust of the flesh, and the lust of the eyes, and the pride of life, is not of the Father, but is of the world. And the world passeth away, and the lust thereof, but he that doeth the will of God abideth for ever." That is man's world, the world of sinful man, motivated throughout by enmity against God, full of corruption and unrighteousness, which is not the object of the love of God, and may not be the object of our love. On the one hand, we read that "God was in Christ reconciling the world unto Himself, not imputing their trespasses unto them," II Cor. 5:19; and on the other hand you hear the Saviour say: "I pray not for the world," John 17:9; and again: "If the world hate you, ye know that it hated me before it hated you. If ye were of the world, the world would love his own: but because ye are not of the world, but I have chosen you out of the world, therefore the world hateth you." John 15:18, 19. The one is God's world, the other is the world of man. On the one hand, we hear the Word of God declare: For God sent not his Son into the world to condemn the world, but that the world through him might be saved,"

John 3:17; on the other hand we hear the Saviour solemnly declare: "Now is the judgment of this world." These two worlds are temporarily one, as the wheat and the chaff are one; for all are by nature in Adam, and all are under sin and condemnation; but God saves His world out of the world of man, and that, too, in the way of justice and judgment.

Now, when the Saviour declares: "Now is the judgment of this world," He speaks of the world of man, of fallen man. Of this world Satan is the prince, not because he has any rightful authority or power, nor because he ever actually succeeded in dethroning God, but because man, who was originally created king of the earthly creation, in order that with all things he might serve the earthly creation, in order that wiith all things he might serve his God, rebelled against the Most High, allied himself with the devil, and ever since performs the will of the devil, and subjects all things to the service of sin and iniquity. It is the world as it exists always, in every age of history, and as we very clearly may behold it in our own day. It is the world with its power and might, its knowledge and wisdom, its commerce and industry, its science and art, its culture and civilization, without God and in opposition to Him; the world with its pride and self-exaltation, its trust in man and in the power and wisdom of man, its hatred of God and of one another, its covetousness and lust for power and love for the glory of man; the world with its lust of the flesh, its idolatry and adultery, its profanity and deceit, its striving after pleasures and treasures, its music and dancing, its shows and vanities; the world, too, with its strife and debate, its unrest and revolutions, its wars and destruction. And it is the world, this too must be stated, with its righteousness of man, its self-righteousness and imaginary or self asserted goodness, its man-made religion and piety. For always that world, with all its iniquity and corruption, puts on a cloak of righteousness and goodness; with all its hatred it speaks of love; with all its injustice and shedding of blood it speaks of its own justice. That beautiful, mighty, powerful, glamorous, boasting, self righteous, proud, thoroughly corrupt world, that painted and adorned harlot, the Lord has in mind, when He says: "Now is the judgment of this world; now shall the prince of this world be cast out."

Let us note that in that hour of judgment this evil world was well represented. This must needs be so. For, you understand that in that one moment of its history the entire world, the world of all ages, from the beginning of its history to the time of its culmination in the antichristian beast, was judged once and for ever. When, therefore, the world is called before the bar of divine justice, it must be represented by what is admittedly the very best it could possibly produce. When the world rejects and kills the Son of God, it may not be represented by a tribe of ignorant and savage cannibals, or by a band of criminals, for whose act of sacrilege and cruel murder it need not claim any responsibility. On the contrary, the very best, the most just, the noblest and wisest, must be delegated to that court of justice where the world will be judged and condemned. The cross of Christ may not be erected in some forsaken corner of the world in the wilds of Africa, but must be exhibited in the very center of the world. It could not appear at any moment of history, but must needs be realized in the fulness of time. That center of the world in that fulness of time was Jerusalem in the year thirty-three of our era. It was there and then that the whole world of all ages appeared in all its culture and civilization, in its wisdom and human philosophy, in its power and human justice, in all the splendor of its natural light, as it stood in the pride of the rebellion against the living God: the world at its best! But there is more. Not only the world of culture and philosophy was represented in Jerusalem in the year thirty-three of our era, also the world of religion, the same rebellious and corrupt world, but now as it was in the Church, and came into contact, had come into contact for many centuries with the light of God's special revelation in the law and the prophets, with the Word which God had spoken at sundry times and in divers ways through the prophets, and finally spoke through His Son!

Was there ever a moment in the history of the world more favorable for her to appear before the bar of highest justice? Was there ever a place more completely and centrally representing all the culture and religion of the world at its best than Jerusalem? There were the leaders of the Jews, the chief priests and elders, the scribes and Pharisees, the theologians of those days, the men that knew the law, and scrupulously kept it. And there was the

official court of the Roman empire, famous for its knowledge
of what is just and true among men, and enlightened and adorned
by the wisdom and refinement of Greek culture and civilization!
There were Caiaphas and Annas, there were all the Sanhedrists,
members of the highest Jewish tribunal; there were Herod the
Tetrarch, and Pilate the Roman governor, the representative of
Roman justice. There was Judas who had been in close contact
with the Lord for three years. And there was the Jewish people,
whose were the fathers, and the covenants, and the promises, and
the lawgiving. All these constituted "the world" of which the Lord
speaks at this time, that is about to be judged, and whose prince
will be cast out! And they represent the world of all times, and
in whatever form it may appear.

But, you say, in what sense is the hour of Jesus' suffering and
condemnation by the world, His crucifixion and death, the judgment of the world? I would like to call your attention especially
to three elements in this judgment of the world through the cross
of Christ. First of all, there is the element of the trial. Through
the suffering of Jesus the world was put on trial. It was summoned before the bar of God's justice, it was publicly tried and
exposed in its real character, it was found wanting and condemned.
This is an essential element in all judgments: the defendant must
be summoned and tried by the judge. It is no different with the
judgment of the world by God. The world must be publicly tried,
its guilt, its corruption, its worthiness of eternal wrath and condemnation must be clearly set forth. Not, indeed, as if God had
need to find out what is the real spiritual ethical value of the
world. He knows that the world, the wicked world as it stands
in alliance with the devil, in spite of all its culture and show of
goodness, and wisdom, and justice, and religion, is filled with
pride and corruption, with enmity against God, and is, therefore,
worthy of damnation. But God must be justified before the whole
creation. Every mouth must be stopped, and all must acknowledge
that He is just and righteous when He condemns the world. Therefore, the world must be exposed. Its mask of culture and religion,
its self righteousness and show of goodness must be torn away
from her, and she must be made to show herself in all her naked
shame and corruption. For this purpose she must be tried. And

this trial God institutes through His Son in the flesh, His holy Child Jesus. All the world must be placed before the question: what think ye of the Christ, and what will ye do with Him? For Christ is the revelation of God. The Father He had clearly revealed. He had come to witness the truth. The light He presented in a world of darkness. And as this Christ, in the hour of His trial, stood before the world as a weak and helpless man, without power and without defense, the world principally faced the question: What will ye do with God's representative, with the Son of God, with God Himself, if He should stand before you in the form of a helpless man?

O, they meant to avoid this public trial! They would rather not answer any questions at all. For it was their intention to kill Jesus secretly, without any formal trial or judicial procedure. And it must not be on the feast day! All publicity must be avoided. As opportunity presented itself the traitor was to deliver Him to them, and somehow they would do away with Him by subtilty. But this might not be. Publicly the Lord must be tried. For clearly and definitely they must answer the question, not their own, but God's question: what will ye do with the Son of God? And so their plans are frustrated. And in the most official way, in the most public place and on the most public day of all, the feast of the passover, all the world gives its answer to God's question in this hour of judgment. Several factors were conducive to this frustration of their own plan, and this realization of the purpose of God. To some of these we hope to call your attention in detail in future discussions. There was the raising of Lazarus and the resulting growing popularity of Jesus, which caused the wicked leaders of the Jews to become excited and to hasten their wicked schemes. And there was, in the night in which He was betrayed, the Lord's dismissal of the traitor, who certainly had no plans to perform his dark deed that night, but who was forced to do quickly what he planned and had sold himself to do, by the sudden exposure of his hypocrisy in the upper room, and his dismissal by the Lord. However this may be, not in secret but in the way of a public trial by all the world, not in a forsaken corner of the world, but in the most public place of all the world and of all times, on the feast of the passover and in Jerusalem, the whole world was placed

before the question: what will ye do with the Son of God? And
all the world answered with one accord: If we can ever get hold
of God we will surely kill Him! Away with Him, crucify Him!

In the second place, upon that world whose mask of culture
and goodness had thus been torn off, and that had become exposed in all its wicked enmity against the living God, God poured
out the vials of His wrath. The sentence of God's just wrath was
executed against the sin of the world. Only, in that hour of wrath
and desolation, this same Christ, the Son of God in human flesh,
proceeded to the place of execution, in order to represent His
own, whom the Father had given Him, His own world of which
He had been appointed the Head from before the foundation
of the world, the world of God's everlasting love. For His own
people, and His own world, were in that old world of sin and
death and corruption, were one with that world, one in guilt and
condemnation, and must be redeemed from it. And to redeem
His own, He, the Lamb of God, must take away the sin of the
world. And to take away the sin of the world, He must willingly
and obediently make His way to the place of wrath and judgment in the hour of the condemnation of the world, and there
in His own flesh bear all the suffering and agony of the wrath of
God to the bitter end. And so He went to the cross. O, indeed,
He was nailed to the cross by wicked hands, and that the "world"
thus crucified the Son of God is the everlasting condemnation
of the world. Yet, He made that cross His own, the altar upon
which He brought the perfect sacrifice of Himself. And God
transformed the cross of men into the place of execution of His
righteous wrath against the sin of the world, and poured all the
vials of His wrath over the head of His only begotten Son. The
world had been tried and exposed and condemned. The sentence
was executed. But in the place of execution stood the Son of God.
God was in Christ reconciling the world unto Himself.

And so, while the old world was judged and condemned, and
the prince of that world was, indeed, cast out, deprived of all his
power to reign; and the day will soon come when this condemnation of the old world and its prince will be finished and fully
executed; the new world emerged from the terrible fire of this
judgment, the world of God's eternal love in Christ Jesus our

Lord. For He proved Himself to be the obedient Servant of Jehovah even unto the bitter death of the cross, and by His obedience He fully satisfied for sin, and obtained an eternal righteousness for that new world whose eternal Prince He is. From the hour of the judgment of the world of sin, He emerged, justified, in His resurrection from the dead. And He ascended into heaven, and was exalted at the right hand of God endowed with power to destroy the old world, and to establish the new in eternal righteousness. And by the power of the faith He giveth unto us we turn away from the world that is judged and condemned, and are liberated from the bondage of its prince, in order even now to become servants of righteousness under the lordship of the Prince of Peace! Blessed are all they that put their trust in Him!

CHAPTER 2

The Judgment of the Church

Whosoever shall fall upon that stone shall be broken; but on whomsoever it shall fall, it will grind him to powder. — Lu. 20:18.
Then the high priest rent his clothes, saying, He hath spoken blasphemy. — Matt. 26:65.
They answered and said, He is guilty of death.
— Matt. 26:66.

The cross and resurrection of our Lord Jesus Christ are the judgment of this world. In the trial of the Saviour the world confronts the question: what shall we do with the Son of God? And its answer is: we shall kill Him! The world of fallen man is condemned, and its prince is cast out through the judgment of the cross. But God's world is justified in the resurrection of the Lord, and its Prince is exalted at the right of the Majesty in the heavens.

Now, as we are studying some phases of this judgment of the cross, we notice that the first and chief defendant that appears before the tribunal of the Most High to be examined and judged is the Church, the House of God! It occupies a chief position, it plays a leading part in the crucifixion of the Son of God! Judgment must needs begin at the House of God. This had been foretold by the prophets of old: "Behold, I will send my messenger, and he shall prepare the way before me: and the Lord, whom ye seek, shall suddenly come to his temple, even the messenger

11

of the covenant, whom ye delight in: behold, he shall come, saith the Lord of hosts. But who may abide the day of his coming: and who shall stand when he appeareth? for he is like a refiner's fire, and like fullers' soap: and he shall sit as a refiner and purifier of silver." Mal. 3:1-3. Hence, it had been said of that day of the Lord, that "it shall burn as an oven; and all the proud, yea, and all that do wickedly shall be stubble: and the day that cometh shall burn them up, saith the Lord of hosts, that it shall leave them neither root nor branch." Mal. 4:1. Yet, on the other hand, unto them that feared the name of Jehovah the sun of righteousness would arise with healing in his wings. Mal. 4:2. The coming of Christ, therefore, would be a judgment for the house of God, for the Church as it was then present in Israel, and represented by official Jerusalem. The Church would be tried, judged, condemned; the vials of the wrath of God would be poured out upon her. And in and through the separating and refining process of this judgment, the sin of that Church would be exposed as never before, the chaff would be burned, the wheat would be gathered into the garner. Thus John the Baptist had announced His coming, Matt. 3:1ff.; Luk. 3:7ff. Thus grayheaded Simeon had prophesied with the child Jesus in his arms: "Behold, this child is set for the fall and rising again of many in Israel, and for a sign that shall be spoken against . . . that the thoughts of many hearts may be revealed." Lu. 2:34, 35. And thus the Lord Himself had not only clearly expressed more than once, but had also plainly obsignated when twice He had come to the temple to drive out those that made of the house of God a den of robbers.

The judgment of the world, therefore, through the cross of Christ must begin at the Church, in order that God's Church in Christ may be justified and saved, while man's Church is condemned and destroyed. For even as we distinguished in the previous chapter between God's world and man's world, so we must now distinguish between God's Church and man's church, the true and the false church, the faithful bride and the adulterous woman. The one is called Jerusalem, the city of the living God, the daughter of Sion; the name of the other is Sodom and Gomorrah, even though in the world she appears as Jerusalem. To the one the Lord says: Ammi, My people; to the other He says: Lo

Ammi, not My people. They are Jacob whom God loves, and Esau whom He hates. In the world they are always one to a certain extent, like the wheat and the chaff. Especially was this the case in the old dispensation, when the church was under the law and confined within the limits of Israel's theocracy. Also in the new dispensation the false church constantly arises in the bosom of the true; and always that false church seeks to gain the ascendancy, the controlling influence in the church in the world. It seeks the pulpit that it may corrupt the truth of the gospel; it wants a ruling position that it may deliver the Church to the world and to the devil. But in the new dispensation the true church can always maintain purity of doctrine by separating from the false, apostate church in the world. In the days of the Old Testament this was impossible. There was one throne of David, one temple, one king, one service of God according to the law, one institute, and if the wicked were in power, occupied the throne and served officially in the temple, the true Church had no means of expressing itself. Then the temple was defiled, the idols were introduced into the land, the righteous were persecuted, and the blood of the prophets of Jehovah was shed. Thus it was in the desert, when they could not enter into the land of promise because of unbelief. Thus it was frequently in the period of the Judges, and later during the reign of the kings; think of the days of wicked Ahab and the service of Baal. Nor is there a more wicked, abominable, hypocritical, self-righteous, self complacent, outwardly pious and inwardly corrupt part of the world whose prince is the devil than the false, apostate church, that wicked adulteress that denies that Jesus is the Christ! It is that church that stones the prophets and then builds their tombs, that kills the righteous and then garnishes their sepulchres; it is that church that is compared to a whitewashed sepulchre, beautiful without but within full of dead men's bones and uncleanness; it is that ungodly, abominable, antichristian harlot that sheds all the blood of the saints, that crucified Christ, and always crucifies Him again!

That world, that apostate Church was, at the time of Jesus, represented by the leaders of the Jews, particularly the Jewish council, whose president was the high priest. And it is these leaders of the Jews that lay their hands on Jesus, and that, in spite of themselves, are compelled to stand in judgment, and to give a clear answer to the question: "what will ye do with the Christ, the Son of God?" Let us follow the history of this trial, which appeared to be the trial of Jesus by the Sanhedrin, but in reality was the trial of the apostate church, that had always stumbled at the stone God laid in Sion, always had, and always does and will kill the prophets, the trial of that part of the world that was represented by carnal Israel.

On Wednesday of the same week in which Jesus was crucified, these leaders of the Jews held an informal meeting to consult how they might kill the Lord. At that time, that is, just a day before they actually captured and tried Jesus, they seemed to have been quite convinced that they could do nothing against Him in the way of a legal procedure. Yet they had always hated Him; and especially since His reappearance in and about Jerusalem, and the enthusiasm that was caused among the people by the raising of Lazarus, they were incensed against the Saviour, and became more and more determined to kill Him. So they had met on that last Wednesday afternoon, not in formal session, but rather as a band of conspirators against Jesus' life. For they consulted how best to remove Him from their way. Two things had been established by them at that informal gathering: they would try to take Jesus by subtilty and kill Him secretly; and they would not make an attempt to murder Him on the feast day, for they were afraid of the people's enthusiasm for the Lord. If their plan had succeeded, Jesus would never have been publicly and formally tried and condemned and crucified. It is in this scheme that Judas who that same day appeared before them to offer his evil services, had his proper place. And, no doubt, he left them under strict orders: "not on the feast day, lest there be an uproar among the people."

However, God's purpose was different. Jesus' must be publicly tried and condemned. And all the plans of the Jewish council were completely frustrated. One of the main factors in the frustration of their plans was, no doubt, the dismissal of the traitor from the upper room, where Jesus had prepared to eat the last passover with His disciples. Judas also had taken his

place among the disciples that night, although the traitor's reward was already in his pocket. No intention he had to deliver
Jesus into the hands of His enemies that night, for his orders
were: "not on the feast day." But the Lord had revealed in that
upper room that He was fully acquainted with Judas' evil purpose, and had sent him out in the night to accomplish it quickly.
The result was, that when the traitor reported his experience
to the leaders of the Jews that same night, these realized that
now they would be compelled to follow the way of legal procedure, and that for such procedure they were not at all prepared.
And so, they obtain a band of soldiers from the captain of the
guard, and proceed to Gethsemane, armed with swords and staves
to take Jesus captive. And thereupon followed Jesus' trial and
condemnation by the Jewish council which belonged to the condemnation of the world, the judgment of the false church.

To understand how this was accomplished we must again call
attention to the fact that the false church was well represented
at this time, and the Jews were well qualified to give an answer
for the carnal church of all ages to the question: "what think
ye of the Christ?" First of all, the Sanhedrin was an august body.
It was the highest Jewish tribunal. There were, indeed, smaller
sanhedrins in every town with a certain number of Jewish inhabitants; but the supreme court was the Sanhedrin in Jerusalem.
It consisted of seventy-one members, the high priest always pre-
siding over its sessions. It was a self-perpetuating body, for it
appointed its own members. At an earlier date this supreme
council of the Jews appears to have had power to try and settle
all kinds of cases, both political and ecclesiastical, but its power
had been considerably curtailed by the Romans. Capital offenses
it had no longer authority to try, and capital punishment it could
no longer inflict. However that may be, the Sanhedrin was a very
able representation of the Jews of that time. It consisted of the very
ablest men of the nation, the high priest and the chief priests,
the elders and scribes, Pharisees and the Sadducees, men that
were versed in theological questions, and that knew the law. And
they certainly were well qualified to give an answer to the question: what think ye of the Christ? For they had been in direct
contact with Jesus of Nazareth. Often they had sent delegations

to watch Him. Besides, Jesus had taught openly in the synagogues and in the temple. And they had been eye witnesses of many of His wonderful works. Well were they able to represent the church of man in giving answer to the question: what shall we do with Jesus, the Son of the living God?

In the second place, let us notice three outstanding results of this trial of the Saviour by the Jewish court: 1. The entire trial very strongly sets forth both the evil design of the judges and the innocence of Jesus of Nazareth. 2. The whole trial culminates in the question of the high priest, whether Jesus be the Christ, the Son of God, and the Lord's affirmative answer. 3. And when they condemn Jesus to death on the basis of His testimony that He is the Christ, they have, in spite of themselves, given a plain answer to the question: what will ye do with the Christ of God? The court judged and found guilty. The false church is for ever condemned.

Let us examine the court records to see how they established the wickedness of the court, and the innocence of the Son of man. First of all, the records show that these judges condemned Jesus the day before, and had wickedly covenanted with a traitor for thirty pieces of silver to deliver Him into their hands that they might kill Him. This proves that in their own consciences they were convinced that they had no case against Jesus. Secondly, it is evident that the entire procedure on the part of the Sanhedrin was illegal. This is true of the session of the court at this time. The Jewish court was not allowed to conduct trials at night, or even to begin a case in the later afternoon; but Jesus' case was begun in the hollow of the night. There were, it appears, four different sessions that night and early morning. There was a session in the apartments of Annas, where a preliminary hearing and examination of the Saviour took place. This was arranged, most probably, because no meeting of the council had been summoned until they were sure that Jesus had been taken captive. Not being permitted to begin a session in the hollow of the night, they postponed calling such a meeting until Jesus had been captured. Annas, who was not the high priest that year, but his father-in-law, no doubt welcomed the opportunity to subject the Lord to a hearing of his own, which, however, led to nothing.

Then followed the session of the council as it had been hastily summoned in the night, and from which we may well imagine men like Nicodemus and Joseph of Arimathea were absent. It was in this meeting that an attempt was made to find an accusation sustained by witnesses against the Saviour, an attempt which absolutely failed. There was, according to Luke 22:66ff. a third session early in the morning, in which Jesus was put under oath by the high priest and placed before the question whether He were the Christ, the Son of the living God. It was then that the Saviour was condemned to death. And, lastly, a meeting was held in the absence of Jesus, to discuss the matter whether or not they should bring Him to the Roman governor to have him confirm their sentence.

Examining the court records of these different sessions, we come to the conclusion that the entire procedure was illegal. It was such for three reasons at least. First of all, they had no authority to try cases that involved capital punishment. Yet, even before the case was opened they had determined that they would pronounce the death sentence upon Jesus. And this is also their actual verdict. The Jewish council condemned the Lord to death, a fact which is not altered by their seeking the confirmation of this sentence through the Roman governor. Secondly, the trial was begun at night, which they were not permitted to do, and which plainly characterizes their entire procedure as a work of darkness. It is only when men are convinced in their own hearts that they conspire to do evil, that they avoid the light of day and publicity. And, thirdly, they evidently gathered in the palace of the high priest, rather than in the council chamber, the only legal place for official sessions. The motive was again to work in private, and to avoid their evil works' becoming known to the people. In all these respects, therefore, the trial of Jesus by the official representatives of the Church was their own condemnation. Already they were drawn before the bar of God's justice, were exposed in their evil character and purpose, and were answering God's question: What think ye of the Christ?

But there is more. Also the trial itself served only to establish the innocence of the Saviour, and their own wickedness. The records clearly reveal, first of all, that when the Saviour appeared

before Annas and later before the Jewish council, they had no
charge against Him! There was no accusation! They had come
against Him with swords and staves, they had bound Him, and
led Him captive, but when He stood before their tribunal, there
was not even an indictment against Him! Not only that, but
from Matt. 26:59 we learn that they deliberately sought evidence
of such a nature that would be sufficient to put Him to death.
Then, secondly, they had no witnesses, and they could not find
them. The Sanhedrin was accustomed to an elaborate system of
witnesses. These witnesses had to be examined separately, and
at least two of them had to agree before their testimony could
be accepted as valid. But it is evident that in Jesus' trial no witnesses were at hand. The court deliberately looked for witnesses
from their own body, and that, not to sustain or corroborate a
charge, but to bring an indictment on the basis of which they
might condemn the Lord to death! And even in this they failed
miserably. For when two witnesses did appear introducing an
indictment concerning a statement of the Lord's about rebuilding the temple, they did not agree. No accusation, no witnesses,
there were; and yet they had captured the Lord with the deliberate intention to put Him to death! Surely, the trial of Jesus
by the Jewish council merely served to accentuate Jesus' righteousness, and the wickedness of the Sanhedrin. The judgment
of Jesus was the judgment of the world as it was present in the
carnal old dispensational church.

But the case may not rest here. The matter must be definitely
settled. In God's courtroom the Sanhedrin must give a clear and
definite answer to God's question: what think ye of the Christ?
What will ye do with Him, the Christ of God, if ye can lay your
hands on Him? The matter may not be left in doubt, for the Sanhedrin represents the false church of all ages. The blood of all the
prophets must be on their head. It is evident that they would
rather evade the issue. For they like to maintain their appearance
of righteousness. They are very religious, as the false church
always is. And they prize their reputation. They seek the honor
of men. If at all possible the Christ-question must be avoided.
Jesus must be exposed as a malefactor, and as such He must be
condemned. Even after they have killed Jesus they must be in a

position to place an extra wreath on the graves of the prophets they had killed. And so they seek other evidence. But God will not have it so. All their efforts fail. The high priest becomes irritated and angry when Jesus maintains a continual silence and answers not one word to all the false and foolish accusations they seek to bring against Him. And finally, all their efforts to incriminate the Lord having failed, the high priest and the council realize that they must face the issue. And by mouth of their worthy president, they adjure the Lord to tell them, whether He be the Christ, the Son of the living God. This time the Saviour breaks His long silence, and replying affirmatively, He solemnly adds, that henceforth they shall see the Son of man, sitting at the right hand of God, and coming with the clouds of heaven!

Upon this they condemn Him to death! What does it mean? It means nothing less than that they had been summoned before the tribunal of God, and had been confronted with the question: what will ye do with Christ, the Son of God? What will ye do with God's anointed, and, therefore, with the living God Himself if He appears before you as a defenseless man? And with one accord they answered, "We will kill Him! He is worthy of death!" O, it is true, they still attempt to keep up their appearance of righteousness and piety! They feign indignation. They pronounce the Lord a blasphemer. The high priest rends his high priestly robe. And well might that born prophet-in-spite-of-himself do so, for the death of Jesus meant the end of his high priestly office. The council maltreat the Saviour, smite and buffet Him, spit upon Him, blindfold and mock Him. But all their show of religion and indignation will avail them nothing, and will never suffice to cover up the fact that they reject the Christ of God! That is their condemnation. For they speak the language and do the work of Antichrist! He that denies, not that a certain Christ will come, but that *Jesus* is the Christ, is moved by the spirit of Antichrist. And why should not Jesus be the Christ? Why should it be blasphemy on the part of this Jesus to confess that He is the Messiah, the Son of God? Had He not revealed the Father in all His teachings? And did they not know? Was He not the Son of David? Did He not have the testimony of John the Baptist, of Moses and all the prophets? Had not the

Father borne witness of Him? Did not all His mighty works corroborate His claim that He is the Christ, the Son of the living God? Yes, they knew Him. They had heard Him. They were acquainted with His doctrine. They had seen His mighty works. Yet, they did not want to accept this man Jesus as the Christ! Another Christ they wanted, not Jesus. A Christ after their own heart, of their own imagination, Who would never testify that their works were evil, Who with them would walk in darkness and seek the honor of men, they desired and sought. Because *Jesus* is the Christ they condemn Him to death! God's question was clearly answered. And they were condemned! "Now is the condemnation of the world!" The Church rejects the Son of God! Judgment must needs begin at the house of God!

And presently the sentence, God's sentence upon an ungodly church is executed. The vials of His wrath are poured out in that hour! But again, in that hour Jesus Himself, God's own anointed High Priest, willingly went to the place of execution, that He might bear the wrath of God against the sin of the Church, and bear it away for ever! For even though the form of the house of God, as it was represented by the high priest and the Jewish council may and must perish, there is within that corrupt institution, within man's church, the true Church of God. And it may never perish! Hence, when men nail Him to the accursed tree in the hour of judgment, He transforms that cross into God's altar, upon which the Good Shepherd lays down His life for the sheep. And so the false church is forever condemned and shall presently perish, perish in the destruction of old Jerusalem, the old temple and all that was connected with it; perish again when the day of the revelation of the righteous judgment of God shall arrive; but, nevertheless, Sion is redeemed through judgment. The true Church presently emerges, justified, in the resurrection of Jesus Christ from the dead, ascends into glory, is exalted with Christ to reign with Him. Jerusalem, Mt. Sion, the temple, the High Priest and the priesthood are now in heaven! And presently she shall be presented as the glorious Bride of Christ, without spot or wrinkle to the Father, to dwell with Him in God's house for ever!

CHAPTER 3

The Judgment of the Political Worldpower

And having spoiled principalities and powers, he
made a shew of them openly, triumphing over them.
— COL. 2:15

Let us remember that in the Lenten weeks we are considering
the cross and resurrection of our Lord Jesus Christ from the
viewpoint of their being the judgment of this world. This was
announced by Jesus Himself a few days before His assumption
in the words: "Now is the judgment of this world, now shall the
prince of this world be cast out." God's world must be justified
in Christ, and saved; man's world must be condemned and destroyed. In the last chapter we called your attention to this judgment of the world as it is represented by the false church, the
church of man, the apostate church, the adulteress. It was judged
and condemned forever, when it was clearly placed before the
question: what will ye do with Jesus Christ? For the false church,
represented by the Sanhedrin of that time, answered: "we deny
that Jesus is the Christ. Crucify Him!" But, even though judgment must needs begin at the house of God, the false church
cannot adequately represent the whole world of man. Another
important and mighty representative of the evil world of fallen
man is the State, the political world-power in the hands and
under the dominion of the man of sin. To the judgment of the
ungodly world-power we must now call your attention.

21

Government is not an invention of man, but is of divine ordination. The State is an institution of God. By this we do not mean that at a certain moment in history God instituted government and established the State by a special act of revelation. On the contrary, in principle the institution of the State was given with the creation of the human race as an organism, and is based upon the authority of the parents in the home. From the family as its basic unit the human race developed into tribes and nations, and the authority of the home was accordingly extended to the authority of the head of the tribe, and the magistrate or king of the State. But when we say that government is a divine institution, we emphasize that there is not and cannot be any authority except from God. No man, nor group of men, can have authority in themselves. God alone has authority. He alone is Sovereign in Himself. And unless He confers authority upon men, they have no power to rule. The head of the State, therefore, whether he be king or emperor, president or dictator, stands in the place of authority that is established and instituted by God. And this remains true no matter in what way he was established in that position, whether as heir to the throne in a monarchy, or as the legally elected president by the vote of the people, as in a democracy. In his office he represents authority conferred upon him from above. His calling is to seek and apply the will of God in the sphere of his authority. And to God he is responsible for all he does in his official capacity as the head of the State.

To this must be added that the State bears the sword, which represents the power of the government to execute justice and judgment, for the protection of them that do well, and for the punishment of evil doers. This sword-power is necessary because of sin. The State as such is not instituted because of sin, as it is often alleged. Government there is even among the angels. And government would have developed even if the human race had never fallen away from God. But that the political powers bear the sword certainly must be attributed to the entrance of sin into the world. And this sword is symbol not only of the power of the State to punish evil doers and protect the good within its own domain, but also to wage righteous war. Thus the Word of God instructs us with respect to the institution of

government: "Let every soul be subject unto the higher powers.
For there is no power but of God: the powers that be are ordained of God. Whosoever therefore resisteth the power, resisteth
the ordinance of God: and they that resist shall receive to themselves damnation. For rulers are not a terror to good works, but
to the evil. Wilt thou then not be afraid of the power? Do that
which is good, and thou shalt have praise of the same: For he
is a minister of God unto thee for good. But if thou do that which
is evil, be afraid; for he beareth not the sword in vain: for he
is a minister of God, a revenger to execute wrath upon him that
doeth evil." Rom. 13:1-4. The Christian, therefore, is not an
insurrectionist. He is in obedience to the higher powers for God's
sake and for conscience' sake, as long as this obedience does
not require of him to obey men more than God. And again that
same Christian will fearlessly refuse obedience to the power of
the State for God's sake and for conscience' sake, the moment
the higher powers would demand of him to disobey God and
violate His precepts. This truth may sound somewhat old fash-
ioned, and may be considered obsolete in our age that loudly
proclaims the sovereignty of man, is strongly characterized by
a general lack of respect for authority, and often fails to distinguish between liberty and licentiousness, but it remains the truth,
nevertheless, a truth which a nation and a government can disregard only to its own destruction.

Such then is, in brief, the State as instituted by God. But even
as this power of the government is a mighty power for good
as long as it functions according to the will of God, so it becomes
a tremendous instrument of corruption under the influence and
dominion of sin. And it is usually from this viewpoint that the
Bible pictures the political world-power. The sword-power is a
mighty force. And we need not be surprised that the prince of
this world, through the agency of fallen and corrupt man, often
succeeds in laying hold on this power, and employs it in his own
wicked service and for his own evil design. More than through
any other agency or institution, it is through the political power
of the State that the devil is the prince of this world. Under his
rule, and through sin which corrupts all things, the State becomes
the chief power of evil. It becomes ungodly, antichristian. In-

stead of using its power for the protection of the good, and the punishment of evil doers, it then causes the wicked to triumph in the land, and the righteous to suffer. It becomes a power of oppression, boasting of its own strength, usurping all authority, lording it over all, the almighty state. Using its mighty sword, it seeks to dominate in every sphere of life, in home and school, in church and society. Always it is the tendency and strife of the ungodly, antichristian State of fallen man to transgress the limits of its own proper domain, and to become totalitarian. It usurps the power to determine what we shall eat and drink, how we shall educate our children, whom and how we shall worship, and what we shall preach and believe. And it always seeks to establish the world-state. To realize one mighty, universal worldpower, lording it over all nations, and dominating every department of life, — that is the ambition of the ungodly political worldpower, whose prince is the devil, and whose agent is fallen man!

This ungodly, antichristian political worldpower, that seeks to gain universal dominion, is always in the world. Its attempt at world dominion was frustrated already at the time of Nimrod and the building of the tower of Babel, where God by His mighty power separated the human race into separate nations. And ever since, the same attempt was made by the mighty tyrants of this world, the result of which was the succession of a series of world empires in their rise and decline and fall, such as Assyria, Babylonia, Persia and Media, Greece and Rome. And Scripture teaches us plainly that before the coming of our Lord Jesus Christ this dream of world empire will for a time be realized in the kingdom of Antichrist, the Beast of Revelation 13. Then there will be the great tribulation for the people of God, such as was not from the beginning of the world, so that no one will be able to buy or sell, unless he receive the mark of the beast and worship his image! Such is the State of fallen man!

That State, that wicked political worldpower, with its oppression and tyranny, its mighty power and proud boast, its slogan that might is right, its bloodshed and persecution of the righteous, its trust in its chariots and horses, its hypocrisy and show of justice, its speaking of peace while it means war, its boast of liberty while it aims at aggrandizement, this mighty Babylon with its riches and pleasures, this terrible antichristian Beast, — is already judged and condemned, and shall surely be destroyed. For God has anointed His own King over Sion, and sits in the heavens to laugh at the vain fury and ravings of the nations. His is the kingdom forever. He shall rule the world in righteousness, as the faithful Servant of God. The question who shall be universal King over all things, Christ or Antichrist, is already decided, not by the power of man, but by God's eternal decree. And through the cross and exaltation of the Son of God the wicked political world-power of Antichrist is already judged.

Yes, indeed, Christ, the anointed King over all, also was brought before the tribunal of the world-power, as it then existed in the mighty Roman empire, and as, in Jerusalem, in the year 33 of our era, it was represented by Pilate, the Roman governor. Both according to the prophecy of Daniel and the book of Revelation, the Roman Empire belongs to the succession of political world-powers that constitute the ungodly, antichristian beast. And a better representative than Rome at the time of Christ, the world-power could hardly have desired. Having conquered practically the entire world by its mighty legions, so that its territory extended from the Atlantic to the Euphrates, and from the Rhine and Danube to the sands of the Sahara, Rome under the emperors, especially beginning with Augustus, now boasted of its peaceful intentions. To establish and maintain a world empire characterized by peace and prosperity, offering the highest degree of liberty to all, and governed by justice and righteousness, these were the avowed aims of the Roman world-power especially since the republic had been replaced by the empire. That world-power had also conquered the land of Canaan, and ruled over the people of Israel at the time of Christ. And when Christ stands before the Roman governor, Pontius Pilate, it is the world-power that is called to express its judgment of Jesus, and to answer the question as it was put by Pilate himself: "What shall I do then with Jesus, Who is called the Christ?" Let us study the outstanding features of this trial of the Saviour by the Roman governor.

First of all, it draws our attention that this proud representative of Roman justice, who wields the sword in the name of Caesar, emphatically and repeatedly pronounces the Lord innocent. The

Sanhedrists who in their early morning session had decided to bring Jesus before Pilate, realized that the Roman judge would care nothing about the accusation, on the ground of which they had condemned the Saviour, that He claimed to be the Christ, the Son of the living God. It appears that at first they hoped to obtain from Pilate the confirmation of their death sentence by merely stating that they found Jesus to be a malefactor. But in this they were mistaken. For the Roman governor confronted them immediately with the question: "What accusation bring ye against this man?" And when the Jews proudly attempted to overawe Pilate with the answer: "If he were not a malefactor, we would not have delivered him up unto thee," the Roman replied that, in that case, they had better take Jesus and judge Him according to their own law. John 18:29-31. Realizing, however, that they would not have the power to put Jesus to death, they then invented the charge that Jesus claimed to be a king, and that He perverted the nation, forbidding to pay tribute to Caesar. There was, of course, in this accusation a semblance of truth, for Jesus was King. Yet, the accusers deliberately distorted the truth, and misrepresented the kingship of the Christ, placing it on a par with, and putting it in the same category as the kingship of Caesar. It was necessary, therefore, that this misunderstanding be removed. Jesus might not be condemned as a common rebel against the authorities, as one that resisted the higher powers. And, therefore, when the Roman governor examined Him on this point, He does admit that He is a King, but at the same time makes clear, that He is not merely another king, next and in opposition to Caesar, that would attempt to usurp the world-power by the power of the sword, for His kingdom is not of this world. Quite in opposition to the ungodly kingdoms of this world, His dominion was founded upon the truth, and every one that is of the truth is a willing subject of that kingdom. And although the Roman governor contemptuously asks: "What is truth?" he nevertheless perceives that the charge of the Jews against Jesus is false, and openly tells His accusers: "I find in him no fault at all." John 18:33-38.

And this verdict is repeated several times. From this it plainly appears that, although Pilate is the judge and is supposed to try Jesus, he here stands before the judgment seat of the Most High, and is confronted with the question: "What will the justice of the world-power do with Jesus, who is called the Christ?" And in order to give a clear answer to this searching question, he must clearly see, and openly declare that Jesus is a righteous man. And this he is compelled to do. In ordinary circumstances he would not have hesitated simply to deliver a defendant to the will of the Jews, for he prized the friendship of Caesar, and he was willing to please the Jews if necessary for his own position. But he was afraid of Jesus! No doubt, he had heard of this Man. His wife certainly was acquainted with Him. And the dream of his wife, together with her earnest prayer that he would have nothing to do with this righteous man, had made matters worse. And, therefore, he sought to release the Lord. And so he repeatedly examines Him, and as often returns to the Jews with the open declaration: I find no guilt in Him at all! And to the very end of the trial this remains his official sentence as judge, as he openly declares before the Jews by washing his hands of the entire case!

Secondly, let us notice, that Pilate, the representative of Roman justice is not at all motivated by love of the truth or justice, but merely by his own carnal ambition. The desire to remain friend of Caesar dominates him in all his actions. His hesitation to deliver Jesus to be crucified cannot be explained from the fear of God and the desire to do justice. His own safety, his own name and position, his own honor and power are uppermost in his mind and heart. In this he is, indeed, a worthy representative of the ungodly world-power. As judge, as representative of the higher power that wielded the sword, he was called to protect the good, and to punish the evil doers. As such his calling in this particular case was clear, and he knew it. Jesus must be protected, justified, acquitted; the wicked Jews must feel the avenging power of his sword. In the light of the "work of the law" that was written in his heart, he clearly perceived this. But he did not hesitate to hold the truth under in unrighteousness! "What is truth?" That he hesitated, nevertheless, had its root in the same selfish, sinful, corrupt ambition. He was afraid of Jesus. Yet he was afraid of the Jews! And he was afraid above all of Caesar! This is plainly evident from the several attempts, as unjust as they were weak, to release Jesus! He attempts to secure the release of the Lord by leaving the accusers the choice between Jesus and Barabbas. But thus the Roman judge trampled all justice under foot. What right had he to put the innocent on a par with the guilty, and leave the decision with the accusers? He scourged the Lord, he had Him mocked by the soldiers, he tried to make Him such an object of pity that the hatred of the accusers might be appeased without the death sentence. But here the world-power deliberately scourged and maltreated the righteous, and plainly expressed its disregard of all justice! What will the mighty, proud, boasting, hypocritical world-power do with Jesus, Who is so plainly the righteous? It will persecute Him, scourge Him, mock at Him for the satisfaction of its own ambition!

But this is not the end. All these attempts of Pilate to release the Lord simply represent so many vain attempts to avoid the ultimate answer to God's final question: What will you do with My Anointed, Who here stands before you as the righteous? The Roman governor, driven to and fro by many conflicting motives, carnal though they all were, himself puts the question rather concisely: "What shall I do then with Jesus which is called Christ?" O, but indeed, this is the question! This is always the question. It is the question that cannot be avoided, and the answer to which is equally unavoidable! What shall I do *then* with Jesus? Yes, but what *can* you do *then?* What can you do, if you must have nothing of His kingdom, if you hear not His voice, if you despise the truth, if you seek your own honor and ambition. Can you go half way with Him? Will you prefer Him above Barabbas? Will you scourge Him and release Him? Will you enshrine Him in the temple of your modern idolatry, and make Him a good man, a noble man, a wonderful example, a great teacher, whose golden rule and sermon on the mount you take to heart? Will you hail Him Prince of this world, even, and create a wonderful world order for Him, in which in His name you may save your hypocritical face, and continue to pursue your antichristian ambition? Will you offer Him all the kingdoms of the world, if only He will worship the devil with you? O, but what shall I do then with Jesus who is called Christ? The question always returns! It must have an answer! It wants an ultimate, a decisive answer. It wants an answer that reveals the thoughts of your inmost hearts! Here you cannot compromise!

Off with the mask of your hypocrisy, of your pretended wisdom, and righteousness, and justice! Summon the help and witness of all your gods, of all your power and wisdom, of all your civilization and culture, of all your religion and piety, and then answer, but by all means answer clearly and ultimately: what will you do with Jesus which is called Christ? Yes, call to help the false church, that already worships the beast and his image, and let her answer first. But you, too, antichristian Beast, and your image that always speaks, must answer for yourself: If the Righteous, the Son of God, Jesus the Christ, stands before you as a helpless man, what will ye do with Him? . . . .

The answer comes from the false church, oh yes, of course, from the false church even now, for from her the antichristian world-power must learn its answer: "Let him be crucified." Matt. 27:23. "And Pilate gave sentence that it should be as they desired," . . . and "he delivered Jesus to their will." Luke 23:24, 25. Now is the condemnation of the world! The world-power had been tried, exposed, found wanting, condemned! Ah, of what avail is it for Pilate still to maintain his appearance of justice? Even as the high priest had made such an attempt by rending his robe, so Pilate now attests his innocence by washing his hands! But to no avail. The answer is clear: Jesus the Christ is righteous, but if He stands in the way of the selfish ambition of the world-power, He must be killed! Crucify the Innocent!

And what shall Jesus do? Shall He cause His power and glory to flash forth to consume His enemies? Shall He give them a mighty proof of His divine power and royal majesty? But no; this may not be. It is not the hour of power and glory as yet. It is the hour of judgment. He is King, indeed; but only as the obedient Servant of the Lord. He must establish His kingdom, to be sure; but only in the way of the righteousness of God. He stands at the head of His own, who also belong by nature to this rebellious kingdom of fallen man. These He must redeem. And they must be redeemed through justice. He must bear their sin, even as it is exposed in this judgment of the world-power. And, therefore, when the vials of God's wrath are poured out in this hour of judgment, He must be present at the place of execution. Yes, indeed, Pilate's sentence must be executed. He must be crucified.

But God will nail His own sentence to that cross of Pilate, the handwriting of our sins. And that divine sentence He will receive and bear willingly, removing the handwriting of our sins that was against us. And so the King dies, humbling Himself as the obedient Servant of Jehovah. And thus He battles His way into His own kingdom. For God hath highly exalted Him, and given Him a name that is above every name, that in the name of Jesus every knee should bow and every tongue confess that Jesus is Lord, to the glory of God the Father!

And what shall you, what shall I do with Jesus? You either crucify Him, or you are crucified with Him through His grace! It is either—or. Nothing less, nothing else you can do with Jesus which is called Christ!

CHAPTER 4

The Judgment of the People

Then cried they again, saying, Not this man, but Barabbas. Now Barabbas was a robber.—JOHN 18:40.

There are certain unchangeable, inalienable principles, to which the higher powers, the government, even in a republic, is subject, which it may not violate, and that cannot even be submitted to the vote of the people, or the will of the majority, principles which any government can only disregard and violate to its own destruction. Higher than the highest powers in this world, is the eternal and unchangeable objective law of God, and beyond the reach of the power of the State is the Word of God as contained in the Holy Scriptures. To maintain the law of God in its own domain, and to leave room for the free course of the Word of God, is certainly the obligation and calling of the higher powers. The government has not the power to determine whether or not the parents shall exercise proper authority in the home, nor whether or not they shall educate their children in the fear of the Lord. The government has not the authority to determine whether or not the citizens shall have the right to kill and murder, to steal and rob and deceive and blaspheme. The government has no power to violate the unchangeable law of God concerning the marriage relation, to make laws providing opportunity for legal divorce and remarriage on the flimsiest grounds rather than on the ground of adultery alone. I realize, of course, that these evils are committed, and that also the higher powers in our own land trample the eternal law of God concerning the matrimonial relationship under foot, till marriage is made a mockery. But I protest that no government can have the authority to make laws contrary to the law of God, and insist that by doing so, nevertheless, it destroys the very foundations of society and of the State. No government can have the authority to determine whether or not the Church shall worship according to the Word of God, and whether or not it shall confess in all its implications that Jesus is the Christ, that He died for His people, that He rose on the third day, and that He shall come again to judge the quick and the dead. The government does not make truth, but is subject to the truth. The State does not create principles of righteousness and justice, but it must ask for the will of God.

Nor may these eternal and unchangeable principles of righteousness and truth be submitted to a vote of the people, as if the will of the majority could have the right to set aside the law of God, or have authority to determine what shall be regarded as the truth. True liberty consists in harmony with the will of God, never in violation of it. And real political freedom does not exist in that State where matters pertaining to the eternal and immutable principles of truth and justice are submitted to the vote of the people, but where the government itself honors that will of God, and protects the rights of its citizens to worship and preach, to confess and to live in every domain of life according to the Word of God. And woe unto that State that violates this truth! If the majority must decide whether Jesus is the Christ, they will ultimately always vote against Him! This is the application of what happened when Pilate, the Roman governor, in an effort to avoid the responsibility of deciding this question himself, submitted it to the vote of the people by placing them before the choice of Jesus or Barabbas!

How clearly the control of things connected with the suffering and death of the Saviour had been taken out of the hands of the conspiring enemies! We remember that they had decided to take the Lord by subtilty and to put Him to death secretly, without any form of legal procedure; and that, moreover, it was not to be on the feast day, when the city of Jerusalem was overcrowded with

people, and easily an uproar might be caused among them! And
yet, all their evil plans failed. They had been compelled to take
Jesus captive that night with the help of Roman soldiers, so that
the matter was known to the Roman governor. They had been
forced by circumstances to conduct a form of legal trial by the
Sanhedrin, the highest Jewish tribunal, the result of which had
been that they pronounced the death sentence upon Jesus. And,
because of the fact that the matter was known to the Roman
authorities, seeing that they had employed Roman soldiers to
take Jesus captive, they now could not avoid His being brought
before the Roman governor, for they did not have the power to
pronounce and execute the death sentence. And so, the Saviour
was brought before the representative of Caesar. However, Pilate,
as we saw previously, felt little inclined to take the responsibility
of deciding the case. He knew that the Lord was righteous, and
that they had delivered Him out of envy. And he stood in awe
of Him. On the other hand, he was afraid of the Jews, and above
all of Caesar. The result was that he sought to release Jesus without endangering his own name and position, and provoking the
hostility of the Jews. And one of the attempts to shift the responsibility that rested upon him in this case as Roman governor
is the choice he gives the people between Jesus and Barabbas.

The multitude gathered before the Praetorium was momentarily
increasing. And well may we surmise that on this day of the feast
they represented the Jewish people from all over the land. They
must have been acquainted with Jesus of Nazareth. Many, if not
all of them, had been witnesses of His mighty works, and had been
in the audience when the Lord was teaching the things concerning the kingdom of God. Many of them had known the time that
they were filled with enthusiasm about the Rabbi of Nazareth, and
had been prepared to proclaim Him the king of the Jews. For
they all looked for a Messiah, that would deliver them from the
obnoxious yoke of foreign dominion, and that would restore the
throne of David to its former renown and glory. And occasionally,
it had appeared to them, that this Jesus of Nazareth had, indeed,
all the qualifications requisite to be the Messiah. But these moments
of popular enthusiasm had not been lasting. Always the Lord had
disappointed them. Ever and again He had estranged them from

Himself. And the result had always been that they were offended in Him. For it was especially in such moments of the rising tide of popular enthusiasm that the Lord had taken special pains to impress on their minds and hearts that His kingdom was not of this world. Thus it had been in Nazareth, whose people had twice rejected Him. Thus it was at the height of His popularity in and around Capernaum, where the people, especially after the sign of the feeding of the five thousand, had clamored for His exaltation to the throne, and had meant to make Him king by force; but to whom the Saviour on the next day had delivered such a hard speech, that all became alienated from Him. And had not some, perhaps even, most of the multitude that was gathered on that passover morning before the Praetorium, been with those who, but a few days before this, had met Him as He made His royal entry into the Holy City, shouting: "Hosanna, blessed is He that cometh in the name of the Lord"? But more than ever they were disappointed in this man now, as He stands there, helpless and bound, in the power of His enemies. Yes, they wanted a Christ, a Messiah, but it must be one that would meet their demands, and would establish a kingdom of this world! But a Christ that meant to represent the cause of God, and to establish the kingdom of heaven, could only be the object of their hatred and contempt.

However, also they, the people themselves, must be brought before the bar of God's justice in this hour of the judgment of this world. They, too, must give an answer to the question: "what will ye do with Jesus that is called Christ?" It is true, they had been represented by their leaders. and in and through them they had already given their answer to the question. But this is not sufficient. They must be left without excuse. They must not be able to complain that the leaders had rejected Jesus as the Christ, and they themselves had never been confronted with the critical question. They, too, must therefore be exposed in the deepest intents of their hearts. And so, they are drawn irresistibly to the Praetorium on that passover morning. not only to be eye-witnesses of the trial, but, as is evident from Mark 15:8, also to demand of the Roman governor that some prisoner should be released unto them. For it appears to have been the custom that on the Pass-

over the Roman governor would release unto them some notorious
prisoner, that had been condemned to suffer the extreme penalty.
And for this they now begin to clamor. The Roman governor here
sees another opportunity to avoid the necessity of sentencing Jesus.
For there "was one named Barabbas, which lay bound with them
that had made insurrection with him, who had committed murder
in the insurrection." Mark 15:7. And as the multitude began to
clamor for the release of some prisoner, Pilate saw his opportunity.
He made a nomination of two. He prepared, to speak in modern
terms, a ballot, and gave the people the opportunity to determine
by vote whether he should release unto them Jesus or Barabbas!
And thus the people themselves were very clearly and definitely
placed before God's question: "what will ye do with God's
Anointed, with Jesus of Nazareth, Who is called Christ?"

Let us clearly understand the significance of the choice before
which the people were now placed. On the one hand, they stand
before the choice of releasing Barabbas, that is, of giving him
back his freedom, and welcoming him once more in their society.
Now this Barabbas was what in our day we would call "public
enemy No. 1." His name signifies "son of a father." It is not
improbable that this means that he was the son of a rabbi, in which
case he came from a good family, and must have had a good
religious education and bringing up. If this surmise is correct, he
had deliberately despised the way of God's covenant, and knowing
the way of righteousness, he had chosen to walk in the way of
iniquity. From Luke 23:19 we learn that he was guilty of sedition,
and at the head of a band of robbers he had instigated an up-
rising in Jerusalem against the Roman authorities. And in the course
of this rebellion he had committed murder. This we also learn
from Mark 15:8. John, with characteristic emphasis simply
states: "Now Barabbas was a robber." And Acts 3:14 expresses
the awful contrast between the two that were here placed on
nomination by saying: "But ye denied the Holy One and the Just,
and desired a murderer to be granted unto you." Matthew
describes him as a notable prisoner. This, then, constitutes the
one alternative before which the people are placed: a criminal,
one from the lowest strata of society, an outstanding representative
of the world of sin and iniquity, a child of darkness, public enemy

number one, that is worthy of death according to the law of God and man. On the other hand, there is Jesus, the Holy and Just One, the Anointed of God, as widely famous for His having done good throughout the land, as the other was notorious for his works of darkness.

Let us consider this nomination for a moment from the viewpoint of the people that are here called to express their preference. It is true, there was an element of ignorance on their part. For so the apostle Peter declares later: "And now brethren, I wot that through ignorance ye did it, as did also your rulers." Acts 3:17. But make no mistake, this ignorance was not so complete as to render them excusable, or incompetent to understand their clear duty when they were placed before the choice of Jesus or Barabbas! To be sure, they did not and they could not consider Jesus in the light in which we are able to see Him now. They could not behold the Lord in the light of the cross and the resurrection, as the Lord of glory. He stood before them in the likeness of sinful flesh, without form or comeliness, and when they saw him, He had no beauty that they should desire Him. Isa. 53:2. But this does not alter the fact that they were perfectly competent, as far as their knowledge was concerned to understand their calling in this case. They did know that Barabbas was a criminal, and they also knew that the Lord was the Holy One and Just. They were aware of the fact that Barabbas was a murderer, and that Jesus had revealed unto them the Father, had proclaimed to them the gospel of the kingdom of heaven, and had done many wonderful works. They were perfectly aware that here they were placed before the choice between the perfectly righteous, and the most notorious bandit, between Him Who claimed, and Who had a right to claim to be the Anointed, the Son of God, and him that was worthy of death. The very nomination was an abomination. It could not even be accepted. Their plain calling it was to protest loudly against this choice, and to reject the nomination. But they accept. There is no protest against this plain perversion of justice on the part of the people. The will of the people is not offended.

And Jesus? Does He not protest? Does He not decline to appear on this ballot with Barabbas, and to be submitted to the vote of the multitude? Perhaps, you say that He had no choice? O, but He did! He, more than anyone, felt keenly the offense of being thus reckoned with the malefactors! He stood there in the full consciousness of being the Anointed of God, the Well-beloved Servant of Jehovah, Who had done no iniquity, and in Whose mouth there was found no guile. He knew Himself to be the Holy and Just One, Whose meat it always had been to do the Father's will. Nay more, He stood there in the full consciousness of being the Son of God, the only Begotten, Who even at this very moment was in the bosom of the Father according to His divine nature. O, the shame of it! The abominable corruption of it! The unspeakable wickedness of it! Man, mere man, who is less than a dust of the balance, here places the very Son of God on a par with the lowest representative of the fallen and sinful and damnable world! The will of the people is about to make a choice between very God and public enemy number one! Will He, too, will the very Son of God also accept this nomination? O, do not say that He has no choice! He might simply have dropped His bonds and disappeared. Or He might have caused His divine glory and majesty to flash forth to consume these wicked enemies, that loved darkness rather than light! But He is silent! Voluntarily He so deeply humbles Himself that He allows Himself to be numbered with the lowest transgressors! And why? Because He knows that it is the hour of judgment of the world! Clearly He perceives that even at this moment God is sitting on the judgment seat, and the "world," the world of the "people," the "world" of the majority, stands before the tribunal of the Most High! He is trying them. He is submitting them to His searching examination. He is placing them before the question: If ye must choose between the Holy One and Just, and a murderer, between light and darkness, between righteousness and iniquity, between the Christ of God, and your own wicked world, what will be your preference? And being conscious of all this, the Lord remains silent, and also accepts the shameful nomination!

The question as put before the people by the Roman governor, is recorded in two different forms. Perhaps Pilate repeated the question, and the people took time to consider what they would answer. In the gospel according to Matthew we read: "Therefore when they were gathered together, Pilate said unto them, Whom will ye that I release unto you? Barabbas, or Jesus which is called Christ?" According to Luke the governor appears to have assumed a bolder attitude, and simply to have stated that he found no guilt in Jesus, and that, therefore, of the two, Jesus or Barabbas, he would release the former. In the gospel according to Mark and John both, we read that Pilate asked the people: "Will ye that I release unto you the king of the Jews?" At any rate, the alternative was clearly put. If there were any need of it, the question by the Roman governor favored the choice of Jesus, and clearly suggested that this was the only proper preference they could express in this case. It was a choice between the criminal and the Christ, between the murderer and their King!

And what is the will of the multitude? How do the people vote? What is the preference of the majority? They prefer the murderer! "Whether of the twain will ye that I release unto you? They said, Barabbas!" And when Pilate asked them again: "What shall I do then with Jesus which is called Christ? They all say unto him, Let him be crucified." And when the Roman judge still presses the matter, and asks them: "Why? what evil hath he done?" the answer of the whole multitude comes surging back with a great and angry roar: "Let him be crucified!" Matt. 27:21-23. It is true that the leaders of the Jews moved among the multitude persuading them to choose Barabbas and demand Jesus' blood. Always theirs is the greater guilt and the greater damnation. But the instigation of the chief priests does not render the multitude irresponsible. The choice remains their own. The preference expressed is theirs. Quite consciously they prefer a murderer to Jesus who is called the Christ! And very definite is their choice: the murderer they receive in their midst and take to their bosom, but Jesus they cast out to be crucified!

"Now is the judgment of this world!" The will of the people had spoken. No, indeed, it was not at all proper that a question such as whether Jesus be the Christ, the Son of God, should be submitted to a vote of the people. A shameful act it was on the part of Pilate to present the nomination of Jesus and Barabbas, and leave the preference to the will of the people. By the very act he had trampled all justice under foot. But it had been done.

And, no doubt, God so willed it. For also the people, the majority of the world, must have an opportunity to express themselves on the crucial question: what will ye do with Jesus, the Christ, the Son of the living God? And, let us not become pious, and exalt ourselves above the multitude that made this choice and expressed preference for a murderer above the Holy One. Let us not draw the wrong conclusion that the multitude before the Praetorium who preferred Barabbas above Jesus were an ignorant lot, a mob that knew not what they were doing, and that if only we had been there instead, we of the enlightened twentieth century, we, who are so much more refined, civilized, educated, religious, we would have condemned Barabbas to the cross, and voted in favor of Jesus! For then you and I would only deceive ourselves. The voters that cast their ballot for Barabbas, the murderer, were fully capable of representing any group of voters of all times, casting their ballot for or against Jesus, the Christ. They were religious people. They had Moses and the prophets. The Word of God was entrusted to them. They were well informed. And their choice represents the choice of the whole world apart from grace, the will of the natural man! Always, when the question concerning Jesus that is called Christ is submitted to a vote of the people, to be decided by the will of the world, the answer must be: Give us Barabbas, and let Jesus be crucified! And always, when this Jesus who is called Christ is presented to the will of the natural man, he will surely prefer darkness to light, the murderer above the Holy One, Barabbas to Jesus, the world above Christ! "Now is the judgment of this world!" By its own testimony it is condemned! Now shall the prince of this world be cast out!

O, let that world put on a cloak of righteousness and justice now, it will be of no avail to them. Let them refuse to enter into the Praetorium, lest they become defiled and incapable of eating the passover, all their religiousness cannot alter the fact that they stand forever exposed as friends of the murderer, enemies of the Holy One. Let them take two other malefactors, yes, by all means, let them take two thieves and crucify them together with Christ, to attest to their own severe justice and hatred of all unrighteousness, no number of executions can undo the fact that they have revealed themselves as lovers of unrighteousness, and haters of that which is good! Sin is forever exposed to be sin through the cross of Jesus that is called the Christ! Now is the judgment of this world!

With that sin upon Himself, Christ proceeded to the place of execution! For such is the mystery of the cross: in the hour of judgment the rejected and despised Servant of Jehovah bears the sin of the hostile world that rejects Him and prefers a murderer. He did so by divine appointment before the foundation of the world, as the Head of His Church. And with that sin upon Him He willingly travels all the way of the cross, by His perfect obedience bringing the sacrifice that taketh away the sin of the world. And having made atonement for sin, and having been exalted at the right hand of God, it is He Who by His Spirit and grace changes our wicked preference for Barabbas and all he represents, into a profound and everlasting delight in the friendship and service of the living God!

CHAPTER 5

The Hour of Execution

And behold, the veil of the temple was rent in twain, from the top to the bottom; and the earth did quake, and the rocks rent; and the graves were opened; and many bodies of the saints which slept arose, and came out of the graves after his resurrection, and went into the holy city, and appeared unto many. — MATT. 27: 45, 46.

In our series of Lenten lectures, we consider the hour of Jesus' suffering from the viewpoint of its being the judgment of the world. God's world must be saved, man's world must be judged and condemned. And this was accomplished through the suffering and death of Jesus Christ our Lord. In the hour of the Saviour's suffering all the world is gathered before the tribunal of God, the world of Jew and Gentile, the religious world and the world of heathendom, and that whole world is exposed in its essential wickedness and ungodliness, its hypocrisy and enmity against God. The thoughts of the heart are exposed. The mask of Man's righteousness and piety and goodness is torn off. For man is confronted with God's searching question: what will ye do with Jesus that is called Christ, the highest revelation of the Father, the Son of God? And we have seen that Man's world, the fallen world, answered with one accord: Away with Him, let Him be crucified!

That world, whose prince is the devil, was well represented in that hour. The very best of the religious world, and the noblest of the heathen world stood before the bar of God's justice. Representatives of the religious world of Israel, whose were the covenants, and to whom the oracles of God were entrusted; and representatives of the Graeco-Roman world, proud of its culture and civilization, its power and human wisdom, answered God's question. And all without exception, Judas and the Sanhedrin, Pilate and Herod, the soldiers and the people, replied that the Son of God should be killed, that the Righteous should be trampled under foot, that a murderer should have the preference over the Holy and Just One. And when it was rendered quite clear that the world of man was worthy of wrath and condemnation, Christ Himself, the Lamb of God, went to the place of execution, in order that He might make of man's cross God's altar, sacrifice Himself obediently upon it, and take away the sin of God's world that it might be saved.

We now turn our attention to the cross itself, in order to find out, if possible, whether the scene of the crucifixion actually appears to be the judgment of the world. We would expect some indications of this in the narratives of the gospel that speak of the suffering and death of our Lord on the cross. And in this expectation we are not disappointed. We read in the gospel according to Matthew: "Now from the sixth hour there was darkness all over the land unto the ninth hour. And about the ninth hour Jesus cried with a loud voice, saying, Eli, Eli, lama, sabachthani? that is to say, My God, my God, why hast thou forsaken me?" 27: 45, 46. And again: "Jesus, when he had cried again with a loud voice, yielded up the ghost. And, behold, the veil of the temple was rent in twain, from the top to bottom; and the earth did quake, and the rocks rent; and the graves were opened; and many bodies of the saints which slept arose, and came out of the graves after his resurrection, and went into the holy city, and appeared unto many." So dreadful and awful were these signs of judgment, that even the Roman centurion and they that were with him "feared greatly, saying, Truly, this was the Son of God." Luke gives us the following account of Jesus' death and its effect upon them that stood by: "And it was about the sixth hour, and there was a darkness over all the earth until the ninth hour. And the sun was darkened, and the veil of the temple was rent in the middle. And when Jesus had cried with a loud voice, he said, Father, into thy hands do I commend my spirit: and having said thus, he gave up the ghost. Now when the centurion saw what was done, he glorified God, saying, Certainly this was a righteous man. And all the people that came together to that sight, beholding the things that were done, smote their breasts, and returned." 23:44-48. Plainly, all these signs, the darkness, the earthquake, the rending of the veil of the temple, the splitting of the rocks, and the opening of the graves, reveal to us the cross of Jesus as the judgment of the world. And that in this hour of the wrath of God the Saviour bore the sin of God's world, and suffered the wrath of God in full and to the very end, is evident from His outcries: "My God, my God, why hast thou forsaken me?" and: "It is finished." Let us consider these details a little more closely.

It appears that the six hour period of the Saviour's suffering on the cross is rather sharply divided into two halves, the division being caused by the darkness that descended upon the scene at about the sixth hour. Before that hour, the cross appears emphatically as Man's cross. Men have overcome, it seems, the Son of God, and He is utterly in their power. In the meantime, however, God is still continuing His trial of sinful man. The world is still answering the question: what think ye of the Christ? this time quite spontaneously, and in a manner that reveals all the fury of their hatred against God and His Anointed. For, even though He is completely in their power now, and although they performed all their evil will upon Him, so that Jesus is nothing but a helpless victim, powerless and naked, suffering agonies of soul and body on the accursed tree, yet they mock and jeer at Him, and fill Him with reproach, as if their hatred is inexhaustible. The rulers and the people, the passers-by and the soldiers, — all join in deriding Him and adding shame and reproach to His suffering. But at about noon the scene changes. Darkness descends upon the land, at first a horrible and dreadful gloom, in which a weird light was mingled with the darkness, and the pale disk of the sun was still distinguishable in the firmament; then it, too, disappeared, and the darkness of night enveloped all. It is at the beginning of this second period of the crucifixion that Jesus cried out: "My God, my God, why hast thou forsaken me?" Then, for three hours nothing is heard. No other utterance is heard from the cross till almost the end. A hush has fallen upon the crowd of spectators. No more jeering and mockery is heard. They realize somehow that here is far more than their own evil work. The cross is taken out of their hands. It has become God's cross. Already they begin to feel that God has come down in His anger to execute judgment upon a wicked world. And they are getting ready presently to leave this dreadful spectacle, smiting their breasts in despair! The trial is over, and the hour of execution has come.

For, let us notice that darkness in nature is a sign of God's wrath and of His coming to execute justice and judgment. Just as the joyful light of the sun is a symbol of the light of God's countenance and His blessed favor, so darkness witnesses of wrath and vengeance. Thus it was with the darkness that enveloped the land of Egypt, when Jehovah was about to deliver His people Israel from the house of bondage. Thus we read of God's coming for judgment upon the enemies of His servant David: "There went up a smoke out of his nostrils, and fire out of his mouth devoured: coals were kindled by it. He bowed the heavens also and came down; and darkness was under his feet . . . And he made darkness pavilions round about him, dark waters and thick clouds of the skies." Darkness enveloped Mount Sinai when God sounded forth His holy law from Horeb. Of darkness as symbol of God's righteousness and justice we read in the Psalms. "Clouds and darkness are round about him, righteousness and judgment are the habitation of his throne." Ps. 97:2. The day of the Lord is described as: "A day of darkness and of gloominess, a day of clouds and of thick darkness." Joel 2:2. And as the day of judgment approaches, "the sun shall be turned into darkness, and the moon into blood." Joel 2:31. And at the opening of the sixth seal, "there was a great earthquake, and the sun became black as sackcloth of hair, and the moon became as blood." Rev. 6:12. Darkness in nature, therefore, symbolizes that God is present, that He is about to pour out the vials of His wrath upon a wicked world. This, then, is also the significance of the darkness that fell upon the land of Canaan in the hour of the cross. It meant that God was present there in His justice, that He has come down to execute judgment upon the wicked and to wreak vengeance upon His enemies. Now is the judgment of this world!

The terrible reality of this wrath and judgment of God is evident from the outcry of Jesus: "My God, my God, why hast thou forsaken me." No, indeed, the cross of Golgotha is not man's cross. It never was. Even though wicked men must needs be instrumental in erecting it, and wicked hands must take hold of the Servant of Jehovah and nail Him to the tree, yet the cross is God's place of execution. It is the embodiment of God's curse. Upon Him that hangs on that cross God is pouring out the vials of His fierce wrath against the sin of the world. As man's cross, it is the everlasting evidence of his wickedness and hatred of God; as God's cross it is the revelation of His righteous judgment upon the world whose prince is the devil. But it is, at the same time, the greatest manifestation of the love wherewith God loved His world: For God so loved the world that He gave His only begotten Son! Hence, in the hour of the judgment of man's world, God's Son is delivered over unto death and hell, in order that God's world may be saved. The cross is not man's but God's judgment. And the Saviour knows. Willingly He went to this place of execution in this hour of judgment. And obediently He shed His blood from the very beginning of His cruel suffering. Yet even so, the suffering becomes more intense as the end approaches; the burden of the wrath of God becomes heavier, the darkness deepens as He descends into lowest hell. He becomes perplexed, amazed, even to the extent that His prayer becomes a question, and the question an outcry of agony: "My God, my God, why hast thou forsaken me?"

Who shall ever fathom the depth of agony expressed in this paradoxical outcry? How shall we ever comprehend the mystery of the cross? Here, in the depth of hell struggles the Son of man, the obedient Servant of Jehovah, perplexed by His agonies of soul and body. And from the depths He still cries to God as His God! He is amazed. He does not understand. He cannot penetrate the darkness. Waves of wrath and desolation pass over

His soul. Yet, He still knows Himself the obedient Servant of Jehovah, and cries out to Him: Eli, Eli! And, no doubt, even in this moment, God in heaven is well pleased with His Anointed, Who is willing to be consumed by the zeal of God's house. And yet, this same Son of God, in Whom God is well pleased, in Whom, if we may so speak, He was never more pleased than in this hour, is the object of God's wrath. On Him God pours out all the vials of His fierce anger against the sin of the world in this hour of judgment. And He, the Son, the Servant of the Lord, complains that God has forsaken Him! The Son of God, Who even at that moment is in the bosom of the Father, forsaken of God in the flesh! The beloved Servant of the Lord the object of God's wrath!

For this is, indeed, the meaning of being forsaken of God: the Son of man has descended into lowest hell! To be forsaken is not the same as to be separated. Separation from God in the local, physical, essential sense of the word is quite impossible. For in God we live and move and have our being, wherever we are. For "Whither shall I go from thy spirit? or whither shall I flee from thy presence? If I ascend up into heaven, thou art there: if I make my bed in hell, behold, thou art there." Ps. 139:7, 8. God is everywhere, and always we have to do with Him. And God was on Golgotha. If He had not been there, the cross would not have been the accursed tree. He was in the darkness, He was in the cross, He was in the nails that pierced the Saviour's hands and feet. He was in Christ's soul and body. For God is in hell itself, and hell would not be the place of eternal desolation but for His presence! O, Christ was deeply conscious of God's presence in this hour of judgment. But He knew Himself forsaken in this hour of His deepest woe, first of all, in the sense that not the dimmest ray of God's favor penetrated His soul at this moment. God had taken His grace from Him. The sweetness of His fellowship He did not taste at all in this moment. Even as the sun had become darkened, so the light of God's countenance was hid from Him. And, secondly, instead of the favor and loving kindness of His God, the Saviour now experiences all the pain and sorrow and anguish of soul and body, that is the result of God's fierce anger against sin. The light of God's favor is completely extinguished; the darkness of God's wrath envelops His soul. In this awful moment, the only moment of that kind in all history, Hell is on earth. In the hour of judgment the Son of man suffers the agonies of hell in utter desolation! And because this Son of man, even in this darkest hour of His suffering, is still obedient, and still bears the terrible wrath of God voluntarily; and because this Son of man is also the eternal Son of God, Who is able to taste the depth of eternal death in a moment; therefore, eternities of desolation are pressed into that one moment of His agony, that wrath of God is fully borne by Him, the justice of God is satisfied, the darkness passes, and presently He rises out of the depths and victoriously announces: "It is finished!" The world of Man is condemned forever; the world of God in Christ is justified and saved!

Plainly, that is the meaning of the signs that accompany the death of the Saviour. Briefly, we may express the significance of these accompanying signs by saying that, when Jesus' flesh splits, everything shakes, and moves, and rends: the new world of God is pressing to break through the old world of man! Everything announces that, in the judgment of God, man's world is to be destroyed, to make room for the justified and glorified world of God in Christ!

This is true, first of all, with respect to the religious world, as is indicated in the rending of the veil. You know that the temple building proper was divided into two apartments: the holy place, and the holy of holies. In the former the people of God dwelled symbolically, though only the priests ever entered it, in the golden candlestick, the table of shewbread, and the altar of incense. In the latter, the Most Holy Place, there was the ark of the covenant, with its mercy seat; and there, even though it is said that after the captivity the ark never returned, God dwelled among His people. The whole was, therefore, a beautiful picture of the idea of God's covenant: God dwelling with His people in intimate fellowship of friendship under the same roof, in the same house. But the two apartments were separated by the veil. And this, according to the epistle to the Hebrews, signified "that the way into the holiest of all was not yet made manifest, while as the first tabernacle was yet standing." The way into the fellowship of God was not yet prepared by the blood of the eternal testament. The veil, therefore, was a very essential part of the temple. On the one hand, it closed off the dwelling place of God among His people. Behind the veil God dwelled. Everything depended upon the closed veil in the old dispensation. All the service of the temple, the sacrifices, the burning of incense, the light of the candlestick, and the dedication of the loaves on the table of shewbread, was directed and dedicated to Him that dwelled behind the veil. Jerusalem was the City of God because of that holiest of all; and Israel was the people of God as a nation, because God dwelled between the cherubim in the holy of holies. Remove the veil, and Israel had lost its peculiar place, Jerusalem was no longer the city of God, the temple was destroyed. On the other hand, that veil was also the real symbol of the imperfection of the old covenant. For it plainly testified that the way into the inner sanctuary was not yet open. The temple was a promise of better things to come, when we might enter with boldness into God's fellowship through the blood of Jesus.

Now, then, that veil was rent, at the same time that Jesus' flesh was rent in death. It was rent by God. For the text tells us, that it was rent from top to bottom, and no human hand could thus have torn the heavy veil in twain. What does it mean? In the first place, it signified that God no longer dwelled in the temple made with hands. He had left the earthly sanctuary! One might look directly into the most holy place and discover that it was empty! It means that the earthly temple, and all its service, its priesthood and sacrifices, was very really destroyed by God Himself. It signified that Jerusalem was no longer the City of the living God, and that Israel had ceased to be God's peculiar people. Old things had passed away! Judgment had been executed upon the house of God! But, secondly, it also had a positive meaning. For that rent veil is a picture of the flesh of Jesus Christ, the way into the presence and fellowship of God is now opened, and we may draw near with boldness, being now justified and cleansed through His blood! Man's world had been destroyed, the world of God was justified and saved!

But there is more. There is an earthquake. And earthquakes, according to Scripture, are signs of God's judgment. They remind us that we are living, not in an unmovable, but in a movable world. And they are a prophecy of the time when God will yet once more "shake not the earth only, but also heaven. And this word, Yet once more, signifieth the removing of those things that are shaken, as of things that are made, that those things which cannot be shaken may remain." Heb. 12:26, 27. These things that cannot be shaken are the eternal kingdom in the new creation, which God gave to His Son, and which is founded in the righteousness of His perfect obedience. Small wonder then, that at the death of Jesus the very foundations of the earth are shaken! O, as yet they cannot be completely demolished, for the time for the perfection of the eternal kingdom is not yet. But the earthquake is, nevertheless, a rumbling of the distant thunder of God's final judgment, that will shake the heavens and the earth, and cause the very elements to melt with fervent heat, to make room for God's eternal world: the new heavens and the new earth, in which righteousness shall dwell! Now is the judgment of the world, now shall the prince of this world be cast out!

And, finally, as the earth quakes, and the foundations are shaken, and the rocks rend, the graves are opened! They were opened in preparation for the saints that slept in them to accompany the Lord as a sort of first fruits in His glorious resurrection. Thus, no doubt, we must read the text in Matthew. The saints that slept in these opened graves did not arise at the time of Jesus' death, but after His resurrection. It were better to put a period after the sentence: "And the graves were opened." And then read on: "And many of the bodies of the saints which slept arose and came out of the graves after his resurrection." At the moment of Jesus' death, then, the graves were opened! O, what a mighty and blessed sign! And how appropriate, and full of significance is this sign in connection with the death of Christ! For the grave as such is sealed. It has only one exit: into eternal death! There is no way out of that grave and its power of death! They that enter there can never find their way into the light of life again! And that which strengthens the jaws of death and the grave is sin, and the wrath of God against it. But, behold, now, when our Lord dies, the jaws of the grave are paralyzed. They open up! And, mark you, they open into life, into resurrection life, for no doubt, these saints were raised with Christ into glory. And, therefore, the grave opens never to close again! There is an exit to death! And the exit leads to life eternal through the resurrection of Jesus Christ from the dead! What, then, does it mean, that at the moment of Christ's death the graves are opened? It signifies that the death of Christ is the deathblow to death itself! For even as the sting of death is sin, and the strength of sin is the law, so the death of our Lord Jesus Christ is the perfect answer to God's demand upon the sinner, the answer of perfect obedience given in the depth of hell, and, therefore, the perfect satisfaction for sin and the paralyzing of the jaws of death!

Now is the judgment of this world! O, mighty, marvellous, glorious cross of Christ! By it the world, man's world, is for ever condemned. Let us, then, not love the world, neither the things that are in the world, the lust of the flesh, and the lust of the eyes, and the pride of life, for then we are condemned with that world! By it the way into the inner sanctuary is opened! Let us, therefore, brethren, have boldness to draw near upon the blood-sprinkled way, through the death of our Lord! By it the grave is for ever opened into life! O death, where is thy sting? O grave where is thy victory? Thanks be to God, who giveth us the victory, through our Lord Jesus Christ! By it all things are shaken, to make room for the unmoveable kingdom! Wherefore, brethren, "we receiving a kingdom which cannot be moved, let us have grace, whereby we may serve God acceptably with reverence and godly fear!"

CHAPTER 6

Risen Indeed

The Lord is risen indeed, and hath appeared unto Simon. — LUKE 24:34.

"But now is Christ risen from the dead!" Thus the apostle Paul writes in I Cor. 15:20. And the context in which this triumphant declaration occurs shows clearly that the resurrection of Jesus Christ from the dead is considered to be the very heart of the gospel, the indispensable basis of all preaching, the cornerstone of the Christian faith. For a moment the apostle had considered the situation of the apostles and their preaching, and of the believers and their faith, in case the Lord had not risen from the dead. And he had stated quite radically that then all preaching would be vain, and the Christian faith would be vain also. And this is self-evident. If Christ is not raised, then there is no power in the cross, then the blood of Jesus is no different from any other blood that was ever shed, and it does not cleanse from all sin; then there is no justification, no forgiveness of sin, we are still in our sins. If Christ is not raised, then He was swallowed up of death, He does not live, He is not the quickening Spirit, nor is He the Son of God come in the flesh. If the resurrection of Jesus Christ is not a fact, then the Incarnation is not true, the Son of God did not die on the cross, the exaltation of the Lord at the right hand of God is a figment of the imagination, and in vain

51

do we look for His coming again in glory to establish His kingdom for ever. If Christ is not raised, then all the experience of believers is an illusion, for then He does not live in them by His Spirit and grace, regeneration is an invention, faith is a mere opinion, the love of Christ is auto-suggestion, and the joy of hope is the product of an overheated imagination. But now is Christ risen from the dead! Preaching is very real though it may be foolishness to the natural man. And the faith of the Church is not vain. The resurrection of our Lord is the way out of darkness into light, out of death into the glory of eternal life!

This basic truth of the gospel is strongly and abundantly attested as a fact, and it is to this testimony by faithful witnesses of the fact of the resurrection that I would like to call your attention in this chapter. Not as if it were my purpose in any way to apologize for the Christian faith in the risen Lord, or to render the fact of the resurrection of Jesus Christ rationally credible. This is neither possible nor necessary. There is no more unreasonable act than to deny the credibility of the resurrection. For as the apostle Paul puts the question to King Agrippa, so we would present it to all that have ever attempted to overthrow the truth of the resurrection of our Lord: "Why should it be a thing incredible with you, that God should raise the dead?" If God is the Lord, He certainly must be the Lord of life and death, and He is able to quicken the dead. And if it pleased Him to reveal Himself in all the glory of His divine wisdom and power and grace, there certainly is no more efficient medium through which this revelation of the living God could be made to us than the resurrection of the Son of God in the flesh. To deny, therefore, the credibility of the resurrection of Christ, is to deny the very existence of God. And, therefore, it cannot possibly be my purpose to demonstrate the credibility of the resurrection of the Lord. Not with the possibility, but with the fact of the resurrection I am now concerned. And facts must be attested. There must be witnesses for them, these witnesses must be faithful, and they must be able to produce proper evidence. And one can hardly refer to a historic fact that is better attested, by more faithful witnesses, and by more indubitable evidence than the fact of the resurrection of Jesus Christ from the dead.

In order, however, that we may be able to appreciate properly these witnesses of the resurrection of Christ, and the evidence they present in their testimony, we must first of all have a clear conception of the fact that is supported by their testimony. Jesus Christ, the Son of God come in the flesh, Who died on the cross, and Who was buried in the sepulchre in the garden of Joseph of Arimathea, is raised from the dead. What does this mean? It means, to be sure, that in the same human nature, in the same body in which He died, He was quickened into new life. The resurrection of Christ was a resurrection of the body. It was real. We do not agree with those who would idealize the resurrection of the Lord, as if it meant that He was glorified merely in a spiritual sense, or that He arose in the minds of the apostles, and through the preaching of the gospel continues to live in the consciousness of the Church. On the contrary, in the very body in which He suffered death on the accursed tree, He arose from the grave. And the reality of the bodily resurrection of the Saviour was revealed to faithful witnesses. However, this is not all. The resurrection of Christ was not like that of the young man of Nain, or of Lazarus, the former of whom had been recalled to life by the Lord from the bier that was to bear his body to the grave, while the latter had been raised after he had been in the grave four days. Had the resurrection of the Lord been no more, the testimony concerning it would have been rather simple. For these men were called back into their earthly life. In their case the jaws of death were forced to give up their victims, in order that they might return, in their mortal, corruptible bodies, to their former earthly existence. They arose from the grave on the earthly side. Lazarus returned to his home in Bethany, to his sisters, Mary and Martha, to his friends and acquaintances that had bemoaned his death. They met him as before. They talked with him, and ate and drank with him. And all could witness that he had been dead and lived again. But that is not true of the resurrection of Jesus Christ our Lord. He arose, to be sure, but not in order to return to us. He went on. He went through the grave. He issued forth from the grave on its immortal, heavenly side. In His case the resurrection meant complete victory over death. Death was swallowed up by Him. Mortality had been swallowed up of life. This corruptible had put on incorruption, this mortal had put on immortality, and the natural had been replaced by the spiritual. In the image of the first Adam, the image of the earthly, the Lord had died and had been buried; but with the image of the heavenly He arose. The result was that the risen Lord in His glorified resurrection body no more belonged to our earthly sphere of life and existence. The former fellowship had been broken forever. Not again could He walk about with His disciples in the same manner as before His resurrection. They can no longer come to Him: He must come to them. If there are to be witnesses of the resurrection, it can only be through the revelation of the risen Lord Himself. And we must expect that the witnesses of this revelation will speak, not only of the real bodily resurrection of the Saviour, but also of its otherness and marvel.

Now, who are these witnesses that became the media of the revelation of the risen Lord, and whose testimony was preserved infallibly for us in Holy Writ?

There is, first of all, the testimony of the women, who, early in the morning of that wonderful first day of the week, had taken their spices and made their way to the garden of Joseph, to see the sepulchre and to complete the embalming of the body of their Master. Witnesses they had been of the burial, but they had not seen, evidently, that Joseph and Nicodemus, within the tomb, had quite finished the preparation of Jesus' body, and with the spices had wound it in linen clothes according to the Jews' manner of burying. And so they made their way to the sepulchre to perform their last service of love to their Lord Whom they loved. On the way they face the serious problem of the stone that had been rolled before the entrance of the tomb, and which was too heavy for them to remove. But as they approach, and view the grave from a distance, they notice to their amazement that the stone is already rolled away. The grave is open! It must have been at this moment that, characteristically, Mary Magdalene at once jumped to the conclusion that they had stolen the body of her Lord, and without taking time to investigate further and to view the grave, returned in haste to report to the apostles. The other women, however, continued, saw a vision of angels, who preached to them the first resurrection gospel, and viewed "the place where the

Lord lay." When Mary Magdalene returned to the grave the
women had already departed. And we know how Mary was the
first recipient of the revelation of the risen Lord, Whom she
recognized in His calling her by name. Yet, also the other women,
as they returned from the sepulchre, were favored by an appearance of the resurrected Christ, and they worshipped Him.

But on that same day several more became witnesses of the
resurrection. Upon the report of Mary, Peter and John hasten to
the garden of Joseph, inspect the vacated grave, and become witnesses of the wonder of the linen clothes, and of the place where
the Lord had lain. It probably was soon after that Peter, who was
so sorely in need of a special token of his Lord's favor, could
report to the rest of the apostles that he had seen the Lord, and
that He was risen indeed! Lu. 24:34; I Cor. 15:5. Then, in the
afternoon of that first day of the week, the risen Christ joined
the company of two disciples on the way to Emmaus, as they were
busily discussing the things that had taken place in Jerusalem,
and the several reports concerning His being seen which by that
time were being circulated in the city. And He expounded to them
from all the Scriptures, that the Christ must suffer thus, and
enter into His glory! And as their hearts were still burning within
them, He became known to them in the breaking of the bread. In
the evening of the same day, finally, He suddenly appeared in
the midst of a congregation of the disciples, the apostles without
Thomas, and others, and convincing them of His identity, instructed them in the things concerning the kingdom of God. Once
more He appeared in the midst of the apostles, a week later, now
for the special purpose of convincing the profoundly sorrowing
and hopeless Thomas that He had risen indeed! He went before
them to Galilee, as He had announced before His death. And
there He appeared, not only through the marvellous draught of
fishes to seven of the apostles at the Sea of Galilee, but also to
more than five hundred brethren at once. Paul makes mention
of an appearance to James, the brother of the Lord. And, having
returned to Judaea, the eleven apostles went with Him to the
Mount of Olives, whence He was taken up from them into heaven.
"Last of all," the apostle informs us in I Cor. 15:8, "he was
seen of me also, as one born out of due time." Hundreds of

witnesses, therefore, could testify in those days, that the Lord had risen indeed!

What is the value of their testimony, even when we consider them from a human viewpoint? The forces of unbelief have united and often sharpened their wits, to prove that the testimony of these numerous witnesses deserves no credibility, but their attempts in this direction could only serve to expose their own folly. How foolish was the story of the watchmen that fled in consternation from the grave they had been guarding, and were bribed by the hard-hearted leaders of the Jews to spread the report, that the disciples had stolen the body of Jesus while they slept! But equally foolish are all the efforts of unbelief to undermine and expose as false the testimony of the witnesses of the resurrection of Christ. Some were not ashamed to maintain that these witnesses were the inventors of deliberate falsehoods, a statement which bears the stamp of absurdity on its very face. Others have tried to explain that the disciples were subject to hallucinations. So strongly did they expect that the Lord would rise from the dead, that the expectation became the father to the conviction that the Lord had risen, and they sincerely but mistakenly believed that they had seen the risen Christ. But all these explanations to deny the truthfulness of the testimony of the witnesses of the resurrection, simply show to what lengths of folly unbelief will go to gainsay the resurrection of Jesus from the dead. Were all these witnesses subject to the same hallucinations? Did the women as they went to the grave on that early morning of the first day expect that Jesus had risen from the dead? Did any of the disciples? We know better. They did not even remotely think of it. Never had they understood the word of Jesus concerning His suffering, death, and resurrection on the third day. Was Thomas likely to be subject to hallucinations, who said that he would not believe unless he should touch the very scars of Jesus' suffering and death? Is it probable or even possible that the disciples were dreaming when they drew the net to shore containing one hundred and fifty-three fishes, which they had caught at the word of the risen Lord? Or did the apostle Paul, perhaps, expect to become a witness of the risen Christ on the way to Damascus? If ever there were true and faithful witnesses, that recorded just exactly what they saw and heard, and whose testimony is reliable, they are the men and women who reported that the Lord is risen indeed! And let us not forget that most, if not all of these witnesses sealed their testimony with their own blood. Trusting in the risen Christ they gladly suffered martyrdom for His sake!

What then is their testimony, and what is the evidence they are able to produce to sustain it? They all witness with one accord that Christ is really risen from the dead, and that He never returned to this world in and through His resurrection, but went on to glory and immortality. This truth was clearly revealed to them on and after the third day. And what is their evidence? Or let us rather ask: how was this truth of the resurrection revealed to these faithful witnesses?

There was, on that first day of the week, first of all, the testimony of the open and empty grave. Let us recall that the next day after the burial of Jesus, the chief priests and Pharisees had appealed to the Roman governor that the sepulchre might be made sure until the third day, "lest his disciples come by night, and steal him away, and say unto the people, He is risen from the dead: so the last error shall be worse than the first." Matt. 27:64. This request had been granted by Pilate. The sepulchre had been sealed. The stone had been secured to the main body of the grave by a steel chain, bearing the Roman seal, and, besides, a watch of Roman soldiers had been stationed at the sepulchre to guard it until the third day. Thus the enemy had themselves furnished evidence beforehand that their own invention was a lie, and that the body of the Lord could never have been removed from the tomb by human hands. Yet, when the women came to the grave in the morning of the first day of the week, they found the tomb open and empty! That open grave, that had been so securely sealed, and so strongly guarded, was the first medium through which the light of the revelation of the risen Lord broke through the darkness of their gloom and sorrow.

Secondly, there was the appearance of angels, that explained to them the empty grave, invited them to inspect it, and proclaimed to them the glad tidings that Christ had risen from the dead. An angel had come down from heaven on that early morning, accompanied by the sign of an earthquake, and he had rolled

the stone away from the sepulchre. This was done, not indeed
that the way out of the grave might be opened for the living Lord,
for of this the risen Christ had no need, and He had risen probably
much earlier on the third day, which had begun at six o'clock the
previous evening; but in order that the grave might be opened and
preserved for inspection for the witnesses of the resurrection. And
it was by the mouth of this heavenly messenger that the gospel of
the risen Lord was first preached to the astonished and perplexed
women: "Fear not ye: for I know that ye seek Jesus, which was
crucified. He is not here: for he is risen, as he said. Come, see
the place where the Lord lay." Matt. 28:5, 6.

Thirdly, these witnesses reported the marvel of "the place where
the Lord lay." The women had seen this place in the tomb and
had been amazed. And after they had reported it to the disciples,
two of them, Peter and John, proceeded to the tomb, not merely
to verify for themselves that it was empty, but more especially to
see the "place where the Lord lay." Now what was so wonderful
and remarkable about this place? It was the sign of the linen
clothes. To these special attention is called. We read that, when
John came to the sepulchre "and stooping down, and looking in,
he saw the linen clothes lying." And again, when Peter, who followed John, arrived, and had gone in the sepulchre, he also saw
the linen clothes lie. And he noticed particularly that the napkin
that had been about Jesus' head, was not lying with the rest of
the clothes, but lying wrapped together by itself. And finally, we
read, that John also went into the tomb, saw the same thing, and
believed. John 20:4-8. Now, why should special attention be
called to the "place where the Lord lay"? And why should the
linen clothes attract so much attention? And what was there about
these linen clothes that caused John to believe that the Lord had
risen from the dead? There can be only one answer: these linen
clothes that had been wrapped about the body of Jesus at the
burial, limb for limb, lay there in the tomb exactly in the shape of
the body that had been wrapped in them, but that was now departed, and for the same reason the napkin that had been twisted
around Jesus' head lay in a place by itself! They had not been
disturbed, though the body of the Lord was in them no more.
And thus they clearly marked the place where the Lord had lain,

and were a silent and most astounding testimony of the wonder of the resurrection of the Saviour!

And, finally, as the culmination and seal upon all this testimony there were the appearances of the Lord Himself. And also these appearances were, on the one hand, very real; yet, on the other hand, they were very strange and marvellous. Appearances they were, not in the sense that Jesus for a time assumed a body, but in the sense that He showed Himself in the spiritual resurrection body to the disciples. And they established beyond a shadow of doubt that the Lord had risen indeed. For they were very real. The Lord was plainly visible to them, and that, too, as the same Jesus that had been crucified, for the prints of the nails in His hands and feet were plainly seen. They were with Him for a while, and He spoke to them, and instructed them in the things of the kingdom of God. He became known to them in the familiar breaking of the bread, or in the equally unmistakable wonder of the draught of fishes at the Sea of Galilee. He even ate before them. And yet, though the risen Lord was very real to them, there was something very strange about Him. He was quite different from the Jesus of Nazareth with whom they had walked for three years. He was with them no more, even though occasionally He appeared within the sphere of their perception. Suddenly He would stand in their midst, though the doors were closed, and just as suddenly He would disappear again. So different was He, that in their faith they marvelled, that in their assurance they questioned, that in their wonder and amazement they sometimes doubted still. For so we read: "And none of the disciples durst ask him, Who art thou? knowing that it was the Lord." John 21:12. And again: "And when they saw him, they worshipped him: but some doubted." And through it all they received the revelation of the risen Lord. He had risen indeed; and He had risen, not to return to them, but in glory and immortality: death had no more dominion over Him!

But now is Christ risen from the dead! That cornerstone of the gospel is firmly laid through the revelation of the risen Lord Himself as attested by many and faithful witnesses! And the truth of this gospel is corroborated by the experience of the Church, of believers of every age! He lives! Raised He was by the Father, and His resurrection is God's own answer to Christ's "It is finished." Just ask the thousands upon thousands that found no peace in their own righteousness, that were troubled because of their sins, and that were ingrafted by faith into Jesus Christ, crucified and raised. They found peace with God through Him! Why? Because the Christ, Who was delivered for our transgressions, and raised for our justification, entered their heart, and they by grace heard God's Word of righteousness through the resurrection of Jesus Christ from the dead. He lives! Just ask the countless throng of believers, who in themselves are dead in trespasses and sins, but who have died and have been raised with Christ, who have been delivered from the bondage of sin, and now have become servants of righteousness. How? Through the power of the living Lord! He is risen, and is become the firstfruits of them that slept! Christ is the first-begotten of the dead! He went through the grave into the glory of eternal life as the Head of the Church! *The* resurrection is begun! And it cannot possibly stop until all that belong to Him, and believe on His name, and look for the city that has foundations, have followed Him in that glorious resurrection. O, death! where is thy sting? O, grave! where is thy victory? Thanks be to God, who giveth us the victory through our Lord Jesus Christ!

THE
AMAZING CROSS

Part II:

Amazing Obedience

CHAPTER 1

Laying Down His Life

*Therefore doth my father love me, because I lay
down my life, that I might take it again.*—JOHN 10:17.

A very proper custom it is of the Church on earth to direct
her attention especially to the passion and death of her Saviour
in the weeks preceding Easter, the so-called lenten season. Proper
this custom is, because the vicarious suffering of the Lord must
needs occupy a central place in the consciousness of faith, and in
the preaching of the gospel. On the death and the resurrection of
our Lord Jesus Christ depends all our salvation. In this respect
the name of Jesus is quite different from any other name. Other
names are remembered by men because of the illustrious lives and
mighty deeds they represent; the name of Jesus is a perpetual object of grateful adoration especially because of the great significance of His death. There is power in that death of Christ, power
of redemption, power of forgiveness and eternal righteousness, the
power of everlasting life and glory. Of a mere man it is sometimes
said that his life was a great blessing for the world, that the world
would be much the worse had he not lived and labored; but of the
Saviour it is true that He would have no significance at all if He
had not died. For had He not died, He would not have risen. And
if He is not raised, our faith is vain, we are yet in our sins. I Cor.
15:17. And, therefore, we are not surprised that the Church never

63

grows weary of concentrating her attention upon the cross of Jesus, and contemplating by faith the suffering of her Lord. In the cross of Christ she glories. To her the Word of the cross is a power of God unto salvation.

We will follow this custom in our discussions, and for the next few chapters make the passion of the Lord the main theme of our discussion. However, we will have to limit this theme if we are to convey a definite message. The suffering of the Lord is as many-sided as human sin and redemption; it is as deep as hell and as high as heaven; it is as rich as the love of God. And we may notice, too, that a comparatively very large part of the gospel narratives is devoted to the passion and death of the Saviour. We must, therefore, confine our discussion to one definite aspect of this suffering, and consider it from a certain particular viewpoint. And the specific aspect of the passion of our Lord which we have chosen to discuss in all our lenten meditations is that of Christ's voluntary suffering. Christ's suffering was a sacrifice. And this implies that He suffered and died voluntarily, by which I mean, not merely that He was wholly resigned to, in agreement with His way of sorrow and grief and death, but that His passion and death were acts of His will. Distinction is often made between the active and passive obedience of the Lord. And this distinction may stand, if we only remember that also His passive obedience was very really obedience. His suffering was an act. He suffered because, before God, it was His will to suffer. He died because it was His will to die. As the Lord Himself expresses it in the words to which I would like to call special attention in the present chapter: "Therefore doth my Father love me, because I lay down my life, that I might take it again. No man taketh it from me, but I lay it down of myself. I have power to lay it down, and I have power to take it again. This commandment have I received of my Father." John 10:17, 18.

Christ laid down His life in order that He might take it again. We should not separate these two clauses, for they are intimately related, and the first can be understood correctly only in the light of the second. Christ did not merely lay down His life, but emphatically He laid down that life in order that He might take it again. A suicide lays down his life, but to no purpose and from

a thoroughly sinful motive. In a certain sense it may be said of one
that he lays down his life for another. A mother may die for the
babe of her love; a friend may die for his friend; a soldier may die
for his country. But in all these cases death is the end of the
self-sacrifice, and the sacrifice bears no other fruit, yields no other
benefit than that which the death as such could profit the other.
But with Christ this is different. He laid down His life for the
very purpose that He might take it again. The main thought is
after all, not the death of Christ, but His resurrection. The
resurrection is the goal that must be attained. For Christ is here
speaking as the Good Shepherd. Sheep were given unto Him by
the Father. He has been appointed the Shepherd of the sheep
whom the Father loves. Christ has a flock. And that flock must
be saved. These sheep, whom the Father gave to Christ, are in
themselves in the midst of death. They have sinned, and as sinners
they are under the just wrath of God and delivered over unto death.
But the Father has ordained that they should have life, and what
is more, that they should have it more abundantly than ever they
had life before. In Adam they possessed an earthly life, and the
image of the earthy they bore. But it is God's purpose to give
them the eternal life of the resurrection in heavenly glory. To give
them that life the Father appointed the Son, even from before the
foundation of the world, as their Good Shepherd. He will give
them that life. But in order to be able to give them this more
abundant life of heavenly glory, He must first obtain it Himself,
and become the quickening Spirit. Only as the risen Lord, the
heavenly Lord, can Christ give the more abundant life to His sheep.
And in order to attain to that glorious life of the resurrection
which He is to impart to His sheep, He must first die, or rather,
He must lay down His life, in order that He might take it again.
Therefore, then, does His Father love Him, because He is willing
to lay down His life in order that He might take it again, and thus
become the living Good Shepherd that is able to give life to His
own more abundantly.

Yes, Christ laid down His life that He might take it again.
And let us understand first of all, that the life He takes again is
not the same as the life He laid down. The life He laid down was
earthy, mortal, corruptible, the life of flesh and blood that can-

not inherit the kingdom of God. The word that is translated "life" here is literally: *soul*. Yet, the translators have rendered it quite correctly by life. For, as I have remarked previously, the word *soul* does not always have the same connotation in Scripture. It sometimes denotes the whole man, for man is called a living soul; in other passages it clearly means the spiritual part of man in distinction from the body; and then again it means the life which man lives in this world, his life as a living soul. And it is in this last sense that the word is used here. Christ had assumed our human nature in the incarnation. The Word was made flesh and dwelled among us. John 1:14. In that human nature, body and soul, Christ, during His earthly sojourn, lived our life. He was like His brethren in all things, sin excepted. He lived our human life. And that life was earthy, weak, mortal and corruptible. O, it is true, that Christ is the life and the resurrection, but He is this, not by virtue of the life He assumed when He became flesh, but because He is the Son of God, Who has life in Himself in the divine nature. In His human nature He lived our life. He ate and drank, He labored and grew weary. He saw and heard earthly things, He spoke an earthly language, He lived in the midst of earthly relationships, and that earthly life was subject to suffering and death. That life He laid down. But when He took it again in His resurrection, it was not in that earthly form, mortal and corruptible, but in the glory of immortality and incorruptibleness. Also Christ's body was sown in weakness, but raised in strength; it was sown in dishonor, it was raised in glory: it was sown in corruptibleness and mortality, it was raised in incorruption and immortality. And when the Lord says that He lays down His life, that He might take it again, the meaning is that He willingly puts down the life He assumed, in order that He might take it again in the glory of the resurrection. The seed must fall into the earth and die before it can bring forth fruit!

But if Christ, as the Good Shepherd, was so to die that He would through death attain to the glorious life of the resurrection, the more abundant life, His death must have special significance. For, He represented His people, the sheep which the Father gave Him. He took their place before the face of God in judgment. All their sins He took upon Himself. And the punishment for their sins He must bear. He died for them, that is, instead of them, and in order to give them life. But if His death was to have that power, the power of redemption, the power to blot out sin and to bestow eternal life, it must be a sacrifice, a perfect and complete sacrifice, satisfying fully the justice of God with respect to sin. And this implies, first, that in laying down His life He should taste death in all its terrible agony as the expression of the wrath of God against sin. Christ must not merely die: He must taste death. The terrible wrath of the infinitely holy God must be poured out over Him, must pass through every nerve and fiber of His existence. In dying He must fully taste the very agony of hell! And, secondly, this death, in order to be a sacrifice and an atonement for sin, must be an *act* on Christ's part. We, too, die, but our death is inflicted upon us without and against our will. The lost in hell also suffer the eternal wrath of God, but in this suffering there is no atonement, for the simple reason that it is not an act of loving obedience. But Christ must bring a sacrifice. He must suffer all there is in death and the wrath of God voluntarily. He must want to die for God's righteousness' sake. He must descend into the depth of hell, and there, experiencing the awful wrath of God against sin, He must be able to say: "Willingly I give Myself a sacrifice to Thy righteousness, O, God! and even here in the darkness of deepest death I love Thee, and it is My meat to do Thy will!" And it is this that is expressed in the words of the Good Shepherd: "I lay down my life, that I might take it again."

Hence, the Lord speaks of a commandment He received from His Father. "This commandment," He says, "I have received of my Father." The commandment He received was that He should lay down His life that He might take it again in glory, in order that, as the Good Shepherd, He might give life to His own, and give it to them more abundantly. Hence, the commandment implied that He should take upon Himself the sins of His people and so bear the punishment for them, that He might take them away forever, blot them out, satisfy the justice of God, and merit for His own eternal righteousness and life. And again, this implied that He had received a commandment voluntarily to walk the way of death and hell and to bear the punishment of sin in perfect and loving obedience. "Thou shalt love Me!" That is the eternal and unchangeable demand of God upon man. "Thou shalt love Me with all thine heart and mind and soul and strength," that is the whole law! And it was God's demand for man in the state of righteousness in paradise. But the first man violated the covenant of friendship, and transgressed the commandment of God. He refused to love God in the midst of the abundance and joy of paradise. And if ever atonement was to be made for sin, someone must come who is able to love God perfectly, but now in the manifestation of His righteousness and justice: He must love God in hell! That is the commandment Christ received: Thou shalt die in love to Me! This commandment Christ received from before the foundations of the world. It was not a commandment that was revealed to Him for the first time at some moment during His sojourn on earth. On the contrary, all His life and work was in obedience to this commandment of the Father. To obey this commandment He came in the fulness of time, assumed our flesh and blood, and dwelled among us. In obedience to this commandment He endured reproach and shame all the time He was on earth, and when He was reviled He reviled not again. In obedience to this commandment He set His face to Jerusalem, that He might be betrayed into the hands of sinners and be crucified and slain. It was in obedience to that commandment, that in the night of His betrayal He sent away the betrayer into the darkness of that darkest of all nights with the message: what thou doest, do quickly! And from there on He descends voluntarily into the depth of hell, the way becoming narrower and more difficult to travel as He descends: from the upper room to the garden of agony, from there to the meeting of the Sanhedrin to be rejected by His own, thence to the Roman governor to be judged and condemned by the world-power, and, finally, to the Hill of the Skull, that He might be lifted up on the accursed tree!

It was all an act of voluntary obedience. "No one taketh my life from me, but I lay it down of myself." O, indeed, superficially considered this would seem different. Did not, after all, men take His life from Him? Was He not crucified by wicked men and slain? Was it not the evil machinations of the chief priests and elders and the dark treachery of the traitor that led Him to His death? Was He not taken captive by a band of soldiers and men,

and does it not appear that He is quite helplessly in the power
of His enemies, when He is bound and led to Annas and Caiaphas,
when He is smitten and spit upon and buffeted? Does it not
appear as if the world is triumphant over Him and takes His
life away from Him, when He is judged by Pilate, mocked by
Herod, scourged by the Roman governor, cruelly crowned with a
crown of thorns by the soldiers, condemned to death and led
away to be crucified? Does it not appear on the way to Golgotha
as if He will die on the road, so that someone must carry His
cross behind Him? And do not men take away His life, when
strong arms of Roman soldiers stretch His weary body on the
cross, and hammer the cruel nails through His hands and feet?
And when He is finally lifted up between two malefactors, do
not the enemies still rail at Him, mocking and jeering, and
challenging Him to come down from the cross if He can? Are
not then that suffering and death of Jesus giving the lie to His own
words: No man can take it from me, but I lay it down of myself?

Indeed, it appears so. But, first of all, do not forget that none
of all these wicked enemies, that play their part in the drama
of the crucifixion, could have laid hands on Him, could have
touched Him with a finger, had He not voluntarily surrendered
Himself to their will. How often this had been proved during the
three years of His public ministry, when they tried to take Him,
but could not, "because His hour had not yet come"! And if we
but study more closely the incidents connected with His capture
and trial and death, it will become abundantly evident, that they
could not have taken His life had He not willed it. After all, was
He not the Son of God? Did He not have power over life and
death? Had He not cast out devils, rebuked storms and angry
waves, raised the dead? Could He not have scattered the wicked
members of the Sanhedrin with a look of His eye, and could He
not have laid the proud Roman governor prostrate before Him?
Or would it have been beyond His wondrous power to release
Himself from the tree and come down? Yes, the enemies were
instrumental in causing His death, and that is their terrible guilt;
but after all, never could they have taken His life, had He not
willed it. But, and this is the second element that must be considered, in all His suffering and death Christ was in perfect har-

mony with the will of His Father. Surely, the enemies inflicted the pain of death upon Him; and God poured out His wrath upon Him for the sins of His people; but in all this Christ suffered willingly, freely, obediently, in love to the Father. If I may express myself thus: His lifeblood was not taken from Him, He shed it! In every drop of blood that trickled from His hands and feet there was a conscious act of obedience, an act of perfect love. And so, on the cross He fully realized His own words: "I lay down my life, that I might take it again. No man taketh it from me, but I lay it down of myself. I have power to lay it down, and I have power to take it again. This commandment have I received of my Father."

Yes, indeed, power Christ had to lay down His life in order that He might take it again! Had it not been so, His death would still have been vain, and could not have had the value of a sacrifice blotting out our sins. No one could possibly offer his life as a vicarious sacrifice, unless he had been authorized by the Judge of heaven and earth. Christ, however, had power so to lay down His life that He might take it again in glory, and that by this voluntary death He might obtain forgiveness, eternal righteousness and life for His own. The idea that must have the emphasis here, according to the meaning of the original, is that Christ had received *authority* to lay down His life, and to take it again. To be sure, Christ also had power in the sense of ability and strength to lay down His life as a sacrifice; for He is the eternal Son of God, and as such He is the Lord of life and death. And He was in a position to give His life as a sacrifice for sin, for He was without sin, and was not Himself under the sentence of death. We have no life to give away or to offer as a sacrifice to God. We are under the death sentence. How could a criminal, sentenced to death and about to die on the gallows, stipulate that his death should be received as a sacrifice for his fellow criminals? But the Saviour knew no sin. He was, therefore, in a position to offer His life to God as a sacrifice for the sins of others. And He was capable of bringing the perfect sacrifice, as an act of perfect obedience, because it was His meat to do the Father's will. He was the perfect High Priest, Who not only had a sacrifice to offer without blemish, but Who could also make the offering

an act of perfect love of God. And even as He was capable of
laying down His life as a sacrifice, so He had power to take it
again, for He is the life and the resurrection!

Yet, the idea that He had authority to lay down His life and to
take it again, must have all the emphasis. Of what avail would
it be that a man would deprive himself of his life, or take the
place of another on the gallows, if such a sacrifice were not
authorized and accepted by the judge? Christ was authorized,
officially appointed and empowered to lay down His life and
to take it again. He was God's High Priest, appointed to bring
the atoning sacrifice instead of His people. And so, the cross is,
indeed, the manifestation of the great love of the Good Shepherd
for His sheep, but it is ultimately the revelation of the unfathomable, eternal and unchangeable love of God to us. The cross is
not the cause of the love of God to His people, but the outflow
and central revelation of that love. "For God so loved the world,
that He gave His only begotten Son, that whosoever believeth on
him should not perish, but have everlasting life." Surveying the
wondrous cross by faith, we are assured that on that accursed
tree "God was in Christ reconciling the world unto Himself, not
imputing their trespasses unto them." II Cor. 5:19. And relying
on that eternal love of God revealed in the cross of His Son,
we have righteousness in the midst of our present sin and guilt;
peace with God, transcendent, victorious peace, in the midst of
the present unrest; and eternal life and glory even while we still
lie in the midst of our present death! And so, the church, contemplating the death of her Lord, may, indeed, sing:

> "When I survey the wondrous cross,
> On which the Prince of glory died,
> My richest gain I count but loss,
> And pour contempt on all my pride.

> "Were the whole realm of nature mine,
> That were a present far too small;
> Love so amazing, so divine,
> Demands my soul, my life, my all!"

CHAPTER 2

Voluntarily Serving the Father's Glory

Father, glorify thy name. — JOHN 12:28.

In these weeks of lenten season, as we especially remember the passion of our Saviour, we were to call particular attention to those phases of the suffering of Christ which clearly reveal that, even though He suffered through wicked hands, He walked all the way of His grief and sorrow and death voluntarily. And I find one of those instances in the remarkable words the Saviour spoke shortly before His death on the cross: "Now is my soul troubled; and what shall I say? Father, save me from this hour: but for this cause came I unto this hour. Father, glorify thy name." John 12:27, 28.

It was but a few days before the final Passover, the last that could ever be properly celebrated. Jesus was in Jerusalem into which He had made His royal or triumphant entry as the King of Sion. Everything reminds Him of the nearness of "the hour" of which the Lord spoke frequently, and which He also mentions in the words just quoted. And as the hour approached there were moments in Jesus' life and consciousness when the dark shadows of it crept over His soul. For the Lord was truly human. There were, no doubt, even in these last days of His life and ministry moments when His consciousness was concentrated upon other matters, and when the apprehension of the approaching

73

suffering would be forced into the background of His conscious life. But there were also other moments, when the anguish of the hour would overwhelm Him, so that He felt the need of pouring out His soul before those that were about Him, and, especially, before the Father. Such a moment it was when He spoke the remarkable words to which we call your attention in this chapter. The hour was approaching fast. In fact, the Lord refers to it as having come already. And as the awful reality of it rushes upon His soul, He complains: "Now is my soul troubled, and what shall I say?"

The context tells us about a peculiar incident that was the special occasion of Jesus' soul trouble at this moment. Some Greeks had come to Jerusalem to worship on the feast of the Passover. And they had expressed their desire to Philip, one of Jesus' disciples, that they might see Jesus. And after Philip had talked the matter over with Andrew, the two had conveyed the request of the Greeks to the Master. The text does not inform us whether or not the request was granted. But it does tell us of the effect it had upon the Lord. In it the Saviour, evidently, beholds a beginning, or at least, a prophecy of the realization of the promise given Him by the Father, that He would see His seed, when His soul should have been made an offering for sin. Isa. 53:10. This is evident from the entire context. The Son of man shall be lifted up, and then He shall draw all men unto Him, i.e., His sheep not only from the fold of the Jewish nation, but also from all the nations of the world. In that He shall be glorified. But before all this can be realized He must die the death of the cross. For: "verily, verily, I say unto you, Except a corn of wheat fall into the ground and die, it abideth alone: but if it die, it bringeth forth much fruit." vs. 24. And in the prospect of bringing forth this abundant fruit, the Lord rejoices. Nevertheless the way to that glory is dark. It is the way of the cross. It is the way of suffering the wrath of God against the sin of His people. His hour is come and its anguish overwhelms Him for the moment and He expresses the fearful apprehension of the awful suffering that awaits Him in the words: "Now is my soul troubled!" However, even though His soul is now troubled, He is perfectly prepared to do the will of the Father, as is evident from the rest of this prayer in which His troubled soul finds relief, and which closes with the well-known words: "Father, glorify thy name."

Yes, in this hour of trouble, the Servant of the Lord never hesitates, but makes the glory of the Father His greatest concern and chief objective, even though that glory requires of Him to travel the deep and dark and amazing way of the cross. This is the great significance of this prayer. The Saviour prays: "Glorify thy name, O Father!" And in His mouth at that particular moment the words had a tremendous meaning. We may notice that this petition is the same in contents as the one the Lord placed at the head of the series of petitions He taught us to pray in the Lord's Prayer: "Hallowed be thy name." Only in passing can we explain the general meaning of this prayer. It really asks that God may glorify His own name through us and all things, and that we, too, may glorify that name and serve the purpose of revealing its glory. The name of God is God as we know Him, as He has revealed Himself to us. God is the invisible One. We cannot see Him, touch Him, perceive Him. We could never know Him, unless He had revealed Himself to us. But we know Him through His name, that is, through God's own revelation of Himself to us. God's name, therefore, is God Himself. Often in the Bible the name of God is identified with Himself. When it speaks of God's name being near, it means that He is near; when it tells us that the name of God is a strong tower, it assures us that God is a strong refuge for those that flee to Him for safety. Wherever His name is revealed, there He Himself is near us; and to lay hold on that name, to believe in that name, to trust in the name of the Lord is to lay hold on, to believe in, to put our confidence in the God of our salvation. That name is revealed in all the works of His hands; it is centrally revealed in Jesus Christ, our Lord, and that, too, as the God of our salvation; and this is the name of God we know from the Holy Scriptures. To glorify that name is to bring out and extol the infinite beauty and goodness of that name of God. God is good, He is the implication of all infinite perfections; He is a light and there is no darkness in Him at all. He is truth, righteousness, holiness, love, grace, mercy and lovingkindness. And the radiation of that infinite goodness of God is His glory. Hence, the shining forth, the clear revelation of God's infinite goodness and perfection is His glory. Hence, when the Saviour here prays: "Father, glorify thy name," the general meaning is: "Father, so let thy name be revealed, that it becomes manifest to men that thou art infinitely good, righteous and holy, true and just, merciful and gracious, mighty and wise, the implication of all perfection!"

This is the general meaning of this prayer. It is in this general sense that we often utter the same prayer, when we say: "Hallowed be thy name, our Father which art in heaven." And it is exactly because we do not always realize what it would mean if God would hear this prayer, that we can so easily let it flow over our lips. Our soul is not at all troubled at the amazing implication of this prayer. In our general, self-complacent religiousness we seem to be perfectly willing to serve the purpose of that glory of the Father's name, little realizing at the moment that this often implies self-denial, suffering for Christ's sake, loss of our position and goods in the world, and that it frequently meant martyrdom for the faithful. Yet, so it is. If we would really receive grace from the Father to make the glory of His name the first and highest purpose in our lives, we must expect that in the world we shall have tribulation. And so, if we always fully understood the implication of this first petition of the Lord's Prayer, we would, to say the least, pray it only with fear and trembling, and our soul, too, might be troubled. Well, the Lord at this particular moment perceived clearly the amazing significance of His petition, when He said: "Father, glorify thy name." In His mouth the petition has a very specific content. For, He means to say: "Father, glorify thyself through me, regardless of the way I must travel, the depths of suffering into which I must descend, the burden of sin I must bear, the agonies of hell I must endure!" This is the specific glorification of the Father's name the Lord has in mind. For He stands here praying as the Mediator deeply conscious of His mediatorial calling and of the deep way of suffering that lies before Him. It is "the hour." All the recent events, the anointing by Mary in the house of Lazarus, the royal entry into Jerusalem, the coming of the Greeks, — all convey the same testimony: the hour is come when the Son of man must be glorified and the Father must be glorified in Him. The seed must fall into the earth and die before it can bring forth much fruit. And in the clear consciousness of the approaching hour the Lord here prays: "Father, glorify thy name."

The way of this revelation of the Father's glory is that of the suffering and death of the Son. Christ must glorify the Father and the Father will glorify Himself in Him in the way of the cross. Through the dark vale of death lies the Lord's own way to the glory of the resurrection. Another way to glory there is none. For as Mediator, as the Head of His Church, Christ must enter into glory. He cannot enter alone. He is anointed from before the foundation of the world to be the firstborn of every creature, and the firstborn of the dead, the Head of the Church, and as such He must be instrumental to lead many sons unto glory. But to lead these many sons of God to glory He must redeem them, for they lie by nature in the midst of sin and death. And in redeeming them He must glorify the Father. As the captain of their salvation, leading His people from sin and death into everlasting glory, He must travel the way of the Father's glory. And the Father's glory is revealed only in the way of righteousness. Christ, therefore, must fulfill all the righteousness of God with respect to sin. And in order to fulfill all the righteousness of God, He must travel the way of God's justice; and the way of God's justice is that of full and complete satisfaction for sin; and the way of perfect satisfaction for sin is that of voluntarily descending into the depth of death and hell in the love of God and for His righteousness' sake. Another way there is not. Voluntary suffering, the willing sacrifice,—that is the price of our redemption. That way Christ must travel. Only in that way will the Father glorify Himself. And at this moment the Lord is deeply and clearly conscious of this way of suffering. And it is in that clear consciousness of the awful way He will have to travel for the revelation of the Father's glory, that He prays: "Father, glorify thy name." He chooses the way of the Father's glory, even though it leads Him through hell!

This is the meaning of atonement. It is voluntary obedience unto death. If it were possible for a man to go through hell obediently, to suffer all the agonies of hell willingly, in the love of God, to travel that deepest way of God's just wrath against sin, and then to say constantly and with a perfect heart: "Father, glorify thy name"—that man would atone for his own sin and by this act of obedience he would redeem his soul from hell! But nothing less would deliver him. We often speak of atonement and satisfaction without understanding the real implication of these terms. Atonement, we say, is satisfaction for sin; and satisfaction for sin is the bearing of the punishment of sin. And this is true, provided you mean by the bearing of the punishment for sin an act of obedience, and not mere passive suffering. When a murderer dies in the electric chair, we sometimes say that he atones for his murder. But this is not true. Capital punishment is simply inflicted upon him. He probably sought to escape it. He hired an attorney to fight the case for him. But it was of no avail. His guilt was proved without a shadow of doubt and he was sentenced to death. And when the sentence is executed and the guilty party finally dies in the electric chair, death is inflicted upon him against his will. And that is no atonement. Atonement is sacrifice. And sacrifice implies that we lay our life upon God's altar willingly and in obedient love, even though that altar of God is placed by God's justice in the depth of hell. This is the reason, too, why there is no atonement in hell. The lost in hell surely bear the punishment of sin, but they cannot bring a sacrifice of love. And again, for the same reason the sinner can never atone for himself. He can bear the punishment of sin. And the punishment of sin he will bear unless he is redeemed in Christ, for God is eternally just, and He is terribly displeased with all the workers of iniquity. But the sinner can only increase his guilt daily. Never can he pay the ransom for his soul for the simple reason that he cannot bring the perfect sacrifice of willing obedience. And this only is atonement.

This sacrifice Jesus brought. He laid down His life for the sheep. No one took it from Him, but He laid it down of Himself. Voluntarily He walked through the depth of hell and sacrificed Himself to God. And a clear proof of this we have in the words we are now considering. His soul was troubled in the anticipation of the suffering that was before Him. The darkness of "the hour" crept over His soul. Very clearly He saw the cross and understood all its awful implication. For Jesus this was quite possible. With

us this is different. We cannot and need not bear the suffering of
tomorrow or of next week. The future is hid from our eyes. If
tomorrow will bring suffering and sorrow, we need not bear it
today. Every day is sufficient as to the evil thereof. But Jesus
knew all the way from the beginning. He knew exactly how and
what He would have to suffer. He could see the way He had to
travel. He knew that Judas would betray Him, that Peter would
deny Him, that He would be filled with reproach, be beaten and
buffeted and spit upon, be crowned with a crown of thorns; He
could see how they would hammer the cruel spikes through His
hands and feet, and lift Him up on the cross, a spectacle to all
the world. And above all, He knew that He would have to bear
the wrath of God in death on that accursed tree, and that the very
agonies of hell would pass through His soul. All this He could
anticipate. And the awful reality of it all overwhelmed His soul
at this very moment, so that He had to cry out: "Now is my soul
troubled."

Did the Lord hesitate to proceed on the way? Was there even
a moment of doubt in His soul as to His willingness completely
to devote Himself to the service of the Father's glory and to choose
the way of suffering? Is that perhaps the implication of His words,
when He says: "and what shall I say? Father, save me from this
hour?" There are those who detect such a moment of hesitation
and doubt in these words. The words, then, would mean: "Father,
excuse me from this hour." For a moment His troubled soul recoiled from the cross, hesitated to proceed on the way of obedience.
He would rather not continue. But this doubt and hesitation lasted
only a moment. For immediately after He realized that this would
mean disobedience to the Father. And, therefore, He took hold of
Himself and with a firm determination to do the will of God as
the Servant of Jehovah, He said: "but for this cause came I unto
this hour." And He ends with the prayer of perfect submission and
obedience: "Father, glorify thy name." But this interpretation does
not satisfy us. It presents Christ as having been disobedient in
heart and mind and desire. I cannot see it in another light. If that
had been the implication of the Lord's words, that one moment,
that split second during which He desired to be excused from
continuing on the way of suffering and obedience, would have been

the fall of the second Adam. That would have been the last of
Jesus as the Saviour of His people. But this is absurd. Jesus was
never disobedient to the Father, not even in His inmost desires,
and not for the twinkling of an eye. He never did, He never
could ask to be excused from finishing His work, which the
Father had given Him to do. And, therefore, this interpretation
of the Lord's words seems impossible. Realizing the impossibility
of this, others have tried to put the words of Jesus in the form
of a question, which He immediately answers: "What shall I
say? Shall I pray to be saved, to be excused from this hour? God
forbid, for unto this purpose came I unto this hour?" But the words
are not in question form; they contain a positive request. And
this request could never mean that the Lord really recoiled from
the way of obedience. Even a few days later, when again His
soul was troubled but in a much more intensified form, so that He
was exceedingly sorrowful even unto death, the thought of disobedience never entered His mind. And, therefore, the words
must be explained as a positive request, as a prayer that was
surely heard, and that is an essential part of the petition: "Father,
glorify thy name." The words: "save me from this hour" do not
mean: grant that I may not have to pass through this hour, for the
Lord realizes very keenly that because of this, that is, because
the name of the Father must be glorified in His suffering and death,
He came unto this hour. But they rather imply: "when I obediently
plunge myself into the darkest depth of this hour, so that I descend
even into hell, then deliver thou my soul from hell, save me out
of all the affliction and death of this hour." It is a prayer for the
resurrection, for the glory the Father promised Him before the
foundation of the world. Unto this hour, this hour of suffering and
death, He came into the world. Steadfastly He had travelled His
way with a view to this hour. Now He would enter into it, in order
that the Father might be glorified in Him. But before He descends
He casts Himself upon the Father in perfect confidence and cries
to Him for salvation: Father, save me out of this hour!

And that prayer is heard. And the promise comes even now,
at the moment of Jesus' prayer, from heaven, that it will be heard.
For we read, that a voice came from heaven, saying: "I have both
glorified it, and will glorify it again." vs. 28. And we do well to

heed this voice from heaven, in the light of it, to look at the cross of Christ, lest we think its preaching foolishness, or interpret it after our own philosophy. For in the cross of Christ God glorified His name! He had glorified it in Jesus before. To the glory of His name the Son of God became flesh. To the glory of that name Jesus had both preached and worked all the time of His public ministry. But He would glorify the Father, and the Father would glorify His name again, now in the death and resurrection of Jesus Christ from the dead. For therein God would show forth His power and glory, His righteousness and everlasting love and mercy and grace, His infinite wisdom and unfathomable knowledge. Through that cross and resurrection He would reveal Himself as the Lord of life and death, mighty to save and to overcome all the powers of darkness! Yes, indeed, in and through the voluntary suffering of His Servant His mighty arm would bring salvation. He would glorify His name again!

Let us heed this voice from heaven. At the time when it was uttered, some people thought that it thundered, even though the voice must have spoken some very clear and intelligible language, for it was meant for the people that stood by. But some people always say that it thunders when the Word of God is heard, in order that they may continue in the lie of their own philosophy and be damned. They make the cross of Christ of none effect. But if we look at the cross, and at the resurrection of Jesus Christ from the dead, in the light of this voice from heaven, and in the light of the whole gospel as we may possess it today, we will understand that Christ descended voluntarily into the depth of hell, in order that the name of the Father might be glorified, His justice might be satisfied, His righteousness and mercy might be revealed in sweetest harmony. For, God was in Christ reconciling the world unto Himself, not imputing their trespasses unto them. Be ye, therefore, reconciled to God!

CHAPTER 3

Forcing the Issue

That thou doest, do quickly. — JOHN 13:27.

A very clear proof of the fact that Jesus suffered voluntarily, that no one took His life from Him, but that He laid it down of Himself, is found in His dismissal of Judas from the upper room in Jerusalem in the night in which He was betrayed, and of which Scripture significantly says that it *was* night. John 13:30. For to one who studies the narrative of that dismissal as it is told us in the gospel according to John, 13:21-30, and who considers this dismissal in the light of the circumstances and of the events that were fast taking shape, it must become evident that the Lord took matters in His own hand, that He forced the issue, that He not only voluntarily laid down His life for His sheep, but that He also controlled both the hour and the way of His suffering. We are all acquainted with the narrative. Jesus was gathered with His disciples in some upper room in Jerusalem, perhaps in the house of John Mark, in order that He might celebrate the very last possible passover with the apostles. Over everything the Lord does in that upper room heavily lies the gloom and shadow of His approaching suffering and death. Prophetic of the services He was to perform for His own on the cross was the foot washing that had just been accomplished, before the traitor was dismissed. Portentously He had declared that even though all were included

83

in this service of the foot washing, yet they were not all clean: was not one of them a devil? And now they are reclining at table, ready to celebrate the last passover. And we read that the Lord became troubled in spirit. A few days ago His soul had been troubled. Now the trouble is of a higher, spiritual character. Then His troubled soul expressed itself in prayer. This time the troubled spirit must unburden itself in action. Ominously His words sound through the now painfully still room: "Verily, verily, I say unto you, that one of you shall betray me." And after the disciples had inquired, and looked upon one another in sad amazement, wondering who this traitor could be; and after the Lord had clearly pointed out, at least to John, who would commit this foul deed by giving Judas the sop, He speaks the words of dismissal to the latter: "That thou doest, do quickly." And immediately the traitor went out into the dark night to accomplish his satanic mission. The Lord had forced the issue!

In order to understand the import of this dismissal, we must bring before our mind the circumstances and try to visualize the entire situation at that time with relation to the suffering and and death of the Saviour. The leaders of the Jews had definitely plotted to bring Jesus to death as soon as opportunity offered itself. But we must remember that their plans were quite different from the determined counsel of God regarding Jesus' suffering and death. For, first of all, they had no intention to bring Jesus to death by way of a public trial. To pass an official death sentence upon the Saviour, either by the Sanhedrin or through the Roman governor, constituted no part of their plot. Nor had they decided that Jesus should die the death of the cross. If a public trial and an official verdict of death had been in their minds, it is difficult to see what need they would have had for a traitor. But now it was their intention to take Him by subtilty, secretly. They intended to come upon Him unawares, perhaps while He was sleeping the sleep of the righteous, in order then to stab Him to death and remove His body under cover of darkness, so that no one of the people might have knowledge of their evil deed. For we read, that the chief priests and the scribes and the elders had assembled together and consulted that they might take Jesus by subtilty, and kill Him. Matt. 26:4. How this was to be accomplished, they had not definitely settled. But kill Him they would, and this had to be done in secret, for the Rabbi of Nazareth was still very popular. And, secondly, and in intimate connection with this first part of their plan there was the second element of their conspiracy, namely, that it should not be done on the feast day, lest after all it should become known and there would be an uproar among the people. Matt. 26:5. And in the realization of those plans Judas could, indeed, play an important part. And we can readily understand that a devilish joy filled their hearts, when one of the most intimate followers of Jesus offered his wicked services, and covenanted with them for thirty pieces of silver to betray Him and deliver Him unto them. But even so they made him promise that he would watch his steps and abide his time, so that he might deliver Him in the absence of the people. Lu. 22:6. Thus the plans were laid. Jesus was to be put out of the way secretly, without any legal procedure and they were to wait till the feast of the passover was past, lest there be an uproar among the people. And Judas was looking for an opportunity to betray his Lord.

In that program we can give to Judas a reasonable and important place. As the history of Jesus' suffering and death actually unfolded itself, it appears as if the leaders of the Jews might just as well have done without him. For why could they not have obtained a band of soldiers and discovered where Jesus was and captured Him without the aid of the traitor? But now it was different. Judas' part in the drama was to watch for a proper opportunity. He was to sneak away from the company of the disciples, in the hollow of the night preferably, when the Master was asleep, so that he might inform the enemies and these might kill the Lord before He could even defend Himself. In the light of this difference between their plans and the actual sequence of events, we can also understand the evident confusion in the Jewish council after they actually captured Jesus. They were not at all prepared for any definite action. They captured Jesus, but knew not how to proceed to kill Him! They had no definite accusation. Nor were there proper witnesses. And after they themselves had condemned Him to death, they still had to deliberate upon the question, whether they should bring Him before the Roman governor or execute the death sentence themselves.

For their program was not in accord with the determinate counsel of the Most High. It was the will of the Father, not that Jesus should be put to death secretly and without any form of trial. Nor might He be stoned to death or cast from some height into the ravine. No, it was the Father's will that all the world should be placed before the question: what think ye of the Christ? For the cross was to be the judgment of the world. The thoughts of many hearts had to be revealed. And for this reason He, the Christ of God, had to stand before the highest court of His own people, of the Church, as well as before the Roman governor, the tribunal of the world. And it was the Father's will that He should be made a public spectacle and die the accursed death of the cross. And, quite contrary to the expressed will of the Jewish leaders, the hour was fixed by divine decree on the feast of the passover. And, of course, the counsel of the Lord must stand. Jesus is to suffer and die, not according to the program of the powers of darkness, but according to the will of the Father. And in the Father's way and at the Father's hour the Son of God is crucified and slain by wicked hands.

Several factors contributed to this frustration of the plans of the enemies, of which the raising of Lazarus was not the least important. A careful reading of that wonderful twelfth chapter of the gospel according to John will show that this mighty miracle had a tremendous influence upon the rapid succession of events in that last week of Jesus' life. It hastened matters considerably. It brought the leaders to a state of excitement in which they were liable to put Jesus to death at any price. For that last miracle had filled the people with enthusiasm for Jesus. The people that had been witness of this marvellous work met Jesus as He made His triumphant entry into Jerusalem, together with crowds of others that had heard about it, and they shouted: "Hosanna. Blessed is the King of Israel, that cometh in the name of the Lord." John 12:15, 17, 18. Many had come to Bethany, not only to see Jesus, but also Lazarus. John 12:9. And the priests had already consulted to put Lazarus to death also. John 12:10. But when the multitude went to meet Jesus, enthusiastically hailing Him as the King of Israel, the Pharisees had gone mad with envy and said among themselves: "Perceive ye how ye prevail nothing? behold, the whole world is gone after Him." John 12:19. It is evident that the raising of Lazarus and the resultant enthusiasm among the people had raised the mad hatred of the enemies to such a pitch that they were ready to do anything to put Jesus to death. It was an important factor in bringing about the "hour" at the Father's time.

But now let us return to the upper room, where the Saviour is gathered with His disciples. Judas also is among them. In his heart is hid the dark plot to betray Jesus, for already he offered his services to the chief priests and elders, as the traitor's reward is in his pocket. But just what is in his mind at this moment? Does he contemplate to carry out his evil deed that very night? Is it his intention presently to leave the company of the disciples in order to betray the Lord? It will now have become evident that no such idea is in Judas' mind as he sits with the Master at the table of the last passover. Had not the leaders of the Jews definitely told him that it should not be done on the feast day, lest there be an uproar among the people? There is plenty of time, therefore. But the Lord takes matters in His own hands. He knows the way the Father would have Him travel, the way of the cross; and He knows too, that on the morrow it is the Father's hour. And, therefore, He forces the issue. He makes it impossible for Judas to tarry any longer. For clearly He reveals that He is thoroughly acquainted with the wicked plot against His life and with the part Judas promised to play in it. And so, when He has plainly indicated that He knows who would betray Him, He sends the traitor out into the dark night with the commission: "That thou doest, do quickly." From now on Judas understands that he must act now or never!

How evident it is from this dismissal of the traitor that the Saviour voluntarily travelled His way to the cross. Indeed, He is the Good Shepherd that lays down His life for the sheep, that He might take it again and give unto them the abundant life of the resurrection! No one took His life from Him. He laid it down of Himself in perfect obedience to the Father, a sacrifice for sin. He might easily have kept silent and let matters run their own course. He might even have exposed the traitor and made it impossible for him to commit his foul deed. Then He would not have been publicly tried and condemned. He would not have died the death of the cross. But He knew "the hour," both as to the time and as to its contents, the awful shame and suffering it implied. And He knew that "the hour" was the will of the Father. Only by His travelling the way of the cross, He knew, could the world be condemned, could His people be redeemed, could the justice of God be satisfied, could the righteousness of God be set forth, could the Father be glorified. And so He forces the issue, sends the traitor away, and virtually says to him: Judas, now or never; for I must travel the way of my Father!

No one who reads the narrative of the dismissal of Judas in that night of Jesus' betrayal, can fail to marvel at the method the Lord employs to accomplish His purpose. That purpose was not to expose the traitor. This, indeed, was done by others more than once on similar occasions. How easily the Lord might have exposed Judas! And would not the disciples have cast themselves upon him and torn him to pieces? But that might not be, for such was not the will of the Father. In this hour force was not to be opposed to force, nor was the strategy to be matched with strategy. The question that was to be answered was not who was the strongest. It was the question of the righteousness of God that was to be decided once and for all. And this meant that the Saviour must walk all the way of obedience, of suffering unto the death of the cross, that the world might be condemned and His own might be redeemed. And, therefore, the traitor must not be exposed. But he must be dismissed, for he must not tarry, but finish his evil work that very night. And this dismissal must be accomplished in such a way, that, on the one hand, all the disciples are witnesses of it, yet on the other hand so that at the moment they do not understand what was taking place. They must be witnesses, in order that after the resurrection they may remember the scene and understand that the Lord travelled the way of the cross voluntarily; yet they must not understand, lest they would rise to prevent so foul an act. And it is evident from the narrative that both these purposes are reached. The disciples learn enough about the matter in the upper room to understand that the Lord knew all about the traitor's plot, and that He voluntarily walked the way of suffering. Yet, at the moment they fail to grasp the situation, for when Judas sallies forth into the dark night, they think that he is sent to buy some things for the feast, or to give alms to the poor. Judas is dismissed without being publicly exposed!

How is this accomplished? On the one hand, by the general announcement of the Lord: "Verily, verily, I say unto you, that one of you shall betray me." This general statement is sufficiently clear to make them all recall later that the Lord was not deceived by Judas' treachery. Yet, on the other hand, it did not point out the traitor in person. General consternation follows the announcement. On every side the question is asked: "Lord, is it I?" And even Judas attempts to seek cover by asking the same question. But in the meantime there is a private transaction by which the traitor is dismissed, while the rest of the disciples, with the exception of John, fail to understand what is taking place. To comprehend how this was possible, we must try to visualize the assembly around the table in the upper room. Imagine, then, a table in the shape of a horseshoe, or of a rectangle open at one end. Around this table, that is, on the outside, the divans or couches were placed on which the Lord and His disciples reclined. The open end of the table was used by him that served at the table. Now, if in your imagination you take your position at that open end of the horseshoe or rectangle, so that you face the table, then the place of the host, in this case of the Lord, was the second divan on your left. We know from Scripture definitely, that John, the disciple whom Jesus loved, was reclining in Jesus' bosom, and as the reclining guests rested on their left arm, this indicates that John occupied the very last divan at your left. And as Jesus gave the sop, after He dipped it, to Judas first, and as it was customary to give the sop first to the guest of honor, we may conclude that Judas was reclining on the other side of Jesus, the third from the end on your left, which was the place of honor. Hence, on your left, as you face the open end of the table, reclined in order John, Jesus, Judas. From the conversation that took place between the two disciples, we surmise that at the other end of the table, the last place to your right, and, there, directly opposite from John, sat Peter. This was the lowest place at the table, and it is not impossible that Peter had occupied it, after their favorite dispute as to who would be the greatest among them, which they seem to have carried on even in the upper room and for which Jesus rebuked them. Lu. 22:24ff. Now, during the general consternation and confusion wrought by Jesus' sudden announcement, Peter whispered across the table to John, that he should ask the Lord who it was that should betray Him. John 13:24. And Jesus, being privately asked by John regarding the person of the traitor, gives John a sign by which he may learn to know who it is, while the sign would arouse no suspicion in the hearts of the other disciples: "He it is to whom I shall give a sop, when I have dipped it." It was a common custom to give the sop first to him that sat on the place of honor, so that this sign could be given without drawing the attention of the rest of the disciples. And thus it came about that only John and Judas knew the meaning of the sign, and that Judas was dismissed without being exposed to the entire assembly.

This, then, in our opinion, is the true answer to the question: why did Jesus choose the sign of the sop to dismiss Judas in that night of His betrayal. It is explained often, that this sop was meant as a final offer of grace, a last attempt on the part of Jesus to bring Judas to repentance. But how contrary to the entire narrative and how impossible is such an interpretation! Not one of the gospel narratives contains even the slightest suggestion that the Lord intended to bring Judas to repentance. There is not even a warning, although the Lord does express that it were better for that man, that was to betray Him, that he had never been born. Nor is there any mention of the Lord's prayer for Judas, such as He speaks of when He announces Peter's impending denial. And how could there be? Judas was the son of perdition, and the Lord knew it. Judas was thoroughly hardened under the same influence and instruction the other disciples had enjoyed. And the Lord could not possibly have intended to prevent Judas from committing his evil deed, for He knew that the traitor belonged to the way of the Father. That way Jesus must travel to the end in willing obedience. And it is an expression of that perfect obedience that He hastens the traitor on his way into the dark night by the words: "That thou doest, do quickly."

In this light, how well we can understand the Saviour's own commentary on this event in the words: "Now is the Son of man glorified, and God is glorified in Him." John 13:31. A few days ago His soul had been troubled in apprehension of the deep way of suffering that lay before Him, but He had prayed: "Father, glorify Thy name." Now the Father had strengthened Him to force the issue, to send Judas on his way, and deliberately and obediently choose the way of the cross. Through that cross the Father would be glorified, for on it atonement would be made for sin, and atonement is the satisfaction of the justice of God, and satisfaction required the descension into lowest hell by the Son of man as an act of voluntary obedience in the love of God. This way the Son of man had now definitely begun to travel. God would be glorified in Him. And He the Son of man, too, would be glorified. For the way of the cross was the way to the glorious resurrection, and to the exaltation of the Son of man at the right hand of God. Already Jesus looks forward to that resurrection and glorification. Glorified He will be, not only in Himself, but as the Good Shepherd, that lays down His life for the sheep in order that He might take it again. And when He has laid it down in perfect obedience to the glory of the Father, and taken it again in immortality and incorruptibility, He will draw all His own unto Himself, impart unto them His own perfect righteousness and abundant life, and take them with Himself in the Father's house forever. Then will the Son of man be glorified in the Church, and the Father will be glorified in all!

CHAPTER 4

Before the Gates of Hell

Nevertheless not as I will, but as thou wilt.
— MATT. 26:39.

This time our contemplation of the voluntary suffering of the Saviour takes us to the garden of Gethsemane in the night in which Jesus was betrayed. It is "the hour." The battle of the ages is soon to be fought and to be decided once for all. It is the hour in which the conflict is to be finished that was announced immediately after the fall of man in paradise: "I will put enmity between thee and the woman, and between thy seed and her seed; it shall bruise thy head and thou shalt bruise his heel." The conflict it is, in which God will reveal that He is God, and that there is no God beside Him; that He is the Lord even over the powers of darkness. In that conflict He will reveal Himself in all the glory of His righteousness and holiness, His justice and equity, His faithfulness and truth, His everlasting mercy and grace over His people. He will glorify His name, redeem His own, long grieved by sin and shame; He will establish His everlasting kingdom and maintain and perfect His covenant. And He will judge and condemn the world, and openly triumph over the forces of darkness, their principalities and powers. It is the hour of the crisis of all history, of the entire universe. Such is the conflict that is presently to be decided on the "Hill of the Skull."

And in this conflict Christ, the Servant of Jehovah, must needs stand alone. There may be no one with Him. Apparently mighty forces have been marshalled against Him and now stand in battle array, ready to strike the first blow. The devil is represented by all the powers of the world: Judas, the Jewish council, the Roman governor, soldiers with swords and staves. But God's representative, the revelation of God's arm of salvation, stands alone, without human help; and that, too, without the power of the sword. He must risk the battle with God alone, and put His confidence in Jehovah of hosts. For, on His part, the battle is not against flesh and blood, nor in behalf of flesh and blood, but against principalities, against powers, against the host of spiritual wickedness in high places, and in behalf of the eternal righteousness and glory of the Father.

The hour of this conflict is now approaching, and its dark shadows are already reaching out for the soul of Christ. The forces are gathering for the conflict even now, as the Servant of Jehovah enters the garden of Gethsemane. They are gathering, however, not according to the plans of the powers of darkness: already they had been frustrated by the unexpected dismissal of the traitor a few hours ago. The public trial by the Sanhedrin and before the Roman governor, Golgotha, that most public of all places in the world, the cross, — all these had no place in the counsel of the enemies. They had conspired to take Him by subtlety and to put Him away secretly. Nor was this their hour, for they had decided to wait till after the feast, lest there might be an uproar among the people. But after all, this was God's conflict and His alone. He determines, therefore, the place of the battlefield and the hour of the battle, and He, too, decides on the mode of the conflict. It is the Father's hour. And thus it happens that, quite contrary to their own plans, they are gathering for the conflict now. Judas had already gone forth in the darkness of the night on his evil mission. He will summon the powers of darkness and lead them to the place where the conflict must begin. And soon after, Jesus, too, left the upper room, where He had celebrated the last passover with His disciples, in order to meet the enemy. The gates of hell they will open before Him, in order that He may voluntarily and obediently descend into utter desolation and there finish the battle. And there, in the garden, before the very gates of hell that will presently be opened before Him, a great sorrow overwhelms His soul. Even now He is cast into the crucible of trial and temptation in which He appears to be consumed, but from which He emerges as the obedient Servant of Jehovah, ready to walk all the dark way of His suffering voluntarily.

A deep, an unfathomably deep sorrow it was, indeed, that enveloped in its dark folds the soul of the Saviour in the garden of Gethsemane, a sorrow to which no other human sorrow can ever be compared, and which, for that very reason we shall never be able fully to explain. This is evident from the very prayer which the Saviour prays. He had entered with three of His disciples into the garden, evidently feeling the need of their proximity and companionship in this hour of agony. Then, however, realizing that He must suffer His grief alone, He had separated Himself even from these three and had gone deeper into the garden by about a stone's throw. And there He "kneeled" down. So we read in the gospel according to Luke, 22:41. Matthew tells us that "he went a little farther and fell on his face." Matt. 26:39. And Mark explains: "And he went forward a little and fell on the ground." And in His amazing sorrow He begins to wonder about the possibility of another way of suffering and obedience than the one whose gloom even now encircles Him, and He prays: "Father, if thou be willing, remove this cup from me: nevertheless, not my will, but thine, be done." Lu. 22:42. Matthew records of this prayer of agonizing sorrow the words: "O my Father, if it be possible, let this cup pass from me: nevertheless, not as I will, but as thou wilt." Matt. 26:39. And Mark gives the prayer in the following form: "Abba, Father, all things are possible unto thee; take away this cup from me: nevertheless, not what I will, but what thou wilt." Mk. 14:36. And the very fact that in this hour the Saviour implores the Father for another way, shows the darkness and depth of the sorrow into which His soul is now plunged. It is the sorrow of the shadow of the cross that grips His soul. And if the shadows were so amazing, what unspeakable agonies did our Saviour suffer for us on the accursed tree itself?

Then, too, we must consider the other details in order to understand a little of the greatness of this wave of sorrow that swept over His soul in the garden. In the gospel narratives of Matthew and Mark we read, that as He entered the garden with the three most intimate of His disciples, "he began to be sorrowful and very heavy;" Matt. 26:37; or, as Mark expresses it: "he began to be sore amazed, and to be very heavy." As yet He had given no expression to the grief and amazement that began to creep over His soul. But somehow the disciples noticed that a change came over Him as He entered the garden. Perhaps they could read the agony in His countenance in the pale moonlight. And, perhaps, the earnest desire to know the reason for this amazement was reflected in their own anxious faces, for immediately the Lord explained: "My soul is exceeding sorrowful, even unto death." Matt. 26:38; Mk. 14:34. Notice the strong adjectives in which His sorrow is described: He is sore amazed; He is very heavy; His soul is exceeding sorrowful. So great, so overwhelming, so agonizing is this sorrow, that it appears to lead Him to the very verge of death. Hardly is His human strength sufficient to bear up under it. Luke adds: "And being in an agony he prayed the more earnestly; and his sweat was as it were great drops of blood falling down to the ground." Lu. 22:44. And He informs us that it was necessary in this dark moment for an angel to come down from heaven to strengthen Him. Lu. 22:43. All these details combine to impress upon our minds that this was an hour of great sorrow, such as no human soul ever experienced, nor is able to bear. For the Saviour it was an hour of amazement and perplexity. He, who but a little while before this had comforted His own disciples and exhorted them that their hearts should not be troubled, now was sore amazed Himself! A load of suffering oppresses Him which He can hardly bear! He does not understand the way, and He gropes for light and comfort!

In Gethsemane we may see the shadow of the cross, and from the effect of the dark shadow upon Jesus' soul we may learn a little about its awful suffering. We feel that in Gethsemane the Saviour passes through one of the crucial moments of His suffering. And to characterize this moment and understand its significance somewhat, we can do no better than to say that in the garden the Lord stands before the very gates of hell. Still they are closed. But presently they will be opened, and this opening of the gates of hell will occur right here in the garden. This is the place, from whence the steep descent into the lowest depth and most terrible darkness of utter desolation must begin. And this, too, is the hour. Already the forces of darkness to which He shall be delivered are on the way to the garden. And the Lord is deeply conscious of this fact. As He enters the garden with three of His disciples He suddenly realizes that this is the starting point of His awful way of suffering. Here and now He stands before the very gates of hell! And this explains why we read so significantly that, as He entered the garden, He *began* to be sore amazed and very heavy!

Yes, indeed, before the gates of hell the Saviour here stands. Only when we look at Gethsemane from this viewpoint can we obtain a glimpse into the depth of sorrow and amazement which our mighty Goël here experiences. Never can the mere outward form of the cross explain this agony of soul. Truly, even from a mere outward and human viewpoint the suffering of the Lord was very great. If we pass in review the different stages of that passion, and think of His being taken captive in the garden, of the reproach and shame He endured before the Jewish council, of His condemnation, His trial by Pilate, the mockery He suffered by the hand of Herod, the scourging by the Roman governor, the mockery and maltreatment by the soldiers, the cruel crown of thorns that was pressed on His brow, and then, finally, the dreadful suffering of the cross, — we wonder that in so short a time human frame could endure so much. Yet, this is merely the external aspect of the passion of our Lord, the suffering which men could and did inflict upon Him. And we recall that others have endured similar sufferings with a song on their lips. And, therefore, in order to understand at all how the Lord's soul could be so exceedingly sorrowful even unto death in the garden, in order to comprehend a little of the depth of His sorrow there, we must remember that there is another side to the death and passion of our Saviour on the cross. There is an inner meaning to that external suffering. For the Lord must atone for sin, for the sin of all His people. And atonement cannot otherwise be made than by satisfaction of the just demand of God with respect to sin. That demand of God upon the sinner, that unchangeable demand is that man shall love

Him, the living God, with all his heart and mind and soul and
strength, love Him as God, wherever and howsoever God reveals
Himself. For the guilty sinner this means, that in order to atone
for his sin he must bear the just wrath of God, and suffer all the
sorrow and agony and death implied in this bearing of the wrath
of God, so that he descends into the darkness of desolation and
suffers the very agonies of hell, and that even then, and even in the
depth of hell he shall love God in His righteous wrath, and willingly bring the sacrifice of love. Such is the mystery of Golgotha.
Thus the Servant of the Lord must descend into the lowest parts
of the earth. So descending in voluntary obedience of love, God
will love Him even while pouring out the vials of His judgment
and wrath over His head! That is the Word of the cross!

And thus, here in Gethsemane, the Saviour stood in the full
consciousness of what was awaiting Him. He knew all. He could
taste the bitter cup of His suffering in anticipation. And in this
hour He lived through all the horror of the approaching cross.
Yet, let us remember, that even now He walks the way of His
grief voluntarily, by an act of His own will, in free obedience to
the Father. Obediently He had chosen to take the way to the
garden, knowing, indeed, that it would bring Him face to face
with the very gates of hell, that there these gates would be opened
unto Him by wicked hands, and that from there He would descend
into its lowest depth. How easily the Lord might have escaped!
How simple it would have been for Him, after He had dismissed
the traitor from the upper room in Jerusalem, to take another way,
instead of coming to the garden of sorrows! But He had come
unto this hour in order that the Father might be glorified in Him.
And knowing that this garden was the place where the gates of
His suffering would be thrown wide open, He had come hither in
perfect obedience. And as He entered the garden billows of sorrow and amazement flooded His soul. Yet, He does not return. He
remains in the garden. Might He not have departed and fled
from this gate of hell even now? But He stays. Willingly He had
come to the very gates of hell. And though their aspect fills His
soul with agony and sorrow even unto death, and though He is
fully aware of the terrible agony that awaits Him once those gates

are opened, He voluntarily remains. That is the meaning of Gethsemane!

Then, too, let us consider that Gethsemane is a clear revelation of God that there is no other way than the way of the cross. Here in the garden it is none other than the beloved Son of God in the flesh that in unspeakable fear and sorrow and agony of soul cries to the Father and asks the question: "O my Father, is there no other way?" Such is the significance of Jesus' prayer. He would have the Father consider the possibility of another way. He prays that the cup may be removed from Him, if it be possible, and if it could be done in harmony with the Father's will. And that cup refers to the bitter suffering of the cross. Some would deny this and look for another interpretation of the prayer of the Lord, on the ground that Jesus could not possibly pray that He might be excused of the suffering of the cross. But the words allow of no other interpretation. The cup which He was appointed to drink is the suffering of the wrath of God on the accursed tree. The gospel according to Mark even tells us that He prayed that, if it were possible, the hour might pass from Him! And the meaning of His prayer is not that He would rather be excused of serving the purpose of the Father's glory; that He would rather withdraw from the obligation of redeeming Sion; or that He would rather not serve the purpose that the world should be condemned through Him. But the question asked in this earnest prayer is, whether to attain the same purpose of the Father's glory, and the redemption of the Church, and the condemnation of the world, there were no other way, less awful and dark and horrible than that which from this moment will open up before Him. Such is the question. The Lord cries out to the Father in agony of soul: "I know, O Father, that Thou must be glorified, and that my people must be redeemed; and for this purpose I now stand before the very gates of hell; darkness has overwhelmed my soul, and I am sore amazed, exceedingly sorrowful, even unto death; and now I ask: Is this the only possible cup? It there no other way, O my God, for Me to travel to attain the same purpose?" This is the question of Gethsemane!

And the answer comes from heaven: "No, another way there is not!" And the answer is very emphatic. No, indeed, this answer did not come from heaven in audible words. But emphatic is the answer, because the Father opens no other way for His only begotten Son in the flesh, His beloved in Whom He is well pleased. Emphatic is the answer in the measure that the prayer is very urgent, and is sent to the throne in heaven from a soul sore oppressed and very heavy, and almost dying with sorrow! Emphatic is the answer, too, because three times the Lord went and returned to His disciples, and three times heaven remains as it were deaf to His cries! O, indeed, He receives an answer to His prayer, and that, too, to the very prayer He sent to the Father. But the answer is, that He travel the way of the cross, that He must drink the cup to its bitterest dregs, but that the Father will sustain and strengthen, and love Him in that way. Even now an angel is sent to Him to strengthen Him to the battle. If ever there was an answer to the question, whether there is another way of redemption than that of the cross, which led through the depth of hell, it may be found in Gethsemane. And the answer is negative. There is no other way.

That is the meaning of Gethsemane also for us. If there were no other way opened to the Son, even in the hour of His deepest woe and sorrow of soul, than the way to the cross, how could there be any other way of righteousness and life for us, than that of faith in the righteousness which He merited for us on the accursed tree? Gethsemane spells the end and hopelessness of all our own righteousness, and leaves no other way than the righteousness of God, which is by faith in Jesus Christ!

No other way; but this way of Christ crucified is quite sufficient. Also this is implied in the meaning of Gethsemane. It is a clear revelation of the truth that the Son of God in the flesh voluntarily descended into the lowest depth of hell, there to bring the perfect sacrifice that would atone for our sin and merit for us eternal righteousness and life. For it is evident that even here in the garden there is not a moment of disobedience on the part of the Saviour. It is His meat to do the Father's will even now, and no matter what the way and will of the Father may be for Him. The thought of disobedience never entered His mind; the desire of disobedience was never in His soul; the will to obey in Him was never hesitant, even for a moment. It is true that with evident refer-

ence to the suffering of Jesus in the garden, the writer of the Hebrews explains that "though he were a Son, yet learned he obedience by the things which he suffered." Heb. 5:8. But this cannot
mean that He was ever hesitant or unwilling to obey, so that He
had to learn to become obedient; but can only signify that He
learned from experience to fathom the awful depth of obedience
to the living God. Had there been only one moment of disobedience
or rebellion in His soul, that moment would have been the victory for the powers of darkness. But this could never be. The
question in Gethsemane never was, whether the Saviour would
obey or disobey. Throughout His experience in the garden it was
firmly established that He would obey. The Father must be
glorified in Him!

That this is true, is evident from His very presence in the
garden. As we said, voluntarily He came thither, voluntarily He
remained. A simple matter it would have been for Him to take
another way. But even in this hour of His deepest sorrow He
chooses the way of the Father. This is evident, above all, from
the contents of the Saviour's prayer. It is the prayer of perfect
obedience. Absolutely and unconditionally He denies His own
will, and prays that it may not be done. No other way does He
desire, unless it is the Father's will, and unless it leads to the
fulness of the revelation of the Father's glory. And throughout
the prayer He seeks the Father's will. Thy will be done! That is the
real meaning of the Lord's prayer in the garden. And that is the
prayer of unconditional surrender to God, of most perfect obedience.

And so, Gethsemane from its dark shadows throws light upon
the cross. It assures us that in His greatest sorrows and agonies
of hell the Saviour was the obedient Servant of the Lord, and
that His suffering and death were acts of His voluntary surrender.
The Good Shepherd did, indeed, lay down His life of Himself. No
one took it from Him. The perfect sacrifice for sin He offered on
the accursed tree. The perfect answer to God's "love Me" He gave
from the depth of hell! He is, indeed, our righteousness! Considering Him with the eye of faith, we may truly say: "Being justified
by faith, we have peace with God through our Lord Jesus Christ!"

CHAPTER 5

Voluntary Self-Surrender

I am he. — JOHN 18:5.

In the night when Jesus was betrayed the enemies had made a desperate attempt to make it appear as if Jesus were a dangerous criminal, whom they overpowered and captured by sheer force of numbers and of arms. After having been dismissed by the Saviour from the upper room, Judas had hastened on his dark and evil mission. Understanding that delay would mean failure, he had immediately proceeded to the chief priests and Pharisees, and, no doubt related to them what had happened, and convinced them that they must act promptly. The leaders of the Jews had most probably appealed to the captain of the guard, and on the pretext that a desperate malefactor was to be captured, had obtained from him a band of men and officers. Perhaps, they had first taken their way to the upper room, where Jesus had eaten the passover with His disciples, supposing that He might still be there; but finding that the Saviour had already departed thence, Judas led the band to Gethsemane, for he knew that Jesus often resorted thither. There they found Jesus and His disciples, and there they finally bound the Saviour and led Him away.

Now, I said a moment ago, that the powers of darkness tried to give to their deed the appearance of being the capture of a criminal that could only be overpowered by main force. Let us notice, that they made a mighty show. A strong force went to capture the Lord. John merely speaks of a band of men and officers. Luke tells us that it was a multitude that went to the garden that night. And Matthew and Mark even speak of a great multitude. Lu. 22:47; Matt. 26:47; Mk. 14:43. And not only were they strong in number, but they were well prepared, for both Matthew and Mark inform us that they were armed with swords and staves. The significance of this is evident. It left the impression that they came against Jesus as if He were a thief and a murderer. The enemy knew better. Daily the Lord had been with them, but never had He given any reason to believe that He was a malefactor, or a dangerous revolutionary. He had been a teacher, and openly had He taught the people in the temple. But, no doubt, only under the pretext of the purpose to capture a criminal had they obtained the band of soldiers from the captain of the guard; and now their original plan to take Him by subtlety and to avoid public commotion having been frustrated, they were quite willing to have it so. If a public trial would prove to be necessary, it would be to the advantage of their evil purpose to give to the Lord the appearance of a public enemy from the start. But, secondly, the fact that they came against the Lord with a strong force, suggested that they expected a strong opposition and desperate resistance. It left the impression that Jesus would fight for His freedom to the last. And if He should surrender without battle, it could only be because He saw the uselessness of resistance against so overpowering a force. Quite against His own will He was captured and led away. Where, then, was His boast that no one could take His life from Him, but that He laid it down of Himself; that He had power to lay it down and to take it again?

However, even in this respect the counsel of the wicked perished, and the plans of the enemy were frustrated. There are a few important details connected with the capture of Jesus in Gethsemane that establish it beyond all doubt, that the enemy could have had no power against Him at all had He not willed it, and that He voluntarily surrendered Himself to His would-be captors. The Lord makes it very plain: 1. that He had a power of Himself which, if He would but employ it, would make it utterly impossible for the enemies, no matter how strong in number they might be or how well armed, to lay hands on Him; 2. that He refused, on His part, all human help and all physical force to defend Him; and 3. that He refrained from calling upon the heavenly host to help Him, although He could have had this help for the asking. Let us look a little more closely at these important details.

The first of these, as we would expect, is recorded in the gospel according to St. John, 18:4-6. It appears that the enemies had failed to notice the sign of the kiss upon which they had agreed with the traitor. We can understand readily that Judas performed this part of the agreement rather hastily, and that, having kissed Jesus, he fell back and stood in the crowd that had come to capture the Lord. Thus we read in John 18:5: "And Judas also, which betrayed Him stood with them." At all events, the sign of the kiss had not served its purpose; they had not recognized the Lord in the darkness of the garden. Hence, Jesus took the initiative. He stepped forward to meet His captors, separating Himself thus from the disciples, and asked: "Whom seek ye?" The question was a perfectly legitimate one. For, although Jesus knew, of course, that they had come to capture Him, they certainly could not expect Him to draw the inference from their appearance that they were seeking Him! Whom, therefore, have ye come to seek, ye, who are so strong in number and so heavily armed? And they answered Him: "Jesus of Nazareth." And when the Lord had thereupon plainly told them: "I am He," they all went backward, and fell to the ground!

How must this be explained? Was their sudden prostration an act of natural terror and awe, caused by the contrast between their expectation to find a desperate criminal, who would fight to the last ditch to gain his freedom, and this bold revelation on the part of Jesus of His majestic, yet defenseless, fearlessness? Thus some recent expositors would explain the incident. But how utterly inadequate is such an interpretation! How impossible that by the simple word of a man, identifying himself as the one they had come to capture, a veritable multitude, Roman soldiers included, would not only fall back for a moment, but one and all without exception lie prostrate before their intended prisoner, and re-

main in the humble attitude until the same voice spoke again!
It is rather evident that here we have to do with a revelation of the divine power of Jesus as the Son of God. Upon the
wings of that brief announcement: "I am He," there was carried
out to His captors a sudden flash of the majesty and power of
His divinity. Through the humble form of a servant His real divine
Presence caused itself to be felt. And in utter amazement the
enemies fell back and prostrated themselves before Jesus on the
ground, thus assuming the attitude of humble worship. How long
they remained in that attitude the narrative does not say, but
long enough to prove beyond a shadow of a doubt that He, Whom
they had come to capture, was completely Master of the situation.
For not until Jesus broke the spell, and once more put the question to them: "Whom seek ye?" could they arise to finish their
work. And the meaning of the incident is plain. It flatly contradicted the testimony implied in those swords and staves. By
these they had created the appearance that Jesus was a desperate
criminal, that must be overcome by force of arms. But here, before the Lord surrenders Himself to their will, He utterly destroys
this appearance and by His act of divine power clearly tells them:
"I am able, if I will, not only to prevent your laying hands on
Me, but to subject you to My sovereign will. However, I came
to do the Father's will, and according to that will I voluntarily deliver Myself up into your hands. For, I am the Good Shepherd,
and the Good Shepherd layeth down His life for the sheep. No
man taketh it from Me; I have power to lay it down, and power to
take it again!"

But there is more. That the Saviour was not taken prisoner
against His will, is evident, not only from the fact that He refused
to exercise His divine power against His captors, but also from His
decline of all human help, as well as from His refraining to ask for
help from heaven. So dreadful, so superhuman, so contrary to all
the inclinations of the human heart was this determination of
Jesus to remain defenseless, that as soon as this had become
clear to the disciples they all forsook Him and fled. Thus we
read in Matt. 26:56. This is significant. For what is the reason for
this precipitate flight? They certainly did not flee because their
Lord was now about to be captured. That the enemy would at-

tempt this they had known for some time, and they had prepared themselves for the occasion. Nor can it be said, that they were physical cowards, for then they would not have remained until the exact moment when Jesus forbade them the use of the sword; and, besides, the act of Peter in defense of his Lord proves that they were ready to fight. Nor can lack of a sufficiently strong love and devotion to their Master be assigned as the reason for their flight. They all had expressed their readiness to go with Him into the prison and into death, and they certainly meant it. No, there can be found only one reason why it was at that particular moment that they forsook the Lord, and that is, that Jesus took the sword out of their hand, and insisted that on His side of the conflict no physical force should be employed whatsoever. Give a man a chance to fight and a good sword, and he will show his courage. But to decline all human help, and to stand utterly defenseless in the face of relentless enemies, that seek your destruction because you represent a righteous cause — that is contrary to all human nature!

But let us follow the narrative. As has been said, the disciples had prepared themselves for a possible attack upon their Lord, and had taken swords with them to the garden that night. The Lord, fully aware of the awful implications of His "hour," had warned them that they would all be offended in Him that night. But they had not believed His word, and through Peter they had asseverated in the strongest terms that they would never be offended: they were prepared to go with Him into prison and into death. And there is no reason to doubt their sincerity. They loved their Master, and they knew the righteousness of His cause. And they proved their sincerity. It must have been the moment when the enemies, at the second question of Jesus, arose from the ground, and when they were about to lay their hands on Him, that Peter gave what may be regarded as a signal for a general attack, by drawing his sword and striking off the ear of Malchus, the servant of the high priest. It is evident that Peter meant business. That blow was never intended for Malchus' ear: it was dealt with the intention to split his head. But then came the moment of the offense; for do not forget that the Lord had definitely foretold them that they would be offended in Him. The Lord rebukes His disciples for handling the sword, and firmly refuses all help. "Put up again thy sword into his place," thus the Lord addresses Peter, "for all they that take the sword shall perish with the sword." We must not misunderstand this word of the Lord. It is not an argument in favor of pacifism. The Lord does not condemn here the use of the sword by the proper authorities, either for the punishment of the individual evil doer, or in righteous warfare. But He was now face to face with that very sword-power. The proper authorities had come to take Him prisoner. They were represented by the soldiers and the leaders of His own people. And to take up the sword against those divinely ordained authorities, even though His cause were perfectly righteous, would be rebellion. Had He done so, He would have become worthy to perish with the sword. And this may never be. And, therefore, He not merely rebukes Peter and bids him to refrain from any form of violence, but He also performs what was to be His last miracle before His death: He healed the ear of Malchus! And we may be sure that the healing was performed perfectly. When this battle for the righteousness and justice of God was finished, and the Servant of the Lord had done His work, no battle scars may be found on the enemy. The scars of violence must all be on the Christ of God, in His hands and feet, and in His side! And, therefore, the Lord must be willingly defenseless. All human help He must refuse. Voluntarily He surrenders Himself to the power of the enemy!

The third detail in this narrative of the capture of the Saviour that proves His voluntary surrender, is mentioned by the Lord Himself in His answer to Peter's act of violence. He calls the attention of His disciple to the folly of the attempt to defend Him by the power of the sword. "Thinkest thou that I cannot now pray to my Father, and He shall give me more than twelve legions of angels?" How puny, how utterly useless and foolish, then, appeared the attempt of the disciples to defend Him by the power of the sword! It ought to have been perfectly evident to them, that if the Lord were bound and led away by the enemy this night, it was not because the enemy had power over Him against His own will, but because He voluntarily walked in the way of the Father, and willingly surrendered Himself to the power of darkness and its fury and violence. That should have been evident even from the majestic act of the Lord by which He laid the enemies prostrate before Him just a moment ago. But, if this were not sufficient, did they forget that He had but to ask the Father, and a multitude of angels would come to His rescue? These words of Jesus must not be taken absolutely and apart from their proper context. They do not mean that even at this moment God's counsel could be altered, and that the Lord could enter His glory alone. He was the Good Shepherd, and the Father had given Him sheep. And for these sheep He must lay down His life. In that absolute sense it was not true, that the Father would send Him twelve legions of angels to rescue Him from the power of darkness at this hour. Nor is it true, that the Saviour could have asked the Father for such a heavenly force to come to His rescue. He knew the Father's will. And He could not pray anything contrary to that will of the Father. And His sheep He loved to the very end. Nor is that the meaning of His words. They are to be taken in connection with Peter's attempt to defend his Master by the power of the sword. That act, and the attitude of the disciples, revealed that they conceived of the battle that must be fought by their Lord as one that was to be decided by force. To them it was, evidently, still a question as to who was the most powerful. And to this attitude the Lord replies. The folly of it He clearly exposes. And His words, therefore, may be paraphrased as follows: "Do you not yet understand that my battle is not a question of power or might? Do you not consider, that if that were the case, if the question were, how I could be delivered from the power of these my enemies, that I could pray the Father, and He would send me at once twelve legions of angels to destroy the forces of darkness that rise up against Me? Do ye not understand that I refrain from using My own power, that I refuse to receive help from your swords, and that I decline to ask My Father for the help of His holy angels, only because My battle cannot be decided by force, but demands that I voluntarily walk in the way of My Father even unto the end?" And the disciples, failing to understand this completely at this moment, became offended in a Master Whose cause they might not defend by the sword. And they forsook Him and fled!

But why must the Lord refrain from using all power, human

or divine, earthly or heavenly, and voluntarily deliver Himself into
the power of the enemies? The Lord supplies the answer when
He adds: "But how then shall the scriptures be fulfilled that thus
it must be?" And to His captors He says: "all this was done, that
the scriptures of the prophets might be fulfilled." The Scriptures
are the Old Testament revelation of God concerning the Christ,
and the purpose of His coming. From the very dawn of history,
ever since the first announcement concerning the seed of the
woman that would crush the head of the serpent, God had revealed the gospel concerning His Son. In direct prophecies, through
dreams and visions, by signs and symbols, through types and
shadows, He had spoken before of the coming of His Son, by
Whom the world would be condemned, Sion would be saved, and
through it all the glory and power, the unfathomable wisdom
and knowledge, the holiness and righteousness, the everlasting
love and mercy of the *Father* would be made manifest. That
gospel was the main theme of the Old Testament Scriptures. And
those Scriptures must be fulfilled. And to serve the fulfillment of
the Scriptures the Christ, the Servant of Jehovah had come into
the world. By Him the world of which the devil was prince, the
world in its rebellion against God, in its iniquity and ungodliness,
must be judged and condemned. And through Him the Church
must be redeemed from sin and death in the way of God's
righteousness and justice.

And in order that both these purposes may be reached, the
Servant of the Lord must be utterly defenseless over against the
enemy, and voluntarily drink the cup His Father gave Him to drink,
and walk the way of the cross. For, on one hand, through Him
the iniquity of sin must be exposed in all its horror. And that this
may be done, the world must have full opportunity to reveal the
inner attitude of their heart over against God. The mask of their
hypocrisy must be torn from their faces; the thin coat of varnish of
outward piety and self-righteousness must be removed from them;
and they must be made to answer the question: What will ye do
with God? To this end the Son of God came into the world, and He
clearly revealed the Father. He is the revelation of God in human
flesh. And He stands before them, not in the majesty of His divine
glory, so that they need be filled with terror, but in the weakness

of a mere man, helpless, defenseless, refusing all power in His defense. And thus they are confronted with the question: "If God would stand before you, in His truth and goodness, His righteousness and holiness, but without power and defenseless, what would ye do with Him?" And the answer to that question came in the cross! All the world replied: Then we will kill Him! To give that answer freely, without coercion, the Lord must stand defenseless before His enemies, and voluntarily surrender Himself!

But on the other hand, He must also save His own. They have sinned. They are in the power of sin and death. They must be delivered from the dominion of sin and be made worthy of righteousness and eternal life. But this must be accomplished in the way of God's justice. And, therefore, He, their Lord, must satisfy that justice of God. And to satisfy that justice He must bring the perfect and all-sufficient sacrifice. He must not merely be killed, but His death must be an act of His own. He must seek death and hell for God's righteousness' sake. He must taste death in obedience to the Father, as an act of love to the Most High. The altar of God, on which He must bring this sacrifice of His life, stands on the bottom of hell. Thither He must descend. And there He must taste all the bitter contents of the cup which the Father gave Him to drink. There all the vials of God's wrath will be poured over His head. And there He must be able to say: "Even here it is My meat to do Thy will, O My God! I love Thee even in Thy righteous wrath!" And this He did. He is, indeed, the Good Shepherd, Who laid down His life for His sheep. No one took it from Him; voluntarily, in love of God, He laid it down of Himself, as became evident even from the narrative concerning His capture. And so we may be assured, that His blood cleanseth from all sin, and that in His cross God was reconciling us unto Himself. Be ye, therefore, reconciled to God!

CHAPTER 6

Refusing to Come Down

Save thyself, and come down from the cross
—MARK 15:30.

The night in which Jesus was captured and tried by the Jewish
council was, as far as the action of the enemies is concerned, a
night of hopeless confusion. Eager though they were to put the
Lord to death, they were not at all prepared to execute their
wicked plans. The capture of Jesus had been precipitated. And
even after they had taken the Lord prisoner in the garden, they
had no definite plan of procedure to realize their evil schemes. The
reason for this lack of a definite program and concerted action
according to plan, we pointed out in a former chapter. Their own
plan had been frustrated, and the Lord had taken matters in His
own hand. They had intended to postpone all action against Jesus
until after the feast day; and, besides, they purposed to avoid a
public trial. But the dismissal of the traitor that night had upset
their entire program: they were forced to take action before they
were thoroughly prepared. And this explains why their action from
the moment they had captured the Lord was characterized by
confusion and indecision. It appears that there was a sort of preliminary hearing of Jesus before Annas, the father-in-law of
Caiaphas, which was decided upon, probably, on the spur of the
moment, to create an opportunity for the Sanhedrin or, at least,

part of the council to assemble. In the meantime notice must have been sent to the Jewish council in Jerusalem that Jesus had been captured, together with a summons to meet. As soon as a sufficient number of the Sanhedrists had arrived, Jesus must have been transferred from the apartments of Annas to those of Caiaphas, occupying another wing of the same building. Then there followed a hearing before the Jewish council, which must have lacked official capacity, because the Jewish council was not allowed to commence a trial at night, and which was marked chiefly by the vain attempt to find false witnesses against the Lord. In the morning there must have been a formal convocation of the supreme court of the Jews, and it was then that Jesus was found guilty of blasphemy and condemned to death. Lu. 22:66-71. And, finally, there was still another gathering of the council in the absence of Jesus, to decide upon the question whether or not they should bring the Lord before the Roman governor. How easily they might have taken matters in their own hands, and stone Jesus to death, as they did in the case of Stephen! But, after all, it was the feast day, and they were afraid of an uproar among the people. And so they decided to lead the Lord to the Roman governor and to insist that he would confirm the death sentence they had already pronounced. Thus the Father's purpose was realized, that the Saviour should die on the cross.

To the scene of that cross our present meditation takes us. We take our stand among the crowd that is gathered at the foot of the Hill of the Skull, and listen to the conversation that is carried on, and watch the crucified Son of man. Particular attention we wish to pay to the reproach and mockery that is even now cast into Jesus' teeth, to the cutting jibes men of all classes and stations in life address to that Sufferer on the central of the three crosses that have been erected on Calvary. There is, in this respect, a marked difference between the first half of the six hour period of the crucifixion and the second half. It was about nine o'clock in the morning that Jesus was nailed to the tree. And about noon the sun began to be darkened, and soon the entire scene of the cross together with all the surrounding country is enveloped in the darkness of night. A hush falls over the crowd standing by. Fear, amazement, terror clutches at their hearts. From now on, they realize, that cross is no longer their work alone: God Himself has come down to make the cross His own. It is the hour of the judgment and divine wrath. But during the first half of this period, before the sun was darkened, the scene on Calvary appeared to be a common execution. And the witnesses mock and jeer. Even criminals are wont to evoke some pity from the hearts of the witnesses when they are led to the place of execution. But with Jesus this is different. It seems as if even at His cross, though they had apparently fulfilled all their evil counsel upon Him, their fury has not assuaged. They must still pour out the vials of their contempt and hatred over His head. And mockingly they challenge Him to come down from the cross and to save Himself if He can!

One of these challenges came from the passers-by. We read in Mk. 15:29, 30: "And they that passed by railed on him, wagging their heads, and saying, Ah, thou that destroyest the temple, and buildest it in three days, save thyself, and come down from the cross." Strange, how well they had remembered this reference of Jesus to the destruction of the temple, they, who could not hear the word of Jesus, and did not accept it! And yet, it was not so strange, if we consider that this particular saying of the Lord concerned the earthly temple, the symbol of all that was dear to the carnal leaders of the Jews; symbol, that is, as they had made it, of their external form of religiousness, without justice and mercy, of their religious conceit and pride, their greed and covetousness! It was on the occasion of the first cleansing of that earthly house of His Father, now three years ago, that the Lord had spoken the words which these passers-by now cast in His teeth. When He had found in the temple those that sold oxen and sheep and doves, and the exchangers of money, He had made a scourge of small cords, and driven them all out of the temple. And when the Jews had demanded of Him a sign of His authority to do these things (as if, forsooth, the act itself had not been a sufficient revelation of authority), the Lord had referred to Himself as the Lord of the temple and the true temple-builder in the words: "Destroy this temple, and in three days I will raise it up." But, as is usually the case when your enemies and enemies of the truth spread the report of your words, this saying of the

Lord had been distorted until their real meaning had been changed into its very opposite. Different versions of it were given. Some reported that the Lord had said: "I am able to destroy the temple of God, and to build it in three days." Matt 26:61. Others alleged that they heard Him say: "I will destroy this temple that is made with hands, and within three days I will build another made without hands." Mark 14:58. And these passers-by find time to shout at Him: "Thou that destroyest the temple, and buildest it in three days, save thyself and come down from the cross!" All these reports differed from one another. But they all agreed on the fundamental point that Jesus had presented Himself as the one that would destroy the temple and rebuild it in three days.

They were people that passed by who thus mocked at Him and challenged Him to come down from the cross. The cross was erected near one of the main roads that led from the north to Jerusalem. And so, the cross was a public spectacle. These passers-by were probably Galileans that came to celebrate the passover. They knew Jesus. They had seen His mighty works. There had been a moment even when they had confessed that Jesus was the prophet that was to come, and when they had intended to take Him by force and make Him their king. But the Lord had bitterly disappointed their fondest hopes, that all concentrated around the idea of an earthly king and earthly prosperity, when He had revealed Himself as the One Who through His death would become the Bread of life to them! John 6:14ff. And they had become His enemies. However this may be, on Golgotha they act in the capacity of mere passers-by. They have no time to stop and survey the cross. The cross of Jesus of Nazareth is not of sufficient interest to them. After all, a crucifixion is not an uncommon occurrence. So they pass by. Only, as is the case with many a superficial passer-by, who takes no time to investigate and knows not what he is talking about, they do slacken their pace for a moment, long enough to look up into the face of the crucified Christ, shake their head at Him and cast their mockery and reproach in His teeth. How they hate Him in their hearts! Pity for Him in this hour of His agony they know not. They wag their heads at Him. And by doing so they express their profound contempt of Him, their utter disapproval of His case, their opinion, as people that have long been acquainted with Him and that, therefore, ought to know, that He is a contemptible fool who has but Himself alone to blame for His utter failure in life and His disastrous end! And by their expressed challenge they deny His power: Thou that destroyest the temple, save thyself, come down from the cross! They mean to imply that Jesus' claim that He would destroy the temple and rebuild it in three days, had been the boast of a demagogue that would by such a sign rouse the people to insurrection against the Roman authorities! Now, then, let Him make good His boast, save Himself, and come down from the cross! It is now evident that He is a vain boaster, powerless even to deliver Himself!

Will He come down? Will He take up the challenge, deliver Himself from the tree to which He is nailed, and thus expose His enemies as boastful liars? But no, this is impossible! He will remain on the cross, not because He lacks the power to come down, but because He has a work to do in this hour, a work that can be finished only on that cross. He is busy! Yes, indeed, He is suffering agonies of body and soul, but in this suffering He is active, and He is occupied with a work that requires all His attention, all the strength of His will, all the energy of His being. And, strange though it may seem, He is in this hour doing the very thing which His enemies challengingly deny that He can do: He is rebuilding the temple! He is laying down His life, and in doing so He is co-worker with God in the laying of the foundation-stone of the temple that will never be destroyed again, the House of God, the tabernacle of God with men. On that cross He is engaged in the realization of the Word of God, that the stone which the builders despised must become the head of the corner! Looking at the cross in this light, we may say that all that are present there are really engaged in the same work of God: the building of the temple. The powers of darkness, the leaders of the Jews, Herod that fox, the Roman governor that delivered Him up to be crucified, the soldiers that hammered the cruel spikes through His hands and feet — all are engaged in the building of the house of God! True, they do neither know it nor mean to build the temple. They hate God and His Christ and they imagine a vain thing. Building the temple they will go to hell, if they do not repent. But the fact remains that every creature, willing or against his will, must be subservient to the counsel of the Most High; and that here, on Golgotha, the powers of darkness serve that purpose of the Almighty in destroying the temple that is made with hands in order that the eternal tabernacle of God with His people might be established forever! But He, that is affixed to that central cross, is the Servant of the Lord. Willingly, in the love of the Father and of His own, He is engaged in the building of the house of God. And, therefore, when through these passers-by the Prince of darkness makes a last forlorn attempt to destroy the work of God, and to persuade the Christ to come down from the cross, He will surely refuse. For the work of God must be finished. The temple must be built!

The temple as to its idea and essence is not that building made with hands that adorned Mount Sion. It was but a shadow. The true temple is the dwelling of God with His people. The essence of the temple is the spiritual bond of fellowship and most intimate communion of friendship between God and men, the relation in which God blesses His people with all spiritual blessings in heavenly places in Christ, and they know Him, enter into His secrets, taste His grace and loving kindness, and forevermore behold the beauties and pleasures there are at His right hand. It is the relation according to which God walks among them and talks with them, and calls them His sons and daughters, and they love Him with all their heart and mind and soul and strength, and serve and glorify Him forever! That temple once existed in earthly form in the first paradise. For man was made after the image of God, and placed in covenant relation of friendship to his Maker. God revealed Himself to him there, and he knew his God in the wind of day and tasted the goodness of God's house in the fruit of the tree of life. But man proved himself to be the destroyer of the temple of God. He sinned. He opened the house of God to the devil. He made it even then a den of robbers. But God, Who gives His glory to no other, had provided some better thing for us, and purposes to rebuild His house in Christ, and that, too, in greater beauty than it ever could have attained in the first Adam. Of this new, heavenly, eternal house of God the building of Jerusalem was but a shadow. God dwelt in the Most

Holy Place, between the cherubim and over the mercy seat, while the people were represented by the candlestick, the altar of incense, and the table of shewbread in the Holy Place. That temple of God, that most intimate fellowship of friendship between God and His people, is centrally realized in the incarnation of the Son of God, in Immanuel: God with us. For in Him God and man are united in the unity of the divine Person of the Son. That temple is further realized in the Church, through the outpouring of the Holy Spirit, through Whom God dwells in Christ with His people spiritually. And that temple will be finished and revealed in all the heavenly glory and beauty of its everlasting perfection, when in the new heaven and earth the tabernacle of God shall be with men, and God will dwell with them, and they shall be His people, and God Himself shall be with them, and be their God. "And God shall wipe away all tears from their eyes; and there shall be no more death, neither sorrow, nor crying, neither shall there be any more pain: for the former things are passed away." Rev. 21:3, 4.

The realization of this heavenly temple would involve the destruction of the temple in Jerusalem. What reason or place would there be for the shadow after reality had come? But still more. The building of the eternal house of God would require, too, the destruction of the temple of Christ's body. For the house of God must be founded on God's eternal righteousness: He can have no fellowship with sin. And, therefore, the justice of God with respect to sin must be satisfied, and satisfaction for sin is the voluntary suffering of death as an act of perfect obedience. He that would lay the foundations of the tabernacle of God with men in righteousness must lay down His life for God's sake. Through the veil, that is through His own flesh, broken and rent on the cross, Christ would forever open the way into the inner sanctuary of God!

And so, the words Jesus had spoken three years before His death, and which were changed into a taunting challenge by those that passed by the cross, are perfectly clear and full of meaning. "Destroy ye this temple," He had said, and had referred to the temple of His body. Yet, as is evident from the connection in which these words were spoken, reference to the temple of

Jerusalem was not altogether absent. The destruction of the one implied the tearing down of the other. And both, the temple of His body and the temple of Jerusalem they, the enemies, were destroying at this moment, as they were destroying the temple of Christ's flesh on the accursed tree. No, they did not intend to destroy the temple of Jerusalem. They had no idea that they were instrumental in the realization of the eternal temple of God. They merely desired in cruel hatred and furious anger to destroy Jesus of Nazareth. Yet, even so this is just what they were doing, fulfilling the counsel of God. For when the body of Jesus was destroyed, the temple of Jerusalem had no more significance and reason to exist. And while they were destroying the temple, Jesus on the cross was already busy rebuilding it. Already He was fast becoming the chief corner stone of the house of God. Even while they are mocking and distorting His words, He is willingly laying down His life before the face of God, laying down His life for His sheep, that He might forever open for them the way into the house of God's everlasting covenant of friendship. And presently He will appear through the resurrection as the central realization of the glorious temple of God. For, they may destroy this temple, but in three days He will rebuild it!

And so, He will not come down from the cross! Even though all hell break loose and come to Golgotha to mock and jeer, and to challenge Him to save Himself, He will not come down. O, indeed, in that first period of the crucifixion, when God still caused His sun to shine upon the righteous and the wicked alike that were present there on Golgotha, it appeared as if He were, indeed, powerless to take up their challenge; as if He were held to the cross by the power of the enemies, rather than by His own will. Or who would endure such contradiction of sinners against himself, as did our Saviour on the cross, if he were not utterly in their power? Everybody mocked! The chief priests, the scribes and elders, the theologians of those days, sarcastically suggested that He saved others, but now could not save Himself; mockingly they shouted that they would believe that He was the King of Israel, if He only would come down from the cross; cruelly they reminded Him that He trusted in God as the Son, and that even God would not deliver Him in this hour of His agony! And even the malefactors that were crucified with Him, or at least one of them, appealed to Him in bitter mockery to save Himself and them! And the passers-by took time to stop and to wag their heads, and to challenge Him to come down and destroy the temple and rebuild it! Even the Roman soldiers heaped contempt upon a king that was so utterly in the power of his enemies! Who would endure all this, if he were not powerless to escape it, or to overcome the mocking mob? Indeed, in this hour there is no name left to the Son of man! There is no beauty that we should desire Him! The impotent victim of the powers of darkness He appears to be! He cannot come down from the cross, even if He would!

But at this hour, we remember His Word, and recall the many incidents that took place on His way to the cross, and believe that even now He has power to lay down His life and to take it again; that, as far as His power is concerned, He could descend from that cruel cross and put to shame the mockery of the enemy; and that, therefore, it is because He wills to suffer and to die, that He endures even this contradiction of sinners against Himself! We remember that He spoke of Himself as the Good Shepherd, that lays down His life for the sheep, whose life no one could take from Him, but who laid it down of Himself, that He might take it again. We recall His prayer, when His soul was troubled in anticipation of this hour, that the Father might glorify His name through Him; and the earnest supplication in the garden that the Father's will might be done. We bring back to our mind the dismissal of the traitor in the upper room, the act of His power in the garden, whereby He laid His would-be captors prostrate in the dust before Him, His refusal of all human or heavenly help to prevent His being taken by the enemy. All this we now recall, and we know, that even in this hour of the cross He is the mighty Lord of life and death. The fact that He did not come down from the cross is no proof of His impotence, of the triumph of His enemies over Him, but rather of the certainty of the atonement by His willing sacrifice. But no, we do not even need to recall the former manifestations of His power, for we may now look at the cross in the light of His glorious resurrection. That resurrection is God's seal on the sacrifice of Christ and on the perfection of His obedience. "It is finished," — thus announced the Saviour from His cross just before He gave up the ghost. "It is finished!" — such is the testimony of God from heaven in the resurrection of Jesus Christ from the dead! And by faith we receive that Word of God, and though all things of our present experience testify against us, we respond: "Indeed, finished forever!"

CHAPTER 7

The Place Where the Lord Lay

Come, and see the place where the Lord lay.
— MATT. 28:6.

The Lord is risen indeed! That is the shout of joy with which
the apostles meet one another on that glorious first day of the week,
when it had become evident to them that their crucified Lord
had broken the bonds of death. That becomes the very heart of
the gospel they carry into the world, after their risen Lord had
been glorified and they had received power through the outpouring
of the Holy Ghost upon them on the day of Pentecost. Even on
that very day of the first fruits, Peter standing with the eleven
preached the Christ, Whom they had taken, as He was delivered
by the determinate counsel and foreknowledge of God, and Whom
they had crucified and slain, but "Whom God had raised up, having
loosed the pains of death, because it was not possible that he
should be holden of it." Acts 2:23, 24. And again: "This Jesus
God hath raised up, whereof we are all witnesses." Acts 2:32.
When on the occasion of the miracle performed upon the impotent man at the temple gate that was called Beautiful, Peter
preaches the gospel to the people, he emphasizes that the Jews
"killed the Prince of life, whom God hath raised from the dead;
whereof we are witnesses." Acts 3:15. And when the apostles on
the day following are called to give account of their deed before

the rulers of the Jews, Peter boldly testifies: "Be it known unto you all, and to all the people of Israel, that by the name of Jesus Christ of Nazareth, whom ye crucified, whom God raised from the dead, even by him doth this man stand here before you whole." Acts 4:10. And when they were released from prison we read of them: "And with great power gave the apostles witness of the resurrection of the Lord Jesus." Acts 4:32. In Perga Paul preaches that the rulers of the Jews condemned and slew Jesus: "But God raised him from the dead. And he was seen many days of them which came up with him from Galilee to Jerusalem, who are his witnesses unto the people. And we declare unto you glad tidings, how that the promise which was made unto the fathers, God hath fulfilled the same unto us their children, in that he hath raised up Jesus again; as it is also written in the second psalm, Thou art my Son, this day have I begotten thee." Acts 13:30-33. And in that well known fifteenth chapter of his first epistle to the Corinthians the apostle Paul writes: "Moreover, brethren, I declare unto you the gospel, which I preached unto you"; and this gospel testified: "how that Christ died for our sins according to the Scriptures; and that he was buried, and that he rose again the third day according to the Scriptures." I Cor. 15:1, 2, 4.

Christ is raised from the dead! That is the gospel of our redemption, the Word of God concerning our justification. For "if thou shalt confess with thy mouth the Lord Jesus, and shalt believe in thine heart that God hath raised him from the dead, thou shalt be saved." Rom. 10:9. O, indeed, the apostles preach Christ crucified; and in the cross of Christ we glory, — but what is the cross without the resurrection? A vain thing! For "if Christ is not raised, your faith is vain; ye are yet in your sins." I Cor. 15:17. He was, indeed, delivered for our transgressions, but He was also raised for our justification. Rom. 4:25. The resurrection is the divine answer to Christ's next to the last cross-utterance: "It is finished." With and for our sins He died and entered into lowest hell. Never could He have risen from that darkness unless He had been the Son of God; never could God in justice have raised Him from the dead, and given Him life and glory and immortality, unless He had fully atoned for all our transgressions. Besides, we need a living Redeemer, Who is able to deliver us from the power of death, and make us partakers of His resurrection life. And through the resurrection of Jesus Christ from the dead we are begotten again unto a lively hope, according to the abundant mercy of our God. I Pet. 1:3. Christ is the resurrection and the life. And in His resurrection we have the earnest of our final glorification. For Christ is risen, and is become the firstfruits of them that slept, and as in Adam all die, so in Christ shall all be made alive. I Cor. 15:20, 22. In the cross of Christ, therefore, we glory, but in that cross, not as it stands in the gloom of Golgotha's darkness, but as it is illumined by the glorious floodlight of the resurrection!

The resurrection of our Lord Jesus Christ from the dead as a fact is well attested by many faithful witnesses, as the apostle Paul emphasizes in that same fifteenth chapter of first Corinthians from which we already quoted. In my estimation, there is in all Scripture nothing more marvelous, nothing more exquisitely beautiful than the resurrection narratives. They bear the undeniable stamp of truth. No one who reads them can deny that here we have the testimony of faithful witnesses, who simply and truthfully recorded what they heard and saw of what in itself far transcends all human experience: the resurrection of their Lord. They are the rock of the gospel narrative upon which all the attempts of unbelief to gainsay the truth of God concerning His Son must needs suffer shipwreck. Often, indeed, ever since the crude story the soldiers were instructed by the Jewish leaders to tell, that, namely, the disciples had stolen the body of Jesus while they slept, the attempt has been made to relegate the resurrection narratives of the gospel to the sphere of myths, but just as often these attempts have failed. No human artist, were he of the most consummate skill, could have designed them. And the reason for this very evident truthfulness of these narratives must be found in the fact, that, while the apostles certainly witness of the *reality* of the resurrection, they, nevertheless, witness at the same time of the transcendence, the "otherness" of this wonder. They did not expect their Lord, yet He meets them. He is the same Lord, witness the scars in His hands and feet, and in His side, yet He is different. He is with them again, yet the former earthly fellowship is never again established. They believe, yet they wonder. They know that it is the Lord, that stands at the shore of the Sea of Tiberias, yet they would like to ask Him: "Who art thou?" It is the element that lends to these narratives the indelible mark of the truth. Clearly and undeniably they testify that the Lord is *risen,* and that He is risen *indeed!*

For, mark you well, these two elements in the resurrection of Christ must be attested by those who are its witnesses; its reality and its "otherness." Yes, the resurrection of our Lord is real. It is a fact. The Lord is risen indeed! His resurrection is not the product of the imagination of apostles, who so intensely desired that resurrection that they finally believed it. It is not a spiritual resurrection in the sense that He arose in the hearts and minds of the apostles, and that now He lives forever in the grateful memory of the Church. No: He is risen! He was in death, and He lives! His body was in the grave, and it is there no more. But the second element in that resurrection must no less be emphasized: He is *raised!* His resurrection may not be put on a par with the raising of the young man of Nain, or of the daughter of Jairus, or of Lazarus. These were but shadows of the real resurrection. Their resurrection was a return. Lazarus was called forth from the grave, but only to return to his former, earthly and mortal existence. To the same side of death and the grave whence he had entered it, he returned. His resurrection was no victory. But Christ went through the grave! He entered it on the side of things earthly, corruptible, mortal, physical; He issued forth from it on the heavenly side, into the sphere of the spiritual, the incorruptible and immortal. Historically real, yet far transcending all that eye can see, and ear can hear, and that can arise in the heart of man, — such is the resurrection of the Lord Jesus Christ from the dead.

How, then, was the fact of the resurrection of our Saviour attested? Several factors together constitute the revelation of the risen Lord. There are, of course, the appearances of the Saviour after the resurrection to several of His disciples, ten in number, not counting the heavenly vision Paul received on the way to Damascus. But these alone would not have been sufficient to establish the reality of the resurrection. The risen Lord, as He appeared to them, was altogether different from the Jesus they had known before the awful crucifixion, and with Whom they had enjoyed daily communion. He showed Himself to them, was with them for a few moments, and mysteriously disappeared again, and they knew not whither He went. And even these appearances ceased after the fortieth day. Might they not have concluded that the Lord was merely alive according to the Spirit, had there been no other evidence of His resurrection? How easily a shadow of doubt as to the reality of His resurrection might have lingered in their hearts and minds is evident from what we read of their attitude of His appearance on a mountain in Galilee: "And when they saw him, they worshipped him: but some doubted." Matt. 28:17. There was, however, in the second place, the word of the angels, that waited for the disciples at the open grave on the morning of the momentous first day of the week, and who preached to them the gospel of the resurrection: "He is not here; He is risen!" Also in the case of the resurrection of the Lord the spoken word accompanied the "Word that had come to pass," and who else could be the bearers of that message than the heavenly spirits? And then, finally, there is the testimony of the open, vacated grave, and of the place where He had lain, a testimony which is so important and marvellous, that we may well call special attention to its message.

Fact is that on the resurrection morning the vacated grave is first of all and chiefly the object on which the attention of all is centered, and the wonder of which fills the witnesses with awe and amazement. It is, no doubt, to watch over the open grave, and to guard its silent evidence from being destroyed and obliterated by rude, profane hands, that an angel came down from heaven to roll the stone from the sepulchre and to sit upon it. For thus we read in the gospel according to Matthew: "And, behold, there was a great earthquake: for the angel of the Lord descended from heaven, and came and rolled back the stone from the door, and sat upon it." Let us take note of this. Had human imagination invented this narrative, it would no doubt have concluded this statement quite differently. It would have pictured Jesus issuing forth from the grave in all His glory and putting the watch of the Roman soldiers to flight. In fact, we almost feel somewhat disappointed at the apparently lame ending of this statement: "and sat upon it." We were prepared to read: "the angel of the Lord descended from heaven, and came and rolled back the stone from the door, and . . . Jesus issued forth in glory." Perhaps, we would have liked to be present with our cameras and take pictures of that wonderful sight! But nothing of the kind, evidently, took place. The angel rolled back the stone, and sat upon it! The Lord had already risen, and no one witnessed the resurrection as such! The reason is, evidently, that the Lord in His resurrection body had no need of stones' being rolled away to issue forth from the grave, and that there would have been nothing for our cameras to record, had we been present. How utterly foolish was the seal that had been attached to the sepulchre, was the chain with which the stone had been fastened to the main body of the grave, were the watchmen that were appointed to guard the resting place of Jesus' body! As if stones and seals and chains and mere men could prevent the Lord of glory from issuing forth from the place of corruption! But the angel that rolled back the stone from the grave, sat upon it. That grave must be preserved, its evidence must be kept, until proper witnesses shall have arrived and inspected the grave, and shall have heard the gospel of their salvation: "He is not here; He is risen!"

These witnesses were, first of all the women, that went to the sepulchre with the evident purpose to complete the embalming of the body of the Lord! They were Mary Magdalene, "the other Mary," Joanna, Salome, and "other women with them." And it is by the guiding hand of God's providential care that on this blessed morning they leave their homes, in order to visit the sepulchre in the garden of Joseph of Arimathea, though the Lord's purpose with this visit was quite different from their own. They had loved the Lord. And they had followed Him during the latter part of His public ministry, in order that they might render unto Him such service as only a woman's hand can perform. Witnesses they had been of His death. And they had belonged to the small funeral procession that took their way into the garden of Joseph on that late Friday afternoon of Jesus' death. They had beheld the sepulchre and saw "how His body was laid." Luke 23:55. However, they had not seen that the body of Jesus was quite thoroughly prepared for the burial by Joseph and Nicodemus, the reason being probably that this was done within the sepulchre itself, hid from the eyes of the women, who waited without. That this had been done is, nevertheless, evident from the statement in John 19: "Then took they the body of Jesus, and wound it in linen clothes with the spices, as the manner of the Jews is to bury." vs. 40. In order to understand the significance of the "place where the Lord lay," we must remember that it was customary to wrap the body of the deceased limb by limb separately in linen clothes together with the spices that had been prepared for the purpose; while a special napkin was twisted around the head. All this had been finished by the two rulers of the Jews on Friday afternoon. Had the women known this they would not have gone to the sepulchre early in the morning that first day of the week, for they also had prepared spices and ointments, and intended to finish the embalming of Jesus' body. But it was in God's providence that they were ignorant of the thorough work done by Joseph and Nicodemus, for they must needs be witnesses of the empty grave, and of the place where the Lord had lain. What is more, had they attended to the Word of the Lord when He was still with them, and had they believed His Word, they would probably have been far from Jerusalem by this time, for Jesus had plainly foretold them that He would be delivered to the chief priests and elders of the people, be crucified and slain, that He would rise again the third day, and that He would go before them into Galilee. But this they had evidently forgotten, and so it happens that on this first day of the week they go to the sepulchre to perform a last labor of love on the dead body of their beloved Lord.

Of the fact that the sepulchre had been sealed, and that a watch had been placed around it, they must have been ignorant. But as they approached the grave they do remember the heavy stone that closed the entrance of the tomb, and they are afraid that there will be no one about to roll it away. However, as they drew nearer they noticed that the grave was open. It appears that Mary Magdalene upon the sight of the open tomb immediately drew the conclusion that they had stolen the body of Jesus. She was not with the women anymore when they reached the sepulchre, but had turned around to tell the disciples that the body of her Lord had been removed. The other women, however, proceed to the grave, and entering into it stood perplexed at the sight. "And as they were much perplexed thereabout" (Luke 24:5), the angel that had rolled away the stone from the sepulchre preached unto them the first resurrection message: "Fear not ye, for I know that ye seek Jesus, which was crucified. He is not here: for he is risen, as he said. Come, see the place where the Lord lay!" Matt. 28:5, 6.

But why this special invitation to see the place where the Lord had lain? Does the angel merely want them to make sure for themselves that the grave was empty? But that had become plain to them at first glance. The mere fact that the body of the Lord was not in the tomb anymore was in need of no special investigation. And why should the angel call special attention to the place where the Lord had lain, had not that place within the tomb been especially discernible? What, then, was peculiar and worthy of special attention about this place?

Before we answer this question we must briefly recall another incident that stands connected with the vacated tomb of the risen Lord. As we said, Mary Magdalene at the sight of the open grave had drawn her own conclusions, and had run to Peter and John with the message: "They have taken away the Lord out of the sepulchre, and we know not where they have laid him." Her conclusions were, of course, wholly erroneous, but again the Lord used her false report to bring two more witnesses to the grave of the risen Christ. Peter and John run to the grave. John being the younger of the two outruns Peter, arrives at the sepulchre first, stoops down and inspects the grave, and immediately notices the linen clothes lying. When Peter arrives, John must have invited him to pay special attention to those linen clothes, and Peter enters the tomb, and not only notices the linen clothes lying, but now also sees that the napkin that had been wound about Jesus' head, was not lying with the rest of the linen clothes, but in a place by itself. "Then went in also that other disciple, which came first to the sepulchre, and he saw, and believed." John 20:8.

Now why all this emphasis on the position of the linen clothes, and of the napkin lying by itself? And why did John believe on the basis of the evidence of these linen clothes? That he believed, not the story of Mary Madgalene, but that Jesus had risen from the dead, something which they had not as yet known from the Scriptures (vs. 9), is evident. The very expression "and believed" can mean nothing less. But why should he believe the resurrection of Jesus on the basis of the evidence of these linen clothes? And again: why had the angel invited the women to "see the place where the Lord lay"? There can be but one answer to this question: the wonder of the resurrection was evidenced by the wonder of those linen clothes! In other words, those linen clothes lay in the grave, not all neatly folded up as some would have it, but in the very position in which they had been wrapped around the body of the Lord! They had not been disturbed! This explains why the napkin was lying by itself, as it had been wound around the head of the Saviour. This explains the special emphasis of the angel on the place where the Lord had lain. And this alone explains all the attention paid to those linen clothes by the two apostles, as well as the fact that John saw and believed! Even as the risen Lord had no need of the stone's being removed from the tomb in order to issue forth from it, so He could leave those linen clothes that had been wrapped about His limbs without disturbing their position in the least. In the very shape of His body they lay there in the tomb, silent witnesses to the wonder of the resurrection!

And so, let us see the place where the Lord lay, and believe! The Lord is risen indeed! And He is risen in glory! He is no longer here, neither will He ever return to the sphere of our earthly and mortal existence. He has gone on! He has gone through the grave and overcome its power of corruption! He is victor! Death hath no more dominion over Him! In Him corruption did already put on incorruption, mortality put on immortality, and He shows forth the image of the heavenly. And He is the firstfruits, the firstbegotten of the dead. His brethren shall surely follow Him! For He has the power to make all things like unto Himself! Also our humiliated bodies He will surely make like unto His most glorious body. In those bodies we shall inherit the kingdom of God, dwell in God's eternal tabernacle forever, know Him even as we are known, and see Him face to face!

BOOK TWO

THE

ROYAL SUFFERER

CHAPTER 1

The First Encounter

Get thee behind me, Satan . . . — Lu. 4:8.

In the revelation of Jesus Christ, His suffering occupies an essential place. Eliminate the cross as an indispensable and strictly necessary element from that revelation, and you have no Christ left. For Him there was no crown without the cross, no glory without shame, no life except through the resurrection, and, therefore, through death. As He Himself expresses this necessity of His suffering after His resurrection to the sojourners to Emmaus: "Ought not the Christ to have suffered these things, and to enter into his glory?" Lu. 24:26. All His earthly sojourn was characterized by suffering. For Him to suffer was not something incidental, something to be avoided, but it belonged to the work which the Father had given Him to do, and, therefore, must be deliberately chosen, preferred, and accomplished to the end. For He came into the world as the Servant of the Lord, at the head of a sinful people, to fulfill all righteousness, the righteousness of God with respect to sin, and thus in the way of righteousness to redeem them whom the Father had given Him. And this meant that He had to satisfy the justice of God, to bear the wrath of God and the punishment of sin in perfect obedience of love. And so, in all His work He suffers, and in His suffering He works. As God's prophet in the world He suffers, enduring shame and contradiction

135

for His name's sake; as the Lamb of God and our High Priest
He brings the perfect sacrifice, pouring out His soul unto death;
as the divinely anointed King He must battle His way into His
kingdom, and overcome the powers of the devil, sin, and death,
not by might, nor by the power of the sword, but by voluntarily
choosing and traveling the way of the cross. He is the "Royal
Sufferer" in an altogether unique sense of the word. And we wish
to consider some of the Scriptural passages in which He appears
in this capacity, as the King that rejects all the glory of the world,
deliberately chooses the way of suffering and death, and so lays
the foundations of His kingdom in His own blood.

The first of these passages we find in Lu. 4:5-8: "And the
devil, taking him up into an high mountain, shewed him all the
kingdoms of the world in a moment of time. And the devil said
unto him, All this power will I give thee, and the glory of them:
for that is delivered unto me, and to whomsoever I will I give it.
If thou therefore wilt worship me, all shall be thine. And Jesus
answered and said unto him, Get thee behind me, Satan: for it is
written, Thou shalt worship the Lord thy God, and him only
shalt thou serve." We are, of course, all acquainted with the
occasion of this first encounter between God's anointed King and
the Prince of this world. Jesus was about to begin His public
ministry. Already He had been baptized, and received testimony
from heaven that He was God's beloved Son. And now the Spirit
that had descended on Him at the time of His baptism, led Him
at once into the wilderness, in order that there He might begin the
battle with the enemy that must be overcome, a battle that is to be
brought to its victorious consummation only through the cross
and in the resurrection of the Servant of the Lord. We are reminded at once of a similar encounter that had taken place centuries before in the first paradise. But we notice, too, that there
are important points of difference between that first temptation and this encounter. The former took place in paradise;
the scene of the latter is the desert. In the former man is
in possession of the dominion of the world over which his God
had appointed him king; in the latter the devil appears as Prince
of the world, in possession of all its kingdoms, while Christ, Who
is God's anointed King has not even a place where He can lay

His head. In the former the devil takes the initiative, and invades Paradise to bring man to his fall; in the latter, however, it is the Son of man that seeks out the Prince of the world in his own abode, the desert, to test his strength and commence the battle. And, finally, in the former the God appointed king of creation suffers defeat through disobedience; in the latter the Son of man scores a decisive victory. For the rest, we may pass in silence several questions that might arise in connection with this temptation of our Lord, in order to concentrate all our attention upon its central significance: the initial and decisive victory of the royal Sufferer over the Prince of this world.

Let us, first of all, take a brief look at the opposing parties in this mortal conflict, and their relative position. They are the Christ of God, the anointed King over Zion, the Servant of the Lord, Whom God ordained from before the foundation of the world to be the Head over all things; and the devil or Satan, the adversary of God and of His cause in the world, the Prince and ruler of this world, who appears here especially in that capacity, as is evident from his vaunted boast. To understand his position over against our Lord as he offers Him all the kingdoms of the world, we must remember that God had created this world a kingdom, with man as its king. Adam's position before the fall was that of friend servant of God, and as such he was king of the earthly creation, and dominion was given him over all things. All creatures were to serve him, that he might serve his God. But Satan launched his attack upon this king-servant of God, and tempted him to become unfaithful to his Lord and Creator, violate God's covenant, and to submit himself to his, the devil's lordship. In this he succeeded. Man became disobedient, rejected the Word of God, and made an alliance with Satan. Henceforth he would still stand at the head of the earthly creation, but in enmity against God and friendship with the Prince of darkness, to subject all things to him in the service of iniquity. In this ethical sense, the devil is the prince and ruler of this world. Through man he has dominion over the kingdoms of this world. He is the world's prince, not because he has any right to rule, nor because he can ever wrest the reins of government from the hands of almighty God, but because he reigns in the sphere of iniquity, and in that sphere fallen man serves him.

God, however, in His eternal good pleasure, had anointed His own King over all things from before the foundation of the world. And through the power of this King, His only begotten Son in the flesh, He purposed to destroy the works of the devil, reveal the glory of His own name, and redeem and deliver all things in heaven and in earth, to reconcile them unto Himself, and to raise them to the highest level of the eternal kingdom of heaven. And in spite of himself the devil must serve this purpose, nor can he ever serve any other purpose with all his wicked devices against the living God. What is more, immediately after the fall God openly announced this purpose and declared the decree to the devil himself in the well-known words: "I will put enmity between thee and the woman, and between thy seed and her seed; it shall bruise thy head, and thou shalt bruise his heel." It was the announcement of his utter defeat through the promised Seed. And the devil understood. And all through the centuries of the old dispensation he had made a desperate attempt to destroy this seed of the woman before the final Seed could be born. He tries to destroy this seed in the very beginning, through the murder of Cain upon Abel, but God raises up another seed in Seth. You may see this design of the devil in the persecution and temptation of the prediluvian church, till only eight of them were left, but God saves His church through the flood. And all through the ages after the flood, in the attempt to build the tower of Babel, the murderous design of Pharaoh upon the little children of Israel in Egypt, the continuous fury of the nations against Israel and the house of David culminating in the Babylonian captivity, the plot of wicked Haman to destroy all the Jews and obliterate them from the earth, the cruel persecutions instigated by Antiochus Epiphanes, that old dispensational Antichrist — throughout this history you may clearly see the design of the devil to destroy the holy seed, and prevent the coming of the promised Seed that would crush his head. That is the reason why always "the heathen raged, and the people imagined a vain thing, the kings of the earth (did) set themselves, and the rulers (did) take counsel together, against the Lord, and against his anointed." But He that sitteth in the

heaven laughed, and had them in derision, and spoke to them in
His sore displeasure: "Yet have I set my king upon my holy hill
of Zion." Ps. 2:1-6. God's counsel was realized. Although it
looked very dark indeed for the seed of David in the fulness of
time, God fulfilled His promise. The great Seed of the woman
was born. One last attempt was made to kill Him while He was
still an infant, when Herod murdered the little children of Bethlehem, but it, too, had been frustrated. And now they stand together,
face to face, on a high mountain, these two: the Prince of the
world of man, and anointed King of Zion, Who had come to crush
the other's head, to destroy the kingdom of darkness, and to
establish His own kingdom, the kingdom of heaven on the
foundations of divine justice and righteousness.

But how shall they fight? What manner of war shall they wage?
Shall the issue as to who shall be ruler of the world be decided
by brute strength, by main force, by the power of arms? But no,
that is impossible. The question was not one of might. If it had
been, the devil would surely have been crushed, destroyed by
the Word that proceeds out of the mouth of the King of Zion.
For He is the mighty Son of God, co-equal with the Father and
the Holy Ghost. But He has assumed our nature, and here, on the
mountain of temptation, He appears as the obedient Servant of
Jehovah. He must receive His kingdom from the Father. And
only in the way of obedience can He enter into the glory of His
kingdom. He must suffer for His own. He stands at the head of
a sinful people that must be redeemed, in order that through
and with Him they may inherit the kingdom of heaven. Therefore
must He suffer, become obedient even unto the death of the cross.
Deliberately He must choose and travel to the end of the way of the
cross. For the question is one of righteousness, of the righteousness
of God. Hence, the battle that is fought on this high mountain, and
that is finished finally on the cross, is a spiritual warfare, that
must be waged with spiritual means, and with spiritual ends in
view. If the devil can but persuade this Servant of the Lord to forsake the way of obedience and suffering, he will overcome Him and
once more become the victor.

And thus he makes his attack. He offers the Son of man a
proposition. He would make a covenant, an alliance with Him!

His proposal is as shameful as it is bold! To make this proposition as concrete, real, and attractive as possible he had taken Him to this high mountain. He showed Him all the kingdoms of the world in a moment of time! How such a panoramic view of all the kingdoms of the world could be obtained even from a high mountain, is a question we need not pause to answer now. Suffice it to say that in a sense these kingdoms were actually his. It is more than mere boast when the devil claims that these kingdoms and their power and glory had been delivered unto him, and that to whomever he would he could give them. His world, the world of sin and rebellion against God, he showed unto the Saviour! In that world his will, the will of the flesh, was being done. He was its spiritual lord. And it was also true that this world had its power and glory! Man, even in his sin, had ruled over it, had belabored it, had cultivated it, had brought to light its hidden treasures, had subdued it. It was the world of culture and civilization, of man's power and glory, of pleasures and treasures, of n.an's art and science, man's industry and commerce, man's wisdom and ingenuity, which the devil here offered to Zion's King. But it was also that same world with all its power and glory subjected to and pressed into the service of sin, the world as it stood in enmity against God, the world full of the lust of the flesh, the lust of the eyes, and the pride of life. That world the devil now offers the Servant of the Lord! He can have it! He may become its lord for nothing! Why, then, should there be enmity between Him and the devil? Why should Christ travel the deep way of the cross, seeing the devil is ready to surrender his throne to Him without a struggle?

But there was an important condition to this proposition of the devil: "If thou therefore wilt worship me, all shall be thine." Always the devil's offers are conditional, and always the condition is the same: forsake God and acknowledge Satan as lord! And therefore, it is always either—or. You cannot serve God and Mammon! You must love one and hate the other! Before this alternative, Christ, too, is placed. How could it be different? The devil was king of the world only in the moral, ethical sense, in the sphere of iniquity. To be sure, he *would* not, but neither *could* he offer anything to Christ *as the Servant of the Lord*. Only if

Christ would become *his* servant, if he could persuade the Christ
to become the antichrist, could Satan make good his promise, and
surrender to Jesus the kingdoms of this world. Such was the
audacity and shamelessness of the devil's proposition!

You say, perhaps, that the temptation was not real, and that
the Lord could never have been attracted by such a proposition.
To this I would answer as follows. First of all, if you mean that
there was not the slightest possibility that the Lord would yield
and fall for the temptation, you are right. Christ could not sin,
and that not because He was without sin, but because He was the
Son of God in human nature. From this viewpoint the temptation
could only serve the purpose to manifest His faithfulness, and
to reveal the devil's defeat. Secondly, if you mean that apart from
its ethical implication the proposition did not appeal at all to
Jesus' human nature, so that there was not even an element of
trial, I must differ. And how could we possibly have the right thus
to minimize the reality of Jesus' temptation and suffering? How
often are we tempted by but a very small part of that world that
is here offered to Jesus, to become unfaithful and serve the devil!
This the Lord could never do, but let us not forget that He very
really dreaded His way of suffering, and that another way than
that of the cross must always have appealed to His human nature.
The temptation was real in as far as it placed before the Lord
the alternatives of human glory and the way of the cross!

"Get thee behind me, Satan!" Christ's rejection of the devil's
proposition is both indignant and final. There is no room for
discussion here, for it is written: "Thou shalt worship the Lord
thy God, and Him only shalt thou serve." That principle was
written, not only in the Scriptures, but also in the heart of the
Servant of the Lord. His meat it was to do the Father's will. That
will would lead Him to the cross, through the depth of hell. Hence,
all the glory of the world He would gladly reject, in order to
choose the way of obedience unto death. The Royal Sufferer He
would be, trusting that the Father would give Him the kingdom.
And in this He was not put to shame. For He was raised from the
dead, exalted to the highest glory, and will appear again as the
King of kings and Lord of lords unto salvation, that all that
love His appearing may share in His glory!

CHAPTER 2

The King and the Bread Question

I am that bread of life. — JOHN 6:48.

There was a principal and profound difference between the conception of the kingdom of God as Jesus came to establish it, and the conception of that kingdom as it was in the minds of many of the Jews during the time of the Saviour's sojourn on earth. After all, the latter was very little different from the kingdom Christ was offered by the devil on the mount of temptation. The Jews expected an earthly kingdom. The earthly throne of David was to be restored and even raised to unknown heights of glory and splendor by the expected Messiah, and the nation of Israel was to be victorious over its enemies in that earthly sense, and rule over the nations of the world. And not only had they formed an earthly and rather carnal conception of the Messianic kingdom, and of the Christ that was to come, but they had set their heart on it. That the kingdom was to be a spiritual commonwealth, embracing all the nations of the world equally, that its blessings were to be spiritual blessings of righteousness, holiness and truth, the forgiveness of sin and eternal life, and that the kingdom would not be finally realized here in this world, but in the world to come — this they did not understand. Even the inner circle of Christ's disciples had this earthly and carnal conception of the kingdom of the Messiah, as is evident from

143

their entire attitude to Jesus before the cross and the resurrection.
For a king that must suffer to enter into His glory, or at least,
for one that had to suffer as Christ would have to be delivered,
crucified and slain, they had no room in their conception and hope.
When the Lord predicted to them this suffering, they either
strenuously opposed the idea and contradicted their Lord, or His
words simply failed to register in their minds. And constantly
they were discussing the question who would be the greatest in
the kingdom of heaven.

No wonder then that there was a constant conflict between
Christ and the carnal Jews on this score. For His kingdom was
in no sense of the word of this world. He did not come to
establish a natural, but a spiritual kingdom, and His kingdom
was not earthly, but heavenly. His coming into the world had
nothing to do with earthly prosperity and peace, earthly power
and glory. He had come to establish the kingdom of God, i.e.
that commonwealth in which God reigns by grace in the hearts of
the subjects, and they acknowledge Him as their God and delight in doing His will. To become citizens of that kingdom men
had to be redeemed, for they had no right to its citizenship. And
to redeem them Christ had to pay the price of their redemption
by His obedience even unto death. And to enter into that kingdom men had to be delivered from the dominion of sin and the
devil, and translated from death into life, from darkness into light.
But the conception of such a kingdom is directly opposed to
the carnal desires and expectations of the natural man. He does
not want to be redeemed and to be delivered from the power of
sin, but in his sin he wants a kingdom of this world with an
abundance of peace and prosperity. Thus it is today. And thus
it was in the days of Christ's sojourn on earth, even though this
carnal conception assumed a more specifically Jewish form and
aspect. And the more clearly carnal Israel apprehended that
Jesus would have nothing of their earthly kingdom and carnal
expectations, the more they were disappointed in Him, hated Him,
denied He was the Christ, and became ready to reject and to
kill Him. And so, the anointed King of God suffered, not only in
order to enter into His kingdom, but also because of the very
nature of the kingdom He came to establish. Because of it, and

because He could never cater to the carnal desires of sinful men,
He was despised and rejected, the Royal Sufferer.

A very clear illustration of this conflict between the anointed
King and the carnal Jews, which resulted in the latter's alienation from Him, and their rejection of Him as the Messiah, is
recorded in the sixth chapter of the gospel according to John.
To bring the story of this conflict briefly and sharply before your
minds, and to give you an impression of the swift and radical
change that was brought about by it in the attitude of the carnal
Jews to the Christ of God, I will "read" just a few verses of this
chapter. In vss. 14 and 15 we read: "Then those men, when
they had seen the miracle that Jesus did, said, This is of a truth
that prophet that should come into the world. When Jesus therefore perceived that they would come and take him by force, to
make him a king, he departed again into a mountain himself
alone." And in vs. 56 we read: "From that time many of his
disciples went back, and walked no more with him." What a
change! In the evening of one day they acknowledge that He is
the expected Messiah, and they are so filled with enthusiasm
about Him, that they are ready to acclaim Him king, and would
compel Him to ascend the throne of Israel. And on the next day
they are wholly disappointed in Him, and become alienated from
Him, so that they forsake the company of His disciples! They
leave Him alone, and reject Him! What had happened? Briefly
I may answer that the bread-question had been discussed and
explained by the Saviour, and although these would-be disciples
had probably not understood all the Lord had been saying to
them, His speech had been sufficiently plain to cause them
to understand that they certainly had made a fundamental mistake when on the previous evening they had intended to make
Him their king, and that He was not the Christ they expected
and desired. Let us follow for a moment the course of events
that had brought about this change.

It was toward the close of Jesus' Galilean ministry, of which
Capernaum had been the center. To speak in modern parlance,
the Saviour appeared to be at the height of His popularity. Tremendous multitudes followed Him, many of whom might be
counted among the broader group of His disciples that followed

Him wherever He went. For the Lord had not only preached the gospel of the kingdom, but His fame was spread abroad because of the many miracles "which he did on them that were diseased." vs. 2. Especially on the occasion recorded in the sixth chapter of the gospel according to John, many thousands had gathered about Him, for the feast of the passover was nigh, and many that went through those parts to go up to the feast to Jerusalem paused to hear Jesus of Nazareth, and to see His marvellous works. And John makes mention of five thousand men only. They were gathered on the east side of the sea of Galilee, whither the Lord had departed with His disciples. And there something occurred, that raised the already feverish enthusiasm of the multitude to a still higher pitch, something so marvellous and appealing to their imagination, that they confessed that Jesus was the promised Messiah, and made preparations to crown Him king.

What was it that so roused their zeal? Jesus had performed another miracle. Yet, the mere fact as such, that the Lord had performed a wonder, will hardly suffice to explain their present state of enthusiasm for Jesus. Many a miracle the Saviour had performed in their coasts, and most of the multitude had been witnesses of them. He had healed the sick, made the lame to walk, opened the eyes of the blind, caused the deaf to hear, cast out devils, and even raised the dead. Yet, never had the multitude been so deeply moved, never had their emotions been so profoundly stirred, never had their enthusiasm reached such a high pitch, as at the sight of the miracle the Lord had now performed before their eyes. With five loaves of bread and two fishes the Lord had supplied food to that entire multitude of thousands of people, and when they were all satisfied they had taken up twelve baskets of fragments that were left over, enough to feed another multitude! To them this was the climax, the greatest of all miracles they had ever seen, and the one that most strongly appealed to them. It fired their imagination. It opened before them glorious vistas of new possibilities. This man must be the Messiah, the prophet that was to come. He surely is the Messiah after their own heart. And they decide to take action at once, and to make Him a king by force. But the Lord withdrew Himself from them, alone into the mountain. He perceives that this is a time of crisis, that on the morrow He will be called to fight a battle. And as often, so now He desires to be alone with the Father to prepare Himself in prayer, not only for the battle that awaits Him on the morrow, but also to consecrate Himself anew unto the work He came to do in the way of the cross.

What was wrong with the zeal of the multitude on this occasion? They were carnal, and their present enthusiasm for the Lord was carnal. It was their earthly expectations of the kingdom that was roused. They had seen bread, and an abundance of it. True, it was wonderful, miraculous bread they had seen, but still it had been real and honest bread that could fill their stomachs and satisfy their hunger. And they wanted more of it. They had not seen the sign itself. That in multiplying the bread Jesus had revealed Himself as the spiritual Bread of Life, that would feed His own unto eternal life, they had not understood. This is evident from the rebuke Jesus administers to them on the following day: "Verily, verily, ye seek me, not because ye saw the miracles, but because ye did eat of the loaves, and were filled." vs. 26. They wanted more bread! When they had watched Jesus so marvellously multiplying those few loaves, they had seen tremendous possibilities. Surely, this was the king they wanted! Here was a man that had the power to solve the social and economic problems, that could supply them with a full dinner pail, that could bring prosperity to the world, the more abundant life! Was there an end to the power of this man? Was He not the very man that did not only talk about and promise freedom from want, but had given a demonstration of His power to realize it, to bestow this freedom upon men? And is not freedom from want the key to all other freedoms in the world? A mighty, earthly king they saw in Jesus. That this is correct is evident from their very intention to make Jesus king by force. They were going to help Him to the throne, and to support Him in the establishment of the kingdom! Had they understood the nature of the kingdom Jesus came to establish, they would never have conceived of such a thing. For men do not make Jesus king. Nor do they establish His kingdom for Him. He establishes His own kingdom, even as He receives it from the Father. And He establishes it, not through human zeal

or by the power of man, not in the way of earthly pomp and
glory, but in the way of the righteousness of God with respect
to a sinful world, through obedience unto the death of the cross:
He is the Royal Sufferer!

This truth the Saviour impressed upon the hearts and minds
of His enthusiastic would-be disciples on the following day. However imperfect may have been their understanding of what Jesus
taught them on that day in Capernaum, it became very clear to
them that He had not come to bring abundance and prosperity
to the world, but to suffer and die, and that they could never
enter into His kingdom except by believing on Him as the Royal
Sufferer! It became clear to them that this man would reject all
their offers of power and glory, would spurn their carnal zeal,
and deliberately choose the way of the cross! That is the meaning
of the battle that is fought on the following day between the Royal
Sufferer and the carnal Galileans in the form of a conversation.

Let us briefly analyze this conversation. The subject is bread.
And for a while it appears as if they might agree on the subject,
and as if they were talking about the same kind of bread. Jesus
admonishes them that they must not labor for the meat that
perishes, but rather for the meat that endureth unto everlasting
life, and which the Son of God giveth unto them. And they are
ostensibly interested, for they ask: "What shall we do that we
might work the works of God?" Vss. 27, 28. And when the Lord
continued to explain that not Moses had given them the true bread
from heaven, when they had eaten manna in the wilderness, but
that His Father gave them that true bread, and that this true
bread is He that giveth life unto the world, they appear to be
very eager to receive it, and pray: "Lord, evermore give us this
bread." However, from there on it becomes increasingly plain
that there is a deep chasm between Jesus and the Galileans,
and that they have not the same bread in mind. Jesus deliberately
disillusions these would-be disciples. He does so, first of all by
emphatically declaring that He *is* the Bread of life! That upsets
them. That Jesus could *give* them bread, they had witnessed. But
when He declares that He *is* the Bread of life, they perceive that
He is talking, not of physical, but of spiritual bread. And they
care not for it. They begin to murmur. And suddenly they recall

that Jesus is the son of Joseph, and that they know His father and mother. How, then, can He be the bread from heaven? And when the Lord elaborates upon this truth, and emphasizes, not only that they can never come to Him unless the Father draw them, but also that they must eat His flesh and drink His blood, they perceive that He will become spiritual bread in the way of sacrifice, of suffering unto death! And as they have no desire for spiritual bread, they do not want a suffering Messiah, whose flesh and blood they are to eat and drink. They are disillusioned. A hard speech they declare this instruction of Jesus, a speech that no one can hear. And they forsake Him!

The battle was finished, and once more the Royal Sufferer had won the victory, although He was forsaken by men. The issue had been clear. It had been the conflict between the flesh and the Spirit, between physical and spiritual bread, between the kingdom of this world and the kingdom of heaven, between disobedience to the Father in the way of earthly glory and perfect obedience in the way of the cross. And Christ had chosen the latter. In the way of suffering He would receive His kingdom from the Father. And in this He would not be ashamed.

And how about us? At the end of the conflict in Capernaum the Lord placed His chosen twelve before the question: Will ye also go away? What is our answer to this question? What do we want, the kingdom of the world or the kingdom of heaven? What do we seek, carnal or spiritual bread? What do we hunger for, the things of the flesh or the righteousness of Christ? By nature we will surely seek the things of the world with those Galileans. But when it is given us of the Father, we will remain with the Royal Sufferer and answer with Peter: "Lord, to whom shall we go? thou hast the words of eternal life. And we believe and are sure that thou art that Christ, the Son of the living God."

CHAPTER 3

The King Without an Army

Put up again thy sword into his place . . .
— MATT. 26:52.

When the hour of Jesus' suffering arrived, the hour when He was taken by wicked hands to be crucified and slain, it became very evident that the hatred of men against Him was directed especially against His kingship. The Jews did not want Him to be their king, the Gentiles could not conceive of a kingship such as He represented: the Romans despised it, the Greeks considered it foolishness. It is true, that the leaders of the Jews sought to hide the real nature of their opposition against Him as long as possible, and several atempts were made to find false witnesses against Him that might invent some other accusation, but all these attempts failed. And in the end the high priest was forced to adjure the Saviour by the living God to tell them whether He were the Christ, the Messiah, the King that was to come, the Son of the living God. And it was upon Jesus' confession that He was that Christ, that they pronounced Him worthy of death. The conflict between the Christ of God and the carnal conception of the Messiah formed and cherished by wicked Israel, had reached its climax: Jesus was condemned because He was God's anointed King!

But also throughout the rest of the Saviour's trial His kingship

151

was the center of attention and interest. The Jewish leaders made it their chief accusation against Him before the Roman governor, that He made Himself a king, and that, too, in opposition to Caesar, although the hypocrites were perfectly aware of the fact that in that sense He refused to be a king. And Pilate, although from the outset incredulous about this point, investigates the accusation, and examines Him as to His royalty. Before Herod, and by the Roman soldiers, He is robed in purple garments, the thorny crown is pressed upon His brows, and a mock-sceptre is put into His hand, to ridicule this would-be king of the Jews. Pilate even presents His bleeding form to the Jews with the words: "Behold, your King." And the infuriated mob shouts back: "We have no king but Caesar!" And the superscription that was nailed above His head to the cross announced to all the world that He was Jesus, the Nazarene, the King of the Jews. Indeed, all through "the hour" He appears as the "Royal Sufferer"!

But how must we explain this furious hatred that appears to concentrate itself upon the kingship He claimed to possess? After all, what had He done to substantiate His claim to royalty, that could provoke such universal madness against Him in so short a time? He was a just man, and all had to admit it, even in this darkest hour, when all men were against Him. Throughout the land His fame was spread abroad that He did only good. He had healed the sick, caused the lame to walk, cleansed the lepers, opened the eyes of the blind, made the deaf to hear, cast out devils, and even raised the dead. Never had He been found plotting against those that were in authority, whether in Moses' seat or on Caesar's throne. He had been the humblest among the humble, the meekest among the meek, the poorest among the poor. Never had He set greedy eyes on the riches of the wealthy, or had He revealed any ambition to usurp the authority of those that were in power. What, then, was there in His claim to royalty that made Him the object of such deep-seated hatred and universal scorn, and that had induced even His own disciples to forsake Him in this hour of His humiliation? The answer to this question must, no doubt, be that He represented the kingdom of God, that it was not of this world, that it stood diametrically opposed to all the pride and lust of man, and that there was no room in that kingdom for the power of man.

This had been plainly revealed in all the teachings, as well as in the entire appearance of the Lord throughout His sojourn on earth. Always He refused all human power. The confession of the psalmist had become perfectly realized in Him: "Now I know that the Lord saveth his anointed; he will hear him from his holy heaven with the saving strength of his right hand. Some trust in chariots, and some in horses: but we will remember the name of the Lord our God." Ps.20:6, 7. Had they offered Him the help of all the battle forces of our modern world, with all the fearful implements of destruction employed in the present conflict, in the service of His kingdom, He would but have scorned the offer, and preferred to stand alone in the battle for His cause in the world. Or if they had all been arrayed against Him, He would not have been moved, but still would have insisted that in His battle for the kingdom of God He must needs refuse the help of man. This, too, became very evident in the hour of His suffering. He was a king without power, without a sword, without an army.

There must have been a curious mixture of wonderment and scorn in the voice of the Roman governor, when he asked the question of Jesus: "Art thou the king of the Jews?" John 18:33; and again: "Art thou a king then?" John 18:37. There was, he must have admitted to himself, indeed a suggestion of royal majesty in the appearance and countenance of this man Jesus, who stood there before him, meek but without fear, clearly giving the lie to all the accusations that were shouted against Him, yet without attempting to defend Himself, strong in His weakness, glorious in His humility, victorious in His defeat. But it was the reflection of a royalty such as Pilate had never known. All the kingship he had ever become acquainted with was characterized by human power and glory, and was dependent upon the sword of mighty legions for its defense and maintenance. But this man had no one to defend Him. He had no army, had never attempted to gather one, and His whole appearance was such that one could not possibly imagine His leading a host to battle. And there He stood, bound and defenseless, without even a word of protest against the perversion of justice that was evidently being committed. Indeed, there was the wonderment of a hidden fear, but also the scorn of the Roman in his voice, as he asked: "Art thou a king then?"

And the Lord not only caught this note of wonderment, but understood what was in Pilate's soul. Hence, in His answer He explains this uniquely strange phenomenon that there were no chariots and horses, no swords of mighty hosts connected with His person, that He had no servants to fight in the defense of His throne. "My kingdom is not of this world: if my kingdom were of this world, then would my servants fight, that I should not be delivered to the Jews, but now is my kingdom not from hence." The meaning of these words is plain. They explain the fact that Jesus, though He is king, appears without an army, without human help. Armies and swords, chariots and horses, guns and tanks, have no place in the conception of His kingdom. The origin of His kingdom is not in this world, and the nature of His kingdom is such that all display of human power is both absurd and impossible. He and His kingdom could never be successfully attacked and destroyed by force of arms, neither could the latter be employed in the establishment and defense of the kingdom of Christ. And it is well that we constantly bear this in mind even today, when the wars of this world are often presented as if they stood in the service of Christ to usher in His kingdom of everlasting peace. Christ's kingdom is not of this world. He scorns the help of armed forces today as He did in the hour of His suffering. And all the battle hosts of this world cannot prevent the coming of His kingdom. Christ is a king without an army!

This had been made very plain in the night before, when a band of soldiers and men, armed with swords and staves had come to the garden of Gethsemane to capture Him. He had stood defenseless in that hour, and that, too, by deliberate choice. Indeed, had He but chosen to make use of it, there had been plenty of power available to Him to prevent the enemy to lay hands on Him. But He had refused all help, and chosen to fight the battle for His kingship alone.

Consider, first of all, that His eleven disciples were perfectly willing to draw the sword in His defense. And sensing the danger and the seriousness of the hour, they had come to the garden that night prepared to fight for their beloved Master. All had declared that they were ready to die with Him, Matt 26:35. And there is no reason to doubt their sincerity and determination. They deeply loved their Master, and they were no cowards. That they finally forsook Him and fled, was not because they dared not fight, but because the Lord forbade them to use the sword, and refused all help. And they had come into the garden armed, prepared for battle, Lu. 22:38. Not only so, but had the Lord wanted help, many more might have come to His aid in this hour of suffering, for still the enthusiasm of the people could easily be aroused in His favor, and the leaders of the Jews were afraid of an uproar among them, unless they could take Jesus by subtilty. What is more, Peter gave the signal for a general attack, when he drew the sword and cut off the ear of the servant of the high priest, intending, no doubt, to split his head. O, indeed, His servants were willing enough to fight for Him. But He had refused their help. He had healed the lone wound of the enemy inflicted by Peter, and had rebuked the zealous but misunderstanding disciple: "Put up again thy sword into his place: for all they that take the sword shall perish with the sword." Matt. 26:52. His kingdom was not of this world. The sword could serve no purpose in it. He must needs be a king without an army.

Besides, consider what tremendous resources of power He had, and upon what mighty reserves He might have called, had the fate of His kingship depended upon the use of force. In that case, as He reminds His disciples, He might have prayed to the Father, and He would have sent Him twelve legions of angels or more to fight for His cause. And if we remember that one angel of the Lord was able to slay one hundred and eighty-five thousand of the foe in one night, what would all the power of the enemy have availed against twelve legions of them? Moerover, had not the Lord even that very night plainly revealed that He would have no need even of these legions of angels, and that He could have defeated the foe that came to capture Him in the garden in His own power? Had He not laid them prostrate before Him in the dust by the Word of His mouth, so that they could not arise but at His bidding? O, indeed, there was an abundance of power available to overcome the enemy, and to prevent His being delivered to the Jews, had His kingdom been of this world, and had it been a question of brute force and human might. But He had refused to make use of it. Deliberately He had chosen to stand alone in the battle. For the nature of His kingdom rendered all human help and sword-power impossible and absurd. That night it had become very evident that He was a king without an army. He had, indeed, come to the daughter of Zion as her king, riding, not on a fiery battle horse, but on the colt of an ass, meek and lowly, and without defense or display of power!

But why this deliberate refusal of all human help and defense? What, then, is the nature of His kingship, and of the kingdom of God, that makes all employment of force and human power impossible?

The kingdom of God, which Christ came to establish, and which He was to receive from the Father, is spiritual. It is a kingdom of *God,* i. e. a commonwealth in which God reigns as the King that is acknowledged and served by all. In that kingdom God rules, not by His power, but by grace. The chief characteristic of that kingdom is not simply that God is sovereign there, but that His sovereignty is acknowledged, so that His will is the delight of the subjects and citizens of that kingdom. God is absolutely sovereign over all creation, of course. No one can ever dispute His authority. He reigns in the heavens above, and on the earth beneath, and in the depth of the abyss. He rules over the inorganic and brute creation, as well as over all His rational and moral creatures. And He is sovereign over all the powers of darkness, that, in spite of themselves, must still execute His will. But this is not what is meant by the kingdom of God. On the contrary, the specific nature of the kingdom of God is such, that in it God is the Friend-sovereign of all its citizens, and they are His friend-servants. He blesses them with all spiritual blessings, and they love to do His will. He reveals Himself to them, and they have their delight in Him. The fundamental idea of the kingdom of God, as far as the relation of its citizens to God is concerned, may, therefore, be expressed in the word *righteousness.* And unless a man's righteousness shall exceed that of the scribes and Pharisees, he shall in no case enter into the kingdom of heaven. Matt. 5:20.

In that kingdom of God Christ is the chief Priest-King, anointed to that position from before the foundation of the world. He must establish this kingdom, gather and form a company of royal priests in and under Himself, and lead them into the glory of that ultimate manifestation of the kingdom of heaven, in which all things in the new creation shall be subject to Him, and to His people in Him, and with them He shall subject Himself unto the Father, that God may be all in all. But this company of royal priests, over which He has been anointed King and High Priest, are by nature lost in sin, guilty and damnable, corrupt and perverse of heart and mind. In every sense their relation to God by nature is the opposite of that of righteousness. He must, therefore, make them righteous, that they may enter into the kingdom of God. But you cannot make men righteous by the power of the sword. Nor could Christ Himself enter into His kingdom with the help of mighty battle hosts. These have no place in His kingdom. On the contrary, He must suffer and die, willingly, obediently, enter into the depth of hell, and bearing the sins of many under the wrath of God, that He might redeem them, atone for their sins, and thus establish the relation of righteousness to God for all the company of His royal priests given Him by the Father. The Christ must suffer in order to enter into His glory. He must travel the way of the cross, to establish the righteousness of the kingdom of heaven. And His enemies, the powers of darkness, must serve to prepare His way to that cross. Hence, armies of men could not have prevented Him from reaching the cross. Legions of angels could be of no help to Him. He must stand alone. Alone He must battle His way against the forces of sin and death, His way to the cross, that on the cross He might bear the sins of His own, and merit for them eternal righteousness and glory.

And in all His way of suffering and death, He trusted in God, confident that the Father would not leave Him alone, would not leave His soul in hell, but would fulfill His promise to Him, raise Him from the dead, exalt Him to the glory of His kingdom, give Him the Spirit of promise, that in the power of that Spirit He might establish the righteousness of His kingdom in the hearts of His own, and lead a great congregation to everlasting glory. And God fully justified His confidence, and will justify the cause of the Son of God, the King without an army, when He shall come again, the forces of opposition shall be utterly consumed, and His kingdom shall be revealed in heavenly perfection! The King without an army, and He alone, shall have, and even now has the victory. And all that believe on His name are more than conquerors through Him that loved them even unto death!

CHAPTER 4

The King Deprived of His Birthright

*He took his brother by the heel in the womb, and
by his strength he had power with God.* — Hos. 12:3.

To the history of Jesus' final "hour," the hour in which He
was delivered into the hands of the ungodly, tried by them, condemned to death and killed by being nailed to the accursed tree,
also belongs the incident of His appearance before Herod to be
tried by that representative of royalty on the throne of Israel.
We are, of course, acquainted with the main facts of this trial,
as well as with the occasion that led up to it. Already the Lord
had been tried and condemned by the Jewish council, and found
worthy of death. Already He had been taken to the Roman
governor, that this representative of Caesar might confirm their
sentence and execute it. And before the Roman judge the leaders
of the Jews had accused the Saviour of perverting the nation,
forbidding to pay tribute to Caesar, and making Himself a king.
And Pilate had examined Jesus, with the result that he found no
fault in Him at all, and frankly declared this result of his investigation to the Jews.

One would have thought that this must needs be the end of
the trial, and that upon this official verdict of the Roman judge,
the case would have been dismissed, and Jesus would have been
acquitted and set free. But Pilate was by no means determined

159

as to the course he was to follow in this case. The matter would have been simple, of course, had he been motivated by the love of justice and a proper sense of his duty as judge. But this was not the case. The matter of truth and justice did not deeply trouble him. But somehow he was struck with fear of Jesus, partly, perhaps, because of what others had told him of this man, partly because of His extraordinary and majestically tranquil appearance, and partly because of the prayer of his wife that he should have nothing to do with this just man. On the other hand, he was also afraid of the Jews, who seemed to be determined to have Jesus put to death, and who became more vehement and fierce in their demands according as Pilate insisted more firmly that Christ was without guilt. And above all, he was afraid of Caesar. And so, he tried to find a way out of the difficulty. Various attempts he made to rid himself of the case. One of these was that he sent Jesus to Herod, as soon as he learned that the Lord was a Galilean, a matter which was the more easily arranged because Herod was in Jerusalem at the time.

What occurred at this trial of our Lord before Herod may be briefly told. Herod was exceeding glad when he saw Jesus. Whatever may have been the chief cause of this gladness, we may be sure that it was the wicked joy of the ungodly that filled his heart at the sight of Christ. He had heard a good deal about the strange power of this man; and his evil, superstitious heart had been troubled at the thought that this might be John the Baptist, whom he had murdered, risen from the dead. The sight of Jesus probably assured him that there was no cause for this fear. He hoped now that Jesus would perform one of His miracles, but in this he was disappointed. He proceeded to question Jesus with many words but Jesus answered him nothing, from which we may conclude that all the questioning of Herod was quite irrelevant to the case over which he sat in judgment. In the meantime, the Jewish leaders vehemently accused the Lord, which probably had no effect upon the tetrarch at all. But he finally vented his wrath and disappointment upon the Saviour, by setting Him at nought with the aid and in the presence of his soldiers, mocking Him, and expressing his contempt for His kingship by arraying Him in a gorgeous robe. However, after this, he too washed his hands of the case, and sent the Lord back to Pilate.

The question arises: what is the special significance of this brief trial of Jesus before Herod? What is the particular place this brief moment occupies in the hour of Jesus' reproach? This question has, of course, no meaning for those who fail to see in the suffering of Christ a complete program, not arranged by man, but by divine wisdom and sovereign determination. They are, perhaps, interested only in the final suffering of Jesus on the cross, pay little attention to what preceded Golgotha, and see in Jesus' trial before Herod nothing but a delay in the approach to the cross, interesting, perhaps, but quite unnecessary. However, if we believe that there was a definite measure of suffering our Lord had to bear, that He must needs suffer the whole of that measure but no more, and that this measure of Jesus' suffering, as well as every detail of its contents, was determined by the sovereign will of the Most High, we understand also that the way to the cross must needs pass through the court of the Galilean tetrarch. And then the question arises: why? Why must the royal Sufferer meet this wicked descendant of a cruel and blood-stained royal house before He may pour out His soul unto death on the accursed tree?

We answer that there, in the courtroom of Herod, between the cruel king and the Royal Sufferer, the judge and the Defendant, in those few brief moments a battle was fought for Christ's birthright, and, therefore, for His kingship. It is a battle which, on the part of Herod is fought by tempting Him to perform a wonder, a sign, and that, too, while the Jewish leaders vehemently hurl accusations against Him; and by putting Him to nought and mocking Him with respect to His kingship and, therefore, with regard to His birthright, thus making Him feel deeply that according to all human standards of judging the matter, Christ has been deprived of this birthright; while, on the part of Christ, this same battle is fought by His absolute silence, by consistently refusing to show His power by giving them a sign, and by trusting for His birthright absolutely in God alone. Once more, but now in very pressing circumstances, the Royal Sufferer decides to receive His kingdom only in the way of obedience to the Father, i. e. in the way of the cross.

Let us attempt to understand the situation in the light of Scripture.

In Christ and Herod we must see two firstborn, the final representatives of two distinct lines of firstborn, that had fought a mortal battle for the birthright all through the old dispensation. You know that the firstborn of man and beast had special significance among Israel. The firstborn was he that opened the womb, that prepared the way into life for his brethren, that was entitled to a double portion of the inheritance, that had the rule over his brethren, and that, in patriarchal times was heir to the covenant blessing in the special sense of the word. Now, Christ is the First-born, of Whom all the firstborn in the old dispensation were types. He was the Firstborn of every creature, by whom and unto whom all things were created, whether things in heaven or things on earth, Col. 1:15 ff. He was the firstborn among many brethren, Who was to open the way for these brethren, and lead them into the glory of eternal life. And He was to enter into His birthright as the Firstborn out of the dead. His, therefore, was the birthright. Upon Him was the promise. He was to have the rule over His brethren, and He was to be king for ever in the kingdom of God, Lord of all under God. He was the King God had set upon His holy hill of Zion. And to Him the Lord had said according to His eternal decree: "Thou art my Son, this day have I begotten thee. Ask of me, and I shall give thee the heathen for thine inheritance, and the uttermost part of the earth for thy possession." Ps. 2:6-8. Upon Him were the sure mercies of David, and of Him the psalmist of old had sung the Word of God: "Also I will make him my firstborn, higher than the kings of the earth. My mercy will I keep for him for evermore, and my covenant shall stand fast with him. His seed also will I make to endure for ever, and His throne as the days of heaven." Unto Him the Lord had said: "Sit thou at my right hand, until I make thine enemies thy footstool. The Lord shall send the rod of thy strength out of Zion: rule thou in the midst of thine enemies." Ps. 110:1, 2. And had not Gabriel, when he had announced His birth to the virgin of Nazareth, predicted that the Lord would give unto Him the throne of His father David, that He would rule over the house of Jacob for ever, and that of His kingdom there would be no end? Lu. 1:32, 33.

That Firstborn, with that glorious birthright, that legal heir to the throne of His father David, was here standing as the defendant before Herod, the only king that occupied a throne in Israel in those days.

He was the firstborn, not according to the flesh, and not by actual birth, but by God's immutable decree, the firstborn according to God's free election, and according to God's sovereign promise. According to the flesh, He was not the firstborn, for always it had pleased the Most High to let the elder serve the younger, that His purpose according to election might stand. For Christ was of the lineage of David, and David was not the firstborn, but the youngest among his brethren. And David was of the tribe of Judah, and Judah was not the firstborn, but the fourth of Israel, yet of him it was said: "thee shall thy brethren serve." And Judah was of Israel, yet again, Israel was not the firstborn, but Esau was, yet it was declared unto Rebekah: "the elder shall serve the younger." Always the child of the flesh occupied the place of the firstborn, and the firstborn according to election came into the world without the birthright! That firstborn, not according to the flesh, but according to the promise of God, and according to sovereign election, now stands face to face with Herod, the king of Israel! And He stands there without birthright, without a throne, without royal dominion and glory, in fact, without any right whatsoever, bound and humiliated, accused and condemned, the wholly disinherited One, the outcast! The Royal Sufferer!

And He stands before Herod!

Who was Herod? He was the last representative of the old dispensational line of the firstborn according to the flesh. Some would recognize in him a very distant descendant of the royal house of David, and thus they would try to explain the fulfillment of the prophecy of dying Israel, that the sceptre should not depart from Judah until Shiloh should come. But Herod was an Idumaean, a descendant of Esau, the reprobate standing in the place of the firstborn according to election! There was not a drop of Jewish, let alone Davidic, blood in his veins. After the captivity of Judah, the Edomites had occupied the lands south of Judah, and had become known as Idumaeans. Antipater, the grandfather of Herod Antipas, was governor of Idumaea, and was made procurator of Judaea by the favor of Julius Caesar. And his son, the terrible and cruel Herod the Great, was made king after his father's death. And after the death of that bloody tyrant, his son, Herod Antipas, the same to whom Christ was sent by Pilate, received part of his father's dominion, and became tetrarch of Galilee. Herod was an Edomite! He represented the reprobate line of the firstborn according to the flesh, that had always hated the firstborn according to the election of grace.

When viewed in this Scriptural light, one begins to understand the special significance of this moment of Jesus' "hour," the specific nature of the suffering He here endured, and of the battle He here had to fight as the Royal Sufferer. There was Herod, the firstborn according to the flesh, the reprobate, the wicked, the profane, that despised God's covenant, and still preferred the mess of pottage. But he stood in the place of the firstborn according to the election! He was arrayed in royal purple, surrounded by his men of war. He sat on Zion's throne, or at least, on what was left of it. He had lived by the sword, and his sword had gained him the victory and the throne! And before him stands the Christ, the firstborn according to election, the Anointed of God upon Whom were the promises. But He is deprived of His birthright! He stands before the carnal and profane Edomite without power or glory, shackled and humiliated, accused on every side, judged as a criminal, completely overcome by His enemies! According to all outward appearances the promise had failed, election had been defeated, the power of the flesh had won! Christ is here the King without His birthright!

What shall He do?

Shall He use an arm of flesh, and show His power to overcome the profane firstborn according to the flesh? Thus Jacob, who even in the womb held his brother by the heel to gain the place of the firstborn, had done before he reached Peniel. Put at a disadvantage by his second place in birth, he had not put his trust in God, but devised human schemes to obtain the birthright. Shall this final descendant of Israel now do the same? He is, no doubt able! For He is the mighty Son of God in the flesh. One flash of His eye, one word from His mouth, and the enemy will lie prostrate at His feet! And He is sorely tempted. Herod, "that fox," presses Him to reveal His power, and to perform a miracle. Moreover he does all in his power to humiliate this first-born according to the election of grace, to humiliate Him more deeply, to put Him to nought more completely, to expose Him as the king without a birthright, without power and glory and majesty! The firstborn according to the flesh here celebrates his victory over the firstborn according to the promise, and he gloats over it and is exceeding glad! He calls in his men of war to mock the Christ. He arrays the Royal Sufferer in the mock robe of royalty to impress more deeply upon Him His defeat. Shall, then, not the Christ consume these enemies by the breath of His mouth, and take His proper seat on Zion's throne. Shall He not take by force the birthright that is denied Him?

But no!

Even in His deepest humiliation He remembers that the way of force is not the Father's way. Or how shall He become the Firstborn among many brethren, of brethren that of themselves lie in the midst of death, if now He refuses to travel the way of His sorrow and humiliation even to the end? Must He not open the womb of death for those whom the Father gave Him, and must He not become the first begotten of the dead, before He can lead them out into liberty and life and glory? But how shall He become the first begotten of the dead, unless He first descends, voluntarily descends into the depth of death and hell? His way, then, the Father's way for Him, is the way of suffering, the way of death, yea, of the death of the cross. For He must fight the battle for the righteousness of God against sin and death, and against all the powers of darkness. That battle He is fighting even now, as He stands before the vain and cruel reprobate that occupies the throne of Israel; and that battle He will presently fight to the finish on the accursed tree of Golgotha. And even this son of the flesh, this profane reprobate, can but serve to lead Him to that final battle ground.

That is the reason for His silent endurance.

Once more He refuses to use an arm of flesh, and once more He deliberately chooses the way of suffering and death as the sole way into the glory of His royal birthright. And He puts His trust in God. Of the courtyard of Herod He makes His Peniel, where He wrestles in princely fashion with God, until Israel's God shall have blessed Him. And in this confidence He shall not be put to shame. Not the son of the reprobate, but the Child of the promise shall have the ultimate victory. Yet a little while, and God will fulfill His promise unto Him, will exalt Him through the resurrection to the throne of the firstborn in heaven, and give Him a name which is above every name, that at the name of Jesus every knee should bow, and every tongue confess that Christ is Lord, to the glory of God the Father! The silent Royal Sufferer has the victory for ever!

CHAPTER 5

The King Without His Glory

Hail, King of the Jews! — MATT. 27:29.

Glory is proper, is essential to kings. A king without glory is a contradiction in terms. Even as brilliancy belongs to the sun in its noonday splendor, so glory belongs to kings. For a king is vested with authority and power. He is an anointed one. And the radiation of his anointing, the effulgence of his royal power and authority, the shining forth of his majesty and exaltation above the people, is his glory. Are not the powers that be ordained of God? Is not the king a minister of God, a divinely appointed agent for the protection of them that do well, and for the punishment of them that do evil? A king, a real king in the Scriptural sense of the word, appears in the world as a representative of divine justice, and is, indeed, clothed with power and authority from above. For there is no power or authority in man. Before God and in relation to one another, all men are equal. Might does not make right. No man has in himself the prerogative to impose his will on others, the right to rule. Nor dare this power to rule be found in any given number of men together, even though they constitute a majority. God alone has power, and His alone is the kingdom. And He alone can bestow the power to rule upon men. Hence, a king is one that occupies the position of authority among men in the name of God. From God he receives his power, in the name of God he is called to rule, and not his own will, but the will of God he is obliged to impose upon and to maintain among men. And even as the true king is a minister of God, who receives his authority and mandate from the Most High, so the true king is also qualified by the God of heaven and earth to occupy that exalted position, and from Him receives wisdom and understanding, power and might to execute his position. The radiation of this authority, the manifestation of this power and wisdom and understanding is the true glory of kings. Glory is inseparable from the kingship.

Even in the sinful world this truth is clearly recognized, as is evident from the fact that men envelop their kings in a halo of glory by external means and paraphernalia to distinguish them from the rest of the people. Splendid palaces of marble and gold they build for their dwelling places. On thrones they exalt them as a sign of their prerogative to rule. With royal purple they clothe them, expressive of their majesty. A crown they press upon their brows, and a sceptre they give into their hands, as symbols of their authority and dominion. All these external means and insignia of royal power and splendor must, of course, frequently serve to cover up an inner weakness and shame, a moral rottenness and corruption, an utter want of all the virtues that should constitute the glory of kings. Yet even so, by means of these outward signs, this outward display of splendor, the world clearly expresses its conviction that a king must be glorious, that glory is essential to the kingship.

This general truth must be borne in mind in order to understand the real meaning of the action of the Roman soldiers, to whom Pilate delivered our Saviour, when they created for Him the appearance of a mock-king, and filled Him with reproach and shame.

The question concerning Jesus' kingship played an important part in the trial of our Lord before the Roman governor. Here He appears clearly as the Royal Sufferer. By the Sanhedrin He had been condemned on the basis of His claim that He was the Christ, the Son of the living God. But when He was arraigned before the representative of the world-power, the Jews accused

Him of being a revolutionary who aspired after royal power, and claimed to be the King of the Jews. Consequently, the Roman governor was compelled to inquire into this kingship of Jesus, and as he did so, received the answer that His kingdom was not of this world, an answer which implied, however, that Jesus was a king indeed, though it were of a different order from that which lay within the scope of Pilate's comprehension. And when the Roman governor, evidently struck and stupified by the contrast between his own conception of what a king ought to be and the appearance of this strange Defendant, without glory and without power, asked in his amazement: "Art thou a king then?" he received once more an affirmative answer together, however, with the still more amazing qualification: "To this end was I born, and for this cause came I into the world, that I should bear witness unto the truth. Every one that is of the truth heareth my voice." John 18:37.

But if Pilate was at a loss to harmonize his idea of royalty with the appearance of the Royal Sufferer, the Roman soldiers could only be filled with contempt for such a king as this. Witnesses they had been of the trial, and they had heard the Lord's replies to the inquiries of the governor. They had understood that He did, indeed, claim to be a king. But such a kingship as He apparently represented they could only despise. Accordingly, when Pilate delivered Him to their will before He was finally sentenced to death and led away to be crucified, it was particularly this kingship of the Saviour which they made the object of their coarse and ribald mockery.

It appears to have been quite customary, cruel and unjust though the custom was, that condemned criminals were delivered up to the merciless jests and maltreatment of the soldiers before they were finally led to the place of execution. In the case of Jesus this seems to have been done before the governor had delivered his final verdict. From the Synoptics this is not clear. In Matt. 27:26 ff. we read: "Then released he Barabbas unto them: and when he had scourged Jesus, he delivered him to be crucified. Then the soldiers of the governor took Jesus into the common hall, and gathered unto him the whole band of soldiers. And they stripped him, and put on him a scarlet robe. And when they had platted a crown of thorns, they put it upon his head, and a reed in his right hand: and they bowed the knee before him, and mocked him, saying, Hail, king of the Jews! And they spit upon him, and took the reed, and smote him on the head. And after they had mocked him, they took the robe off from him, and put his own raiment on him, and led him away to crucify him." A similar account of this part of Jesus' suffering we find in Mark 15:16ff. From the account in the gospel according to John, however, we learn that after Jesus had been scourged and had been subjected to the ribald mockery of the soldiers, the Roman governor brought Him forth once again to the people, declaring that he found no fault in Him; that he exhibited Him to them in all His misery and humiliation, saying: "Behold, the man!" that in answer to the cries of the chief priests and officers, demanding that He should be crucified, he became, evidently, exasperated, and said: "Take ye him, and crucify him: for I find no fault in him"; that he took Jesus once more into the judgment hall, examined Him, and sought to release Him; and that only after he had been threatened with the loss of Caesar's friendship, and the Jews had emphatically declared that they would acknowledge no king but Caesar, the Roman governor finally passed judgment, and delivered Jesus over to be crucified. John 19:1ff.

But what is the significance of this phase of the suffering of our Lord? Or shall we take the position that no specific meaning is to be attached to it, and that, apart from the general consideration that we here behold the Saviour in His deepest humiliation and shame, the object of reproach and mockery by wicked men, the suffering inflicted upon Him by the soldiers has no special meaning? Shall we, perhaps, assume the attitude of proud condemnation over against those cruel soldiers who, devoid of the commonest human sympathy, called the whole band of soldiers together to participate in what they, evidently, considered a "good time," and, wholly unnecessarily, aggravated the suffering of the Man of Sorrows? Shall we exalt ourselves above a form of civilization that could permit such cruelties, and flatter ourselves that in our advanced age of enlightenment such barbarisms could not be tolerated? Or shall we, at least, by contrast, feel pious and religious, and shed a sympathizing tear for the silent Sufferer as

He stands there, the mock-robe about His shoulders, the mock-crown pressed on His head, the mock-sceptre in His hand, the object of merciless jests, spit upon, and beaten?

O, how we would miss the point entirely of this phase of Jesus' passion, by assuming such a proud and supercilious attitude! How we would fail to see the light of revelation in this part of the gospel narrative, and to hear the Word of God that comes to us through it!

For, first of all, let us not for a moment be oblivious of the fact that all the human agents that took an active part in inflicting upon our Lord His unspeakable suffering of soul and body, were but the representatives of the fallen and wicked world, to which we all belong by nature, and that their acts do but reveal the hidden depths of the corruption, enmity of God, darkness of the lie, and hatred of the light there are in our hearts apart from the redeeming and regenerating grace of God. No amount of culture and civilization can possibly change this. Apart from grace, we are those soldiers! Apart from grace, we would and do cast about Him that purple robe of mockery, press that cruel crown of thorns upon His brow, force that mock-sceptre into His hand, pay Him that mock homage, and then pour upon Him all the vials of our contempt by beating Him and spitting into His face! All our modern world would and does heap the same contempt upon Him the soldiers did! There is no reason here for boasting and self-exaltation, but only for deepest shame and humiliation.

O, we want a king, but that King we hate!

We, too, have no king but Caesar, though we attempt to cloak our modern hatred of God's King in a robe of self-willed piety and religion!

And, secondly, let us recall that there is a measure of Jesus' suffering that must be fulfilled, and that the passion of our Saviour is one whole, every part of which, in its minutest detail, is essential to it. Must not the Christ suffer this in order to enter into His glory? And the necessity of this suffering is not determined by the arbitrary whims of man, but by the wisdom and good pleasure, the righteousness and justice of the God of our salvation. Every phase of Christ's passion is necessary, and, therefore, has its own significance. Hence, the question is as proper as

it is important: what is the special significance of this part of
Jesus' passion? What does it mean that the soldiers thus vent their
wrath and contempt upon the Man of Sorrows?

Three elements in the cruel mockery of the soldiers demand
our attention. First, it is evident that they mean to express their
utter contempt and deep hatred of the kingship Jesus represents.
Secondly, by creating the appearance of a mock-king for the
Saviour, they plainly declare their own notion of what belongs
to the glory of a king. And, thirdly, by heaping their contempt
upon Jesus, they unwittingly create a picture of man as the
fallen king, under the wrath of God, in all his shame and humiliation as servant of the devil.

Let us recall that man is, indeed, a fallen king, deprived of
his proper glory, and that as such he has a distorted and
corrupt notion of what constitutes the proper glory of kingship.
He was created after the image of God, in true knowledge of God,
righteousness, and holiness, so that he was capable of rightly
knowing his God in love, fulfilling His will, and consecrating himself to his Sovereign with his whole being and with all things in
the earthly creation. His relation to God was a covenant relation,
a relation of living fellowship and intimate friendship. Man was
the friend of God. And as friend he was God's servant. And as
God's servant, he was king over all the earthly creation. For God
gave him dominion over all things. In and before all creatures,
he represented God's own sovereignty. God's name he had to
declare in all the world. God's glory he must extol. God's will he
must obey and maintain. In the name of God, as His servant,
and in true liberty as His friend, he was called to reign over all
things. All things must serve him that he might serve his God.
That was man's royal glory by virtue of his creation.

But he rebelled against his rightful sovereign. By willful disobedience he chose the word of the devil, and rejected the Word
of God. And by doing so he subjected himself to the slavery of
sin and the devil. The object of the wrath of God he became.
And he lost all his excellent gifts. His glory was turned into
shame. He was a king without glory. His knowledge was turned
into darkness, his righteousness into unrighteousness, his holiness
into corruption. An enemy of God he became. But still he seeks

to reign and to realize the kingdom of man in the world, a kingship of rebellion against the living God instead of in loving subjection to Him; a kingship characterized by might rather than by right, by brute force rather than by humble obedience to the will of God.

It is this kingship of fallen man that was represented by the soldiers of that Roman world-power whose foundations were laid by brute strength, and whose continued existence was dependent upon the mighty sword of its emperors. And it was their notion of the glory of royalty that motivated them in inflicting upon the Saviour this peculiar form of reproach and humiliation.

For Christ was God's King, His kingdom was not of this world. Anointed before the foundation of the world to be the King of kings and Lord of lords for ever in the new kingdom, the eternal kingdom of heaven in the new creation, He was to wrest the dominion from the Prince of this world and the powers of darkness, and to establish His own kingdom in the glory of the new creation in which righteousness shall dwell. But only as the Servant of Jehovah is He to reign. Only in the way of obedience, of perfect obedience of love, and that too, instead of and in behalf of sinners, could He attain to glory and receive His kingdom from the Father. For the righteousness of God He must wage war against sin and death. By fully satisfying the justice of God against sin can He ascend to His throne. Not by the power of the sword, but in the way of humble obedience even unto the death of the Cross, He must lay the foundation of His kingdom. He must die that He may rise to the glory of His resurrection. He must humble Himself that He may be exalted. He must empty Himself and become utterly without glory that He may receive all power in heaven and on earth.

He is the perfect Servant-King of God!

As such He stands before the Roman governor, who can only be amazed at His claim that He is a king.

The Royal Sufferer!

As such He stands in the midst of the Roman soldiers, those representatives of brute force, who can only despise His kingship, and while plainly expressing their own notion that the glory of a king is his sword and his might, give to God's Anointed the appearance of a mock-king, by means of the purple robe, the reed-sceptre, the thorny crown, in order then to empty the vials of their hateful contempt upon Him by beating Him with His own sceptre, and by spitting in His face!

And yet, who fails to recognize that thus they do create but the real image of sinful man, the fallen king, under the wrath of God? O, they know not what they do, but the fact remains: that mock-king of their own creation is the very picture of the re-bellious sinner. True, man is still king, and he shows his might and dominion over the earthly creation in all the inventions of modern culture: he is a mock-king nevertheless. His crown is but a crown of thorns, symbol of the curse of God, for the wrath of God abideth on him; his royal robe is but a shabby soldier's cloak, that will presently be taken off from his shoulders to ex-pose his miserable being, naked and bleeding with the scourge of God's anger; his royal sceptre is only a common reed that must soon be taken out of his hand that with it he may be beaten with many stripes. Indeed, that appearance of a mock-king which the soldiers created for the Royal Sufferer belongs to fallen man, the rebel-king, who proposes to rule over all things in the service of sin and of the Prince of this world!

And the Lord assumes this appearance of mock royalty!

For, you understand, of course, that no one could have im-posed this form of mockery and reproach upon Him against His will. Had He not humbled Himself, no man could thus have humiliated Him. Had He refused to receive that crown of thorns, no man could have pressed it upon His brow. Had He not will-ingly submitted, no man could have cast that mock robe about His shoulders, nor could they ever have pressed that reed into His hand or beaten Him with it. He willingly submitted to the cruel jests of the soldiers, knowing that thus it was the Father's will. Had He not been sent into the likeness of sinful flesh, in order that in that likeness He might suffer the wrath of God, and satisfy the justice of God against sin for us? In the way of this suffering He must attain to His Messianic glory, and receive His kingdom from the Father. He does not rebel. He knows that it is God that will justify Him. He trusts that in the way of His deepest humiliation He will attain to highest glory for Himself and for His own. He does not cast off that mock robe, because He knows that the Father will presently clothe Him with majesty and honor. He allows that cruel crown of thorns to be pressed upon His head, because He trusts that presently He will receive from the Father the royal diadem of an everlasting kingdom. And He takes the mock sceptre, confident that in the way of the cross He will receive from the Father the true sceptre of royalty, all power in heaven and on earth.

And He was not put to shame.

The Royal Sufferer, Who as the Servant of Jehovah humbled Himself even unto the death of the cross, received a name above all names, that in the name of Jesus every knee should bow, and every tongue confess that He is Lord, to the glory of God the Father!

CHAPTER 6

A Public Spectacle

Jesus of Nazareth the King of the Jews.
— JOHN 19:19.

When a person was condemned to death by crucifixion, it was customary to publish to all the world his crime as the ground for his punishment by preparing a superscription briefly describing his guilt, and affixing it to the cross of the victim. This superscription was written on a little board, sometimes before the victim was led to the place of execution, in which case it was hung on his breast; but more often, as was evidently also the case with the superscription above Jesus' head, it was prepared at the place of the crucifixion and nailed to the cross for all to read. All the gospel writers make mention of the superscription that was nailed to Jesus' cross. Matthew writes: "And set up over his head his accusation written, THIS IS JESUS THE KING OF THE JEWS." Matt. 27:37. Mark has it in briefer form: "And the superscription of his accusation was written over, THE KING OF THE JEWS." Mk. 15:26. Luke informs us that the superscription was written in "letters of Greek, and Latin, and Hebrew," and reports it in this form: "THIS IS THE KING OF THE JEWS." Lu. 23:38. And John, who as we know was a close eye witness of the crucifixion, is most elaborate about his super-

177

scription and the incident connected with its preparation. He writes as follows: "And Pilate wrote a title, and put it on the cross. And the writing was, JESUS OF NAZARETH THE KING OF THE JEWS. This title then read many of the Jews: for the place where Jesus was crucified was nigh to the city: and it was written in Hebrew, and Greek, and Latin. Then said the chief priests of the Jews to Pilate, Write not, The King of the Jews; but that he said, I am King of the Jews. Pilate answered, What I have written I have written." John 19:19-22. All the gospel narrators, therefore, attached special significance to this superscription, and all are agreed on this, that it presented Jesus to the world as condemned and crucified because He was the King of the Jews.

What may be the special significance of this superscription?

In answer to this question, we must consider what was written by the Roman governor as Jesus' accusation, first of all as the truth, that was proclaimed from the cross in all its terrible significance, according to God's own will, and by His own providential direction. Whatever may have been Pilate's motive in writing this accusation exactly in this form, he did write the truth! The Roman governor may have been impelled to write this superscription by hatred of the Jews, and by the desire to humiliate them in the eyes of all the world. Then, too, he may have been impressed by Jesus' affirmative answer so unhesitantly given to his question: "Art thou the king of the Jews?" Certain it is, that as he wrote this particular accusation, and that, too, in the language of the whole world, his hand was directed by God's all controlling providence to write the truth. And it is under the direction of that same providential power that he remains inflexible when the Jews' leaders protest against the form of the superscription, and answers them: "What I have written I have written." The truth was written and published to all the world by this superscription, not according to the distorted and corrupted version of it that was suggested by the Jewish leaders, but according to Christ's own testimony: "I am indeed the King of the Jews."

Thus understood, the superscription conveyed a terrible message, and we need not be surprised that the chief priests insisted that it should be changed into some statement declaring that He *claimed* to be the King of the Jews! For consider what it all meant. First of all, as the matter was presented, it signified that Israel's hope was blasted completely and for ever! For what else was the hope of Israel than the coming of the Messiah, the King of the Jews, that would deliver them from all their enemies and miseries, and lead them on to the glory of the highest realization of the Davidic kingdom? For Israel was the Old Testament form of the kingdom of God. God was their King, and He was visibly represented by the King that sat on David's throne. Yet, all the kings of the old dispensation that occupied the throne of David, the theocratic throne, were but shadows of *the* King that was to come, the Anointed of God, the Messiah. But for Him mount Zion, the throne of David, all that ever sat on it, had no significance at all. There was really only one King of Israel, and that was the promised Messiah. He was the subject of all prophecy, the main theme of every psalm. He was the Seed of the woman that would crush the head of the serpent, the great Seed of Abraham, the Shiloh of which Jacob had spoken, the Lion of Judah's tribe, the King whose shout even Balaam had heard among them as they were encamped in the plains of Moab, and the rising of whose sceptre he had predicted; the root of David, the king that had been set by Jehovah upon God's holy hill of Zion. He was *the* King of the Jews! And according to that terrible superscription that King of the Jews was now breathing His last upon the accursed tree!

Upon the head of that King rested all the promises of God! To Him it was promised that He should have the heathen for His inheritance, and the utmost parts of the earth for His possessions, Ps. 2:8; that His throne should be for ever and ever, and the sceptre of His kingdom would be a right sceptre, Ps. 45:6; that He would have dominion from sea to sea, and from the river to the ends of the earth, Ps. 72:8. They that dwell in the wilderness would bow before Him, and His enemies should lick the dust; and all the kings of the earth would fall down before Him, all nations would serve Him. His name would endure for ever, as long as the sun, and all men would be blessed in Him, so that all nations would call Him blessed. Ps. 72:9, 11, 17. For His reign would be in righteousness, He would save the children of the needy, and crush the oppressor. The blood of those that have no helper would be precious in His sight, and He would redeem their soul from violence and deceit. Ps. 72:4, 12-14. Of Him the inspired poet of Israel taught the people to sing in hope: that God had laid help upon Him, had exalted Him above the people, had anointed Him with holy oil, that God's hand would be established with Him, and His arm would strengthen Him, so that the enemy should not exact upon Him, nor the son of wickedness afflict Him; that the Most High would make Him His firstborn, higher than the kings of the earth, with whom God would keep mercy for ever, and confirm His covenant, Ps. 89:19-28. And a glorious and everlasting reign of righteousness and prosperity was promised Him. For He was the rod out of the stem of Jesse, and the Spirit of the Lord rested on Him, the Spirit of wisdom and understanding, of counsel and might, of knowledge and the fear of the Lord. With righteousness He would judge the poor, and reprove with equity for the meek of the earth. Righteousness would be the girdle of His loins, and faithfulness the girdle of His reins. A kingdom of blessed peace would He establish, in which all creation would share, so that the wolf would dwell with the lamb, and the leopard lie down with the kid; the calf and the young lion and the fatling together, and a young child would lead them. The cow and the bear would feed, and their young ones would lie down together, and the lion would eat straw like the ox during His reign. There would be no more hurt or destruction in all God's holy mountain, for the earth would be full of knowledge of the Lord, as the waters cover the sea. Isa. 11:1-9.

The King of the Jews as the sole, the glorious hope of Israel!

And now read that superscription, Pilate's composition, yes, but by God's directing hand, and, therefore, His revelation. O, how its letters must have appeared flaming symbols of doom to the leaders of the Jews, who were at least perfectly aware that they had delivered Him in their hatred! JESUS OF NAZARETH THE KING OF THE JEWS! *The* King! Not *a* king, but *the* King! The hope, the only hope of Israel! Beside this King of the Jews no other king was to be expected! And He was dying, affixed to the accursed tree, breathing His last! O, but will they

not repent? Will they not beg Pilate to take Him down from the
cross, while He is still alive, before their hope is blasted? But no!
Not He must be released from that cross: the superscription must
be changed. It must be given the lie! But to this they receive only
one answer, God's answer through the Roman governor: it is
irrevocable; what I have written I have written!

But even so the meaning of this superscription is not exhausted.
For mark you well, that superscription is affixed *to the cross!* It
proclaims to all the world, not merely that the King of the Jews,
the only Hope of Israel, is dying, but that He is killed! He is
murdered by whom? By the Romans, yes; for that very cross,
which was a Roman form of punishment, testifies to that fact.
But by the Romans because and as He was delivered to them
by the Jews! The King of the Jews, God's Holy One, upon Whom
were all the promises of God, the only Hope of Israel, murdered
by His own people! Still more! That superscription is not even
a mere announcement that the King of the Jews is murdered; it
means to proclaim to all the world the ground and reason of His
being killed. It states why the Jews kill this Jesus of Nazareth:
He is put to death by the Jews *because He is the King of the
Jews!* . . . .

O, horror!

When God realizes His glorious promise, and sends His Holy
One to His people Israel, they despise Him, reject Him, pour their
contempt upon this gift of God, will not have Him to be king
over them, and say: "This is the Son, let us kill Him!" That is
God's meaning and interpretation of this superscription! It is the
sentence. His sentence of judgment, against the carnal Jews. The
measure of iniquity is now filled. With the death of Christ in the
flesh, the judgment of the old dispensational Church has come.
When the King of the Jews breathes His last presently upon that
accursed tree, Israel according to the flesh dies with Him. Temple
and altar, priest and king, earthly mount Zion and throne of
David, may and must perish with the flesh of Christ, and that, too,
for ever, never to return. *The* King of the Jews in human flesh
perishes on the cross by the hands of carnal Israel: it must needs
perish with Him! No longer is there sense or reason, no longer
is there room for a separate, national Israel. The axe that was

laid at the root of Israel's tree even in the days of John the Baptist, is about to deliver its finishing stroke. And the same wicked hands that murder the King of the Jews must, in God's justice, by killing this King, also swing the axe that will hew down to the ground the proud tree of Israel's theocracy and national existence!

Such is the meaning of the superscription! God's meaning!

But wait! Is this then the end of this King of Israel? Do all the glorious and blessed promises of God then perish with Him on the cross? God forbid! On the contrary, here they find their realization, and that, too, through the instrumentality of wicked, carnal Israel, that kill the King of the Jews! For the Stone which the builders rejected must become the head of the corner! The King of the Jews must perish, in order that the difference between Jew and Greek may be eliminated for ever, and He may become one Lord over all, rich unto all that call upon Him! Rom. 10:12. And this, too, is already dimly predicted by the fact that this superscription was written in Hebrew and Latin and Greek.

I say dimly, for this was certainly not the meaning Pilate intended to put into the superscription, neither did those that watched the cross, or those that passed by there and stopped a moment to utter a curse or a prayer, discern this meaning. Even the disciples would have paid no further attention to this superscription had they not received a new and greater light of understanding the cross after the resurrection of the Lord. That title on the cross was man's word, and man's word was very loud on Calvary. And so, each would put his own meaning into Pilate's writing. Many would read it, for Golgotha was near the city, just aside from the main road from Jerusalem to the north. And it was the passover. Crowds from all over the world, Jews and proselytes, would come and congregate in the holy city, and many would pass the scene on the Hill of the Skull. Hence, the superscription was written in Hebrew, Latin, and Greek, that all might have an opportunity to read. Thus the crucified Lord, the Royal Sufferer, became a universal, public spectacle, and all would explain Pilate's cross-title in their own light. Hebrew was the language of the Church, of religion, and the Jew, looking at that cross and its superscription would hate and despise the Nazarene as an imposter, one who falsely pretended to be the Messiah, but was finally exposed as a liar, and justly put to death as a blasphemer. Though Pilate would not alter what he had written, the Jew would, nevertheless, read the superscription as if it accused the Nazarene of being a false Christ: He said that He was the King of the Jews! Latin was the language of the world-power, and the Roman would look with contempt on such a king, without power, and without glory! And Greek was the vehicle of human philosophy, of the wisdom of the world. And the wise man of the world would consider that cross and its superscription mere foolishness, and its victim a poor fool, that reaped the reward of His folly. And thus the superscription in its triple world-language transformed the cross into a universal spectacle, and exposed the Royal Sufferer to the hatred and scorn of all the religious and civilized world!

Nevertheless, there is also in this triple universal speech, the Word of God, which is especially evident if you read it in the light of still another sentence that is affixed to this cross. For do but look closely, not now with your natural, but with your spiritual eyes, the eyes of faith. Do you not clearly discern a second super-scription, even over that of Pilate, affixed to the cross, not by human hand, but directly by the finger of God? It is the hand writing of ordinances that was against us, together with this title: THE LAMB OF GOD THAT TAKETH AWAY THE SIN OF THE WORLD. That title is God's reason for the cross, His *logos* of the accursed tree. It is God's accusation against this man, yet not against Him personally, but against the world, and against Him only as He came to represent His own, given Him by the Father. And these are not from the Jews only, but from Hebrews, and Latins, and Greeks, from all the nations of the world. For their sake He is the Royal Sufferer. For their sake God has delivered Him. For their sake He allowed Himself willingly to be affixed to this cruel tree, that He might lay down His life, and obtain eternal righteousness and everlasting life for all that believe on His name!

Adorable mystery!

O, the depth of riches, both of the wisdom and knowledge of God. The King of the Jews perishes on the cross in order that out of the depth of that death He may presently issue forth the Lord of all, Hebrews, Latins, and Greeks, and be rich unto all that call upon Him. For whosoever shall call upon the name of the Lord shall be saved!

CHAPTER 7

Victorious in Defeat

It is finished. — JOHN 19:30.

Did ever man appear so hopelessly lost, so completely put to nought, so utterly defeated as our Lord in the hour of His suffering and agony on Calvary? His enemies had triumphed over Him. He was forsaken by His own, condemned by the Church, sentenced by the worldly judge. There was no one to defend His cause. He had been mocked at and filled with reproach, beaten and buffeted and spit upon, scourged and crowned with a crown of thorns. And finally He had been led to the place of the Skull. And there "they crucified him, and two other with him, and Jesus in the midst." John 19-18. He is numbered with the transgressors, exposed as a criminal, in fact, as the chief of them, as public enemy number one! And even so, His enemies know not pity. And all that are present and watch this dreadful spectacle, as well as those that pass by, the chief priests and the people, the soldiers and even the malefactors that were crucified with Him, mock and jeer and taunt Him, sarcastically challenging Him to deliver Himself and come down from the cross, thus contributing to and bringing out in bolder relief the picture of utter helplessness and defeat He presents. And does not God Himself set His seal of approval upon this execution of judgment by men? For darkness envelops the cross, and soon from the darkness the terrible cry of utter amazement is heard: "My God, my God, why hast thou forsaken me?" Was ever man so utterly forsaken by God and men, as this man Jesus as He is hanging on the accursed tree?

But hark! The crucified One speaks once more! He complains of thirst, but the note of amazement that was in His voice a moment ago is gone. And again He cries out. And is there not this time a note of triumph in His voice? Is not this next to the last cross utterance an announcement of victory? "It is finished!" He shouts. And in the consciousness of having finished all, He now beckons death to take His earthly frame, and commends His spirit into the hands of the Father. Surely, this is not the death of a defeated man. He appears to be in perfect control even of the moment of His own death. And in the hour of what seems to be His utter defeat He announces the victory: "It is finished!" And while men slink away from Golgotha smiting their breasts and admitting defeat, God from heaven corroborates with signs and wonders the shout of triumph by His Son on the cross. Indeed, the moment of Christ's utter defeat is the beginning of His glorious victory! He is victorious even in His defeat!

It is finished! This is one of the briefest of the seven cross utterances. Like the immediately preceding one it consists of only one word in the original. Yet, it is one of the most momentous and significant declarations ever made. What does it mean? Surely, it is far more than the announcement of approaching death. In this sixth cross utterance the Saviour does not mean to say that the end is fast approaching, and that He feels Himself sinking away into the mysterious depths of death. Such an interpretation would hardly be in harmony with the facts of Jesus' death. For these facts plainly witness that Jesus was never overcome by death, that death had no power at all arbitrarily to sever the thread of His earthly life; that, on the contrary, the Saviour laid down His own life, as He had said, in His own time, and that death could come in only at His own beck and call. This is evident from the fact that the Lord died much sooner than was and could have been expected. Death by crucifixion was a very slow process of dying. It could last from one even to three whole days. But Jesus died within six hours. And all marvelled that He

had died so soon. Death did not overpower Him. By the strength
of His divine nature the Son of God sustained His human nature
in all its suffering until the work was finished and the battle was
won: then He gave up the ghost. This is evident, too, from the fact
that the Saviour remained fully and clearly conscious to the very
last, and that He cried out with a powerful voice even at the moment
of His departure from this life. The outcry "It is finished" cannot
mean "I feel the end approaching." For no one took His life
from Him. He had power to lay it down of Himself, and He had
power to take it again.

Nor is this the meaning of the word that is used here in the
original. It emphasizes that something is finished, that the end is
attained that was to be reached, that a work had been accomplished. Hardly could this be said by man when death overtakes
him, especially when he is still in the prime of his life, and when
his life is taken from him by the sword of the worldly magistrate.
Death usually takes us away from the stage of our earthly life
and labors when it would seem that there are still many unfinished
tasks. But with the Lord this was different. When He cried out
"It is finished," He did not mean to announce that His earthly
life was ended, but that His work was completed, that the purpose, the end of His earthly life and labors had been reached,
and that now He could leave this world and lay down His life.
This is the meaning of the word the Lord here employs. And
that this is, indeed, the meaning of the sixth cross utterance is
evident, finally, from the context. For in vs. 28 of John 19 we
read: "After this, Jesus knowing that all things were now accomplished, that the Scripture might be fulfilled, saith, I thirst."
The Saviour was conscious that all things were accomplished,
that His work was finished. And as there was neither reason nor
motive for Him to stay in the flesh even one moment longer
than was required for the accomplishment of His work, He bowed
the head and gave up the ghost. John 19:30.

But what is implied in this announcement? Just what was
finished? In general we may answer: all the work which the
Father gave Him to do had been accomplished. Not, indeed, as
if the Saviour is not working even now. To be sure, He has all
power in heaven and in earth, He reigns in might and glory at

the right hand of God, He preserves His people, and causes all things to work together unto the coming of the glorious day when He shall appear as our Saviour from heaven. But, first of all, the Saviour is looking back here upon His life in the flesh, and upon that part of the work that had to be finished in human nature, in the likeness of sinful flesh; He is considering chiefly, no doubt, the program of His suffering and agonies of the last few hours; and with regard to that program of redemption in as far as it must be accomplished by the Son of God in the world, in the state of His humiliation, He here declares that it is finished, and that the end in view, the purpose of it all has been attained. That is why it is an announcement of victory. And for this reason we may also say, in the second place, that in principle all the work of salvation had been accomplished. In the perfect obedience of Jesus on the cross all the work is finished that must bear fruit in the eternal glory of the whole Church, of all the saints in the new creation!

But let us consider this sixth cross word a moment from the specific viewpoint of its being an outcry from the mouth of the Royal Sufferer, Who must enter into the glory of His kingdom through suffering. For it is especially when we view it in this light that we clearly discern in it the note of triumph, and understand it as an announcement of victory.

Jesus suffered and died as God's anointed King. And let us clearly understand the implication and significance of this. For this does not merely mean that He suffered and left His life on the battlefield in defense of His cause and kingdom. This, indeed, may also be said of the kings of this world. They have enemies that attack them and compel them to fight in defense of their kingdom. Or they themselves are motivated by carnal ambition and lust for power and aggrandizement, and go out to battle. And in the battle, whenever they personally went out with their armies to meet the enemy, they would often suffer, and forfeit their lives. In a sense, therefore, it might be said of them, too, that they were royal sufferers: they died as kings. However, their suffering and death were not essential to their kingship. On the contrary, their death is a loss. It may be their defeat. They meant to fight and gain the victory, but they did not intend to die. With the Christ, however, this is essentially different. He suffers and dies to establish His kingdom, and to enter into the possession and glory of it. He does not merely suffer in battle, but His suffering is His battle. He does not simply fight to the death, but by dying He fights. He deliberately chooses the way of suffering. He wants to die! In the fullest sense of the word He lays down His life, and in doing so He fights the battle for His kingdom. Suffering and death are not accidental with Him: they are the essence of His battle. He is the Royal Sufferer because there is no other way for Him to enter into the glory of His Kingdom than through the death of the cross!

For His Kingdom is not of this world. Jesus is the Christ. He was Anointed from before the foundation of the world to be King over all in the new creation. But that new creation, that eternal Kingdom of heaven, over which He was anointed King for ever, is the redeemed world. His kingdom, and the subjects of that kingdom, those whom the Father has given Him, are by nature in the power of the devil, the prince of this world. They are in sin, they are under the wrath and condemnation of God, they lie in the midst of death. From this power of the devil, sin, and death they must be delivered. And Christ is anointed, ordained and qualified by God the Father to accomplish this task. He has His fight not with flesh and blood, but with the powers of darkness. He must break the power of the devil, vanquish sin and death, and so battle His way into His kingdom. But how can sin and death be vanquished, and how can the devil be deprived of his power to rule in the world? Only in the way of the righteousness of God. The guilt of sin must be blotted out. The justice of God must be satisfied with respect to sin. And how can the justice of God be satisfied? Only by a perfect sacrifice. The sentence of God against sin is death. The soul that sinneth shall die. The case against the sinner, therefore, is hopeless as far as he is concerned. For how shall the sinner die and live? How shall the sinner that is himself dead in sin, an enemy of God by nature, sacrifice himself in death unto God? But God anointed His Son to stand at the head of His sinful people, so that He might represent them, take their place, assume responsibility for all their sin, and bring the perfect sacrifice that would satisfy the justice

of God, and for ever blot out the guilt of sin. To bring that
sacrifice and accomplish that perfect redemption, and thus to
establish His eternal kingdom of glory on the sure foundation of
the righteousness of God, the Son of God was ordained from before the foundation of the world.

Thus He came into the world. "The Lord hath laid on him
the iniquity of us all." Isa. 53:6. And with the responsibility for
all our iniquities upon Himself, He said: "Sacrifice and offering
thou didst not desire; mine ears hast thou opened: burnt offering
and sin offering hast thou not required. Then said I, Lo, I come;
in the volume of the book it is written of me, I delight to do thy
will, O my God: yea, thy law is within my heart," Ps. 40:6-8.
And with that delight to do God's will in His heart, and with
all our iniquities upon Himself, He deliberately rejected all other
ways and chose the way of the cross, the way of death and hell!
That is why "He was oppressed, and he was afflicted, yet he
opened not his mouth: he is brought as a lamb to the slaughter,
and as a sheep before her shearers is dumb, so he opened not
his mouth." Isa. 53:7. That, and not because He is powerless, is
the reason why all the mockery and sarcastic invectives of the
enemies cannot induce Him to come down from that cross, and
why He silently endures when the soldiers even cast into His
teeth the taunt: "If thou be the king of the Jews, save thyself."
That cross is His battlefield! That apparently helpless Sufferer,
Who appears so utterly passive, is engaged in a fierce battle. That
apparently impotent victim of His enemies, has the devil by his
throat, is taking the sting out of death, is choking the last accusing
breath of condemnation out of sin. He is fighting the battle for
the righteousness of God into the glory of His everlasting kingdom
at the head of all whom the Father has given Him! That is why
He is more than victor, for even His enemies unwittingly, by
attempting to destroy Him, are instrumental in leading Him on
to victory! And that is why the moment of His apparent utter
defeat is the moment of His final victory, and He is able to
announce to all the world: "It is finished!" The battle is fought!
The foe is vanquished! Sin is blotted out! Eternal righteousness
is obtained for all mine! The devil is for ever dethroned! Death
is swallowed up in victory! The way through deepest death and

hell is wide open and leads into the heavenly tabernacle of God with men! "The kingdoms of this world are become the kingdoms of our Lord, and of his Christ; and he shall reign for ever and ever." Rev. 11:15. It is finished!

Lo! even now, as the Servant of Jehovah, the Royal Sufferer, makes His announcement of victory, and departs from the earthly tabernacle of His flesh, God sustains the claim of His beloved Son with signs from heaven! The Roman centurion gives Him testimony that He was a righteous man, the Son of God, Lu. 23:47; Matt. 27:54. Those that had come to mock now smite their breasts, and return in utter amazement, Lu. 32:48. The veil of the temple is marvellously rent by the hand of Him that dwells between the cherubim, a sign that the old temple is destroyed, and that the way into the true sanctuary, into the presence of God is now opened. When Christ breaks through the flesh in which all our iniquities had been contracted, everything splits, opens up as it were to make room for the new economy of things. The earth quakes, as a prophecy of the day when God shall shake yet once more, not only the earth, but also the heavens, to usher in the eternal kingdom of glory. The rocks rend, and the graves are opened: death must give up its victims unto the glorious resurrection that is to come! O, indeed, victorious in His defeat is the Royal Sufferer! With perfect confidence He even now announces His own victory: It is finished! And God from heaven corroborates His testimony that righteousness is established, that sin is blotted out, that death is overcome, and that the eternal kingdom of His Anointed has been established!

Only by grace, and through faith, we, too, corroborate the truth of that announcement. And receiving this testimony we put all our confidence in Him that uttered it: the crucified and risen Lord! And putting all our confidence in Him we enter into a finished work. Then we enter into a finished righteousness, the righteousness of God in Christ, and we know that, even though all things in this world testify to the contrary, and our own conscience accuse us, we are justified and have peace with God. Then we enter into a perfect victory over sin, the devil and death, for faith is the victory that overcomes the world. Then we do, indeed, still fight a battle in this world, but it is a battle against foes that have been vanquished by the Captain of our salvation. None of our work can add to the perfection of His work; our fighting cannot make His victory more sure and complete. For it is finished! And entering by faith into the finished work of our Lord, we know that we are more than conquerors through Him that loved us even unto death!

CHAPTER 8

Victorious in Resurrection — Glory

He is not here: for he is risen. — MATT. 28:6.

How exuberant with significance is the first resurrection sermon, preached with staccato brevity by the shining messenger from heaven in the dark rock-hewn sepulchre of Joseph, to a few astounded and perplexed women that are holding their breath in sheer amazement because of the marvellous and wholly un-expected things they witnessed! "Fear not ye: for I know that ye seek Jesus which was crucified. He is not here, for he is risen, as he said." Matt. 28:5, 6.

Early in the morning, preventing the first glimmer of dawn, these women had arisen. They were Mary Magdalene, always eager to render the service of love and gratitude of her Lord, Who had delivered her from the devil's oppression, the other Mary, the mother of James, and Salome. And there were still others with them. Rest they had not been able to find, not even in the quiet and worshipful hours of the sabbath that was now past, nor in the dark hours of the night that had followed the sabbath; for their souls had been troubled as in their minds they had re-viewed the events of the last few days without, however, finding a solution of the problem these events presented to them, and their sorrow had kept sleep far from their eyes. They had been witnesses of the crucifixion of their beloved Master. They had

193

looked upon Him, in Whom all their hope was founded, as He was hanging helpless on the accursed tree; they had seen His reproach and shame; they had heard the taunting jeers and bitter sneers, the biting jests and cutting sarcasms of the enemy as they raved in the fury of a never to be satisfied hatred about the cross; they had listened to His outcry of utter perplexity sounding forth in the awful darkness that enveloped the hellish scene on Calvary, and they had watched Him sink into the dark abyss of death, overcome apparently by the powers of darkness that had risen against Him. And they had followed in the sad funeral procession to the tomb in Joseph's garden; and although they had remained without the tomb, and, therefore, had not witnessed the actual preparation of the body for the burial by Joseph and Nicodemus, they had waited until the burial had been completed, and the large stone had been rolled before the entrance of the tomb.

Then they had returned.

And it seemed to them that their hope had been buried with Him in the sepulchre of Joseph. For they had not understood. They knew not as yet, that their Saviour must suffer thus, in order to enter into His glory. They had not understood the meaning of that terrible cross, its reproach and shame, its suffering and death. Repeatedly their Lord had spoken to them of His approaching decease at Jerusalem, and in broad outlines He had foretold them the program of His suffering: how He must be delivered to the leaders of the Jews, be numbered with the transgressors, crucified and cruelly murdered. But His words had not registered in their consciousness. And so, not having understood His word concerning His passion and death, they failed to take hold of His promise concerning His resurrection on the third day, and were unmindful of His injunction that they should go to Galilee where He would go before them to meet them. A great sorrow filled their hearts. And as they returned from the sepulchre to rest on the sabbath day according to the commandment, they agreed among one another that they would return to the grave as soon as possible, to perform a last service of love, and to finish the preparation of that precious body for the burial, which, as far as they knew, had been all too hasty and incomplete. Thus it had come about that, instead of proceeding to Galilee in the

hope of meeting their risen Lord, they made their way, early on
that first day of the week, to the garden of Joseph once more.
Anxious they had been about the great stone that closed the
entrance to the tomb. . . .

And then the wonders had followed one another in quick succession. From afar they had perceived that the stone had been
rolled away from the sepulchre. And at the sight of the open
grave in the distance, Mary Magdalene had at once jumped to
the conclusion that they must have removed the body of her Lord;
and she had returned to tell the disciples that they had stolen
the body of Jesus. The other women, however, had continued
on their way. They had found the grave empty. They had seen
the place where the Lord had lain, that wonderful, that mysterious
place, and the marvel of the linen clothes. And they had heard
the gospel of the glorious resurrection, preached to them by the
heavenly ambassador that had been awaiting them in the empty
grave: "Fear not ye! For I know that ye seek Jesus which was
crucified. He is not here, for he is risen, as he said!"

Fear not ye! Let the enemy now fear! For He is risen! Let
all the powers of darkness now fear and tremble, for His resurrection is His victory over them all, and spells their final and
complete destruction! Already the enemy had been struck with
terror, and fled in confusion in that early morning of the first
day of the week. Even at the grave they had been well represented. The wicked leaders of the Jews had not felt at ease, even
after this strange Jesus of Nazareth had given up the ghost on
the cross before their eyes, and the spear thrust in His side had
proved beyond all doubt that He had succumbed to the power of
death. Had He not spoken of His resurrection on the third day?
If the disciples at this time were not mindful of His words concerning His power to rebuild the temple in three days, they,
His enemies had not forgotten. O, they would not admit, even
to themselves, the subconscious fear of this Jesus of Nazareth that
troubled them even now He was dead and buried. But might not
the disciples come to the grave by night and steal the body of
Jesus, and make the last error worse than the first? And so they
had applied to the Roman governor for a watch of soldiers, and
required of him that the grave be securely sealed. And although

Pilate had replied to them with a touch of sarcasm, their request had been granted. The sepulchre had been sealed, and a guard of Roman soldiers had been sent to watch the grave.

Thus the power of the hostile world was well represented at the grave! Or are these soldiers not a striking representation of the power of unbelief that is always making the futile attempt to deny that Jesus is the Christ, and that, for this very reason, desperately try to keep Jesus in the grave, gainsaying the resurrection? And are not all the wicked endeavors of an infidel philosophy to contradict the report of Jesus' glorious resurrection just as foolish and vain as that first story the soldiers were bribed to circulate, that they, Roman soldiers, had slept on guard, and that, though they had been sleeping, they could report that the disciples had stolen the body of Jesus? Or is it not utterly foolish to claim that the disciples invented the gospel of the risen Lord, of the empty grave, of the place where Jesus had lain, of the wonder of the linen clothes, of the vision of angels, and above all, of the several appearances of the risen Lord Himself? O, but indeed, the power that crucified Him once, that would crucify Him again, now with the more subtle nails of scoffing criticism and unbelieving philosophy; the power that must needs crucify Him always, because it loves the darkness rather than the light, and because it realizes that the resurrection of the Lord of glory is their defeat — that power was represented by this strange death-watch of Roman soldiers at the sepulchre of the crucified One!

Foolish spectacle! As if, forsooth, a chain and a seal, and a band of soldiers could keep in the grave Him Whom the bands of death could not hold, Who had power to lay down His life, and power to take it again, Who is the resurrection and the life! Foolish, too, because it is more than probable that for some time, at least, they were keeping watch around the empty grave. The exact moment of the resurrection of our Lord is not known. It may have been any time after the sabbath which had come to a close at six o'clock the previous evening. In fact, it is quite proper to maintain that death did not hold our Lord a moment longer than was necessary to fulfill His word that He would rise on the third day. Certain it is that the risen One was not in need of having the stone rolled away from the grave to make His exit from Hades. And certain it is, too, that the angel that descended from heaven early in the morning, accompanied by the sign of an earthquake, to roll the stone away from the entrance of the tomb, did so, not to let Jesus out, but to open the grave for inspection, and to guard it against spoliation by wicked hands. And so, the soldiers must have been guarding an empty grave for some time.

But they had also feared. The signs of the resurrection had filled them with terror. For as a sign that the Prince of life had broken the bands of death, and overcome the power of Hades, the earth had quaked and trembled; and to open and exhibit the empty sepulchre, and to preach to anxious and amazed disciples the first gospel of the risen Lord, a heavenly ambassador had descended bringing with him a halo of glory from the very presence of God. And the watchmen had feared, and they had become as dead men. In great consternation they had fled. And in this, too, they are but proper representatives of a hostile world. For the resurrection of Jesus Christ from the dead is God's judgment. It is the sentence of condemnation upon that wicked world that nailed Him to the cross, even as it is the complete justification of the Christ that was crucified. Let the enemy fear, for the resurrection is the incontrovertible evidence that Jesus is the Christ, the Son of God! It is the victory of the Royal Sufferer!

But fear not ye! For I know that ye seek Jesus that was crucified! And surely, they that seek the crucified Jesus will find the risen Lord, not in order to flee from Him in terror and consternation, but to rejoice in His salvation. The way of the cross is the way into the resurrection. O, to be sure, the women had not understood. As far as their conscious knowledge was concerned, and as far as they had acted in clear consciousness and understanding of what they were doing, they had not come to the grave to become witnesses of the resurrection; neither had they come to seek the crucified One: it was only His body they wanted, that they might perform a last service of love upon it. And even now, as they stand in the empty sepulchre, amazement written all over their faces, and listen to the marvellous message of the angel, they do not comprehend. Even as they had not been able to under-

stand the cross, so they do not fully grasp the glory of the resurrection on the third day. But it was, nevertheless, true, that they
had sought Jesus, the crucified One. The enemies had despised
and rejected Him, nailed Him to the accursed tree. But they had
sought Him, followed Him, served Him to the very last; and even
now they had come to seek what was left of the crucified Jesus.
And they had sought Him and followed Him, because they loved
Him, believed in Him, and had fixed their hope on Christ, the Son
of the living God. And thus seeking Him, they had finally come
to the vacated grave and found the risen Lord!

It is always thus. The joy of Easter follows the sorrow of
Good Friday. The defeat of the cross leads to the victory of the
resurrection. The seeking of the crucified One, must needs end
in the finding of the risen Lord! We must seek the crucified Jesus,
but then, indeed, as the crucified One. We must not change the
cross into an emblem of Man's nobility and goodness: for it is the
token of our sin and shame, the emblem of His love and faithfulness. We must not seek Jesus the good man, the wise man, the
noble example whom you follow, the instructor whose precepts
you keep, the modern Jesus that flatters your sinful pride. You will
never find the risen Lord in that direction. In the modern Jesus
there is nothing but death. But you must seek Jesus that was
crucified, of Whom the angel said in the beginning that He would
save His people from their sins, the Royal Sufferer, Who must
suffer in order to enter into His glory, Who was wounded for our
transgressions, bruised for our iniquities, the Good Shepherd Who
laid down His life for His sheep. We must seek Him, not as a
matter of curiosity, but as a thing of life and death; not as an
object of theological inquisitiveness, but to find a way out!

Then we will find the risen Lord, the way out, the victory!

He is not here! He is risen! That is, in brief, the whole gospel,
the gospel of the risen Lord, of the victory of the Royal Sufferer
in resurrection glory, and the victory of all that seek the crucified Jesus.

He is not here! He is risen! He was here once, to be sure!
Here, in our earthly sphere of death He was. He tabernacled
among us in the likeness of sinful flesh. Here He descended into
deepest death, into the nethermost parts of Hades. Here He was

in the place of corruption in weakness, dishonor, mortality, shame, corruptibility, but here He is no more. And that He is no more here is not due to the fact that He is totally consumed by death. But He is risen!

That is the victory!

For consider what it means that He is risen. It means that God has fulfilled all His promises unto Him, and He has raised Him from the dead. But as such it is a testimony of God of His and our justification. He is justified, and we are justified in Him! The resurrection is the victory over sin and damnation. For it was on account of our transgressions that He sank into death. For He had no sin. Our iniquities He bore on the accursed tree and for them He shed His lifeblood and descended into the lowest hell. But He did not disappear in death. He was not consumed of hell. He atoned. He satisfied the justice of God in respect to our sins. And then He ascended out of the darkness of utter desolation. Even on the cross He announced that it was finished. And now, in the resurrection God Himself seals that testimony of His Servant on the cross: it is finished! Finished is the sacrifice of perfect obedience for our sins: the resurrection of Jesus Christ from the dead is God's own act of acceptance of the perfect sacrifice. Finished is the atonement, the blotting out of our sins, the obedience whereby eternal righteousness has been obtained for all whom the Father gave His Christ! Finished for ever is our justification! He has gained the victory over the power of sin, the right to make us free, and to make us partakers of eternal life and glory. That is the meaning of the resurrection!

He is risen! O, glorious victory! For the Royal Sufferer did not simply return from the grave, as did Lazarus whom once He raised from the dead: He went on! He is not here! He did not return into the likeness of our sinful flesh. He is no longer, He is not again in the sphere of weakness: He went on to power. He did not return to the sphere of dishonor: He went through to glory. He is not again clothed with mortality and corruptibility: He has put on immortality and incorruption! He no longer bears the image of the earthy: He stands revealed as the Lord from heaven!

Fear not ye! Rejoice! For He is risen as the first-fruits of them that slept! The full harvest of all His own is sure to follow! For presently this glorious Lord will ascend to His Father and our Father, and will receive the promise of the Holy Spirit. And in that Spirit He will come again, to make His own partakers of His resurrection life. He, the beginning of the resurrection will not rest until He has raised all His own, made them like unto Himself, and taken them with Him in the everlasting, heavenly tabernacle of God with men! He is risen! Fear not ye, but rejoice for evermore!

BOOK THREE

REJECTED

OF MEN

CHAPTER 1

Rejected of Men

He is despised and rejected of men . . . Isa. 53:3

Higher than the heavens, deep as hell, is the mystery of the suffering and death of our Saviour. For higher than the highest heavens is the mercy of God of which it is the revelation; and deep as hell is His Holy wrath and justice against sin that by this suffering is fully satisfied. If you could imagine all the suffering of mankind compressed into one awful agony, you could not fathom or comprehend the passion of our Lord that reached its climax on the accursed tree, and finally pressed from His dying lips the agonizing cry: "My God, my God, why hast thou forsaken me?" Who could endure suffering as He, the Son of God in human flesh, could endure? Who could taste the pains of hell as He, very God and very man, could taste them? Who could feel the anguish of being forsaken of God as He, the Servant of Jehovah, could feel it? To Whom could the wages of sin be more bitter than to Him, Who knew no sin, but was made sin for us? And Who could feel more deeply and keenly the reproach of men than He, Who was the sinless One in the midst of a world of darkness and iniquity? Indeed, whenever we contemplate the passion and death of the suffering Servant of the Lord, we realize that here there are mysterious depths that we can never fathom. We can only stand amazed and worship.

Besides, the passion of our Lord is as manysided as human nature and human life. For He came in the likeness of sinful flesh, He assumed the flesh and blood of the children, in order that, in that flesh, and that, too, in the whole human nature, He might bear the wrath of God against sin. He suffered in body and soul, in mind and spirit, in every fibre of His being. Is there any pain anywhere that He did not endure? Is there ever any sorrow He did not bear? Is there any agony of soul or body with which He was not acquainted? Where, after He suffered and died, shall we ever tread a path of suffering which He has not trod before, or discover a depth of agony in which we do not find His footsteps? He suffered the wrath of God and the hatred of men. He suffered hell and damnation, reproach and shame, anguish of soul and spirit. He is eminently the Man of Sorrows!

Even for this reason it is expedient, as we would reverently contemplate the suffering of our Saviour, that we do not arbitrarily move about at random, but take a certain definite viewpoint, and from that point of view consider a certain aspect of the passion of our Lord. And in the following chapters, we wish to study this suffering of Christ from the viewpoint of His being rejected of men.

Our theme is taken from the fifty-third chapter of the prophecy of Isaiah, a chapter of which it has been said that it might have been written in the shadow of Golgotha, as in a sense it was. In the third verse we read: "He is despised and rejected of men; a man of sorrows, and acquainted with grief: and we hid as it were our faces from him; he was despised, and we esteemed him not." When, several centuries later, the Ethiopian eunuch read this section of Isaiah's prophecy, he asked of Philip: "Of whom speaketh the prophet this? of himself or of another man?" Acts 8:34. And from the standpoint of the eunuch, who could not read this prophecy in the clearer light of the New Testament, as we are accustomed to do, the question was a perfectly natural one. For the prophet is speaking of the "Servant of the Lord." And this Servant of Jehovah is, indeed, the Christ, but only in the ultimate and central sense of the word. The term, however, has different, though closely related connotations. In the broadest sense it is used to denote the nation of Israel, God's covenant people, delivered out of the bondage of Egypt to be God's servant in the midst of the nations. Seeing, however, that not all were Israel that were of Israel, and that there always was a large carnal element among the people of God, the term "Servant of Jehovah" is also used to denote the true spiritual Israel, the remnant according to the election of grace. In a still more limited sense, the term refers to the prophet himself. Yet, Israel could be called the Lord's servant only through and for the sake of Christ, the Holy Seed that was still in their loins. He is the Servant of the Lord *par excellence.* And, therefore, in the ultimate sense the term refers to Him alone. This is emphatically true of the fifty-third chapter of this prophecy, which speaks almost directly of the suffering Saviour. He is the "arm of the Lord" spoken of in the first verse. Of Him the prophet had said that He grew up as a tender plant, as a root out of a dry ground; and that He had no form or comeliness, and no beauty that we should desire Him. He is the despised and rejected One, before Whom we hide our faces.

Consider what this means. He is despised. O, this does not mean that He belongs to those lowly and simple men that occupy a forgotten place in society, that live without being noticed, and die without being missed, to whom no one pays any attention. On the contrary, it presupposes that Christ came into contact with men, and that they expressed an opinion about Him, and treated Him accordingly. In the days of His flesh the Saviour was well known, even as He is universally known in the world of today. Who did not know Jesus of Nazareth? Throughout the land His fame was spread abroad. His name was on the lips of high and low, of rich and poor, of the common people and of those that sat in high places. But He was despised of men. He was considered a worthless fellow, a good for nothing, who was not fit to live in decent and civilized society. No one would offer Him a place in the world, or furnish Him with a recommendation. This contempt of men for Him was so profound, so the prophet declares, that men hid their faces from Him. In modern parlance this means that, as they saw Him, they would pull up their noses in utter contempt.

And He was rejected. This, too, implies that He was well known. It even presupposes that He appeared with a certain claim. He assumed a certain position. He represented a cause. He taught a certain doctrine. But He was rejected. He could find no supporters for His cause. No one took His side. Men forsook Him. They left Him alone. They condemned His cause, and left Him alone. The prophet says that He was rejected of *men*. The emphasis of this word probably falls on men that were outstanding among the people. Men of position and of authority, the leaders of the people, those that were supposed to know what they were about, princes, kings, governors, theologians, scribes and Pharisees, men that were honored for their wisdom and discretion, their piety and religion — they rejected Him. Nevertheless, although there may be a special reference to men of eminent position and authority in this term, it refers, in general, to all men. The leaders took the initiative, but the people followed, and all rejected Him. And the prophet even seems to include himself and his own people, for he repeats: "he was despised," and then adds: "and we esteemed him not." O, it was not only the rabble of men, those that were of no account, that despised and rejected this Servant of the Lord, but *men,* mere men as they are found everywhere in this world, men, exactly in their capacity and character as men that filled Him with contempt, and hid their faces from Him.

Let us make no mistake about this: men rejected Him! Let us not read this prophecy of Isaiah as a mere prediction of an event that was realized some eight hundred years later when wicked Jews and ungodly heathen nailed Jesus of Nazareth to the accursed tree, but that does not necessarily concern us, modern men, the Church and the world of the twentieth century. For then we miss the point. Then we look upon this prophecy as outsiders, as students of theology, or of ethics. Then we probably make an attempt to solve the problem how, more than nineteen centuries ago, men could ever despise and reject such a wonderful man as Jesus, and from the heights of our conceit we look down on the men that crucified Him, and we feel rather secure in our self-righteous condemnation of them. Then we are quite ready to enjoy an evening of mingled aesthetic and religious emotions aroused by the rendering of Handel's Messiah, and to be rather pleased with our own, rather pleasant, feeling of deeply pious sympathy stirred in our soul when this "Man of sorrows" that is acquainted with grief is bewailed in music and song. O, what a pleasant experience it is for us to look down upon Golgotha from the heights of our modern self-righteousness and religiousness! What a self-flattering emotion it is to pity this Man of sorrows, and to feel that if Jesus had only walked our streets, and presented His cause to us, we would never have rejected Him, and nailed Him to the accursed tree!

He was rejected by *men!* Men of all classes, and of all ages, are included in this. Respectable men and men of disreputable character, honorable men and men in dishonor, religious men and men without religion, men of high moral standards and immoral men, professors of theology and ethics and the common people, educated and uneducated men, kings, governors, theologians, scribes, Pharisees, business men, fishermen, soldiers, — all rejected Him! Even one of His own intimate followers betrayed Him and sold Him for thirty pieces of silver, another swore and cursed himself rather than have anything to do with Him, and they all were offended in Him and forsook Him! O, how men hated Him! How deeply they despised Him! How utterly they rejected Him! They called Him a liar and deceiver, a blasphemer and an ally of Beelzebub, a glutton and winebibber, a companion of publicans and sinners! They contradicted Him, cast Him out of their synagogues, buffeted Him, spit upon Him, taunted and mocked Him, and filled Him with reproach, scourged Him and pressed a crown of thorns upon His brow, nailed Him to the cross and set Him up between two malefactors. And even then they still railed on Him, and poured the vials of their inexhaustible fury and contempt upon Him!

O, do you not discern the tremendous significance of this? Do you not understand that you cannot read this Word of God as an outsider, as a mere spectator, as an interested philosopher or theologian? Do you not see that this prophecy of Isaiah must not be understood as the mere prediction of an event that once took place during the first few decades of our era, and that could never occur again, but rather as the statement of a general truth and of a situation that must needs always arise wherever and whenever men come into contact with this Servant of Jehovah? Men despised Him! Mere men rejected Him! It made absolutely no difference by what other name they were called, whether they were of Israel or of the heathen, of the Church or of the world, whether, besides being *men,* they were kings or priests or common people, religious or irreligious, decent citizens or criminals, as *men* they surely rejected Him, and must have nothing of the cause He advocated! Men, as they are found always and everywhere in this world, rejected Him. What happened in the first decades of our era, when Jesus of Nazareth walked among men, is simply an outstanding example of what always happens, and must needs occur, wherever this same Jesus presents Himself and His cause to mere men. You and I, as mere men, reject Him. And however piously our modern world and our modern church may babble about the wonderful Christ, always it rejects the Servant of Jehovah, and crucifies Him afresh! He is ousted from our universities, scourged in our seminaries, robed in mock-purple on our pulpits, railed at by the rabble, cursed in our streets, crucified by the mighty powers of this world!

And why do men reject Him? The answer to this question must be found in the fact that He is the Man of sorrows. Do not misunderstand this. Mere men do not despise and reject their suffering fellows. Even though they are capable of inflicting the most cruel tortures upon one another, under favorable conditions they can also sympathize with one another's suffering. But Christ was not merely a man who, like others, was acquainted with suffering: He was *the* Man of sorrows. Sorrows belong to Him. They are inseparable from Him. They are an essential part of Him. Suffering and death belonged to His calling, to His cause, to the work He had to do. He came into the world with the purpose in His heart to suffer and to die. For He came *for sin.* The sins of His own He freely took upon Himself. The burden of their guilt He took upon His mighty shoulders. And with the sin of the world upon Him, the Lamb of God walked the way of the righteousness of God. He represented God's cause against man's sin. He took the side of God's righteousness against the self-righteousness of man. And for the sin of His own, and to satisfy the justice of God, He bore all the divine wrath, freely suffered all the agonies of hell, and thus brought the perfect sacrifice of atonement and reconciliation. And thus He is the Man of sorrows. And as the Man of sorrows He is and claims to be the arm of the Lord unto salvation. He condemns all the righteousness of man, all his goodness, all his wisdom, all his self-willed religiousness and piety. Always He stands for the righteousness of God over against the unfruitful works of darkness. He never compromised. Consistently He proclaimed that there is no hope in man's work, and that there is no way out except through His own death and sacrifice on the cross. All the pride of man He lays low, in order to exalt the righteousness of God as the sole way of salvation.

That is the reason why men reject Him. For men are enemies of God and His righteousness. They love the darkness rather than the light. Hating the righteousness of God, they seek their own righteousness. They seek salvation through the might and power, the wisdom and ingenuity of man. Hence, they hate the Man of sorrows. He has no place in the world of men. The cross is foolishness to them. And so, it is inevitable that wherever and whenever this Servant of the Lord, this Man of sorrows, appears in the world of mere men, He is despised and rejected. To this there is not a single exception. Mere men always reject the Christ.

What then? Must this be the last word? If all men reject Him, must not the very purpose of His coming necessarily be frustrated? God forbid! For we must apply also here that what is impossible with men, is possible with God. The wonder of grace changes mere men, carnal men, into spiritual children of God, that have eyes to see, ears to hear, and hearts that yearn after the living God. With those eyes they behold Him, not as an object of contempt, nor as someone whom it is but proper to pity, but as the Lamb of God that taketh away their sin. With those ears they hear His voice as the voice of the Good Shepherd that laid down His life for the sheep. With those hearts they yearn after Him, hungering and thirsting for the righteousness of God. They turn to the cross of the Man of sorrows, not to weep over Him and feel pious in doing so, but to beat their breasts in shame and humiliation because of their sins; and to find the way out of sin and death into the fellowship of His righteousness and glorious resurrection. And thus, they that are saved by grace, find in Him that is rejected of men the forgiveness of sins, peace with God, and life from the dead!

Yet, He is rejected of men. And they who by the grace of God come to Him, must needs bear His reproach in the midst of this present world. For they confess His name, love His precepts, keep his commandments, walk as children of light, and condemn the world in its unfruitful works of darkness. They represent His cause, the cause of the Son of God, in the world. And this means that they must bear His reproach. As men rejected Him, so they will reject them; as they despised Him, so they will despise them. But in all this they look forward to the final victory. For if we suffer with Him, we shall also be glorified together! The rejected of men is the Risen Lord!

CHAPTER 2

Hated Without a Cause

But this cometh to pass that the word might be ful-
filled that is written in their law, They hated me with-
out a cause. — JOHN 15:25.

That there is a good deal of hatred in the world is undeniable.
Individuals, social groups, and nations openly express and manifest their hatred of one another. Men hate one another for the
love of money, greed and covetousness, personal ambition and
lust for power, envy and revenge. And Scripture teaches us that
the deepest root of all hatred among men is enmity against God.
Just as the love of one another is principally love of God, so men's
hatred of one another is but an expression of their hatred of God.
However, the sinner is loath to admit this. He understands that
to admit that his hatred of the neighbor is principally hatred of
God, is his condemnation. Hence, he tries to justify himself. He
finds a cause for his hatred, and the cause is always in the neighbor he hates. His neighbor is evil, has wronged him, is an oppressor of the poor, is greedy of gain and ambitious of power, a
cruel tyrant and murderer, one that should have no place in decent
society, and that ought, therefore, to be destroyed. And so he tries
to find a just cause for his hatred, and to present it in the light
of righteous indignation. Nor is it very difficult for man thus
to deceive himself, and to discover such a justifying cause in

211

the neighbor for his hatred of him, in a world of men of which the Holy Scriptures express the judgment: "that they are all under sin; As it is written, There is none righteous, no, not one: There is none that understandeth, there is none that seeketh after God. They are all gone out of the way, they are together become unprofitable; there is none that doeth good, no, not one. Their throat is an open sepulchre; with their tongues they have used deceit; the poison of asps is under their lips; Whose mouth is full of cursing and bitterness: Their feet are swift to shed blood: Destruction and misery are in their ways: And the way of peace have they not known: There is no fear of God before their eyes." Rom. 3:9-18. In such a world, it should not be difficult to find the cause for one's hatred of the neighbor in the neighbor himself, and thus to justify himself before the tribunal of Man, and of Man's God!

However, this state of affairs may not prevail. It cannot be ultimate and final. God must be justified when He judgeth, and all men must be found liars. Every possible excuse must be taken away from them. They must be left without one plea. All the apparent goodness and righteousness and even piety and religiousness must be exposed as fundamentally wickedness and enmity against God. The white-washed sepulchres must be opened, and the stinking and rotten dead men's bones must be revealed. A situation must be provided in which the sinner must himself confess that he hates without a cause, that is, that his hatred has no other cause than his own enmity against God, and that, therefore, he stands hopelessly and utterly condemned before the tribunal of God. And this situation is created when the Son of God Himself becomes the neighbor of men, and tabernacles among us in the likeness of sinful flesh. The Son of God becomes the Son of man! God becomes man's neighbor! He lives with them, He walks among them and speaks to them in their own language, He enters their homes and walks on their streets, He eats and drinks with them, and sits at their feasts, He attends their weddings and their funerals, He enters their sickrooms and stands at their deathbeds, He sings and weeps with them: He is the Son of man, The Neighbor of all!

Here, then, men have their opportunity to prove that they

do not hate unless their hatred of the neighbor has a cause, is justified. For Christ, the Son of God in the likeness of sinful flesh, the Son of man, is the perfect neighbor. He does not at all fall under the condemnation of the passage from the third chapter of the Romans we just quoted. He came to us from without, even though He is flesh of our flesh and blood of our blood. For, though He is born of a woman, He is conceived of the Holy Ghost, without the will of man. The Person of the Son of God in human flesh is without sin, separate from sinners, though He became their neighbor, holy and undefiled. He is the perfect Neighbor! Surely, in Him men looked in vain for a cause of their hatred. No sin was found in Him, no guile was found in His mouth. Surely, if man's hatred of the neighbor is always, or usually, provoked by a justifying cause in the neighbor, they will not, they cannot hate this Son of Man. If they hate Him, they will expose themselves as liars, and as enemies of God. Yet, so it was. For this Son of man Himself complains, pleading His cause before the face of God: "They hated me without a cause."

It was in the night in which our Saviour was betrayed, the very eve of the hour when the hellish fury of this hatred without a cause would seek to spend itself by condemning Him to death, and nailing Him to the accursed tree. Either He was still in the upper room in Jerusalem where He had eaten the last passover with His disciples, or they were already on the way to Gethsemane. And these last moments of His earthly sojourn He rendered valuable by comforting and instructing His disciples, and by praying for them. He warns them that the world will hate them, and persecute them, at the same time explaining that this hatred against them will really be directed against Him. For, thus He addresses them: "All these things will they do unto you for my name's sake, because they know not him that sent me. If I had not come and spoken unto them, they had not had sin, but now they have no cloke for their sin. He that hateth me, hateth my Father also. If I had not done among them the works which none other man did, they had not had sin: but now they have both seen and hated both me and my Father. But this cometh to pass, that the word might be fulfilled that is written in their law, They hated me without a cause." John 15:21-25.

We must not overlook the fact that the Saviour is here quoting from the Old Testament, which He designates by the words "their law." The words occur literally in the Psalms. In Psalm 35:19 we read: "Let not them that are mine enemies wrongfully rejoice over me: neither let them wink with the eye that hate me without a cause." But the reference is, perhaps, especially to that eminently Messianic sixty-ninth Psalm, in the fourth verse of which we read: "They that hate me without a cause are more than the hairs of mine head."

If the Ethiopian eunuch had read these words, he, no doubt, would have asked the same question that arose in his mind as he was pondering the words of Isaiah 53: "Of whom speaketh the prophet this? of himself, or of some other man?" For it is evident that the psalmist also, and even in the first place, speaks of himself. He speaks in the first person. He complains before the face of God of his own suffering. He is one whose enemies are more than the hairs of his head, hate him without a cause, and seek his destruction. Nay, more, we know that the Holy Spirit inspired the psalmist to compose this song, not merely for himself, but for the Old Testament Church, in order that they, too, might take it on their lips, make it their own, and complain of their own suffering, and of their enemies that hated them without a cause. All this was centuries before the coming of Christ. Yet, hundreds of years later, the Saviour declares that these words have reference to Him, and that they have their fulfillment in Him.

What does it mean? And how is this possible? There is only one answer to this question: it is Christ Himself Who is the central subject also in the thirty-fifth and sixty-ninth Psalms, and in all the Law and the Prophets of the old dispensation. It was He Who was in all the godly of the old dispensation, and Who became manifest in them, in their word and walk in the midst of the world. He was in the prophets, priests and kings of Israel, and in all the saints, the whole Church represented by them, and in all the old dispensational people of God, even from the beginning of the world. And as He became manifest in them, He was always hated without a cause. The Lamb is slain from the foundation of the world. And only in as far as Christ was in them, and became revealed in their word and conversation, in their whole life and walk in the midst of an ungodly world, could they complain with the psalmist of Psalm 69: "They that hate me without a cause are more than the hairs of mine head." They were hated thus, but only as the representatives of Christ. They suffered and were persecuted, but only because Christ was in them. They were constantly encompassed by enemies that aimed at their destruction, but only because they were made to stand for the cause of the Son of God in the midst of the world. In His people, Christ was hated from the beginning of the world, and all through the centuries of the old dispensation, until this hatred without a cause was finally completely fulfilled in the fulness of time, when the Son of God Himself walked among us in the likeness of sinful flesh.

Of this suffering of Christ in His saints, of this hatred without a cause, testifies the blood of all the righteous. It is of this hatred that Abel, being dead, yet speaketh, for he offered up a better sacrifice than Cain, thereby testifying of the Christ, and he was killed because he was righteous and his brother wicked. Of this hatred knew Enoch, who witnessed against the ungodly world of his day, and had the testimony that he pleased God; whom they sought to kill, but could not find him, because God had translated him. And all the prediluvian Church was acquainted with the fury of this hatred, and would, humanly speaking, have been destroyed, had not God saved them by the waters of the flood. This hatred without a cause was directed against the people of Israel in the house of bondage in Egypt, when Moses chose rather to suffer affliction with the people of God than to be called the son of Pharaoh's daughter, and to enjoy the pleasures of sin for a season, esteeming the reproach of Christ greater riches than the treasures of Egypt. And all through their history, the people of Israel, in the desert, in their own land of Canaan, in Babylon, and after their return, were the object of this senseless and furious hatred. Still more. Even within the nation of Israel this hatred was revealed, and expressed more furiously and wickedly than anywhere else. For always the carnal seed hated and persecuted the spiritual seed. They killed the prophets, and stoned them that were sent unto them by God. And so, some "had trial of cruel mockings and scourgings, yea, moreover, of bonds and imprisonment: they were stoned, they were sawn asunder, were tempted, were slain with the sword: they wandered about in sheepskins and goatskins; being destitute, afflicted, tormented; (of whom the world was not worthy) they wandered in deserts and in mountains, and in dens and caves of the earth." Heb. 11:36-38. No wonder they could sing with the psalmist: "Save me, O God, for the waters are come in unto my soul. I sink in deep mire, where there is no standing: I am come into deep waters, where the floods overflow me. I am weary of my crying: my throat is dried: mine eyes fail, while I wait for my God. They that hate me without a cause are more than the hairs of mine head: they that would destroy me, being mine enemies wrongfully, are mighty . . . Because for thy sake I have borne reproach; shame hath covered my face." "For thy sake!" Indeed, this hatred without a cause was directed against the Christ in them, and manifest through them!

And yet, this word was not *fulfilled* in them. For, first of all, in their case the enemies might still find an excuse, a cause that would seem to justify their cruel hatred. Even though they stood for the cause of Christ, and suffered for His sake, they were not perfect. The enemy might easily find and point to iniquity in them, and claim that they were worthy of destruction. How easy it would be for the enemy of Christ to discover an excuse for his hatred against a man like David, the singer of Israel, the very one that complains of his being hated without a cause in Psalm 69! Was he not an adulterer and a murderer, and did not the whole nation suffer for his pride? No, it could not become fully manifested in them, that they were hated without a cause. And besides, their suffering did not fill the measure. Not always did they suffer. Occasionally, they even occupied positions of power and honor. They were not uniformly hated. The word, therefore, that was written in their law awaited its fulfillment.

And fulfilled it was in Christ!

Completely without a cause was He hated. Never could the enemy find a cause for hatred in Him, a cause that would justify, or even appear to justify his hatred before the tribunal of God. He was the Son of God in human flesh. He was the perfect revelation of the Father. Always He represented the cause of God. Always He witnessed of Him. Never was sin found in His

person. He could stand in the midst of His enemies, and challenge
them: "which of you can convict me of sin?" So sinless, so undefiled, so perfect was He, that, although they were ever seeking
occasions to kill Him, they could never find a reason. So spotlessly pure was He, that even when they had taken Him prisoner,
and tried Him in their courts, all their attempts to find testimony
against Him utterly failed, and the Roman governor was forced
to admit repeatedly that he found no cause of death in Him at all.
Always He did well. Nor did He ever occupy or seek to occupy a
position of power and glory in the world, that might offer an
occasion of malice and envy to the opponents. He was the lowliest
among the lowly. He had no place where to lay His head!

Yet, how they hated Him! No man was ever hated as He!
His enemies were, indeed, more than the hairs of His head.
Constantly they sought to destroy Him. And when they finally
seemed to succeed in their evil plans, their fury knew no bounds.
It seemed as if their hatred could not be satiated. They mocked
Him, maltreated Him in every possible way, demanded the most
shameful and cruel death thinkable for Him, and even when they
had nailed Him to the accursed tree, they continued to fill Him
with reproach!

Without a cause? Is there then no answer to the question: why
did they hate Him so furiously? O, yes! Listen, He Himself gives
the answer: "He that hateth me, hateth my Father also." And
again: "But now have they both seen and hated both me and
my Father." John 15: 23, 24. That all our hatred is revealed as
hatred of God — that is the meaning of the cross.

But who are these enemies that so cruelly and wickedly hate
Him? The text simply says: "They." But is this not too indefinite?
Must one who makes so serious a charge, and that, too, before the
face of God, not mention his enemies by name? In this case that
is superfluous. "They" is quite sufficient. It means *men, just men,*
men of all classes and positions, *all men* without exception. That
cross means that you and I hated Him without a cause, and that
we are enemies of God, that would destroy God Himself if
we could!

What then? Shall we approach that cross to pity the crucified
One, and to shed a self-righteous, pious tear? God forbid! But

the only proper, the only possible thing to do is to prostrate ourselves before the cross, under the mighty hand of God's judgment, and confess unconditionally and without reservation that we hated both Him and His Father!

But are we not absolutely lost, and do we not sign our own condemnation, if we do so? Must this, then, be our last word? Thanks be to God, no! For, listen! If by the grace of God you thus sign your own condemnation, God will surely justify you! For that Son of man, Whom you crucified, made of that cross God's altar, and in unfathomable love, He bore the guilt of your hatred, and bore it away for ever! And, therefore, at that cross you may also cry out: "God, be merciful to me, a sinner!" and return to your house, cleansed from sin, and justified for ever!

CHAPTER 3

A Stranger Unto His Brethren

*I am become a stranger unto my brethren, and
an alien unto my mother's children.* — Ps. 69:8.

When the author of the sixty-ninth psalm complains that he
is become a stranger unto his brethren, he refers to a profound
difference between these and himself, of a deep chasm that
separates from him those that should be united with him in the
bonds of natural love. And this alienation of himself from his
own kin is a cause of much grief and deep suffering on the part
of the poet.

To be a stranger *among strangers* is not so serious, and need
not be a matter of distress, or a cause of misery. A traveler may,
for a time, sojourn in a foreign land. He is a stranger in the land
of his sojourn. There are natural differences between him and the
inhabitants of that land. He does not belong to them. He differs
from them in appearance, in dress, in personal habits. He speaks
a different language. His citizenship is not in that land. He has
no home there. He merely sojourns among them for a time, in
order then to return to his own country. But his being a stranger
in that land is not a cause of distress and grief to him. It is true,
he is marked as a stranger. Perhaps, he may occasionally feel lone-
some, and a longing for his homeland may steal into his soul.
But for the rest he does not suffer any inconvenience. He is

known as a stranger, and accepted as such. Perhaps, he is received and treated with extraordinary deference, kindness, and hospitality. The inhabitants of the strange land put forth special efforts to make him feel at home, and are eager to make a good impression on this stranger among them. Must one not be hospitable to strangers? And is it not true that people that are rude to their own kin often put themselves out to be polite and kind to strangers, especially if these be men of some standing, and to make a favorable impression on them?

However, to be stranger *to men,* and particularly, to be a stranger to one's *brethren,* is something quite different, speaks of a far more serious and profound alienation. It is not natural, but spiritual. It refers to a chasm which even the most intimate ties of natural love and blood relationship cannot bridge. If one is a stranger *unto* men, as the psalmist complains that he is, he dwells among his own kin. From a natural viewpoint he is like them. There is every possible affinity and kinship between them and himself. He is flesh of their flesh, and blood of their blood. He is their fellow-citizen. He speaks the same language as they, has his home among them, comes into daily contact with them, is met on their streets, in their public places, in their shops and factories. He buys and sells among them, he eats and drinks with them. From a natural viewpoint, he lives the same life as they. And he is well known to them. They know his father and his mother, and remember where and when he was born, and how he grew up among them. And if he is a stranger, not merely to *men,* but to his *brethren,* the natural affinity is as close as possible. The same blood is coursing in their veins. They were brought up from earliest infancy in the same home, sucked the same breasts, ate at the same table, slept in the same bed, had the same education, and should, according to every natural law of kinship be thorough acquaintances and close companions of one another.

And yet, he is a stranger to them!

There is a profound difference between them and himself, a spiritual difference so deep and radical, that even the closest blood relationship is not capable of overcoming it. Those that ought to know him do not understand him. They that should be his companions according to every natural law, separate them-

selves from him. His walk and conversation is different from
theirs, and they cannot explain them. He does not seem to fit
in their world of thought. He is motivated by different principles,
he strives after different ideals, he walks in a different direction.
He is out of step with the world. He cannot accommodate himself to the ways of his fellowmen. Though, from a natural viewpoint, he is like his fellows, from a spiritual point of view he is
totally different. He is a stranger, not *among* men, but *to* men.
They know him well in a natural sense, but spiritually he is an
alien to them. They misunderstand and misinterpret him. He is
a stranger to his brethren!

And this spiritual alienation from one's fellowmen, from one's
own kin, is a cause of suffering. For what man is there in
whose heart there is no need of fellowship? Who does not yearn
for association and companionship with his fellowmen? Who does
not long to be congenial with them, to live in agreement with
them. Who does not feel a deep need of the love of those that
are his kith and kin according to the flesh? And who does not
suffer when those that should be his intimate companions treat
him as an alien, misinterpret his actions, ascribe evil motives to
him, consider him odd, a fool, a misfit in society, separate themselves from him, cast him out of their fellowship, and heap upon
him reproach and shame?

Such a stranger among His brethren according to the flesh is
the Christ!

For there can be no doubt that also in the eighth verse of the
sixty-ninth psalm it is Christ that is speaking of His relation to
men, and of His suffering among them and from them. Indeed,
as we said before, the subject that is speaking here is also
the poet himself, and he is complaining of his own estrangement
from his brethren. Moreover, the psalm was sung by the Old
Testament people of God, and is still sung by the Church of the
new dispensation. Throughout the ages of history, God's people
are strangers in the earth, and they can, indeed, take these words
of the sixty-ninth psalm on their own lips: "I am become a
stranger to my brethren, and an alien unto my mother's children."
Abel was a stranger to Cain when he offered the better sacrifice
and was accepted. Enoch was an alien to his fellowmen, when

he witnessed against the ungodliness of his age, and prophesied of
the coming of the Lord to judge. Noah had brothers and sisters,
children of his mother, but he was a stranger and fool to them
when he became a preacher of righteousness, and built the ark,
for he alone of them all was saved. Abraham became a stranger
in the earth when he obeyed the Word of God, and sought the
city that hath foundations, whose builder and maker is God.
And so one might go on, and pass in review the lives of all the
saints of the old dispensation, of Jacob in relation to Esau, of
Joseph and his brethren, of Moses in Egypt and in the desert, of
Gideon, and Jephthah, and Samson, of David and his father's
sons, of all the prophets that were despised, and tortured, and
stoned to death. And are not the people of God in the new
dispensation strangers in the earth? Is it not true that, the more
they reveal themselves as children of God, and stand for the
cause of the Son of God in the midst of the world, the more
they must stand alone, and become strangers unto their fellowmen and their brethren according to the flesh? And did not the
Saviour say that "the brother shall deliver up the brother to death,
and the father the child: and the children shall rise up against
their parents, and cause them to be put to death"? Matt. 10:21.
And again: "He that loveth father or mother more than me is
not worthy of me: and he that loveth son or daughter more than
me is not worthy of me." Matt. 10:37. Indeed, the words of the
sixty-ninth psalm have a general application, and refer to all the
saints in the world. They are strangers unto their brethren.

And yet, this is true only because, and in as far as Christ is in
them, and becomes manifest in them. The real speaker in the psalm
is Christ. In Him these words are fulfilled.

First of all, these words may be applied to Him in their most
literal, historical sense: in the days of His flesh He was a stranger
to His nearest kin, to His mother, to His brothers and sisters.
There are those who insist that Christ had no real brothers and
sisters according to the flesh. When these terms are used in relation to Jesus, they have a wider meaning, and refer to more distant relatives, according to them. They consider that it was but
proper that Mary should remain a virgin, and bear no other
children than the Son of man. But we can not agree with this.

Christ was not an only child, but the firstborn of Mary, even as
He is firstborn among many brethren. Besides, Scripture definitely
speaks of His brothers and sisters, speaks of them in the same
breath with His father and mother, and mentions His brothers
by name. "Is not this the carpenter's son? is not his mother called
Mary? and his brethren, James, and Joses, and Simon, and Judas?
And his sisters, are they not all with us?" Matt. 13:55, 56. And
the idea itself that He should have been an only son is not
Scriptural at all, nor does it appeal to us. Scripture much rather
emphasizes that He became like unto us in all things, which implies that He entered into every possible human relationship, and
lived our whole life. He was a son in relation to His parents, a
brother in relation to His brothers and sisters.

But He was a stranger to them. He grew up in their midst,
in the home of Joseph and Mary in Nazareth. Daily they must
have had contact with Him. They became acquainted with Him.
And even then He must have impressed them as being principally
different from them in a spiritual sense, though in all other respects He was like unto them. How could it be otherwise? Was
He not the Son of God in the flesh, and even in His human nature
without sin? Never did He commit an act of disobedience to His
parents, never did He perform a sinful act, never did an idle
word leave His lips. He was perfect in all His ways. How painfully different and strange He must have been, even as a child,
to His brothers and sisters!

And this was emphasized and accentuated when He entered
upon His public ministry. No doubt, their mother had informed
His brothers and sisters about His wonderful birth, and about the
marvelous things that were spoken of Him by the angel. He was
the expected Messiah! Yet, even in the light of this knowledge,
they could not explain Him. He was radically different from any
conception of the Messiah they had formed, and wholly different
from what they wanted Him to be. They, no doubt, expected
Him to rise to earthly glory, and would fain share in His glory.
But soon after He began His public ministry, it became evident
to them that in this they were to be disappointed. He did not seek
earthly glory. He did not aspire to an exalted position. On the
contrary, by His severe preaching He soon antagonized the men

of power and influence, the chief priests, and scribes, and Pharisees. His brethren wanted Him to go to Jerusalem, and to perform His wonderful works, and reveal His mighty power to the leaders of the nation, in order that they might acclaim Him as the expected King of Israel. They said to Him: "There is no man that doeth anything in secret, and he himself seeketh to be known openly. If thou do these things, shew thyself to the world." John 7:4. For even then it was already true that "neither did his brethren believe in him." Even His own mother did not understand Him. At the wedding feast of Cana, she wanted Him to show His power, and reveal Himself as the Messiah, for her hour was always there. When by His teaching He antagonized the leaders of the nation, His friends considered that He was mad, and they tried to lead Him away by main force. Mark 3:21. And for the same reason and purpose, His mother and brethren came on the scene, sending messages to Him, and calling Him, that they might take Him with them. Mark 3:31ff. They sought His earthly exaltation. They would have Him be popular with the great and influential of the nation. And now everything went wrong. He was ruining His own reputation. He was fast working out His own destruction. He traveled the way of death! He was a stranger unto His brethren!

But, of course, the text of the sixty-ninth psalm has a wider application. It means that He was a stranger to men. Emphatically it means: "Even to my own brethren, those that are nearest to me of kin, those that should know me, and love me, I am become a stranger! How much more am I a stranger to all men! If my own father and mother, and brothers, and sisters, do not understand me, how can it be expected that I am anything but an alien to men in general?" And so it proved to be, indeed, in the days of His flesh. The more He spoke, and worked, and revealed who and what He was, and what He came to do, the wider and deeper the chasm yawned that separated Him from the men of His day. On the one side of this chasm He stood more and more alone, a stranger to, and forsaken by men; on the other side stood men of all classes and stations in life, revealing their alienation from Him in various ways. When He sought to save that which was lost, they called Him a companion of sinners; when He came

eating and drinking, they said that He was glutton and a winebibber; when He cast out devils, they attributed His power to
Beelzebub; when He did well on the sabbath, they called Him
profane; when He taught the people, they said that He was a
deceiver; when He claimed to be the Son of God, they accused
Him of blasphemy. Others were offended in Him, and forsook
Him. And finally He stood completely forsaken, wholly alone, a
stranger to all, so that when His enemies took hold of Him, to
condemn Him to death, He had no one to support Him, and to
defend His cause. He had become a complete stranger to all.

Let us not fail to grasp the import of this, and to understand
what the Word of God has to say to us here. For it concerns us
very deeply. We must beware, lest we contemplate this alienage
of the Christ of God from the heights of our modern religiousness, in order then to flatter ourselves that in our modern world
and to our modern men He is no longer a stranger. There is a
Word of God here. And the Word of God in this case is that
Christ is always a stranger to all men, to men as they are in this
world, mere, natural men, no matter whether they be Jew or
Gentile, rich or poor, civilized or outside of the pale of our
civilization. He is a stranger to you and to me as we are by nature,
apart from grace. Nor must we fail to understand the true character of this alienation. It is spiritual. The situation was not such
in the days of His flesh, that men did not understand Him in
the natural sense, and that they completely failed to grasp His
teaching, and the purpose of His coming, as far as their natural
understanding was concerned. But the more they understood, the
more they became alienated from Him. The reason is, as He
Himself expressed it in the sixty-ninth psalm: "For the zeal of
thine house hath eaten me up." He came in behalf of God's house,
God's eternal covenant. He came to represent the cause of God
in the world, and to establish God's Kingdom in the way of God's
righteousness, which for Him was the way of self-humiliation and
death, even the death of the cross. But they were carnal, and
minded carnal things. And thus it is always. He is heavenly, we
are earthly; He is spiritual, we are carnal; He represents the
cause of God, we are enemies of God; He seeks God's righteousness, we seek our own righteousness; He came to reveal the

light of life, we love the darkness rather than the light. He is a stranger to His brethren, to all men, always and everywhere, to you and to me, because He is the perfect revelation of God, and God, the living God, is a stranger to us! That is our condemnation. Let us confess it!

Nor is this the last word. For He came to make us, who are by nature alienated from Him, His brethren! He died as a stranger to the world, but of His death He made a perfect sacrifice, blotting out the guilt of our sin, that He might bring us to God. And God justified Him, raised Him from the dead, glorified Him at His right hand, and made Him the quickening Spirit. And by the power of His grace He quickens us, enlightens us, calls us out of darkness into the light, and makes us His brethren in the spiritual sense of the word. And thus we know Him, saved by grace, and when He declares the name of God unto His brethren in the midst of the church, we join Him in singing the praise of Him Who loved us, and washed us in the blood of His Son. The Stranger to all is the Firstborn among many brethren in the congregation of the redeemed!

CHAPTER 4

Reproached by the Ungodly

The reproaches of them that reproached thee are fallen upon me. — Ps. 69:10.

As long as we contemplate the suffering of our Lord Jesus Christ as innocent bystanders, deeply interested, perhaps, in that awful spectacle, and even sympathetic, we cannot hear the Word of God that comes to us through that suffering. Then we fail to see in that sufferer the Son of God. All we see is a man in deep distress, the innocent victim of His enemies, a man, perhaps, that had the misfortune of being far in advance of His age, and who was, therefore, misunderstood, rejected, hated without a cause, a stranger to His own kin, and filled with reproach and shame. We feel, no doubt, that we would have taken His part against His enemies, and would have pleaded His cause. We are filled with indignation at those wicked and miserable Jews that hated and constantly persecuted Him, sought occasion against Him, and finally nailed Him to the cross. In that case, the spectacle of the Man of Sorrows, of the passion and death of Jesus Christ has an effect upon us which is precisely opposite to that designed by the Word of God: in our blindness we exalt ourselves above the enemies of Christ, we are hardened in our self-righteousness, and fail to repent and to humble ourselves under the mighty hand of God.

227

We must, therefore, understand that the passion of Jesus Christ is not the suffering of a mere man among men, in regard to which you and I are free to determine our position, to take sides. It is the suffering of the Son of God in the flesh, a suffering which, in as far as it was inflicted upon Him by men, was motivated by hatred against God. Therefore this suffering is wholly unique. There never was, there never will be a sorrow like unto His sorrow. And He stands entirely alone in His suffering. No mere man ever takes it up for Him, or pleads His cause. All men are always against Him, unless the power of grace changes their hearts and opens their eyes to see. For "all we like sheep have gone astray; we have turned every one to his own way." Isa. 53:5. And "there is none righteous, no not one: there is none that understandeth, there is none that seeketh after God . . . For all have sinned, and come short of the glory of God." Rom. 3:10, 11, 23. In order, then, fruitfully to contemplate the passion and death of our Lord we must not look down from the heights of our self-willed religiousness upon the men that caused Him to suffer, but understand that by nature our place is among His enemies. That is our real position. Nor must we flatter ourselves that it is in our power to change that position, for then we would deceive ourselves. Only the sovereign mercy of God can bring about such a radical change. We rejected Him, we hated Him without a cause, we are estranged from Him. And we reproached Him with the reproaches of them that reproach the living God. In all that men did to Jesus is clearly reflected the corruption of our own nature.

Once again we take our theme from that eminently Messianic sixty-ninth Psalm. In verses nine to twelve we hear the Christ complain before the face of God: "For the zeal of thine house hath eaten me up; and the reproaches of them that reproached thee are fallen upon me. When I wept, and chastened my soul with fasting, that was to my reproach. I made sackcloth also my garment; and I became a proverb to them. They that sit in the gate speak against me; and I was the song of the drunkards." Nor can there be any doubt that it is the Christ that is the real subject of this complaint, for the apostle Paul refers to this passage in Romans 15:3: "For even Christ pleased not himself, but as it is written, The reproaches of them that reproached thee fell on me."

Let us analyze this passage for a moment, and consider its different elements in their proper relation to one another, in order then to consider how they are fulfilled in Christ.

First of all, we notice that the poet speaks of his zeal for the house of God as the deepest cause of all his suffering, and of the reproach that is heaped upon him. The house of God is the sanctuary of Jehovah and all it represents: God's covenant and kingdom, the fellowship of His friendship, the glory of Him that sits enthroned between the cherubim, His cause, His righteousness and holiness, His people and their redemption through the blood that was sprinkled upon the horns of the altar, and upon the mercy seat in the inner sanctuary. For this house of God he is zealous. So overpowering is this zeal that it is like a fire in his bones that consumes him.

Secondly, it is evident that the poet beholds that house of God in a deplorable state. The sanctuary is defiled. The altar is profaned. The dwelling place of God has become a den of thieves. And because of this deplorable condition of Jehovah's sanctuary the psalmist suffers. He weeps his soul out. He goes in sackcloth and ashes. He chastens his soul with fasting. The zeal of the house of God in its deplorable state causes him to suffer.

And, finally, in this suffering and evident sorrow and distress because of God's cause he becomes the object of hatred and is filled with reproach and ignominy. For he dwells in the midst of the enemies of the house of God. They are not at all concerned about Jehovah's sanctuary. In fact, they are the cause of its being defiled. Hence, they hate him. And the more he reveals his zeal for God's cause, and his distress because of the defilement of the house of God, the more they express their hatred. They heap reproach upon his head. They make him a byword, a proverb, an example of whatever is worthless. In the assembly of the drunkards he is the theme of their song. And those that sit in the gate, the judges of his people, speak against him as if he were an evil doer. And he complains to God about his distress. For he realizes that in him they mean to revile the living God. The reproaches of God's enemies are fallen upon him.

Now, all this was true of the author of this psalm. He speaks of his own experience. And, what is more, it may be applied to all the prophets of Israel, and, in fact, to all the saints. But it is applicable to them only because Christ is in them, and becomes revealed through them; and, besides, only in a limited sense. But in Christ the words of the psalmist are completely realized. He bore the reproach of men as no other man did. And never did He bear any other reproach than that which was directed against the living God.

Of Him alone it is literally true that the zeal of God's house consumed Him. The disciples were reminded of this when they witnessed His first cleansing of the temple, when He drove out those that made His Father's house a den of robbers. John 2:17. Yet, this act was performed only in the earthly sanctuary, and was typical of what He had come to do. For He came to build the real temple of God, to establish the eternal covenant of God with His people. That covenant of friendship had once been established in Paradise with the first Adam. But man had violated the covenant by rejecting the Word of God and heeding the lie of the devil. He had defiled the house of God. However, God would give His glory to no other. He maintained His covenant, and, according to His eternal good pleasure, purposed not only to restore His house and to cleanse it from all the pollution of sin, but also to raise it through the deep way of sin and death and grace to the higher level of heavenly perfection and glory. Unto that end He had from all eternity ordained His only begotten Son to be the Head over the whole house of God, in order that He might destroy the works of the devil, and build the eternal house of God's covenant. For this purpose He came into the world. Another purpose for His coming there was not. In that one purpose, to establish God's everlasting tabernacle with men, His whole existence and life were bound up. Other interests He had none. Only the zeal for God's house motivated Him. He represented God's cause, God's glory, the honor of God's name, God's righteousness and holiness and justice. And He came to destroy the defiled temple of Man, and to build the temple of God in all its heavenly glory. And that house of God was to be realized in His people, those whom the Father had given Him from before the foundation of the world.

And because of this zeal for God's house, He became the Man of Sorrows. For only on the basis of righteousness, of God's righteousness, and in the way of His justice could God's house be founded and built. And we had sinned, and had become worthy of death and damnation. We were children of wrath. No right we had to dwell in God's fellowship. If His house were to be rebuilt and perfected in those whom the Father had given Christ in His eternal good pleasure, the guilt of their sin must be blotted out, and they must be clothed with an everlasting righteousness. And this required the sacrifice of perfect obedience even unto death. This sacrifice we could never bring. We could only defile and destroy the house of God: never could we cleanse it and rebuild it. But Christ came to satisfy the justice of God, to take all the sins of His own upon Himself, and in their stead to stand in the place of judgment, bear all the wrath of God, bring the perfect sacrifice in tasting all the horrors of death, and thus to lay the foundations of the house of God in His own precious blood.

Hence, He was the Man of Sorrows. He came to suffer, and to die. The zeal of God's house caused Him to make sackcloth His garment, for He came in the likeness of sinful flesh, and He partook of the flesh and blood of the children. And in that likeness of sinful flesh He fasted and wept, He "offered up prayers and supplications with strong crying and tears unto him that was able to save Him from death." Heb. 5:7. His soul became exceedingly sorrowful even unto death, so that His sweat became at is were great drops of blood. He was troubled in soul and spirit, until the amazing cry was wrung from His breast: "My God, my God, why hast thou forsaken me?"

And because of all this He was filled with reproach!

Reproach is itself a keen form of suffering, and a cause of more suffering. One that heaps reproach upon you hates you, and expresses his hatred by attacking your good name, usually by making it an object of contempt and scorn. Every man has a name, a reputation with his fellowmen. By that name he is known from different aspects and in different capacities and relationships, as a father in relation to his family, a workman in the shop, a teacher in the school, a citizen among his fellow-citizens, a member of the church. His name denotes what he is, how he is known among men, from the viewpoint of his ability and moral character. To attack one's name, therefore, is to attack his person, his honor, his very place in the world. And to heap reproach on one is to besmear his name, to make him of ill repute among men, to present him as a worthless fellow, an object of contempt, one that is unworthy to have a place in decent society. And the result is, if the attack is successful, that the victim becomes an outcast, who meets with scorn and disdain everywhere, and cannot find a place in the world.

Literally, this was done to Christ. He, too, had a name. And His name was ordained and given Him of God. He was Jesus, that would save His people from their sins; The Lamb of God that taketh away the sin of the world, the Son of God, the Christ, the promised Messiah that would reign over the house of Jacob for ever, and that would restore and build the temple of God. That was His name. And that name He revealed in His public ministry. For He taught the people. And by the very contents and character of His instruction, as well as by direct declarations, He made Himself known as the prophet that was to come, as the Messiah, the anointed of God, that was sent of the Father into the world to establish the kingdom of heaven, and to realize the everlasting tabernacle of God with men. And He corroborated His teaching, and sustained His claim by His mighty works. For He went throughout the land doing good: He opened the eyes of the blind, the ears of the deaf; He made the lame to walk, He cleansed the lepers, and He raised the dead! And He made it very plain that He came to destroy the power of darkness, and to maintain the cause of the righteousness of God in the way of suffering and death.

And men attacked His name. They destroyed His reputation among men. They called Him a sinner, a liar, a deceiver, a friend of publicans and sinners, a subject of Beelzebub, a blasphemer, a revolutionary. They heaped scorn and derision upon Him. And the astonishing feature of this reproach is that the more He suffered, the more vehement became their attacks upon His name, the more furious they became in their contempt and scorn and bitter hatred. Even when He was in their power they mocked Him, blindfolded Him, spit their contempt upon Him, put Him to nought by means of a purple mock-robe, a cruel crown of thorns, a reed-sceptre, and mock obeisance. Yea, even when He was nailed to the cross, and at the time when even the lowest and vilest criminal would have been an object of commiseration, their fury knew no bounds. Still they heaped their reproach upon Him, challenged Him to come down from the cross and with satanic hatred suggested that even God had forsaken Him!

Was ever man reproached as He? Indeed, He became a by-word and a proverb. His name was the theme of the song of drunken revelers. And those that sat in the gate spoke against Him. No man ventured to defend His name. So reviled He was that even His foremost disciple publicly disavowed any connection with Him!

And what was the reason? Why did they so furiously rage against His name, and heap scorn and contempt upon it? Principally, and in its deepest sense, because they meant to reproach the name of God! For thus He complains: "the reproaches of them that reproach thee are fallen upon me." He represented the cause of God; they stood for the cause of man against God. He defended the honor of God; they sought the honor of men. He maintained the righteousness and justice of God; they exalted themselves in self-righteousness against the living God. He came to destroy the temple of man which they loved; He came to build the house of God, which they hated and defiled. In their reproach of Christ they revealed themselves as utterly profane, as hating and despising the holy things of God and His covenant! Because the zeal of God's house consumed Him they filled Him with contempt! In Him they reproached the living God! That is the condemnation of the world!

And that is our condemnation! For by nature, as mere men, apart from grace, we belong with that profane, scorning, contemptuous, God-reviling world that heaped reproach on Christ. Let us not shed a religious, self-righteous tear of sympathy at the cross of Christ: let us rather confess that we heaped that reproach upon His head. Let us not weep over Him, let us rather weep over ourselves and over our children. Let us not condemn those wicked Jews that so despised their Messiah; let us rather sign our own condemnation before the terrible tribunal of God. Let us, as we contemplate His reproach, not put on a mask of righteous indignation; let us rather mirror ourselves in it to discover what foul profanities there are lurking in the depth of our sinful nature.

Then there is hope. Otherwise we must needs be damned with that God-reproaching world.

Then there is a way out. Not, mark you, because we have the power to change ourselves, or the will to abandon our profane, God-reviling attitude, for we are slaves of sin. But then there is hope, first of all, because He bore the sin of our reproach upon that very tree to which we finally spiked Him; because He brought the perfect sacrifice that blotted out the guilt of our iniquity, and obtained for His own the perfect righteousness. And, secondly, because He was raised from the dead, and became the quickening Spirit, and has the power to deliver us from our profanity, and so to change us, that instead of heaping reproach upon the name of God, we prostrate ourselves before Him in humble adoration, with the prayer on our lips: Hallowed be Thy name! Such is the marvel of His wondrous grace!

CHAPTER 5

Contradicted by Sinners

For consider him that endured such contradiction
of sinners against himself, lest ye be wearied and faint
in your minds. — HEB. 12:3.

In the third verse of the twelfth chapter of the epistle to the
Hebrews the Word of God exhorts us to consider Jesus as the
One that was greatly contradicted by sinners. And the practical
purpose of this exhortation is that by this consideration we may
receive the strength of patience, and be encouraged to stand and
to continue our way as children of God in the world, when otherwise we should be inclined to grow weary and faint in the battle.
For, laying aside every encumbrance, and the sin which doth so
easily beset us, we must run the race that is set before us *with*
patience. And patience is the strength to endure hardship and suffering for Christ's sake. For if Christ be in us, and we have become new creatures in Him, and we walk no longer in darkness,
but in the light of life, we must expect opposition. They hated
Him, they will also hate us. The more faithful we are, and the
more we hold fast to our profession of His name, not only in word
but also in all our walk and conversation, the more this opposition
of the world will reveal itself. The world, carnal men, will contradict us. And if, then, we should grow wearied and faint in our
minds, discouraged, and inclined to hang the harp in the willows,

and to give up the battle, it is time we look upon the Author and Finisher of our faith. It is true, there is also a cloud of witnesses: the saints that have gone before us, that lived and battled and died by faith. They, too, endured the contradiction of all the world. But at the head of them all stands Jesus. He was contradicted more than any other. If, therefore, we are contradicted for His name's sake, we may gather courage, considering, first of all, that exactly in our being contradicted by the world we are in good company; and, secondly, that even as He endured unto glory and victory, so by His grace we may also endure. Let us, therefore, consider Him that endureth such contradiction of sinners against Himself.

And as we consider Him thus, in humble obedience to the Word of God, several questions arise in our soul, and demand an answer. What was it they contradicted in Jesus? How, and to what extent, did they contradict Him? What was the reason and the character of their contradiction? And who were they that so opposed Him? How did our Lord endure this contradiction against Himself? And what is the significance of it all for men as sinners, and for the people of God in the midst of the world?

To contradict is to speak against, to gainsay, to deny the truth of someone's testimony, and to declare the very opposite. And in the text we quoted the Word of God declares that, when God sent His Son into the world, sinners opened their mouth against Him in fierce contradiction. And this contradiction of sinners was part of His suffering, which He patiently endured unto the end.

But just what was the point of their contradiction? Was it a certain point of the doctrine which He taught that was opposed and gainsaid? Was this contradiction a matter of theological dispute, some question of the law, or of the prophets? Did they, perhaps, oppose some claim He made? Or did they impugn some of the works He performed? The answer is: He endured contradiction of sinners *against Himself!* In His case, the contradiction did not concern some particular point of doctrine or life: it was directed against Himself, His person, and therefore against His whole appearance. He is the contradicted One! This had become manifest in the attitude rebellious Israel, who would not hear the law of the Lord, had assumed over against all the prophets, when they said unto them: "See not . . . prophesy not unto us right things, speak unto us smooth things, prophesy deceits: Get you out of the way, turn aside out of the path, cause the Holy One of Israel to cease from before us." Isa. 30:10, 11. And this had been predicted of Him by the gray haired Simeon when, holding the child Jesus in his arms, he prophesied: "Behold, this child is set for a fall and rising again of many in Israel, and for a sign that shall be spoken against." Lu. 2:34 .Thus it was fulfilled during His earthly sojourn, in the days of His flesh. And thus it still is: always it is the Christ that is opposed by sinners, and that is the object of their contradiction.

O, to be sure, they gainsaid His teaching, and men still do. Was ever a man more consistently contradicted than Jesus Who is called the Christ, when He walked among us in the land of Canaan, and taught the people? When He would preach the gospel to the poor, and deliverance to the captives, recovering of sight to the blind, healing to the broken hearted, and liberty to the bruised, they said to Him: "Physician, heal theyself." Lu. 4:16 ff. When He spoke of Himself as the Bread of life, they said: "This is an hard saying, who can hear it?" John 6:60. When He was teaching in Jerusalem, and they felt impotent to resist His doctrine directly, they said: He is from Galilee, "Search, and look: for out of Galilee ariseth no prophet." John 7:53. When He announced Himself as the light of the world, they objected that He witnessed of Himself, and that, therefore, His witness was not true, John 8:13. When He rebuked them, because they did not hear His word, they cast in His teeth: "Say we not well that thou art a Samaritan, and hast a devil?" John 8:48. When He presented Himself as one with the Father, they called Him a blasphemer, and would kill Him, John 10:33. And when He taught the people that the Son of man must be lifted up, they answered Him: "We have heard out of the law that the Christ abideth for ever: and how sayest thou, The Son of man must be lifted up?" John 12:34. And mark you well, the striking and amazing feature of this contradiction is that it is radical and complete. It did not consist in a difference of opinion between Him and His opponents with regard to a certain point of doctrine: they contradicted Him in all His doctrine. No mere man, no sinner

ever agreed with Him. Always He was contradicted by all with
respect to all His teaching. O, indeed, there were those who believed on Him, and who confessed that He spoke words of eternal
life, but they confessed this not through flesh and blood, but by
the grace of God Who revealed it unto them.

Again, His works, too, were the object of the contradiction of
sinners. When He healed men on the sabbath, they accused
Him of transgressing the law of Moses. When He sought to save
that which was lost, they said that He was a companion of publicans and sinners. When, in distinction from John, He came
eating and drinking, they called Him a glutton and winebibber.
When He cast out devils, they explained it from His fellowship
with Beelzebub, the prince of devils. When He cleansed the
temple, they demanded a sign of His authority, and accused Him
of aiming at the destruction of the temple. And when the revelation
of His marvelous power reached its climax in the raising of
Lazarus from the dead, they concluded that He was a danger to
the very life of the nation, and decided to kill Him! John 12:47 ff.
And again, let it be noted, that this opposition to and contradiction of His mighty works, did not concern merely some of the
things He did: the contradiction was radical. No work of Him
was ever approved by mere men. Invariably He was opposed in
all He did. Also in His works He was the contradicted One!

And yet, ultimately, this contradiction against Christ's doc-
trine, and this opposition to His works, was directed against
Himself, against His Person, against Jesus that is called Christ.
For all His teaching and all His works were concentrated in Himself. They were but means of His self-revelation as the Son of
God, Who is in the bosom of the Father, and therefore, of the
Father Himself. In all He spoke and did He became revealed as
the Christ that was sent into the world, the Anointed of the
Father, the promised Messiah that would redeem Israel, and establish the kingdom of God for ever. And all the opposition of sinners against His doctrine and works aimed at this one end:
they intended to contradict that this Jesus of Nazareth was indeed
the Christ! They did not want Him! They would not that *He*
should be King over them. They expected a Messiah, to be sure.
But the very idea that this Jesus was that Messiah that was

to come, and that they need not look for another, they hated with all their heart. Always they allied themselves, with all sinners, furiously raging against Him, and taking counsel together against the Anointed of the Lord, saying: "Let us break their bands asunder, and cast away their cords from us." All their contradiction of His doctrine and works was aimed at Himself. They meant to exterminate His very name from the earth.

It was, therefore, inevitable that their contradiction, instead of being confined to mere words, should translate itself in deeds of violence. Mere words were powerless against Him. Often they tried to argue with Him, and to expose His doctrine as false and evil. But just as often they were completely defeated in debate, so that, finally, no one had the courage even to ask Him a question. They deliberately attempted to ensnare Him in His words, and to tempt Him to say things that would give them occasion against Him. But always they failed. And, what was worse, the more they contradicted Him in words, and tried to dispute with Him, the more they were convicted in their own conscience of their own evil works, and of His truth and righteousness. Mere words were of no avail against Him. Even when they had finally taken Him prisoner and arraigned Him in their highest court of justice, they could not successfully speak against Him: by His very silence they were condemned and pricked in their conscience. And so, their contradiction of His Person must translate itself in deeds of hatred. Often they took up stones to kill Him, but as long as His "hour had not yet come" these attempts at assassination failed. But when His hour had come, and they had overpowered Him apparently, their fury knew no bounds. They contradicted that Jesus was the Christ, by blindfolding Him, and smiting Him, by spitting upon Him, and putting Him to nought. They contradicted that He was the King of Israel, by putting on Him the mock robe and the mock crown, and putting into His hand the mock sceptre, and paying Him a mock homage. All their deeds of violence were calculated plainly to disprove His claim that He was the Christ, the Son of the living God. Even after they had nailed Him to the accursed tree, the reproach and bitter jeers they cast into His teeth were intended unto that end. If He were the Christ, the Son of God, the King of Israel, He would come down from the cross!

Where words had failed, their deeds of violence appeared to be successful: the cross was the contradiction of His claim that He was the Christ! On the cross He hangs as the contradicted One!

And let us clearly understand this: all contradiction of Christ's doctrine and works, in whatever form it may present itself, is aimed at Him! All through the centuries of the new dispensation He is contradicted. Always again, false teachers arose in the Church, "denying the Lord that bought them," II Pet. 2:1. And also in our time, He still is the sign that is spoken against. But whether this contradiction reveals itself in the crass form of atheistic hatred that deliberately seeks to exterminate the Church, and to obliterate the very name of Christ from the face of the earth, such as was the program of Russian Bolshevism, before it was supposed to be in favor of some form of religious freedom; or whether it presents itself in the very name of the Christ it contradicts, and with a form of godliness that is devoid of power, as is the case with modern religiousness; always the contradiction of Christ's word and work is directed against Himself. One is either for or against, not a certain doctrine, but the very Christ Himself!

But why should men be against Him? Why do they contradict His teaching and work? What is the meaning of this contradiction? What is its cause and nature? Did and do men, perhaps, misunderstand Him, and do they, therefore, contradict Him by mistake? If this be the case, men ought to be more fully and clearly instructed concerning Him, and their opposition to Him will gradually disappear and change into agreement. But this cannot be. For the more fully the men of His day understood Him, the more they hated Him. Is it, perhaps, a matter of intellectual disagreement, and difference of opinion, which men ought to respect in one another, and concerning which they must learn to assume an attitude of tolerance? But no: the facts contradict this. There is no more bitter spirit of intolerance than that which characterizes this contradiction against Christ. Witness the fact that they nailed Him to the cross, and hated Him without a cause. The answer is in the text: "consider him who endured such contradiction *of sinners* against Himself."

This explains both the cause and the character of this contradiction. The cause was sin; the nature of this contradiction is ethical: it is a matter, not of the head, but of the heart of man. Let me quote just one of the many passages of Scripture that may be adduced to prove this, that of John 8:42-47: "Jesus said unto them, If God were your Father, ye would love me: for I proceeded forth and came from God . . . Ye are of your father the devil, and the lusts of your father ye will do . . . And because I tell you the truth, ye believe me not . . . He that is of God heareth God's words: ye therefore hear them not, because ye are not of God." There is the answer. Christ was of God, they were of the devil; He did the will of His Father, they fulfilled the lusts of the devil; He was the light, they were blind and hated the light; He came to establish God's kingdom in the way of God's righteousness, they wanted to maintain the devil's kingdom of darkness in the way of iniquity; He came to suffer and die for God's righteousness, they wanted a Christ with power to save them, not from, but in their sin. *Sinners* contradicted Him, not a certain class of sinners, but all sinners, exactly in their capacity as sinners, spoke against, and always do speak against Him. And in this they do but reveal their deeply rooted opposition to, and hatred of the living God. That is the condemnation of sinners! Let us confess it!

If we do not confess this our opposition against God, we are condemned already. If we do, there is salvation in the very blood we shed by our contradiction.

For Christ died for His own, those whom the Father gave Him from before the foundation of the world. He took the *No* of their contradiction against God to the place of judgment, and there, on the cross, He expressed His perfect *Yes* in the sacrifice of perfect and loving obedience He offered as He willingly tasted death and hell in our stead, and in our behalf. By His perfect *Yes,* He blotted out the guilt of our *No,* and obtained for us the forgiveness of sins, and everlasting righteousness, so that in Him we are so perfectly righteous before God as if we had never said *No* but always *Yes* in response to the Word of the living God! And having thus sacrificed Himself, He was exalted through His resurrection and ascension at the right hand of God, and is become the quickening Spirit. He gives us the faith, whereby we confess the sin of our contradiction in true sorrow after God, and lay hold of His perfect righteousness. And He removes the spirit of contradiction, gives us a new heart, and thus causes us to change our *No* into *Yes,* to confess His name, and represent the cause of the Son of God in the world.

Then we, too, endure the contradiction of sinners for His name's sake. And if, as we suffer with Him, we should grow weary and faint in our minds, let us consider Him, and take courage! Consider that the grace of Him who so perfectly endured such contradiction against Himself, is able also to keep us even unto the end; and that, even as He, having endured unto the end, had the victory, and was exalted to the highest glory, so we shall enter into the victory He gained for us!

CHAPTER 6

Cast Out by His Own

*He came unto his own, and his own received him
not.* — JOHN 1:11

The apostle John begins his gospel narrative by speaking of
the eternal Son of God, the Word that in the beginning was with
God, and was God, and by Whom all things are made. This eternal
Word, without Whom nothing is made that was made, dwells in
all creation, and in Him was life, and the life was the light of
men. But men are darkness, and although the light shone in the
darkness, the darkness did not comprehend the light. Loving the
darkness rather than the light, sinful men rejected the knowledge
of God, would have none of it, and held the truth in unrighteousness. The light was in the world, and the world was made by Him,
but the world received Him not. And when the apostle had thus
expounded the eternal glory of the Christ as the divine Word,
he continues: "He came unto his own, and his own received him
not." He was cast out by His own!

Perhaps, you remark that we express ourselves strongly, too
strongly, when we say that the text in John 1:11 means that His
own cast Him out. The text merely declares that they did not
receive Him. But we must remember that no one can assume a
neutral attitude with respect to the Christ of God. You cannot
coldly ignore Him. When He comes to you, you cannot politely

decline to receive Him, as you might do with a caller that seeks
an audience with you at an inopportune moment. For He is the
eternal Son of God, the Christ, the Light of the world. Your
attitude toward Him is always for or against. You love Him or
you hate Him. You cleave to Him, or you despise Him. There
is no middle ground. Besides, always He comes to His own. When
He comes He is not a stranger that has no right to enter: He
comes to His own house. He is not a man that kindly seeks an
audience. He is no beggar that awaits your mercy. He demands
attention. He speaks with authority. He comes to His own! And,
therefore, His word is always with power. By it you are humbled
or hardened. Over against it you obey or you rebel. You receive
Him, or you cast Him out.

And the facts in this case corroborate this truth. When He
came unto His own, and His own received Him not, they cast
Him out. From the very beginning of His coming, and especially
from the time He entered upon His public ministry, until His
"hour" had come, and they nailed Him to the accursed tree on
Calvary, they conspired against Him to cast Him out of His
own house. Jesus is the rejected of men, the stranger to His
brethren, the One that is hated without a cause, that bears the
reproach of the ungodly, and that is always contradicted by
sinners; but He is also the One that, by His own, is cast out of
His own possession and inheritance!

Let us not overlook that this is precisely the point of the text,
and this is exactly the story of His public ministry ending in the
death of the cross: He was cast out of His own house! In our
translation of the passage this meaning of the words is lost, and
the text appears to mean that He came to His own people, and
that they refused to receive Him. In the original, however, two
different forms of the word that is twice translated by "his own"
are used. And while the second time the word occurs in the text
it surely refers to the people, His own people, the first time it
has a different meaning, and does not refer to men, but to things.
We should, therefore, read: He came to that which was His own,
to His own property, His own things, His own inheritance, and
His own people received Him not, would not let Him take

possession of that which was His own, cast Him out of His own house!

The question arises: to what does the Word of God refer when it states that Jesus came unto His own things? What are those things, what is that inheritance to which He came? Is John still thinking of the Christ as the eternal Word, by Whom in the beginning all things were made, and Who in the fulness of time came into the world as the incarnated Son of God? In that case "his own things" refers to the whole world. He came into the world which was His own, and the world did not receive Him. And such an interpretation would be quite possible, of course. It would give us quite a proper conception. For He that came into the world in the fulness of time is, indeed, the eternal Son of God, God of God, Light of Light, co-eternal and co-equal with the Father and the Holy Ghost. As such He is the Creator of the heavens and of the earth, the undisputed Lord of all. All things are His, for without Him was not anything made that was made. Not only so, but even as the Messiah, the Christ of God, the Son of God in human flesh, He is the sole proprietor of all things, of the whole world. For He is, in God's decree, the firstborn of every creature, Who as the firstbegotten of the dead and as the Head of the Church, must have the preeminence in all things. It is God's good pleasure that in Him all the fulness shall dwell, and that all things in heaven and on earth shall ultimately be gathered into one glorious creation, one house of God, under and in Him as the Head over all. As the Christ, He is the Anointed, ordained of God to be King over all forever, to Whom the Most High from all eternity spoke the word: "Thou art my Son: this day have I begotten thee. Ask of me, and I shall give thee the heathen for thine inheritance, and the uttermost parts of the earth for thy possession." Ps. 11:7, 8. And when He came into the world, He came as God's Son, who was appointed heir of all things, Heb. 1:2. To be sure, therefore, it would be quite proper to understand the words of John 1:11 in this sense. Christ came into His own world, which as the Son of God He had made, over which He was absolute Lord; and which, as the Christ, He had received as an inheritance from the Father. Into this world He had come in the beginning, but His own in Adam had not re-

ceived Him, but cast Him out, preferring the lie and the slavery
of the devil. Into this world He came in the fulness of time as the
heir of all things, to reclaim it, to redeem it, and to lead it to
the heavenly level of His eternal kingdom. And when He thus
came, the world received Him not, but cast Him out once more
by nailing Him to the accursed tree. That is the sin of the world.
Always they mean to cast the living God out of His own house!

Nor do I think that this meaning must be excluded from the
text, for the coming of Christ unto His own in Israel, and His
coming into the whole world are intimately related, cannot be
separated. When He came to Israel in the fulness of time He also
came to the world. Yet, it would seem, in the light of the context,
that the passage has more immediate and direct reference to the
fact that Christ came to His own in the nation of Israel. This
seems to be the distinction between this verse and the immediately
preceding one. There we read: "He was in the world, and the
world was made by him, and the world knew him not." And
then, as if referring to something far more specific and serious,
to a far more intimate relation and unexpected refusal, the eleventh
verse continues: "He came unto his own, and his own received
him not." Although, therefore, the general reference to the whole
world as being His own is not excluded, the immediate and special
reference is, no doubt, to the fact that He came to Israel, to all
the things Israel stood for, and that His own people received
Him not, but cast Him out of His own heritage.

In coming to Israel, He came to the Old Testament Church, to
the old dispensational theocracy as it had been instituted and was
based on Moses, and supported by all the prophets, the house of
God that had been supervised by the mediator of the Old
Testament. And that entire house, and all that was in it was
Christ's. When Christ came, He came literally to His own things,
to His own temple, His own altar, His own temple service, His
own sacrifices and offerings, His own sabbaths and holy days, His
own passover and feast of the firstfruits, His own covenants and
promises, His own kingdom and throne, His own law and prophets,
His own priesthood. The whole house was His. And the promised
land and people were His. They were the sheep of His own fold.
They were His by divine right, for the whole house and all that

pertained to it had been given Him by the Father from before the foundation of the world. Moreover, He had founded that house and built it: Moses had only been His agent and representative. It was He that had delivered His own with a mighty arm out of the house of bondage in Egypt, He had led them through the Red Sea, He had instituted the old covenant at Sinai, He had led them through the wilderness, He had been the manna they ate, and the water they drank from the rocks had been supplied by Him. He had led them into the land of Canaan, had established the throne of David on Mount Zion, and the house of God on Moriah, and He had spoken to them through all the prophets. Moreover, all these things were but shadows of Himself. They all pointed to Him, and without Him neither the law nor the prophets, neither the temple nor the altar, neither the kingdom nor the throne of David had any meaning. Indeed, all these things were His own, and He was their Lord, the Anointed over the whole house of God!

And He came to it all in the fulness of time. He came to His own in the incarnation, for He assumed the flesh and blood of the children, and took on Himself the seed of Abraham out of the house of David, and this seed, and this royal house were His own. And by assuming the flesh and blood of the children He came not merely to, but into His own house. He came to His own through His public ministry, for in His preaching and mighty works He revealed Himself as the One that was expected, that had spoken to them through all the law and the prophets, through all the sacrifices and shadows, and that now had come unto His own. When, in the synagogue of Nazareth, the book of Isaiah was handed to Him, He made plain to them that He spoke from His own Scriptures, and that the gospel preached by Isaiah was His own gospel, that was fulfilled by Him. When He cleansed the temple He prophesied that He had come to rebuild the house of His Father in His own body. And thus He came to His own to fulfill all the law and all the prophets, to redeem His own, to change the shadows into eternal realities, to replace the sacrifices of bulls and of goats by His own, perfect self-sacrifice, the earthly temple by the everlasting covenant and tabernacle of God, the priesthood of Aaron by that according to the order of Melchisedec, the old theocrarcy by the kingdom of heaven and its righteousness, the earthly throne of David by the everlasting throne at the right hand of God. He came to remove the shadows and reveal reality, to break down the old forms that the essence might come to light!

Thus He came unto His own.

But His own, that is, His own people, received Him not. For Israel was, indeed, His own people, not merely in the sense that He was of their flesh and blood, but in the far deeper and more intimate sense that they were the sheep of His own fold. They were the Church. They were the people of God. In distinction from all the nations of the world they had been chosen and formed into God's own peculiar possession. They were the people God had given to Christ from before the foundation of the world. For as the apostle Paul writes: they were "Israelites; to whom pertaineth the adoption, and the glory, and the covenants, and the giving of the law, and the service of God, and the promises; whose are the fathers, and of whom as concerning the flesh Christ came, who is over all, God blessed for ever, Amen." Rom. 9:4, 5. They, His own people, who expected Him, and who of all people would be expected to give Him a hearty reception, received Him not, but on the contrary, cast Him out of His own house! Fact is, that they had always done so, when they maltreated and stoned the prophets, all through the old dispensation. But when He came, and they recognized Him, they said: "This is the heir, let us kill him, and let us seize on his inheritance." Matt. 21:38. And always they conspired against Him to cast Him out. Even when, in the beginning of His public ministry, He preached His own gospel from His own Scriptures in His own synagogue, they meant to cast Him down from the precipice. Lu. 4:16 ff. And often they took up stones to kill Him. And when finally His hour had come, they took hold of Him and brought Him into their court, and when they had diligently inquired, and He had declared under oath that He was the Christ, the Son of God, the heir that had come unto His own, they judged that He was worthy of death. And with the help of all the world they led Him outside of Jerusalem, and nailed Him to the cross. They cast Him out. His own received Him not! The Church excommunicated the Christ of God!

But, you ask, how was this possible? How could His own fail to receive Him? And why did they cast Him out? The answer to the first question is found in the words of Romans 9:6: "For they are not all Israel, which are of Israel." Always the line of election and reprobation cuts through the Church, according to God's own sovereign counsel of predestination. Always there is in the Church in the world the spiritual seed of the promise and the carnal seed. And always the carnal seed, those that are of Israel without being real Israel, persecute the spiritual seed, and cast out the Christ. For often the true spiritual Israel, the remnant according to the election of grace, is small, few in number, while the wicked grow as the grass, and are in power. It was so in Israel of old, in the fulness of time, when Christ came to His own. The true flock of Christ was small, the carnal seed abounded, and the latter were in power and sat on Moses' seat. The carnal seed were the leaders of the people, the scribes and Pharisees, the high priest and the chief priests and elders. And they sought their own righteousness, not the righteousness of God. They wanted a carnal Messiah, that would establish a carnal kingdom, in which they could serve the lusts of the flesh, enjoy the honor of men, and continue to cover up their inward corruption by a cloak of religiousness and piety. Hence, they wanted to keep the shadows, and hated the spiritual reality of the kingdom of God Christ came to establish. For they realized that in Christ's kingdom they would be exposed as naked and miserable, and that they would have to repent of their iniquity in order to enter therein. And repent they would not. For they loved the darkness rather than the light. And so they cast the Christ out of His own house, that they might continue to make it a den of robbers!

But mark the unsearchable riches of the wisdom and knowledge of God: it was exactly through their rejection of Christ, through their casting Him out and nailing Him to the accursed tree, that the Most High fulfilled His purpose of redemption! For the stone which the builders despised is become the head of the corner! For of their cross the Christ made His altar! The blood they shed in their hatred of Him, He willingly poured out as the blood of reconciliation! Even as they cast Him out, and through

that very act, He came unto His own, and entered into the inheritance God had given Him from before the foundation of
the world. The shadows they wanted to maintain by casting Him
out find their end and fulfillment in the very cross to which they
nailed Him! And thus were laid the foundations of eternal righteousness upon which the everlasting tabernacle of God is established, and on which the throne of David stands for ever and secure!

And thus also He became the Redeemer of all whom the
Father had given Him, not only of Israel but of all nations. And
while the rest are blinded, the election obtains salvation. Rom.
11:7. They receive Him through the power of His own grace.
And to as many as received Him, to them He gave the power
to become the sons of God! "O the depth of the riches both
of the wisdom and knowledge of God! . . . For of him, and
through him, and to him, are all things: to whom be glory for
ever! Amen." Rom. 11:33, 36.

CHAPTER 7

Denied by His Disciple

I know not the man . . . — Matt. 26:74.

Christ was rejected of men. Mere men always despised Him, hated Him without a cause, filled Him with reproach, contradicted Him, cast Him out of His own house. No flesh ever gloried in Him. To this there was, and to this there is no exception. The leaders of the people and the people themselves, the learned and the uneducated, the rich and the poor, the world and His own, — all assumed the same attitude of opposition. And now we must add that this is even true of the small inner circle of His own disciples, that had enjoyed His fellowship and His instruction, and had been witnesses of His mighty works during the three years of His public ministry. For in the dark hour of His deliverance into the hands of sinners all were offended, forsook Him, and fled; one of them betrayed Him for thirty pieces of silver; another, the very foremost and representative of them all, denied Him, declaring under oath that he knew not the man!

When we speak of the denial of Peter, we must beware lest we be tempted to treat the narrative as mere outsiders that have really no direct interest in the matter; or as judges that are ready to condemn in others what we ourselves are but too ready to do; or to present it as a warning example of an unfaithful friend, who forsook his Master in the hour of need, in order piously to draw from the incident a moral lesson. For then we would miss the point, and fail to hear the Word of God to us. Rather must we take the position from the outset that also in the narrative of the denial of Jesus by His foremost disciple Scripture presents us with the revelation of Jesus Christ. It emphasizes that this revelation of Jesus Christ is so decidedly contrary to all the world that no mere flesh, even in its best form and under the most favorable influences, can ever do anything but reject Him; and that, on the other hand, the suffering of Christ in the hour of God's judgment and wrath, was so unique, so amazing and dreadful, that no flesh could accompany Him into the dark vale of His agony. Nor might He carry with Him into the depth of His grief the consciousness of human sympathy. No flesh might sustain Him. He must walk the path of His sorrows alone. With God alone He must risk the descent into hell. To God alone He must cry from the depths. In the Father alone must be His trust. Of this He was well aware. In the full consciousness of this dread loneliness and forsakenness He had approached His "hour." For even that same night, either in the upper room or on the way to Gethsemane, He had solemnly declared to His eleven disciples: "Behold, the hour cometh, yea, is now come, that ye shall be scattered, every man to his own, and shall leave me alone: and yet I am not alone, because the Father is with me." John 16:32.

The narrative of Peter's denial is well known. When it had become plain that, in the garden, Jesus firmly intended to deliver Himself into the hands of His enemies without an attempt at self-defense, all the disciples had become offended, and fled. Peter, however, and another disciple, whose identity is not revealed, but who may have been John, followed their captive Master afar off. It is difficult to understand just what motivated Peter to follow the Lord, and presently even to enter into the palace of the High Priest, where Jesus was being tried. Certain it would seem, in the light of what had already taken place in the garden, as well as in the light of what followed, that he was spiritually poorly prepared to risk himself into the camp of the enemy that night. It may be that, belatedly, he had been mindful of his boast that, although all would be offended in Jesus, he would never be offended. Then, too, Matthew makes the remark that Peter followed to see the end. This would seem to indicate that he still could not accept the word Jesus had spoken repeatedly to His disciples about His being delivered into the hands of sinners. Still he expected that the Lord would give some token of His power, and as He had done so frequently before, escape from the power of His enemies. However this may be, the other disciple who with Peter followed the band of captors was known to the high priest, and seems to have entered into the palace of Caiaphas the moment Jesus was brought in by the soldiers. And upon his request the gate was also opened to Peter, and he entered into the inner court of the palace.

All the four gospel narratives mention the denial of Peter. There is some difference between them as to the details of this denial, differences that may partly be due to the fact that several persons took part in the tragedy, and questioned Peter as to his identity, or directly asserted that he was one of Jesus' disciples. Partly, however, these several details supplement one another. Matthew and Mark both mention the fact that at the third denial the enemy noticed that even his speech marked Peter as a disciple of Jesus. Mark alone tells us about the first crowing of the cock, to which, evidently, Peter paid no attention. Luke informs us that an hour elapsed between the second and third denials, and it is he, too, that speaks of that significant look of Jesus upon His wretched disciple, simultaneous with the crowing of the cock. And John adds the detail that in the third attack upon Peter a kinsman of Malchus, whose ear Peter had cut off, claimed that he had seen him in the garden with Jesus.

The order of the various denials, therefore, was approximately as follows. The other disciple had entered before Peter, but upon that one's request the latter too was permitted to enter. A damsel opens the gate for him, at the same time addressing the question to him: "Art not thou also one of this man's disciples?" But Peter denied and said: "I am not." John 18:17. According to Matthew and Mark, he answered: "I know not what thou sayest." It was at this moment that the cock crew the first time. Peter advanced into the inner court of the palace, where the soldiers that had taken Jesus captive had built a fire to protect themselves against the chill of the night. Taking his place among them, and warming himself, he is soon attacked for the second time, and again he denies any knowledge of the Lord. After this they seem to have forgotten the miserable disciple for a while, for an hour went by before they troubled him again. But presently a kinsman of Malchus took special notice of Peter, came dangerously near to recognizing him as the one that had intended to kill the servant of the high priest, and said to him: "Did I not see thee in the garden with him?" John 18:26. Others joined the attack, and recognized him as a Galilean. But the more positive their assertions became, the more vehemently Peter denied. And this time he swore and cursed to support his persistent denial of having any connection with Jesus of Nazareth. Perhaps it was at this moment that Jesus was led from the apartments of Annas to those of Caiaphas, along one of the open porches that lined the inner court of the palace, thus giving Him the opportunity to cast that look full of significance and soul-searching power upon His wretched disciple. This look, combined with the simultaneous second crowing of the cock, caused Peter to be mindful of the words of Jesus. And leaving the palace, he wept bitterly.

Let us try to understand the depth of sin into which Peter had fallen in that awful night. As far as he was concerned, all connections with the Saviour were severed. He had disavowed any acquaintance with Him. In the hour of Christ's deepest reproach, he had been ashamed of Him, had pierced His soul by his threefold denial, had taken sides with the enemy that had taken Him prisoner, that condemned Him, and that were about to crucify Him. He had declared that, as far as he was concerned, this man might very well be the evil-doer they claimed Him to be, and that it was, to say the least, a matter of indifference to him, whether they acquitted Him or condemned Him to death. All this he had declared under oath, before the face of God. And he had cursed himself, thus emphasizing that he would be damned rather than have anything to do with this man! Surely, all connections with the Lord were severed for good and for ever, as far as Peter's action was concerned. If the Lord takes Peter at his word, the words He had spoken once will be fulfilled with respect to this disciple: "He that denieth me before men, him will I deny before my Father which is in heaven."

Joining himself to the enemies of his Lord, Peter had utterly rejected Him! And let us add immediately, that it is exactly this we do every time we choose for the world against Christ, whether it is because we are ashamed to confess Him, or seek the honor of men, or are afraid of losing our job or position, and of the suffering for Christ's sake in general.

But what does it mean? What is the Word of God to us in this part of the revelation of Jesus Christ?

First of all, the denial of Peter reveals that the flesh, even the best of it, has nothing in Christ, that the natural man always rejects Him. Do not make the mistake of explaining this narrative as you would any natural story of a man forsaking his best friend in dire circumstances. Peter's denial is the choice of the flesh for the world and against the Christ. Do not misunderstand me. I do not mean to say that Peter was not a child of God, that he was a mere carnal reprobate, that all there was in him was what he revealed of himself, in that dreadful night, in the palace of the high priest. We know better. Peter repented: he went out and wept bitterly. He was restored after the resurrection. He was a true disciple of Jesus. He was a child of God. He was a spiritual, not a mere carnal man. The fact is, however, that it was not Peter, the spiritual man, the rock, but Simon, the carnal man, the old man in Peter, the flesh, that acquired the upperhand over him that night, that motivated him in coming to the palace of the high priest to see the end, and that expressed itself in the threefold denial.

And the flesh, always and everywhere, also in the children of God, rejects the Christ. It stands in enmity against God. It minds earthly things. It seeks the world and its lust. And it wants a carnal Christ, not the crucified One. For the crucified Christ stands opposed to the "world" and condemns it. And Peter being of a sanguine, self-assertive character, his flesh also was quick to act, and strongly asserted itself. In the service of Satan, the old Simon had spoken, and contradicted the Lord long before the final denial, when they were in the borders of Caesarea Philippi, and the Saviour had instructed His disciples concerning His approaching suffering and death at the hands of the leaders of the Jews. For "then Peter took him, and began to rebuke him, saying,

Be it far from thee, Lord: this shall not be unto thee." Matt
16:22. And although Jesus had sharply rebuked him with the
words: "Get thee behind me, Satan: thou art an offence unto
me: for thou savourest not the things that be of God, but those
that be of men," the old Simon had never been overcome. This
had become evident that same night, in the preamble to the
threefold denial. Earnestly the Lord had warned him: "Simon,
Simon, Satan hath desired to have you, that he may sift you as
wheat: But I have prayed for thee, that thy faith fail not." Lu.
22:31, 32. But he had contradicted the Lord, intimated that he
had no need of admonition and prayer, and declared that he was
ready to go with Him into prison and into death. Lu. 22:33.
When Jesus had forwarned the disciples that they would all be
offended because of Him that night, Peter, or rather, the old Simon,
had again contradicted Him, and exalting himself above all the
rest had declared: "Though all shall be offended because of thee,
yet will I never be offended." And when the Lord had foretold
him that he would deny Him thrice, Peter had declared: "Though
I should die with thee, yet will I not deny thee." Matt 26:31-35.

That old Simon, as well as the flesh in all the disciples (for he
spoke for them all), wanted an earthly Christ with earthly glory.
They were offended at the cross. They attempted to prevent the
cross. Sword in hand, they came to the garden that night, ready
to defend their Lord. And it was only when they saw that Jesus
delivered Himself up to His enemies, and that the sword was
taken out of their hand, that they became offended because
of Him. That old Simon followed the captive Lord to see the end,
still expecting that Jesus might show a sign of His power and
escape. That old Simon entered the palace of the high priest, and
was once more offended because of a Christ that was utterly in
the power of the enemies, that chose the cross. And that same
old Simon disavowed the Christ, declared that he knew not the
man, and that he would rather be damned than have anything to
do with Jesus! The flesh, even the flesh in the children of God,
always rejects the Christ. That is the meaning of Peter's denial.

Then, too, in the denial of Peter we behold a reflection of the
deep, the altogether unique, the unspeakably terrible suffering
of Christ. On the one hand, it should be evident from this denial

that no man could endure that suffering, or could even endure to
be in its presence, and to have but the smallest share in it. At
the sight of it, even His foremost disciple fell, and became
offended, broke off all connections with Him. The spectacle of
the deliberate, voluntary suffering of Him Who had the power
to consume His enemies if He so desired; the sight of the Son of
God deliberately seeking death and hell in the love of God, and for
His righteousness' sake, was too awful, too dreadful, too superhuman, too radically contrary to the desires of the flesh, for any
man to endure. All men, even His best friends, must needs forsake Him, and leave Him alone. And, on the other hand, when
the last and foremost of His disciples had left Him alone in His
suffering, and fled from the scene of it, it also had become plain
that Christ alone could, that He alone must and that He alone
did endure that suffering that consisted in bearing the wrath of
God against sin, in satisfying the immutable righteousness of
God, and in bringing the perfect sacrifice of atonement. That
way to the cross and into hell He must travel absolutely alone.
Forsaken by all, He offers the sacrifice of righteousness, and
finishes it all alone. There was no man with Him. To that cross
mere man can only bring his own unrighteousness, the righteousness of it is all of God in Christ. And when the sacrifice is finished
and sealed in the resurrection of Christ from the dead, we must
cease from boasting, beware lest we come to the crucified and
risen Lord with our own goodness and righteousness and religiousness, confess our sin and condemnation, that we may be clothed
with the righteousness of God He alone obtained for us by His
perfect sacrifice. That is the meaning of the denial of Peter.

Finally, the Word of God in Peter's denial also loudly proclaims to us that nothing can separate us from the love of God in
Christ Jesus, and that no one can pluck us out of His hand. You
understand that Peter's denial was divinely determined. It belonged to God's program for Jesus' hour. Christ had read that
part of the program to His disciple before it came to pass. And
the divine purpose of it was, no doubt, directly, to cure Peter
of the sin of his boasting in the flesh and his self-confidence. But
it also meant to be the Word of God to us that even in our deepest
temptation and sin, the love of Christ never fails. Always He

assures us that He took all our sin and denial of Him to the cross to blot it out for ever. Always the cock crows, and always He casts that look, that penetrating, reminding, rebuking look of never failing love upon us. Always He prays for us, until we go out and weep bitterly, then to forgive and to restore us. Nothing can separate us from the love of Christ!

CHAPTER 8

Reckoned Among the Transgressors

And when they were come to the place, which is called Calvary, there they crucified him, and the malefactors, one on the right hand, and the other on the left. — Lu. 23:33.

It was inevitable that the rejection of Jesus by men should culminate in His condemnation and death. And it was equally inevitable that the death should assume the form of the execution of a criminal's sentence, that is, of His being reckoned among, and numbered with the transgressors.

This, that the suffering Servant of the Lord was to be numbered among the transgressors, had been predicted by the prophet long ago, Isa. 53:12. To this the Lord Himself had referred in the night in which He was betrayed, when He had warned His disciples: "For I say unto you that this that is written must yet be accomplished in me, And he was reckoned among the transgressors: for the things concerning me have an end." Lu. 22:37. And thus it was most literally fulfilled. For not only was He formally tried and condemned as a criminal, but also the very form of death that was inflicted upon Him accentuated the fact that He died as an evil-doer, and that He was numbered with the lowest of criminals. This was the meaning of the crucifixion itself. And this was emphasized by the fact that two other male-

259

factors were crucified with Him, the one on His right hand, the other on His left. And the Apostle John adds significantly: "and Jesus in the midst." John 19:18.

We say that this was but inevitable. For, first of all, the rejection of Jesus by mere men, by the flesh, must needs be complete, and must continue to the bitter end. There is no hatred that is deeper and more radical than the hatred of the flesh against Christ. For Christ is the revelation of the living God, Who is GOD indeed. He is the Light, and there is no darkness in Him at all. He represents the righteousness of God over against a world that lieth in darkness. He always and uncompromisingly condemns the evil world and its lusts. And He demands repentance, not in part but complete, not outward but real and from the heart, not of certain sins but of sin itself. He is radical. He exposes the very intents of the heart. No mere outward piety can ever find favor with Him. He opens the white-washed sepulchres and exposes the dead men's bones within. He saves, yes, but from sin. He promises life and glory, to be sure, but only in the way of the righteousness of God. He offers no hope to the sinner that does not repent. He has no program of salvation for a world that loves the darkness rather than the light. Apart from God He knows of nothing but death and damnation. He condemns the very goodness and religiousness of man. Looking at all things in the light of, and in relation to the living God, He was the most radical, the most severe and uncompromising, the most intolerant Preacher that ever spoke to men. With Him all flesh must be condemned that grace alone might abound. That is why the flesh that loves the darkness and will not repent was cut to the quick, and moved to a hatred against Him that could never be quenched, that was bent on His utter destruction. Always the rejection of Christ must end in seeking to destroy Him.

But equally certain it is that in killing Him, unless it can be done in secret, men, mere men, the flesh that hates Him, will number Him with the transgressors. For always the flesh seeks to justify itself, at least in the eyes of men. The whitewashed sepulchres must not be opened. Even though men crucify Christ, they will still be pious and religious. The very day after they nailed Christ to the tree they must enter into the temple to perform the religious rites connected with the passover. In fact, in the very name of man's goodness and religiousness, Christ must be killed! Hence, they cannot openly admit, what in their deepest heart they know, that they kill Him because they are evil and He is good, because He is the light and they are darkness, because He is the revelation of the living God and they are enemies of God. On the contrary, He must be the transgressor! As an evil-doer He must be exposed, and as a malefactor He must die! He must be numbered with the transgressors! That is the deep hypocrisy of the flesh!

But this was inevitable not only as the end of men's rejection of Him, but also as the fulfillment of God's eternal good pleasure. For from before the foundation of the world God had anointed Him to be the Redeemer of His people. He was ordained the Head of the Church, and that Church was in itself sinful and damnable, a race of transgressors. Them He must redeem. And to redeem them He must take their place in judgment, in the righteous judgment of God. All their iniquities He must bear. He must be made sin for them, that they may become righteousness of God in Him. In God's own judgment He must be numbered with the transgressors, and treated as the Chief among them all! Such was the eternal good pleasure of God!

Looking at the scene of the crucifixion in this light, and considering the cross as God's and not man's judgment, we cannot but marvel at the wisdom of God. For then the entire scene is arranged as by His hand. Then it is as by His hand that two malefactors are crucified with Jesus, one at His right side, and the other at His left, and Jesus in the midst of them: He is numbered with the transgressors. Then it is by his own sovereign determination that it is exactly these, and no other, malefactors that are His fellow victims on Calvary. They are His choice. And little did the enemies surmise that presently one of them would confess the Christ, while the other cast his bitter jeers at Him. Looking at the scene in that light, who can fail to see God's sovereign counsel of predestination in it all, the clear revelation of the truth that "God is merciful to whom He will be merciful, and whom He will He hardeneth"? On the one hand, we may behold a last and clear illustration of the fact that the flesh always rejects the Christ, no matter what may be the circumstances. On the other hand, the penitent murderer is a clear demonstration of the triumph of election, the irresistible power of God's sovereign grace. God is the Lord!

Let us consider this revelation of the cross a little more in detail.

During the first three hours of the crucifixion, until the wings of the dreadful darkness that descended at noon cover the scene, the cross appears emphatically as Man's cross, and the crucified One as the rejected of men. It seems that even the cross alone cannot appease their wrath and fury, is to them not a sufficiently clear expression of their hatred, and of their rejection of Him. To the end they want to express their contempt of Him also by the word of their mouth. And especially do they accentuate the fact that they reject Him as the Christ, as the Servant of God, as the Builder of the temple, as the King of the Jews. Perhaps, the superscription Pilate had written and attached to the cross, stating that He *is* the King of the Jews, provoked them to greater fury. All unite to heap their contempt upon Him, the leaders of the people and the people themselves, the soldiers and the passers-by. They mock and jeer and wag their heads, and declare to all the world that the cross is tangible evidence that He was a deceiver, and that He is not the Christ; for if He were, He surely would save Himself and come down from the cross. And now even the malefactors reject Him. Even in the eyes of thieves and murderers He is contemptuous. For one of them opens his mouth, and addresses Him in the words: "If thou be the Christ, save thyself and us." Matthew and Mark make no distinction between the two malefactors, but simply tell us that they too mocked Him, thus emphasizing the fact that He was rejected even by the scum of society. But Luke informs us that there was a distinction, and the other thief rebuked the first, saying: "Dost not thou fear God, seeing thou art in the same condemnation? And we indeed justly; for we receive the due reward for our deeds; but this man hath done nothing amiss." And then he addressed Jesus in the well-known prayer: "Lord, remember me when thou comest into thy kingdom."

What does it mean? What is the special significance of this part of the revelation of Jesus Christ?

First of all, it is a plain proof of the fact that nothing will induce the flesh to accept the Christ. Only grace can do this. The idea is often expressed that circumstances of dire need, and especially of the danger of death, may change a man, and induce him to seek salvation in the blood of Christ. Especially in times like the present stories are circulated as to how in the hour before the battle men learn to pray, even those who only cursed before. Let us not be deceived by such tales. There is no power and no influence in all the world, apart from grace, that can change the flesh, or induce a man to come to Christ. Mere man always rejects the Christ of the Scriptures. Of this the impenitent thief is undeniable proof. Consider that he was in the throes of death. Consider, too, that he was receiving the due reward for his deeds, and that he was facing damnation. And then consider his words: "If thou be the Christ, save thyself and us." If we analyze this brief speech, we discover that it has, indeed, the form of a prayer, the prayer of unbelief, of the wicked: "save thyself and us!" O, we realize that he is mocking: he does not expect that this Christ can do anything of the kind. Nevertheless, he reveals what kind of salvation he desires. He wants to be saved from that cross. He is not sorry for his sin. That he is under just judgment does not trouble him. That he has offended the living God is no cause of sorrow to him. But he would like to escape his just punishment. It is the sorrow of the world he reveals in the words: "save thyself and us!"

And thus he also reveals what kind of Christ he would desire: a Christ that would utterly ignore the righteousness of God, leave him in his sin, and deliver him from its punishment! If this man be the Christ, *his* Christ, He must be able to do just that. He must have power to make him enjoy a life of sin without suffering the consequences, and without receiving the wages of sin! But this Christ, that is suspended on the cross, utterly in the power of the enemy, meek and lowly, that is evidently not able to deliver Himself, and who even prayed for His enemies, he despises with all his sinful heart. The flesh seeks a Christ of this world, that can make of the world of sin a good place to live in, and that regards not the righteousness of God. It seeks the antichrist! But the Christ of the Scriptures it despises and rejects even in the face of death and damnation! Christ is always the Rejected of men!

Secondly, this part of the revelation of Jesus Christ witnesses to us that sovereign grace is always triumphant, and that nothing can prevent it from breaking through the darkness of the sinful mind, and the perversion of the rebellious will of the sinner. For it is exactly the wonder of grace that is revealed in the attitude and prayer of the second malefactor. It is God's elective, sovereign grace, and absolutely nothing else that distinguishes this second thief from the first!

Or, how else would you explain the facts? Would you, perhaps, insist that, while both these criminals had the same opportunity, the one by the choice of his free will made use of it and accepted Christ, while the other rejected Him? But consider then the circumstances, and in the light of them the words and the prayer of the penitent thief. Everything was against him. His own life and career as an evil doer witnessed against him: he was under just judgment, and there seemed to be no hope for him. The position of this man, who claimed to be the Christ, and who had preached the kingdom of God, was against him. As far as he, the penitent thief, by his natural light, could see, the cause of this Christ was lost. For this Christ was in the power of His enemies. He was condemned as a criminal. He was about to die. All the world had disavowed and rejected Him. Moreover, all the mob before the cross loudly proclaimed that He was not the Christ, and pointed to the proof of His being a pretender in the fact that He could not come down from the cross. And remember, there was no preaching here, no altar call. Christ had not addressed one word to this malefactor. He did not beg him to repent and to come to Him. There was merely the sight of this crucified Christ, and His lost cause, mocked at and despised by all!

How, then, would you explain his attitude and prayer except from God's sovereign, irresistible, elective grace? O, you might probably explain from free will the fact that he rebukes his fellow-in-crime. Perhaps, you might interpret his confession, that he is receiving the due reward for his deeds, as well as his defense of the innocence of Christ, from the free choice of his own will, and from the fact that he made better use of his natural light than his impenitent fellow. I would not agree with you, but it might seem as if you could defend such a position. But how would you ever explain his marvelous prayer: "Lord, remember me, when thou comest into thy kingdom"?

Consider what this means! It implies that this dying thief here had a vision of the kingdom of Christ at a moment when, to all outward appearances the cause of that kingdom was lost! It means that this malefactor had more light than anyone present at the crucifixion, the disciples of Christ included. No one, at that moment, could see any light in that Christ. All had been offended. The enemies were triumphant. The powers of darkness had the victory. It was their hour. The disciples were silent. And yet, this dying thief saw the light! He saw the light in the darkness of the cross. He alone in this dark hour dared speak of the kingdom of God! And what is more, he connected the kingdom of God, the kingdom of Christ, with the cross! For in opposition to the entire mob of howling and mocking enemies, he confessed that even now Christ was going into His kingdom! And it is in that light, and not in any natural light, that he prayed: "Lord, remember me, when thou comest into thy kingdom!" He, too, longed to enter into the kingdom of God! He saw the glory of that kingdom. And he saw it on the other side of death, of Christ's death, of his own death, for he, too, was dying. Somehow, he believed in the resurrection of Christ, and in the resurrection of the dead. And trusting in Christ's power and mercy to save, he casts himself upon Him, and pleads: "remember me!" And he believed the forgiveness of sins! For how could he dare to pray that he might be remembered, he who was a criminal, if he had thought of any other remembrance than that which proceeds from God's forgiving mercy?

Would you still attempt to explain this marvellous light, and this mighty hope and expectation from man's free will? As well might you explain the resurrection of the dead from the same free will of man. Whence did this man have this light, this repentance, this expectation of forgiveness, this hope of the kingdom of Christ, when all things were against him, and not even the best of the disciples could discern the resurrection of the dead? Whence did he have all this in distinction from his fellow-criminal who was in the same position, and hated the Christ? Here is the answer: God is merciful to whom He will be merciful, and whom He will He hardeneth!

Yes, Christ is numbered with the transgressors. And dying for them, the promise of God to Him that He shall see His seed is already being fulfilled! The Father gives Him this malefactor as the firstfruits! And when the Father gives Him His own, He receives them, no matter how deeply they have sunk in the mire of sin. Hence, the answer to the thief is still the answer of Jesus to all that repent: "Today thou shalt be with me in paradise!"

CHAPTER 9

The Meaning of the Resurrection

But now is Christ risen from the dead, and become the firstfruits of them that slept . . . — I Cor. 15:20.

That God is the God of our salvation, that He is able, and willing, and that He surely shall save us from our deepest woe in order to make us heirs of everlasting righteousness and life — that is the meaning of the resurrection of Jesus Christ from the dead. He is able to save to the uttermost, that is, from the bottom of hell to the height of heaven. What is impossible with men, is possible with God. And exactly where the situation has become impossible, it pleases God to reveal Himself in the glory of His power. As we sing in Psalm 33:

> *"Not human strength or mighty hosts,*
> *Not charging steeds or warlike boasts*
> *Can save from overthrow;*
> *But God will save from death and shame*
> *All those who fear and trust His name,*
> *And they no want shall know."*

And this power and purpose to save to the uttermost He revealed in the resurrection of our Lord Jesus Christ. For thus the Word of God speaks of "the exceeding greatness of his power to usward who believe, according to the working of his mighty power, which he wrought in Christ, when he raised him from the

267

dead, and set him at his own right hand in heavenly places." Eph.
1:19, 20. Indeed, that God can and will save "from death and
shame" — that is the meaning of the resurrection of our Lord
from the dead.

In the resurrection of Christ, therefore, we lay hold of the
hope of our calling. Apart from His resurrection, there is no hope,
there is only the darkness of despair. For here we lie in the midst
of death, and there is no way out. And in our darkness we are,
indeed, aware that God is, and that He is the Lord Who is to be
feared and glorified. We know Him through the things that are
made, as the One that calls the things that are not as if they were.
And we experience His wrath, and know that we are in judgment.
For "the wrath of God is revealed from heaven against all ungodliness and unrighteousness of men, who hold the truth in unrighteousness." Rom. 1:18. In His wrath we pine and die! But in
the resurrection of Jesus Christ from the dead, we by faith lay
hold of God Who quickens the dead, and Who saves from deepest
corruption and shame, from the very desolation of hell, and that,
too, to the uttermost. For into that depth of darkness, into the
lower parts of the earth, Christ descended when He cried out:
"My God, my God, why hast thou forsaken me?" For He humbled Himself, and made Himself of no reputation, became a
spectacle of reproach and shame and humiliation even unto the
death of the cross. But out of that deepest woe God raised Him
even to the higher level of His resurrection-life and glory. And
clinging by faith to that God, Who raised up Jesus from the dead,
we are saved, and shall be saved. That is the meaning of the
resurrection.

"But now is Christ risen from the dead," thus we read in
I Cor. 15:20. And a very significant *but* it is that introduces this
positive declaration. For it means that through the resurrection of
Christ we are assured that there is a resurrection of the dead.
The two are inseparably connected. You cannot sever them.
There were, evidently, some in the congregation of Corinth who
imagined that such a separation were possible. It seems that they
did not think of denying that Christ was raised from the dead.
And yet, they said that there is no resurrection of the dead, that
the dead are not raised. But the apostle Paul emphasizes that

this is a serious error, that you can never separate the two. If there is no resurrection of the dead, then Christ is not raised. For, apart from the resurrection of Christ there is no resurrection of the dead. And, on the other hand, if Christ is raised, there is a resurrection of the dead. For His resurrection is not, and cannot be an isolated fact. It is not simply an event that is historically recorded, an amazing occurrence in the past, of which one speaks occasionally as a matter of interest, but that, for the rest, has no further effect or significance. The resurrection of Christ does not mean that in the year thirty-three of our era a man, some individual, performed the astounding and inexplicable feat of rising from the dead, an act which no one accomplished since, and which no one is likely to perform ever again. On the contrary, it is Christ that arose, and that was raised. And He is become the firstfruits of them that slept. For He is not a mere individual among others. He is the Son of God, the Lord Himself, in human flesh. And He is the Anointed of God, ordained from before the foundation of the world to be the Head of the Church, and that, too, as the firstbegotten of the dead. He died for His own, and they died with and in Him. He arose for His own, and they are inseparable from Him in His resurrection. If He arose from the dead, it is clear that there is a resurrection of the dead! That is the meaning of Christ's resurrection!

But now is Christ risen from the dead! That is the very heart of the gospel of our salvation. For through the resurrection of Christ we know that God justifieth the ungodly. That mystery is revealed nowhere else, in no other way. Wherever we turn, in whatever direction we look, as far as we can see — always we meet with the inexorable divine verdict of death, eternal death. For God is just. And we have sinned, and are dead in trespasses and sins, and sin constantly. And God is angry with the wicked every day. His justice demands satisfaction. His holiness is a consuming fire. Always He judges us. And His verdict is death. The soul that sinneth shall die! And in His anger and holy wrath He pursues us, encompasses us round about, strikes fear and terror into our soul, casts us into everlasting desolation. And there is no way out. In vain do we look for light in this darkness. All human attempts to discover an avenue of escape out of this dread-

ful death, are without avail. We may scan the heavens, but we find
no mercy. We may peruse all the pages of history, but unanimously
they witness of the revelation of God's wrath and holy anger
against the sinner. We may give ourselves to introspection and
listen to the voice of our own conscience, but the answer we hear
is that we are worthy of death, and shall surely die. There is no
light. If you ask the question: will God justify the ungodly? heaven
and earth, all history, your own conscience, and every voice that
may be heard in all the world will answer loudly: *Impossible!*
We have sinned, and we must die! For we lie under the condemnation of a just and holy God, of God Who is the Lord!

But now is Christ risen from the dead! That is the light in the
darkness of our condemnation and death. For this resurrection is
God's act: He raised Him! And God's act is His Word to us. And
His resurrection-Word in Christ is that He justifieth the ungodly,
His Word of righteousness and salvation to sinners that lie in the
midst of death. For it is Christ that was raised. And again, Christ
is no individual, no mere man among men, but the Head of
all the elect, so that He represents them in life and in death, and
in the resurrection from the dead. He represented them in the
hour of judgment, in the darkness of the wrath of God on Calvary.
For there He was delivered for our transgressions, delivered by
men, yes, but also by God. He was delivered over unto death
and hell in God's just judgment, not for His own sins, for He
was without spot or blemish, the righteous Servant of Jehovah;
but for our sins, which it pleased God to lay upon Him, and which
He assumed voluntarily. And with those sins of His own upon
Him He traveled all the bitter way of death, in the love of God,
in obedience unto the Father, and thus brought the perfect sacrifice
that satisfied the justice of God, and atoned for the sins of His
own. And when He had thus functioned as the perfect High Priest,
bringing the perfect sacrifice, in the sanctuary of God, He announced: *It is finished!* And God gave His own answer to this
declaration of His Servant in the resurrection of Christ from the
dead. For He was raised for our justification, that is, *on account of*
our justification. Never could God have raised Him from the
dead, had He not fully atoned for all our sins, and obtained
everlasting righteousness through His perfect sacrifice on the cross.

Hence, even as the resurrection of Christ means that there is a resurrection from the dead, so the justification of Christ in His being raised from the dead, signifies that there is a justification of sinners. God justifieth the ungodly! Astounding mystery! That is the meaning of the resurrection of Jesus Christ from the dead!

But now is Christ risen from the dead, and is become the firstfruits of them that slept! And even now we live with Him and through Him, and He lives in us. We are dead to sin! For "so many of us as were baptized into Jesus Christ were baptized into his death. Therefore we are buried with him by baptism into death: that like as Christ was raised up from the dead by the glory of the Father, even so we also should walk in newness of life. For if we have been planted together in the likeness of his death, we shall also be in the likeness of his resurrection: Knowing this, that our old man is crucified with him, that the body of sin might be destroyed, that henceforth we should not serve sin." Rom. 6:3-6. O yes, Christ is raised from the dead, and He lives, and His promise is fulfilled that because He lives we shall live also. He is the resurrection and the life, and he that believeth in Him shall live, though he were dead, and believing in Him one shall never die! John 11:25, 26. The hour is come, indeed, that the dead hear the voice of the Son of God, and live. John 5:25. He that is in Christ is a new creature; old things have passed away, behold, all things have become new! II Cor. 5:17. For He Who lives in the resurrection is Christ. And once more, Christ is no individual, but He is the head of the body, His Church. For her, and in her, and through her, He lives. For the risen One is exalted in highest glory, and is become the quickening Spirit. And He Himself, through His Spirit and by His own Word of the gospel, lives in them, quickens them, calls them from death to life, from darkness to light, from sin to righteousness, and thus makes them partaker of His own everlasting resurrection-righteousness, and His own resurrection-life. And now we do, indeed, still lie in the midst of death in ourselves, yet in our death we have life; we still hear all the voices of condemnation because of our sin, but we also hear the voice of the risen Lord, overpowering them, victorious over them all, justifying us and clothing us with an everlasting righteousness; there are still the motions of sin in our members, but there is also the new man in Christ, having a delight in the law of God and walking in newness of life. We have light in darkness, righteousness in the midst of sin, life in the midst of death. That is the meaning of the resurrection of Jesus Christ!

But now is Christ risen from the dead, and is become the firstfruits of them that slept! Glorious gospel! Through the darkness of death immortality is brought to light. Death is swallowed up in victory! And believing in Him we know that we are more than conquerors, victors even over death and the grave, and that even through death we shall live with Him in everlasting, heavenly glory. For He is risen! And His resurrection is not a return to the earthly life in the likeness of sinful flesh, which He had assumed in His incarnation: it is an advance to immortality; death hath no more dominion over Him! He did not return to us, He went on! He did not even return to the level of Adam's life in the original state of rectitude: He was raised to the higher level of heavenly glory. In His resurrection the corruptible did put on incorruption, the mortal put on immortality; that which was in dishonor was raised in glory, weakness was changed into power, the natural was raised into spiritual, the earthly into the heavenly. Death was completely swallowed up in everlasting life. His resurrection is the glorification of the Son of God in the flesh! And again, He was raised as the Christ. He is the firstfruits of them that slept. And even as the firstfruits of the harvest that was presented to God in the Old Testament sanctuary was the beginning of the harvest, a sure pledge of the entire harvest to be gathered in, so Christ is the beginning, the principle of the final, glorious resurrection of all His own, a sure pledge that all shall be glorified with Him. For "the first man is of the earth, earthy: the second man is the Lord from heaven. As is the earthy, so are they also that are earthly: and as is the heavenly, so are they also that are heavenly. And as we have borne the image of the earthy, we shall also bear the image of the heavenly. Now this I say, brethren, that flesh and blood cannot inherit the kingdom of God; neither doth corruption inherit incorruption. Behold, I shew you a mystery: we shall not all sleep, but we shall all be changed, In a moment, in the twinkling of an eye, at the last trump: for the trumpet shall sound, and the dead shall be raised incorruptible, and we shall be changed. For this corruptible must put on incorruption, and this mortal must put on immortality. So when this corruptible shall have put on incorruption, and this mortal shall have put on immortality, then shall be brought to pass the saying that is written, Death is swallowed up in victory. O death, where is thy sting? O grave, where is thy victory? The sting of death is sin, and the strength of sin is the law. But thanks be to God, which giveth us the victory through our Lord Jesus Christ." I Cor. 15:47-57. That is the meaning of the resurrection of Jesus Christ from the dead!

But now is Christ risen from the dead. And He is the firstfruits of them that slept. Yes, but we may add: He is also the beginning of the new creation of God, of the new heavens and of the new earth, and of the eternal, heavenly tabernacle of God that shall be with men. O, well might, at the occasion of His resurrection from the tomb in Joseph's garden, the earth quake, and the watchmen became as dead men, and flee in terror. For His resurrection means that the entire old order of earthly and corruptible things shall pass away, to make room for the new order of God's everlasting kingdom. For Christ, as the firstbegotten of the dead, is also the firstborn of every creature, by Whom and unto Whom and for Whom all things in heaven and earth are created. And it is the Father's good pleasure that in Him should all the fulness dwell; "And having made peace through the blood of the cross, by him to reconcile all things unto himself; by him, I say, whether they be things in earth, or things in heaven." Col. 1:15-20. Of that new order, in which Christ shall be the Head, and God shall be all in all, the Risen Lord is the beginning, the principle. For He has the power to subdue all things unto Himself. Phil. 3:21. And so, looking by faith at the risen Lord, we look forward in hope to the realization of the Word of God in Rev. 21:1-5: "And I saw a new heaven and a new earth: for the first heaven, and the first earth were passed away; and there was no more sea. And I, John, saw the holy city, new Jerusalem, coming down from God out of heaven, prepared as a bride adorned for her husband. And I heard a great voice out of heaven, saying, Behold, the tabernacle of God is with men, and he will dwell with them, and they shall be his people, and God himself shall be with them, and be their God. And God shall wipe away all tears from their eyes; and there shall be no more death, neither sorrow, nor crying, neither shall there be any more pain: for the former things are passed away. And he that sat upon the throne said, behold, I make all things new." That is the ultimate meaning of the resurrection of Jesus Christ from the dead!

Wherefore, my beloved brethren, whatever betide, however all things may appear against you, be ye stedfast, unmoveable, always abounding in the work of the Lord, forasmuch as ye know that your labor is not in vain in the Lord! I Cor. 15:58.

BOOK FOUR

THE POWER
OF THE CROSS

CHAPTER 1

The Word of the Cross

*For the word of the cross is to them that perish
foolishness; but unto us which are saved it is the
power of God.* — I COR. 1:18.

The word of the cross is the power of God!

Is not this the most amazing paradox, greater, deeper, more
astounding even than that of God's revelation in the flesh of the
Babe in swaddling clothes, in the manger of Bethlehem? Is not
the cross the ultimate in human impotency, and does it not sym-
bolize all that is despised and rejected of men? How, then, can
that cross be the revelation of the Most High, a Word of the Lord
of heaven and earth; and how is it possible that this Word of God
in and through the cross is a word of power?

Yet, does not all revelation of the infinite God to the finite
creature necessarily imply a paradox?

God is God, and there is none beside Him. He is the Holy
One of Israel, the incomparable One, infinitely and eternally distinct from all that is called creature. For "to whom then will ye
liken God? or what likeness will ye compare unto him? . . . Have
ye not known? have ye not heard? hath it not been told you from
the beginning? have ye not understood from the foundations of
the earth? It is he that sitteth upon the circle of the earth, and
the inhabitants thereof are as grasshoppers; that stretcheth out the

277

heavens as a curtain, and spreadeth them out as a tent to dwell in: That bringeth the princes to nothing; he maketh the judges of the earth as vanity. Yea, they shall not be planted; yea, they shall not be sown: yea, their stock shall not take root in the earth: and he shall also blow upon them, and they shall wither, and the whirlwind shall take them away as stubble. To whom then shall ye liken me, or shall I be equal? saith the holy One" (Isa. 40:18, 20-25).

An infinite chasm, never to be bridged, there is between the Creator and the creature. He is the I AM, the self-existent One; the creature is utterly dependent. He is the Eternal, the creature is borne upon the stream of time. He is the Infinite, the creature is limited on every side. In all His glorious, adorable virtues, of wisdom and knowledge, of justice and righteousness, of grace and truth, He is infinite perfection; the creature is never more than an infinitesimally small reflection of His glory. And He is the Lord, the only Sovereign of heaven and earth. Of Him, and through Him, and unto Him are all things. To Him must be the glory forever!

When, therefore, it pleases God to reveal Himself to us, that is, when He so comes down to our level that we may know Him, and have fellowship with Him; yet so, that He becomes known as God; known, but as the incomprehensible One; near, yet infinitely far away; immanent, yet transcendent, — He does so by performing wondrous things, those things that are impossible with man.

He does so in creation, for He calls the things that are not as if they were. "Lift up your eyes on high, and behold who hath created all these things, that bringeth out their host by number: he calleth them all by names by the greatness of his might, for that he is strong in power: not one faileth" (Isa. 40:26).

Far more gloriously, however, He reveals Himself as God, as the incomparable Lord, in the work of redemption. In creation, He calls the things that are not as if they were. In redemption, He calls light out of darkness, righteousness out of unrighteousness, the glory of the eternal, heavenly day out of the darkness of the night of sin; and He quickens the dead. What is impossible with man, is possible with God! And lest man should boast in his own power and wisdom, God brings these utterly to nought, will have none of them; and deliberately chooses the weak, and foolish, and base things of the world, yea, and things that are not, to bring to nought the things that are, and to become revealed as the incomparable God, who is the Lord. No flesh may ever glory in His presence!

That is the word of the cross.

Clearly, and with great emphasis, this profound truth is set forth in the first chapter of First Corinthians, from the seventeenth verse to the end. The theme of that passage is: "the power and wisdom of God in the word of the cross." The apostle emphasizes that this word of the cross cannot possibly be preached by means of the wisdom of a human word, for "the preaching (or 'word') of the cross is foolishness to them that perish, but to us that are saved it is the power of God." The power and wisdom of the world God was pleased to put to shame and to bring to nought. Unto the salvation of the world, He will not employ them, nor use them as the medium of revelation for His own power and wisdom, lest man should boast in His presence. On the contrary, it pleased Him through the foolishness of preaching to save them that believe. Man as mere man, as the proud sinner that boasts against God, ever seeks to save himself by his own power, and to solve the problem of the salvation of the world by his own wisdom. Hence, "the Jews require a sign, and the Greeks seek after wisdom." God, however, will not share His glory with the creature. He that glorieth must glory in the Lord. And, therefore, He chooses the foolish things of the world as a means to reveal His wisdom, the weak things of the world to reveal His power, the base things of the world as a medium to reveal His glory, and the things that are not, that He may utterly bring to nought the things that are. And so He chooses the cross to make a crown; and the utterly despised and rejected Jesus of Nazareth, the crucified One, utterly crushed and forsaken, He presents as the Saviour of the world, and makes Him Lord of all! And thus the apostles, and the Church after them, preach "Christ crucified, unto the Jews a stumbling-block, and unto the Greeks foolishness, but unto them which are called, both Jews and Greeks, the power of God, and the wisdom of God."

That is the word of the cross.

But what is this word of the cross that is a power of God unto salvation?

In the eighteenth verse of First Corinthians, the apostle writes: "For the word of the cross is to them that perish foolishness, but to us that are saved it is the power of God." It needed no further definition of "the cross" to indicate that the cross of Christ is meant. Even though His is not the only cross, and though, in the days of Christ's flesh, death by crucifixion was inflicted frequently; yea, though two others, malefactors, were crucified with Him on Calvary, yet there is only one cross that is of any significance for the Christian faith: the cross of Christ. Moreover, we also understand that there is a figure of speech here, and that not the cross, but Christ crucified is meant. When the Scriptures speak of the cross they refer to the historic event that Jesus Christ "suffered under Pontius Pilate, was crucified, dead, and buried, descended into hell."

But what may be the meaning of *"the word"* of the cross?

No doubt, the translation: "the word of the cross," should be maintained, in preference to that of the Authorized Version: "the preaching of the cross." For that is the meaning of the original: *Ho logos tou staurou.* The phrase does not refer to the gospel message *concerning* the cross, in the first place, even though it is true that the preaching of the gospel is the vehicle upon which the word of the cross is carried out to men. It most emphatically does not denote a word that *we,* that mere men speak about that cross. But the reference is to the Word which God speaks in and through the cross of Christ.

The cross is a Word of God.

All things may be said to be words of God. The Word of God is the very essence and meaning of all things that are made. For "in the beginning was the Word, and the Word was with God, and the Word was God. The same was in the beginning with God. All things were made by him, and without him was not any thing made that was made." There is a Word of God in the golden glory of the sun, and in the silvery shimmer of the moon, striking a path across the rippling surface of the lake. There is a Word of God in the humble lily of the valley and in the proud cedar of Lebanon, in the flashing lightning and in the roaring thunder, in the lowly lamb and in the mighty lion, in the murmuring brook and in the tempestuous ocean. That is the reason why the heavens declare the glory of God, and the firmament sheweth His handiwork, day unto day uttereth speech, and night unto night uttereth knowledge. For in all the works of His hands God speaks concerning Himself. We understand this speech no more because of the darkness of sin within, and the curse and vanity of the creature without. But even so, all creation is a Word of God, and the Word of God in every creature is its idea, its essence, its real meaning.

In the same sense, Scripture speaks of the word of the cross. That cross of Christ is a revelation of the living God, a Word of God to us. That Word of God in the cross is its idea, its real meaning; and only as the Word of God it is power. For, mark you well, the word of the cross is the power *of God*.

Nor could we, of ourselves, discern the meaning of that word of the cross, and hear it. The divine logic of the cross is hid from our eyes. Standing on Calvary, the natural man, contemplating the cross in his own light, might discern a relative difference between it and the two crosses of the malefactors that were crucified with our Lord. He may come to the conclusion that the crucified One is a good man, who died for His principles; and he might become religious, condemning the enemies that nailed Him to the tree, and exalting himself above them. But that there is any special significance, that there is a marvelous power in that cross, he can never discover. From that viewpoint, it is foolishness to him. However, God has revealed the *logos,* the word of the cross unto us. He spoke it to the apostles and prophets. And as they received the word of the cross, they proclaimed it in the world. Their word concerning the cross has been preserved for us in the Holy Scriptures. And it is by the light of the Holy Writ, and through the illumination of the Spirit, that the Church still discerns and hears the word of the cross, and preaches the gospel to all the world. Hence, the word of the cross is the Word which God speaks through the crucified One, which He revealed to and spoke through the apostles and prophets, and which He still speaks through the preaching of the gospel, by the Church, according to the Scriptures.

Hence, we must stand at Calvary and, contemplating the cross of Jesus, we must hear what God will say to us.

We must be silent, by all means we must refrain from our own speech, about Calvary. For if we are not completely silent, if we attempt to form our own judgment of that cross, and to philosophize about it, we will never hear the Word of God which alone is the power unto salvation.

And standing in that attitude of the silence of faith, we will hear the word of the cross speaking, first of all and emphatically, of righteousness, and justice, and God's terrible displeasure and wrath against our sin. Watching the cross of Jesus, by faith, and in the light of the Holy Scriptures, we know that God is there on Calvary, and that in the suffering and death of the crucified One, He speaks of His holiness and righteousness, of His unchangeable justice, of His holy anger against all the workers of iniquity, and of the impossibility of salvation except in the way of satisfaction. We see that cross, not as man's word, but as the Word of God; we forget the judgment of Pontius Pilate, of the Sanhedrin, the wickedness of the Jews; and we know that we behold the righteous judgment of God. We no longer hear the jeers and mockery of wicked men: we are struck by the awful thunder of God's wrath, filling our hearts with the fear of death and hell. We understand, as we watch the lifeblood of the Lamb of God slowly dripping from His hands and feet, that every drop is laden with the wrath of God against sin. We behold the dreadful darkness spreading its horrible wings over the scene on Calvary, enveloping Him and us all, and we understand that God is hiding His face from us, and that He has come to execute judgment upon the world. And we are filled with fear. We would like to call on the mountains to fall upon us, and to the hills to cover us, and to hide us from the face of Him that sitteth upon the throne. For we realize that, as far as we are concerned, the situation is absolutely impossible. We hear, through the cross of Jesus, the Word of God as a word of righteousness and judgment and wrath, and we tremble.

That is the word of the cross.

For, as we continue to listen to the word of the cross, we realize that it is not *His,* but *our* sin that is brought into judgment on Calvary. We have sinned, and are worthy of death. We are corrupt, darkened in our understanding, perverse of will, alienated from God, His enemies, hating Him, and hating one another. We are guilty. And we have nothing to pay. And the word of the cross to us is that God demands the last farthing. He demands that we love Him, and we hate Him. He brings upon us death and desolation, and still He demands that we love Him, even in the revelation of His justice and wrath; and we can only hate Him the more, and increase our guilt daily. And so the word of the cross, as a revelation of God's righteous wrath against our sin, loudly proclaims that, if our wisdom and power must provide a way out, the case is hopeless. We can only perish everlastingly. Things have become utterly impossible. All our power and wisdom have been brought to nought.

That is the word of the cross.

But wait! Do not flee in terror from Calvary as you hear the word of God's unchangeable righteousness and holy wrath. Do not depart from the scene, and do not cease to listen to the word of the cross, as soon as you have become convinced that, as for you, all the power and all the wisdom of the world cannot save you. For what is impossible with man is possible with God. And it pleases Him to reveal His great power of salvation exactly then and there when and where it has become completely impossible for us to find a way out.

For the Word of the cross proclaims that the death of Jesus of Nazareth is the death of the Son of God in the flesh, freely giving His life for us, in our stead, and in our behalf. It is the revelation of God's eternal, unfathomable, boundless, and unchangeable love to His people. As you survey the cross of Calvary, in the light of the Holy Scriptures, and by faith, you there behold the God of your salvation. Therein, indeed, lies the mystery, the most amazing paradox of the cross: the offended God is come down into our flesh, is descended into the nethermost parts of the earth, to bear our offenses! God, O mystery of mysteries! in His only begotten Son come in the flesh, bears our sins, dies our death, bears God's wrath, blots out all our iniquities.

Paradox of paradoxes, God in the flesh is forsaken of God: "My God, my God, why hast thou forsaken me?" That is the paradox, yet that is exactly the power of the cross. Deny it, and you have nothing left but a word of man. Deny that there, on the cross is suspended, not mere man, but "the only begotten Son, our Lord," God of God, Light of Light, coequal with the Father and the Holy Ghost, and you have made the cross of Christ vain. But that He is the Son, who is eternally in the bosom of the Father, voluntarily taking our place in judgment, that we might nevermore be condemned — that is the very heart of the word of the cross.

And so, the word of the cross speaks of a wondrous love. It proclaims that God, before the world was, loved us and ordained us unto everlasting life and glory; that, unto that end, He appointed His only begotten Son to be the Head of His brethren, the Church, that He might bear their sins, atone for their iniquities, obtain for them everlasting righteousness, deliver them from all their woe, and lead them into the glory of God's heavenly tabernacle with men. It proclaims that this good pleasure of the God of our salvation was realized in the fulness of time, that He sent His only begotten Son into the world, loaded all the burden of our sin upon Him, delivered Him over unto death, yea, the death of the cross, and thus redeemed us by His own blood. At the cross *our* power and wisdom are brought to nought, but God's wisdom and the power of His eternal love gloriously shine forth. For God so loved the world that He gave His only begotten Son, that whosoever believeth in Him should not perish, but have everlasting life.

That is the word of the cross.

And that Word is power, a power of God! It does not merely *speak* of righteousness and judgment, of love and salvation, of redemption and eternal life; it accomplishes it. By the power of the word of the cross the burden of our sins is rolled from our weary shoulders, the shackles of corruption are cut, death loses its sting; and righteousness and peace, life and glory are bestowed upon us.

It is such a power, exactly because it is the Word of God.

He speaks it.

And when He speaks it to our soul, we are saved. And when we are saved the word of the cross is a power of God *to us*.

Indeed, not to all people is the word of the cross a power unto salvation. For not to all the mighty word of the cross is spoken in its saving efficacy. And the natural man cannot discern the things of the Spirit. They are foolishness to him. Through such a weak and foolish and base thing as a cross, he will not be saved. He seeks power and wisdom. The philosophy of man, rather than the wisdom of God, he will follow. In the power of man, the power of science and invention, of armies and equipment for war, of conferences and peace treaties, he puts his hope for the salvation of the world. He will not humble himself before God as a sinner, but rather boasts in his own goodness. And so, the cross is foolishness to him, a thing that is vain, and that cannot accomplish what it promises. But it is foolishness to him, because he belongs to them that are perishing in their darkness and corruption. And, on the other hand, he perishes, because he loves his own folly and despises the wisdom and power of God, revealed in the cross of the only begotten Son of God.

But they that are saved know and acknowledge the word of the cross as a power of God.

To them that word was spoken, and still is spoken, efficaciously. They are called. It is the Word of God to them. He Himself, through Christ, in the Spirit, by the preaching of the gospel, addressed it to their hearts. They heard the voice of Jesus say: "Come unto me, and rest," and they still hear it. And through that mighty Word they were saved, and they are being saved. They were burdened with sin, and through the word of the cross the load of their sin was lifted from their shoulders. Weary, and vainly laboring in their unrest they were, and at the cross they found rest. Filled with misery in the consciousness of the wrath of God against their sin they were, but hearing the word of the cross they found peace. In the midst of death they lay, but the word of the cross quickened them, and filled their hearts with the hope of eternal life. Light and joy, rest and peace, wisdom and knowledge, redemption and forgiveness, the adoption unto children of God, eternal righteousness and life they found as they heard the word of the cross. They are saved. To them the word of the cross is a power of God, and in it alone they put all their confidence.

And they are being saved through that same word, day by day.

Hearing that word, they go from strength to strength, until the word of the cross shall be fully realized in them through the resurrection from the dead, when they shall dwell in God's tabernacle, and see Him face to face!

O, indeed, the word of the cross is a power of God!

CHAPTER 2

Redemption from the Curse of the Law

*Christ hath redeemed us from the curse of the law,
being made a curse for us: for it is written, Cursed
is every one that hangeth on a tree. —* GAL. 3:13.

Marvelous power of the cross!

The lifeblood of the crucified One, dripping from His hands
and feet, shed voluntarily, obediently, a sacrifice of love on the
altar of God's justice, redeems us from the curse of the law!

And when we hear the word of the cross, and experience its
power by faith, the oppressing burden of that curse is lifted from
our weary souls, and the blessing of the gospel fills our hearts
with the peace that passeth all understanding!

That is the power that is attributed to the cross of Jesus by
the Holy Scriptures in Gal. 3:10-13: "For as many as are of the
works of the law are under the curse: for it is written, Cursed
is every one that continueth not in all things which are written in
the book of the law to do them. But that no man is justified by
the law in the sight of God, it is evident: for, The just shall live
by faith. And the law is not of faith: but, The man that doeth
them shall live in them. Christ hath redeemed us from the curse
of the law, being made a curse for us: for it is written, Cursed is
every one that hangeth on a tree."

By nature we all are under the curse of the law.

287

It is true that, in the passages from Galatians, the reference is, primarily, to the Israel of the old dispensation. They were, indeed, the covenant people of God, and heirs of the promise of salvation. However, on Mount Sinai, the law was, so to speak, imposed upon the promise, and although the former could not, and did not, make the latter of none effect, nevertheless, the covenant people were made to bear the burden of the law, and they became obligated to bear the curse of the law if they did not perfectly keep all the words of the law delivered unto them by Moses. And what is more, they had even covenanted with Jehovah to assume responsibility for that curse. For, according to the command of Moses in Deut. 27:11 ff., when the people of Israel had crossed over Jordan into the land of Canaan, half of the tribes took their position on mount Gerizim, and the other half on mount Ebal. And the Levites read to all the people the blessing and the curse of the law, and both the tribes of Israel responded with a solemn *Amen*. The curse was divided into a series of individual curses, the last one of which covered the entire law: "Cursed be he that confirmeth not all the words of the law to do them." And from mount Ebal was heard the solemn response by which the people voluntarily assumed this curse of the law: *Amen!*

Truly, as many as were under the law, and of the works of the law, were under a curse. For who was able to keep the law of the Lord perfectly? A thousand times, in the course of their history, the people of Israel transgressed, and trampled underfoot the statutes of their God.

Yet, this word is applicable, not only to Israel, but to all men as well. For we, too, are under the law: "Thou shalt love the Lord thy God with all thy heart, and with all thy mind, and with all thy strength." Such is our everlasting and unchangeable obligation. But we transgressed. We violated the covenant of God. In Adam, we trampled underfoot God's holy commandment of love. We are born in sin. And that means that we are born under the wrath of God, and under the curse of the law. For always the Word of God against the transgressors of His covenant is: "The day that thou eatest thereof thou shalt surely die." And "by one man sin entered into the world, and death by sin; and so death passed upon all men, for that all have sinned" (Rom. 5:12). We are, with all the children of our race, born on mount Ebal, where we hear the dreadful thunder of the law: "Cursed be every one that confirmeth not all the words of the law to do them." Nor is there, on our part, a way out. For we can never meet that obligation of the curse and live. On the contrary, we can only increase our guilt daily. For even while we stand in the fearful darkness of mount Ebal, and hear the awful voice of God's holy wrath, cursing us into everlasting desolation and death, we continue to hate Him, to love the darkness rather than the light, and to rebel against His holy commandment. We are, by nature, corrupt, darkened in our understanding, perverse of will, obdurate in heart, willing servants of unrighteousness. How, then, could we ever bring the sacrifice that would redeem us from that curse of the law?

Redeemed we must be, purchased free from the curse of the law. The price must be paid. For God is just. He cannot deny Himself. The demand of His law He cannot change: "Love Me with all thy heart." And there is no mercy without justice. For God is one. His righteousness is His mercy; His mercy and justice are never in conflict with each other. And, therefore, the soul that sinneth must die. And only in the way of death, but then still under the law of love, that is, by way of going through death as an act of obedience to that very law, in love to God, can his soul be delivered.

But the price of redemption he can never pay. The works of the ceremonial law are not sufficient, for the blood of bulls and goats can never blot out the guilt of sin. The works of the moral law of love he cannot, and will not perform; still less can he, under that law, bring his own life a sacrifice for sin.

By the works of the law no man is justified in the sight of God.

The sinner under the law is under the curse.

And let us make no mistake, and imagine that the sentence of the law against us is like the sentence of a human judge that has been pronounced, but the execution of which is postponed until some future day. The law is not a mere code: it is the Word of the living God, the Word which He always speaks, and that, too, a Word of power that accomplishes what it says. When the law pronounces the verdict: "Cursed be everyone that continueth not in all the words of the law to do them," it is the living God that thus speaks His Word of wrath, and pronounces the curse upon us. His own word of wrath and holy anger against the workers of iniquity, — that is the curse. It is the opposite of His word of favor. The latter is His *eulogia,* His pronouncing blessing upon the righteous, upon those that keep His covenant, and love His statutes to do them. In His favor there is fellowship and friendship, joy and peace, light and life: the enjoyment of all the pleasures there are at His right hand. But His wrath means that we are forsaken of Him, cast out of His fellowship, that His face is against us, that He fills us with terror, misery, and death. And this curse of the Holy One encompasses us on every side, and is within us, in our soul and body, and pursues us in all our earthly existence, throughout all our life. "For the wrath of God is revealed from heaven against all ungodliness and unrighteousness of men, who hold the truth in unrighteousness" (Rom. 1:18). The expression, the operation of that wrath, the curse, becomes manifest in all the evils of this present time, in sickness and pain, in sorrow and death, in strife and confusion, in war and destruction, in an ever more deeply sinking into the foul morass of sin and corruption. It pursues us, this curse of the law, until we sink away into the final desolation of being forsaken in hell.

Such is the curse of the law.

And it is from that curse that Christ has redeemed us.

That is the power of the cross! O precious cross of Christ!

He came down to our level. Not by necessity or compulsion, but by His own voluntary choice and determination, He assumed our nature, soul and body, became flesh of our flesh, bone of our bone. For He, let us remember, is the Son of God, the second Person of the Holy Trinity, God of God, Light of Light, Who is, according to His divine nature, consubstantial with the Father and the Holy Ghost, and who is eternally in the bosom of the Father. On this truth depends the whole mystery of our redemption from the curse. He is, according to His human nature, of us, but not through the will of man; by His own will the Son of God assumed the flesh and blood of His brethren: He was conceived by the Holy Ghost, born of the virgin Mary. And descending from

His glory, reaching down to our level to assume our nature, and to enter into our existence and life, He voluntarily assumed His position under the law, and took the responsibility of fulfilling the law upon Himself. For, "when the fulness of the time was come, God sent forth his Son, made of a woman, made under the law, To redeeem them that were under the law, that we might receive the adoption of sons" (Gal. 4:4, 5). And so reaching down to our depth, and coming under the law, He took upon His mighty shoulders the responsibility for the curse of the law.

He, too, heard the thunder of God's law, and the terror of it vibrated through His whole being, His soul and body: "Cursed is every one that continueth not in all the works of the law to do them." Yea, He heard it, as no one else could hear it. He heard it to the end, even so that it was silenced forever, and that we might hear it nevermore. For, first of all, He heard that curse, and let it vibrate through His soul and body, as the Son of God in the flesh. He was able to bear the curse of the law to the very end, even through the very depth of hell. He was capable of bearing that curse as an act, as a sacrifice of love, so that He could satisfy the justice of God, reply to God's demand with His perfect *Yes* to blot out the guilt of our rebellious *No,* remove the curse, and obtain the favor of God, righteousness and life. The mighty Son of God in the flesh was able to fight His way through the curse to the promise, through the oppressing wrath of God to His blessed favor, through death into life, through the depth of hell into the glory of God's heavenly tabernacle.

That is the power of the cross.

For He, the Son of God in the flesh, was in a position to bear this curse in our stead, in our behalf, and to pay the price for our redemption. Not for His own sin did He have to become the object of the curse of the law. He had no sin. He knew no sin. No guile was ever found in His mouth. Being the Person of the Son of God, the sin of Adam could not be imputed to Him: He had no original sin. The dreadful and inexorable line indicated in the twelfth verse of Romans five: "through one man sin entered into the world, and death through sin; and so death passed upon all men," was broken by the incarnation, by the coming of the Son of God into our flesh. Nor was His nature polluted, for He was conceived by the Holy Spirit, without the will of the flesh. And being without guilt and without the pollution of sin, yet coming under the law, and assuming the responsibility for the curse of the law freely, He could bear the sins of others. To do this He had the right; yea, that He should do so was the will of the Father concerning Him, for the Son of God, from before the world was, had been ordained the Head of all His own, the Church, that He might represent them in the hour of judgment, bear their iniquities, and redeem them from the curse of the law.

And so He became a curse for us, in our stead, and in our behalf.

All His life, from the manger to the cross, He bore that curse. For He tabernacled and walked among us in a sin-cursed world. He was conscious of His calling to bear the wrath of God. The shadow of the cross cast its gloomy darkness over His entire way. Yet, in that shadow He walked in perfect obedience to the Father. Every step of His life was an act of love. Bearing the wrath of God vicariously, and suffering the sorrow and misery of the curse, He personally remained the faithful Servant of Jehovah, obedient unto death, yea, even unto the death of the cross. He never failed, never wavered, never slipped, never rebelled. Every moment of His earthly existence, the Father could and did say unto Him: "Thou art my beloved Son in whom I am well pleased."

Under the burden of the curse, all His life was a descent into the dark depth of the death of the cross.

But on Calvary it was finished.

There He became literally a curse for us. There He bore, and removed, finally and forever, the curse of the law.

Exactly in and through that shameful and bitter death of the cross, Christ became a curse for us. For so it is written: "Cursed is every one that hangeth on a tree." The words are a quotation from Deut. 21:22, 23: "And if a man have committed a sin worthy of death, and he be put to death, and thou hang him on a tree: His body shall not remain all night upon the tree, but thou shalt in any wise bury him that day; for he that is hanged is accursed of God; that thy land be not defiled, which the Lord thy God giveth thee for an inheritance." The reference in these words, therefore, is not to capital punishment by hanging, but to hanging and public exposure after death had been inflicted upon the guilty party, either by the sword or by stoning. It was especially the hanging on a tree of him that was found worthy of death that was, according to the word of God, an abomination and a curse.

Hence, the death of Christ must assume the form of crucifixion. For He must become a curse for us. He might not die a natural death; had He died of some disease, or of the infirmity of old age, His death would have been of no avail. Nor might the enemy simply stone Him to death, as they sometimes intended to do, or cast Him from a precipice, before His hour had come; nor might their final intention, with the help of the traitor, to take Him by subtility and secretly put Him out of the way, meet with success. All these attempts were frustrated; and when the hour had come, the Father so directed the course of events that the only and inevitable outcome was the death of the cross. For Christ had to become a curse for us, and the death of the cross was accursed of God.

That cross was and is to us the symbol, the expression, the very embodiment of the curse, and it was such for Christ. The victim of crucifixion was made a public spectacle of shame and contempt. He was an abomination, an outcast. No room there was for him in all the earth: he was lifted up from the earth. In heaven he was not received: suspended he remained between heaven above and the earth below. Men did not want him; God did not receive him. Of God and men he was forsaken. Such is the meaning of the cross of Christ. Suspended on the accursed tree of Calvary, He had no name or position left to Him. He was utterly despised by men, and forsaken of God. By the symbolism of the cross, conceived as God's, not as man's cross, we are assured that Christ became a curse for us.

Yet, for Christ the cross was more than a mere symbol. It was also the medium through which the cursing Word of God was conveyed to His consciousness, and He was made to taste the horror of that curse with His whole being. For also this word: "Cursed is every one that hangeth on a tree," is a Word of God, not of man. It is, therefore, not man's but God's own interpretation of the cross that places the victim of crucifixion in the category of those that are accursed of God. In the category, I say, for the word from Deuteronomy allows for no exception. Also that central cross on Calvary, together with the two others, therefore, belong to that category, according to the Word of God. On Calvary, through the cross, God spoke His own Word to the crucified Christ: "Cursed is every one that hangeth on a tree; cursed art even Thou as Thou standest in the place of sinners!"

That is the word of the cross to Jesus!

And our Lord heard that Word of God.

O, how He heard it! No one else could have heard it as He. And hearing it, He trembled, became amazed and utterly astonished, exceedingly sorrowful, filled with terror, unspeakably miserable. The Word of God's righteous and holy anger against sin was in that cross, and it vibrated through His whole soul and body. As the slow moments of His dying hours were measured by the equally slow trickle of His blood from His hands and feet, He felt the oppressing hand of God's wrath become increasingly heavy. And as every passing moment was more heavily laden with the wrath of God, He responded with loving obedience that filled every drop of blood pressed out of Him, and by Him was sprinkled upon God's altar, and upon the mercy seat in the sanctuary. Accentuated was the Word of God's curse by the darkness that presently spread its horrible wings over the scene of judgment on Calvary; and, in the darkness, the Saviour completely withdrew Himself, wholly occupied, with all His heart, and mind, and soul, and strength, with the task of bearing the curse, and of responding to it in loving obedience, by His dripping blood. Before the darkness set in, He could still divide His attention between His own suffering and the misery of others, in loving sympathy for His own. But during the three hours of darkness, He is completely silent. His intense suffering, the offering of the perfect sacrifice, the laying down of His life in obedience to the Father, the amazing experience of the fierce wrath of God, and the superhuman task of meeting this dreadful expression of God's holy anger without complaint, without rebellion, yea, in the love of God — these now require all His attention, every ounce of His strength.

Thus He descended into the lowest parts of the earth, into the deepest darkness of woe and desolation, ever pursued by the cursing wrath of God, yet constantly bearing it in perfect obedience.

And thus we can somewhat understand that, at the moment when God's oppressing curse pressed Him into the very desolation and agony of hell, at the same time that His love and obedience are most perfectly and mightily expressed, His sudden outcry should become a question of amazement, wrung from His sorely vexed soul: "My God, my God, why hast thou forsaken me?"

Christ is become a curse for us!

That is the word of the cross!

And when we hear that word of the cross, we recognize it as a power of God redeeming us from the curse of the law. Then we stand by faith at the cross of Calvary, and tremble with terror in the consciousness of our sins and of God's holy wrath, and cry out: "God, be merciful to me, a sinner!" Then we know, through the same word of the cross, that it is all finished, that our Saviour took our place on the Ebal of Calvary, that He bore the curse of the law even unto the end, fulfilled all it obligations, and removed it forever. Yea, then we look through the darkness of Calvary into the glorious light of His resurrection, and are assured that God accepted His sacrifice, that the law can curse us no more, that we have eternal righteousness and peace with God, through our Lord Jesus Christ. Instead of being children of wrath, we are now the objects of God's favor, and hear His blessed word: "I will walk with you, and be your God; and ye are my sons and my daughters."

That is the power of the cross!

Hallelujah!

CHAPTER 3

Reconciled by His Death

For if, when we were enemies, we were reconciled to God by the death of his Son, much more, being reconciled, we shall be saved by his life.—ROM. 5:10.

O, adorable wisdom of God, wiser than, and bringing to nought all the wisdom of men!

O, blessed power of divine love, that many waters could not quench, that all the floods of our iniquity were not able to drown, whose weakness is stronger than men, and that puts all the power of men to shame!

We were reconciled to God by the death of His Son, and that, too, while we were enemies!

Was ever such a thing heard among men? Was it ever observed anywhere that men were reconciled to each other at the very moment that the offending party hated him whom he offended, insulted and abused him, slandered him and raved against him with hateful and bitter mockery and blasphemy, plotted to kill him and to obliterate his very name and memory from the face of the earth? Or, to accentuate the paradox, would it be considered possible with men that the offended party turn the blasphemy and abuse, the hatred and murderous assault of the offender into the very means and basis of reconciliation?

Yet, such is the power of the word of the cross!

For listen to this word of God, and let every phrase of it, in all its amazing significance, sink deeply into your soul, and stand clearly before your consciousness: "when we were enemies . . . by the death of His Son . . . God reconciled us unto Himself!"

Connect this evaluation of ourselves that "we were enemies" with the phrase "by the death of his Son," and what is the result? This, that we played our part in that death of the Son of God, and that we revealed, in the most horrible and shameless way, our enmity against God, when we nailed the Son of God in the flesh to the accursed tree! We hated God, and when He sent His Son into the world to dwell among us in our flesh and blood, we revealed all our enmity against Him. We conspired to kill Him, we erected the cross on Calvary, we nailed Him to the accursed tree. We expressed all our contempt upon Him, and filled Him with reproach, spit upon Him, buffeted Him, scourged Him, mocked Him, and cast Him out as one that was not worthy to have a name in human society, as the lowest of criminals. And then, at that very moment, God reconciled us unto Himself. Yea, what is more, through that very cross which we had erected, and by which we revealed our enmity against God, He accomplished our reconciliation. God was in Christ, there in that bleeding and emaciated human form on the tree, in that cross, in those cruel spikes, in that dripping blood, in that dreadful darkness, and in that agonizing outcry of utter astonishment: "My God, my God, why hast thou forsaken me?" When we were yet enemies, He reconciled us, by the death of His Son, that same death which we inflicted upon Him! When we hated Him He loved us, and He bore the expression of our hatred in love, to atone for it. The blood that we caused to flow from His hands and feet, He voluntarily shed, that He might offer the sacrifice of love that could satisfy the justice of God against our sin. And our jeers and mockery He changed into a prayer for the forgiveness of our sins.

When we were enemies, we were reconciled to God, by the death of His Son!

That is the power of the cross!

What does it mean?

First of all, and above all, it means that He loved us, with a sovereign love, that is, with a love that has its fountain in Him only, and that, for that very reason, is a fire that could not be quenched, not even by all the floods of our hatred and iniquity. "Herein is love, not that we loved God, but that he loved us, and sent his Son to be the propitiation for our sins" (I John 4:10). For that cross, that death of His Son, is not the *cause* but the *expression* and *revelation* of the love of God. Reconciliation presupposes the love relation. Thus it is among men. One does not speak of reconciliation of two perfect strangers. On the contrary, to be reconciled to each other there must exist a certain relation between two parties, whether it be that of man and wife, of king and subject, of a friend to his friend. And when we read in Scripture that God reconciled us unto Himself, the implication is that, on God's part, there exists such a love-relation, the eternal covenant of friendship, between Him and His people. Herein is love, not that we loved Him, but that He loved us. And in that eternal love alone must be found the explanation of the very possibility of reconciliation.

For, secondly, reconciliation also implies that the relation between the parties, such as it may be, has been transgressed, violated by one or by both of the parties. The husband or wife committed fornication, thus violating the marriage relation; the friendship is restrained, because one of the friends committed an act of perfidy; the servant is in disgrace with his lord, because he dishonored his name. Thus it is with respect to our relation to God. On our part we are covenant breakers, we violated the covenant relation through sin. In the covenant of friendship with his God, man was created. God revealed Himself to man, opened His heart to him, spoke to him as a friend to his friend, caused him to taste His favor and lovingkindness, which is better than life. And man was God's friend-servant, whose calling it was to glorify the name of his Creator, to consecrate himself and all things to Him, and to serve Him in love. But man violated the covenant of God. He transgressed the holy commandment. Wilfully, he turned himself away from God, rejected himself to the slavery of the devil. He fell in disgrace. He became an object of the just wrath of God. He became an exile from God's house. The covenant relation of friendship ceased to function. As far as we were concerned, we had severed the connection, broken the covenant: we were enemies of God.

Reconciliation, however, means further that, on God's part, the relation was never severed. If it had, reconciliation could never have been accomplished. Itself is an act of love, such an act of love whereby the cause of the alienation, namely sin, is removed, so that the covenant relation of friendship can function once more.

On this truth all emphasis must be placed.

If the fellowship between God and His fallen and sinful covenant people is to be restored, sin must be taken out of the way. With respect to reconciliation between men, this is neither necessary nor possible: repentance on the part of the guilty party, and forgiveness on the part of him that was offended, are all that is required to restore the right relationship, and to bring the estranged parties together again. But with respect to our relation to God this is different. God is righteous and just. He cannot deny Himself. His mercy can never be in conflict with His righteousness. The sinner is under the wrath of God, and must suffer the punishment of death. In his guilt and condemnation, he can never be the object of God's favor. If we are to be reconciled to God, sin must be removed, the cause of our alienation from God must be taken out of the way.

But how can sin that has once been committed be undone? How is it possible that the guilt of sin be expunged? How can the guilty sinner ever be made righteous before God, so that the Most High declares him free from sin and worthy of His favor and life?

The sole answer to this question is: only in the way of satisfaction.

But again, what is satisfaction? What is capable of satisfying the justice of God against sin? Can the sinner bring anything to God, an offering of gold or silver, or of bulls or goats, whereby he may blot out his sin, and be restored to God's favor? Indeed not; for he has nothing to bring, even if such external gifts could have the value of atonement for his sin: the earth is the Lord's and the fulness thereof. What then? Shall he, perhaps, perform some good deeds, and, on the basis of these, plead for a favorable verdict? This possibility, too, is excluded. For, first of all, he is dead through trespasses and sins, and cannot perform one deed that can obtain the approval of the Judge of heaven and earth. He is an enemy of God. And, secondly, even if he could perform that which is good before God, no good work could possibly expunge the handwriting of sin that is against him. If I trade with a grocer, and for a long time run up a bill with him, until I cannot possibly pay my debt, but now begin to pay cash for every item I buy, do I thereby pay off one cent of my debt? How, then, could the sinner pay for the guilt of his sin, and expunge his debt with God, by henceforth living in accord with the will of God, say this were possible? We are obligated to love the Lord our God with all our heart, and with all our mind, and with all our soul, and with all our strength, every moment of our life. If we fail, we become guilty, worthy of death and damnation. And no amount of good works can obliterate the guilt of our sin.

What then can satisfy the justice of God against sin, and restore us to His favor?

Suppose that we suffer the punishment of our sin in death. Can we, by this suffering of death, ourselves atone for our sin, satisfy the justice of God, and become worthy of the resurrection and eternal life? Indeed not. If this were the case, man would be able to suffer his way out of hell, which is impossible. Mere passive suffering of death does not blot out sin.

Only a sacrifice, that is, a giving up of our life in death, as an act of obedience and love of God, a perfect sacrifice, can blot out the guilt of our sin.

Let us remember that the demand of God's law is that we shall love Him. This demand never changes. Even when man falls into sin, and the sentence of death is pronounced upon him, and the wrath of God oppresses him, and curses him into death and hell, God still demands that man love Him. For even in His wrath God is good, holy and righteous, and worthy to be loved and praised. To blot out sin, therefore, requires of man a sacrifice, a perfect sacrifice, an act of love whereby man voluntarily assumes the burden of the wrath of God, voluntarily descends into the depth of death and hell, in the conscious acknowledgment that

God is righteous in His judgment; and he must be able thus to bear the whole burden of God's wrath to the end, in the perfect obedience of love. In opposition to the wanton *No* of sin, he must express the perfect *Yes* of obedience to God!

But man, the sinner, the enemy of God, dead through trespasses and sin, can never do this. He is not able to bear the infinite burden of God's holy displeasure against sin, voluntarily, in love, and deliver himself. As far as man is concerned, there is no way out. He is lost.

But what is impossible with man is possible with God! God is the Reconciler! He alone! For He was in Christ reconciling us unto Himself. When we were enemies, and when, on our part, all reconciliation was absolutely impossible, God reconciled us unto Himself by the death of His Son! He is the Reconciler! Let us be careful, lest we distort this truth. God was not *reconciled;* He *reconciles.* He did not have to be reconciled to us. If this had been the case, reconciliation would have been forever impossible, for where would be the reconciler that was capable of reconciling Him to us? No, but He loved us, when we were enemies. On His part the eternal covenant relation between Him and His people was never broken. He loved us, His own, with a sovereign love, eternal, unchangeable. Nor dare we present this holy mystery as if Christ were the Reconciler, that intervenes between God and us, to bring us together, so that He reconciles God to us and us to Him. For Christ is of God! He is the Son of God, very God Himself. And He is the revelation of the reconciling love of God. He does not reconcile God to us, nor us to Him, but Himself, the offended God, bore the burden of our sins and iniquities on His mighty shoulders, and thus reconciled us to Himself!

That is the mystery of reconciliation!

All things are of God (II Cor. 5:18).

God is the Reconciler!

That is the word of the cross.

Survey the wondrous cross of Calvary. Consider its profound mystery. Contemplate its paradox. That Man there, hanging on the tree of shame, between two malefactors, is the Son of God. He is very God, the only begotten Son, Who, even at this moment when, in the flesh, He is dying on the accursed tree, is, according to Godhead, in the bosom of the Father! In the flesh, God's Son is dying! There, on Calvary, you behold God the Reconciler, the God of our salvation. If this is not your confession, if you do not begin all you have to say about this crucified One with the confession that He is the only begotten Son, our Lord; if you do not prostrate yourself in utter amazement before that profound mystery, and confess that, in that bleeding form, pining away under the oppressing wrath of God, you behold very God, Light of Light, the crucified Christ means nothing to you. For were we not reconciled to God by the death of His Son? Only because He is the Son of God, who came from above, could He voluntarily assume the burden of our sins, and enter into our death. Only because He came from above, and voluntarily took upon Himself our flesh and blood, from the virgin Mary, and through the conception by the Holy Ghost, could He be righteous and holy, without guilt and without defilement, and offer to God the perfect sacrifice of love. Only because He is the mighty Son of God could He bear the full burden of the wrath of God even unto the end, and finish the work of satisfaction. Only because in His cross we behold the death of the Son of God does His perfect sacrifice have that infinite value that can be imputed to millions upon millions unto their everlasting justification.

God of God, in human nature, bearing God's wrath, dying our death, obliterating forever the guilt of sin, reconciling us unto Himself!

That is the paradox, yes, but that is the power of the cross!

And so, reconciliation is an accomplished fact. It is finished. The judgment is past. The debt is paid. Sin is blotted out. Our state of alienation and estrangement from God is changed into that of reconciliation. The covenant of friendship is established firmly and forever in the blood of Christ, in the death of His Son. Nineteen hundred years ago, when we were enemies, and when we revealed our hatred of God by nailing His Son to the cross of Calvary, yea, through that very act, God reconciled us unto Himself. We were not reconciled because we sought reconciliation, asked for it, implored Him for it, but in spite of the fact that we were enemies. And we are not reconciled now, *because* we believe in Him, or seek Him, even though by faith we enter into the state of reconciliation: reconciled we are solely by that act of God accomplished on the cross. And that means that sovereign love and sovereign election are the basis of this sovereign act of reconciliation. God is the Reconciler of all His own, given to Christ from before the foundation of the world, and they are reconciled. For God was in Christ, not opening a way of reconciliation merely but reconciling us by the death of His Son unto Himself. He gave His life for His sheep, given Him by the Father, and not one of them may perish. Long before they repent and believe, independent from their faith and repentance, while they were enemies, God reconciled them all unto Himself. And their sins can never be imputed to them anymore!

Reconciliation is an accomplished fact.

That is the power of the cross!

And that power of the cross is conveyed to us through the Word of the cross, the gospel of reconciliation.

For the Word of the cross is revealed unto us.

Never could we, in our own wisdom, have discerned the divine meaning, the idea, and the power of that cross of Calvary. Nor can human wisdom be trusted to interpret that cross of the Son of God. To us that cross is foolishness. Always we require a sign, a sign of human power, and the cross is the ultimate in human weakness: it has no sign for a wicked and adulterous generation. Always we seek after wisdom, the wisdom of this world; but the cross is the ultimate of human foolishness: it humbles all our pride. But God speaks His own Word, and He interprets His own cross. The Word of the cross, as a word of reconciliation, He spoke, by His Spirit, to the apostles. To them He revealed that He was in Christ reconciling the world unto Himself. And by virtue of this revelation they became witnesses of the cross, and of the resurrection. They preached the word of the cross. And the Church heard and believed, through the same Spirit of Christ, preserved that word of the cross, and, in turn, proclaimed it in all the world. And thus the preaching of the gospel is the ministry of reconciliation. It proclaims that God is the Reconciler, loving us with an eternal love. It preaches that reconciliation is an accomplished fact: God was in Christ, reconciling us by the death of

His Son. And it sends forth the prayer, as if God did be-seech us: "Be ye reconciled to God!"

O, wonder of divine grace!

Glorious light of mercy, shining from the face of God in the cross of Jesus, radiating into the darkness of sin and death that envelops all our present existence in its gloomy shadow!

And as we hear this word of the cross, the Word of God, the Reconciler, we confess our sins, bemoan our alienation from Him, humble ourselves in dust and ashes because of our enmity against Him, and turn to Him for refuge. Through the power of His Word, of His mighty Word of reconciliation, we enter into the state of reconciliation, cast ourselves upon Him in the confidence of faith, believe that He loves us, receive the forgiveness of sins and everlasting righteousness and life, and have peace with God through our Lord Jesus Christ!

The power of the cross has been realized in us!

CHAPTER 4

Death's Tyrant Destroyed

Forasmuch then as the children are partakers of flesh and blood, he also himself likewise took part of the same; that through death he might destroy him that had the power of death, that is, the devil; and deliver them who through fear of death were all their lifetime subject to bondage. — HEB. 2:14, 15.

O death, where is thy sting?

O grave, where is thy victory?

The sting of death is sin; and the strength of sin is the law.

But thanks be to God, which giveth us the victory through our Lord Jesus Christ (I Cor. 15:55-57).

For He, the Lord from heaven, died, and went through death; and by the act of passing through death, He destroyed him that had the power of death, that is the devil, and delivered us from the bondage of the fear of death that pursued us in all our living.

That is, indeed, the foolishness of the cross to them that require a sign, and that seek after wisdom: by dying He overcame and destroyed him that had the power of death.

But that is exactly the power of the cross to them that believe.

And when we hear the word of the cross, and experience its saving power in our hearts, we are liberated from the guilt of sin, from the power of corruption, from the dominion of the devil, and

307

from the bondage of the fear of death. The truth of this is taught throughout Scripture, but is very concisely and beautifully expressed in the words that are quoted at the head of this meditation.

God, so we learn from the context, purposes to bring many sons unto glory. Unto that end, He appointed over them a Captain, to head them all the way, to lead them into the glory ordained for them by the Father. He is called the captain of their salvation, God's only begotten Son, Jesus Christ, our Lord. The children, however, whom God wants to lead to the glory of His everlasting tabernacle, are partakers of flesh and blood, that is, together with all mankind, they exist in and bear the human nature. And in that human nature, by partaking of flesh and blood, they are in the sphere and bondage of death. In death's fortress, so to speak, they are held, hopelessly imprisoned. In that fortress the devil reigns. There, in the darkness of the prison of death, the prince of this world sways his scepter. He is the tyrant of death. The children whom God purposes to lead to glory are under his dominion. The captain of their salvation, therefore, must lead them all the way, out of that prison of death, into the glorious liberty of the children of God. To do this, He must take up His position among them, become partaker of the flesh and blood of the children, descend into their death, overcome him that has the power of death by dying Himself, and liberate the children the Father has given Him. And this He did through death.

And having accomplished this task, He declares: "Fear not; I am the first and the last: I am he that liveth, and was dead; and behold, I am alive forevermore, Amen; and have the keys of hell and of death" (Rev. 1:17, 18).

But what is this death to which we are subject through our partaking of flesh and blood, and in the sphere of which the devil sways his sceptre?

Let us not think too superficially of this grim and dreadful reality that is called death. Above all, let us not attempt to deceive ourselves as to the horror of this reality, by presenting it as something quite normal and natural, as the inevitable end of all life. For then we would be led astray by the philosophy of the world. According to philosophy, we live as long as we are in our present flesh and blood; we die when we leave them. As long as we are in this world, are able to move about and do our work, can see and hear, touch and taste and smell, eat and drink, we live; but presently, when we breathe our last, are put into the coffin, and buried, we are dead. Death means that our heart stops beating, that the organism of our body collapses, and that we return to the dust, whence we are taken.

Now, to be sure, this so-called physical death is a phase of death. And even when we consider it all by itself, it is sufficiently dreadful to fill us with fear. For, in the first place, it is strictly the end of all our earthly existence, of the earthly life of my body and of my soul. In death we are completely unclothed. Through death all our relationships, of love and friendship, our fellowship with men, our connection with the present world, are severed. Death is a complete loss. And it is, as far as our earthly existence is concerned, final. From death there is no return. And even in the sphere of this death we are born, and we know it: this life is nothing but a continual death. The fear of death is in all our living. Secondly, also this phase of death is not the inevitable and normal end of a natural process: it is the expression of the wrath of God against sin, and we know it. In death, God speaks to us: "You have sinned; wantonly you have turned your back upon Me, the sole Fountain of all good; you are worthy of death! You are not worthy even of your earthly life. I repent that I made you: dust you are, and to dust you shall return!" In death we face the wrath of Him Who is a consuming fire. And we tremble. We would like to hide ourselves from the face of Him that sitteth upon the throne. And, thirdly, death is, indeed, the end, but it is also the beginning. It is but the mouth of the dark pit of eternal desolation, into which we must needs sink away forever. For death is no annihilation, and we know it. *I* exist, *I* pass through physical death, *I* sink into the horror of eternal wrath and death. And I may put on a bold front over against the grim reality of physical death, and boast that I can take it, but in my heart of hearts I am aware that I stand powerless over against the grim reaper, that in death the heavy hand of God is upon me. And I am afraid.

But even so all is not said.

Man is more than a sheep. He was formed to be God's image-bearer, and to live in the fellowship of friendship with his

Creator. Life, for man, does not consist in this that he can eat, and drink, and be merry; but in the covenant fellowship with the living God. To be the object of His favor, and to taste that the Lord is good; to know Him in love, and to enjoy the light of His countenance; to will His will, and to serve Him with all his power, and with all things — that is life for man, the image-bearer of God. The opposite is death. To be the object of His wrath, and to be forsaken of Him; to have all our light changed into darkness, to be conscious of His consuming anger against sin; to dwell in the darkness of the lie, to be perverted in our will, polluted in all our desires, and to stand in enmity against God — that is death.

In this death, too, we are born, because by birth we partake of flesh and blood. Once, in the state of rectitude, we lived. For in His image God created us. Endowed we were with true knowledge of God: our mind was enlightened to know Him in love; we were created in perfect righteousness: our will was attuned to the will of God; and from the hand of our Creator we came forth in spotless holiness: our whole nature was consecrated to Him, and we longed for His favor and fellowship. But all this was perverted. We rejected the Word of God, violated the commandment of life, and preferred the word of the devil. Thus we became guilty, objects of God's wrath, and worthy of the just punishment of sin, which is death. And that punishment was inflicted upon us at once, according to the Word of God: "The day thou eatest thereof, thou shalt surely die." In Adam, the representative of our race, and the father of us all, we entered into the state of death. For "by the offence of one judgment came upon all men to condemnation" (Rom. 5:18); and "by one man sin entered into the world, and death by sin; and so death passed upon all men, for that all have sinned" (Rom. 5:12). This death certainly includes physical death. But it also implies our spiritual corruption, the darkness of our mind, so that we are incapable of rightly knowing our God; the perversion of our will, so that we hate the righteousness of God, and are incapable of doing His will; and the pollution of our whole nature, so that we are enemies of God, and follow after the lust of our flesh. In this death we are born: all that partake of flesh and blood, are under its dominion.

And the result is that, throughout our whole life, and in all our living in this world, we are in bondage to the fear of death.

All fear is principally fear of death. Take death away, and there is no room for fear. There is no fear in love, and, therefore, there is no fear in life. This fear of death is, first of all, an apprehension of the just wrath of God, and the realization that death is the penalty for sin; and, secondly, it is the sense of alarm at the wrath to come. For there is no way out for man, and he knows it. All his expectation perishes. From death to death he proceeds. Daily he increases his guilt, and he gathers for himself treasures of wrath in the day of the revelation of the righteous judgment of God. When he looks forward, — and what else can he do, carried away, as he is, on the fast flowing stream of time? — he beholds the Grim Reaper. And when he looks beyond death and the grave, he has the testimony in his conscience that he must appear in the revelation of the righteous judgment of God, that in that judgment his sins will rise up against him, and that he has nothing to hope for but eternal wrath and desolation.

This fear of death holds him in bondage.

It pursues him all his life. Always it is with him. In all his activities it is present. Whether he is at home or in his office, whether he laughs or sings, whether he attends the funeral of a dear one, or seeks a few moments of respite in banqueting and revelry — always there is the voice of this fear of death, now subdued, as an undertone, now, as in the quiet hours of introspection, and in the still hours of the night, clamoring loudly for recognition. As long as possible, he desperately struggles to escape the cruel clutches of physical death, but he must give it up. He sets his face like a flint, and proudly boasts that he is brave, and can take it, but he knows that he is lying. Throughout their life, in all their living, the children that partake of flesh and blood are held in bondage through fear of death.

In that fortress of death, the devil reigns.

For the text tells that he, the devil, had the power of death.

What may be the meaning of this expression? We understand at once that it cannot convey the idea that the devil has the authority to judge and to execute the judgment of death, for that is God's prerogative only. Nor can it mean that he has the power to kill, for life and death are in the power of God alone. He does not have authority to express the death sentence, nor does he have power *over* death, but, having himself been shut up in the prison of death and corruption, he has the power *of* death. In the fortress of death he exercises power. That is his proper sphere. There he is prince and ruler. Over them that are consigned to this prison of darkness and corruption, he reigns, and they are his subjects. Willing slaves they are, to be sure, but slaves nevertheless. They do his will, and they love the darkness rather than the light. Death is the devil's proper power. The children that are partakers of flesh and blood, shut up, because of their guilt, in the prison of death, are in the power of the prince of this world, and the lusts of their father the devil they will do (John 8:44).

Is there then no way out?

There is not as far as man is concerned. On his side, the situation is quite impossible.

But what is impossible with man is possible with God. His mighty arm wrought deliverance out of the fortress of death, for the children He had ordained unto glory.

And this great deliverance was accomplished through death, the death of His Son.

That is the power of the cross.

For the text tells us that He, the Son of God, deliberately entered the fortress of death, destroyed the devil in his power, and delivered them who throughout all their life were in bondage through the fear of death.

Let me, to clarify the meaning of these words, be permitted to present the whole matter in the form of a figure, an extended metaphor.

When man sinned, God shut him up in the fortress of death, of darkness and corruption, as his just punishment. The key He gave to the devil, that is, not the power to open and shut the prison-doors, but the power to rule within the sphere of death, and to lord it over all within its walls. He is the prince of darkness.

Now, into that prison Christ entered. For the text tells us that He also partook of the flesh and blood of the children. By doing so, He came under the law, and in the midst of death. But He is the Son of God. He was not born by the will of the flesh. He came from above. Voluntarily, He descended into the darkness of death's fortress. He *assumed* the flesh and blood of the children by an act of His own, through the Spirit, from the virgin Mary. He was, therefore, personally, not under the sentence of death, neither under the dominion of the devil. He was free, even in that prison, to do the will of the Father. Without sin He was, neither was ever guile found in His mouth. But He came as the captain of the salvation of the children the Father had given Him, to represent them in death, to break the power of the devil over His brethren, and to deliver them from the fear of death. For that purpose, that He might take their sins upon His mighty shoulders, remove their guilt, and thus break the power of the devil, He partook of the flesh and blood of the children.

Pursuing the metaphor, we may say that, the Son of God in human nature thus entered the fortress of death, the devil at once went forth to meet Him, and said to Him: "Here, in the fortress of death, I am lord and king; and you will have to submit yourself to my dominion." But the captain of our salvation replied: "I came to do the will of my Father, even here in the dominion of death. And this is the will of my Father that sent Me, that of all He gave Me I lose none, but lead them all out of this prison into the glorious liberty of the children of God. And so, I am appointed to bring you to nought, and I am going to take that keypower away from you!" But the devil, recognizing Him as the One that had been announced ages ago as the One that would crush his head, preferred to compromise, and so he answered: "There is no need of any conflict between you and me. I recognize that you are an able man. And I am perfectly willing to make you my superintendent in this prison of death. Just bow down and worship me, and recognize my authority, and I will give you all my kingdom: the keypower is yours." But the Lord answered: "Get thee behind me, Satan! For the Lord God alone I worship. From Him, in the way of obedience unto death, in the way of His righteousness, I expect to receive authority to destroy thee, to break thy power, and to secure that key of death and of Hades. Thy power of death over my brethren is based on the guilt of their transgression. But I came to take their sins upon Myself, and so to taste death for them that their iniquities are blotted out, and they are clothed with eternal righteousness. And by so doing, I will destroy thee, and deliver my brethren from the bondage of the fear of death."

And this Christ did.

He destroyed the devil, who had the power of death. The meaning is not that He annihilated him, but that He put him utterly to nought as the tyrant of death. He took the power of death, the right to lord it over the children He must lead to glory, and to hold them under his dominion, away from the prince of darkness.

And this He did through death.

His death is the right to liberty for all His brethren. By His death, He obtained the authority and power to deliver them from the prison of sin, and from the fortress of the fear of death; the right, too, to bestow upon them an eternal righteousness, and to lead them into the glory of everlasting life. For He *tasted* death for every one of them. He tasted all the horror there is in death. Fully He recognized, in death, the heavy hand of God's wrath against sin. There is no agony, no horror, no pain, no sorrow and grief, no amazement and abandonment, no astonishment and desolation, in death which He did not taste. And freely, voluntarily, in the love of God, as the Servant of Jehovah, that was come to do the will of the Father in and unto death, He descended into its dark depth, bore it all, and passed through it into life. For of death He made an act of obedience. Dying, He sprinkled His lifeblood upon the altar of God's justice in the depth of hell!

O, it is true, to the eye of the natural man, the cross of Jesus of Nazareth on Calvary, appears only as man's cross. It is foolishness to him. And true it is, that man played his part to erect that cross. When this Servant of Jehovah had made it quite plain that, even in the fortress of death, He had come to do the will of the Father, that He steadfastly refused to submit Himself to him that had the power of death, that is, the devil, all hell broke loose, all the forces of darkness set themselves against Him, and released against Him all their satanic fury. They took Him, bound Him, condemned Him, spit upon Him, scourged Him, made Him a spectacle to all the world, and nailed Him to the accursed tree. Yet, they but opened the way for Him, that He might voluntarily descend into the gloomy depth of death and hell. Every drop of blood they pressed from His hands and feet He filled with the love of God, and willingly shed upon the altar of obedience to the Father. Thus His death was a sacrifice, the perfect sacrifice of atonement for sin. And thus He merited the right to deliver His brethren from the fortress of death, and to lead them into the everlasting glory of God's tabernacle with men.

Through death, He destroyed him that had the power of death, that is, the devil.

And through death, He obtained the authority and power to deliver them who, through fear of death, were all their lifetime subject to bondage.

And deliver them He does!

Our Redeemer is also our Deliverer!

Through death, He passed into the glory of His resurrection, and of His exaltation at the right hand of God, and is clothed with all power in heaven and on earth. He holds the keys of death and hell. This mighty Lord, through His Spirit, now stretches His strong arm of salvation into our prison of sin and death, to lead us out into liberty. He opens wide the door, breaks the shackles of sin that hold us in bondage to the will of the devil, gives us a new heart, a new life, new love, new light, new knowledge, and wisdom. He gives us the saving faith, the power whereby we may appropriate Him, and all His blessings of salvation. He calls us through the word of the cross, the word of reconciliation, of liberty, of deliverance from the slavery of sin. And we hear the voice of Jesus, the captain of our salvation, calling: "Come unto me, and rest."

And we do come, and find rest; we repent and are forgiven; we believe and are delivered.

No longer do we accomplish the will of the devil, but have a new delight in the law of the God of our salvation.

And no longer does the fear of death hold us in bondage, for in His cross and resurrection we behold the way out, into the final glory of the tabernacle of God with us.

O, amazing power of the cross!

CHAPTER 5

The Power to Purge Our Conscience

How much more shall the blood of Christ, who through the eternal Spirit offered himself without spot to God, purge your conscience from dead works, to serve the living God. — Heb. 9:14.

Most beautifully expressed, I think, is the blessing of the believer's purged conscience, purged, that is, by the blood of Christ, by the Heidelberg Catechism in its sixtieth question and answer:

"How art thou righteous before God?"

"Only by a true faith in Jesus Christ; so that, though my conscience accuse me, that I have grossly transgressed all the commandments of God, and kept none of them, and am still inclined to all evil; notwithstanding, God, without any merit of mine, but only of mere grace, grants and imputes to me the perfect satisfaction, righteousness, and holiness of Christ; even so, as if I never had had, nor committed any sin; yea, as if I had fully accomplished all that obedience which Christ has accomplished for me; inasmuch as I embrace such benefit with a believing heart."

And then, lest the absurd conclusion should be drawn that a purged conscience is a sort of indulgence to walk in sin, it adds in question and answer sixty-four:

"But doth not this doctrine make men careless and profane?"

317

"By no means: for it is impossible that those, who are implanted into Christ by a true faith, should not bring forth fruits of thankfulness."

A purged conscience rejoices in the perfect, imputed righteousness of God in Christ.

And thus it makes us free to serve the living God!

And the power thus to purge our conscience is in the blood of Christ.

Such, in brief, is the teaching of the Word of God in the ninth chapter of the epistle to the Hebrews, the fourteenth verse.

The context points to the excellency of the New Testament high priest above the one that served in the Old Testament sanctuary. The latter served in an earthly tabernacle, a figure for the time then present, in which were offered gifts and sacrifices that could never make one perfect as pertaining to the conscience. Christ, however, came as the high priest in a greater and more perfect tabernacle, not made with hands, the heavenly sanctuary; and He came, not by means of earthly gifts and sacrifices, but by His own blood: priest and offering are one in Him. And thus He did what the Old Testament high priest could never have done: He obtained eternal redemption for us. If there were the power of a typical and ceremonial cleansing in the blood of bulls and goats, and in the ashes of an heifer sprinkling the unclean, "how much more shall the blood of Christ, who through the eternal Spirit offered himself without spot to God, purge your conscience, to serve the living God?"

To purge our conscience from dead works, therefore, belongs to the power of the cross.

What is a purged conscience? And how is this power to purge the conscience in the cross of Jesus?

Let us note, first of all, that the text from the ninth chapter of the Hebrews implies that, by nature, apart from the blood of Christ, we perform nothing but dead works, and that the testimony of these dead works is inscribed in our conscience.

The expression "dead works" appears to be a paradox. For by them are meant works that have their origin in death, that are performed by the dead; that are, as far as their ethical nature is concerned, characterized by death; and that, therefore, work out and lead to nothing but death. But is it not a contradiction in terms to speak of works that have their origin in death? Is not death the state of complete inactivity, the end of all work? It is, as long as we entertain the philosophical notion of death that it is, merely, the end of all earthly existence. But this is not the Scriptural conception. According to the Word of God, all men are dead, not when they breathe their last, but when they are born. So really dead they are that, unless they are born all óver again, they shall never see life. For: "He that believeth on the Son hath everlasting life: and he that believeth not the Son shall not see life; but the wrath of God abideth on him" (John 3:36). And again: "Verily, verily, I say unto thee, Except a man be born again, he cannot see the kingdom of God." For: "that which is born of the flesh is flesh" (John 3:3, 6). It would be of no avail, therefore, for a man, to enter into his mother's womb a second time and be born over: he must be born of the Spirit, from above, in order to live. In the flesh death reigns: "For they that are after the flesh do mind the things of the flesh; but they that are after the Spirit the things of the Spirit. For to be carnally minded is death; but to be spiritually minded is life and peace. Because the carnal mind is enmity against God: for it is not subject to the law of God, neither indeed can be. So then they that are in the flesh cannot please God" (Rom. 8:5-8).

We see, therefore, that a man does not first die when he closes his eyes in physical death, but when he comes into the flesh, when he is born. Moreover, we learn that death is not mere inactivity, but that it is a power, a negative power: it is enmity against God, it is to be carnally minded, so that they, over which this power reigns, cannot please God, but always mind the things of the flesh. It is the power of darkness, of the lie, of unrighteousness and corruption, of defilement and pollution, that works in our entire nature, in our body and in our soul, in our mind and in our will, in our desires and in all our inclination. It is the power of opposition against God, that is enthroned in our heart, and, from that deepest center of our moral nature, controls and directs the issues of our life.

Death is the opposite of life.

Life is the operation of our whole nature in the direction of and in harmony with God. It means that the power of the love of God is enthroned in our heart, and that this positive motive power gives direction to all the issues of our life, controls our thinking, and willing, and all our longing and desires. It signifies that our mind is enlightened with the true knowledge of God, that our will is motivated by righteousness, the virtue of harmony with the will of God, that our whole nature is spotlessly pure and holy, consecrated to the living God; and that, thus motivated by the love of God, and standing in knowledge, righteousness, and holiness, we dwell in God's house, have fellowship with Him, taste His blessed favor, and serve and glorify Him with our whole being, with all our power, and with all things.

Such is life.

In this state of life man was originally created.

And when he fell from his state of rectitude, he died: "the day that thou eatest thereof, thou shalt surely die." Nor does this death into which he fell mean that he was destroyed, annihilated; nor that he become wholly inactive. He did not lose his power to think and to will, to imagine and to desire, to see and to hear, to speak and to act. Even though he, no doubt, lost a good deal of his powers and talents, also from this natural viewpoint, he remained a rational, moral, active being. But the motor of his ethical nature, his heart, was put into reverse. His love of God was perverted into enmity. His light became darkness. His knowledge of God was corrupted into love of the lie. And his holiness was changed into pollution and corruption of his whole nature.

Such is death.

And dead works are those that have their fountain in this death, that are performed by men that are in the flesh, whose mind is enmity against God.

For even as they have their origin in death, so these works are, in their ethical nature and value, dead. There is no life in them, because they are not motivated by the love of God. This is true of all the works of the flesh. We must not imagine that we dare make a distinction between the works of the natural man, as if some were alive, others are dead. The tree is corrupt, and all its fruit is corrupt. "Doth a fountain send forth at the same place sweet water and bitter? Can the fig tree, my brethren, bear olive berries? either a vine figs? so can no fountain yield both salt water and fresh" (Jas. 3:11, 12). Whether a man, without the love of God in his heart, motivated by the carnal mind, holds up a bank, or bequeaths a million dollars to a charitable institution, his works are always dead. Whether he defiles and destroys the sanctuary, or faithfully brings his bulls and goats to the altar, and and pays his tithes, if he is in the flesh, his work is void of the love of God, motivated by enmity, pride, covetousness, or carnal fear, and, therefore, it is dead.

And so, finally, dead works are those upon which rests the righteous judgment, and that, therefore, lead to destruction. The wages of sin is death. That the end of the dead works of the flesh is destruction is evident even from the fruit of man's works in this world. Man that departs from, and is opposed to the living God, rushes into death, and brings destruction upon the whole world. He may attempt to stem the tide of his own corruption, and adapt himself externally, to an extent, to the law of God, but his enmity against God, his malice and envy, his greed and covetousness, the lust of the flesh, and the lust of the eyes, and the pride of life, lead him astray. He commits adultery, and destroys the home, the very foundation of society; and he makes laws that make a mockery of God's holy institution of marriage. He lusts after wealth and pleasure, and creates continual strife. And although he makes a desperate attempt to shackle the god of war with chains of international pacts, agreements, and conferences, the spirit of enmity and revenge that dominates his heart involves him in the most deadly conflicts, that become more universal in scope, and more destructive and dreadful in character, according as an ungodly civilization provides him with more effective and deadly instruments of destruction. And so he demonstrates the truth of the Word of God: "Their feet are swift to shed blood: Destruction and misery are in their ways: And the way of peace have they not known" (Rom. 3:15-17).

Dead works lead to death!

Their end is eternal desolation. Performing his dead works, the natural man increases his guilt daily, and thus gathers unto himself treasures of wrath in the day of wrath, and of the revelation of the righteous judgment of God (Rom. 2:5).

And this righteous judgment of God man knows. For the sentence of God, declaring him guilty and worthy of damnation, is inscribed in his conscience.

The testimony of God against all our dead works is preserved in our conscience, until the day when the books shall be opened.

What is our conscience?

It is not a distinct and special faculty of our soul, next to intellect and will; it is rather to be described as our awareness of, our agreement with, and consent to, the righteous judgment of God over all our works.

God is Judge. He always judges all our works. Constantly, from moment to moment, in all our life and activity, we stand before Him in judgment. He declares a just verdict upon every one of our works. And this judgment and verdict He makes known to us. He inscribes it in our conscience. Through His own revelation, whether in the works of His hands round about us, in creation and providence, or by means of the Holy Scriptures and through the written law, He makes this inscription in our moral consciousness, and that, too, by His Spirit. For even the Gentiles that have not the written law, are a law unto themselves, and have the work of the law written in their hearts, their conscience also bearing them witness (Rom. 2:14, 15). How much clearer, then, is this handwriting of the Judge of heaven and earth in the consciences of those that live under the revealed law and the gospel! Man reads this verdict of God. He cannot but agree with it, however he may attempt to silence the voice of his conscience, and to contradict the verdict of God. He consents to it. He stands condemned, and he knows it, because of the testimony of his dead works. A thousand voices of condemnation arise against him from within. They all pronounce but one sentence: death. His sins rise up against him, and they shall be fully exposed in the day of the revelation of the righteous judgment of God, when the books shall be opened, and everyone shall be judged according as his work shall be!

And now, O glorious power of the cross! the blood of Jesus purges our conscience from dead works!

It completely blots out that otherwise indelible handwriting of God that testifies against us.

Just think of the wonder of it all! Imagine the marvellous paradox! For, as long as we are in the flesh, the dead works are still there. We have sinned, and we know it: for the purging of our conscience does not mean that we are made to forget our transgressions. What is more, as long as we have not attained to heavenly perfection, we still sin, and add to our dead works day by day. But God's sentence of condemnation that is upon all these dead works is no longer there. Or shall we not rather put it this way: the sentence of condemnation that is written in our conscience, as soon as we stand alone, at our own responsibility, apart from Christ, is overcome completely, by another sentence, the verdict of God in the blood and resurrection of our Lord Jesus Christ! It is the voice of Jesus, the voice of grace, that is heard by faith, by which our conscience is perfectly purged from the inscription of God against our dead works!

You understand?

Though our consciences, apart from Christ, accuse us, yet, the blood of Christ overcomes all these accusations, and faith is the victory over all of them, so that I know that I am so righteous before God that I appear before Him as one that never had or committed any sin at all.

Nay more: the blood of Christ, sprinkled upon our conscience, so purges it that now there is inscribed in it the verdict of an eternal righteousness that makes us worthy of eternal life!

No longer can our sins rise up against us, to condemn us and to clamor for our damnation, before the tribunal of God.

No longer can the law curse us.

No longer can the devil, that accuser of the brethren, terrorize us by reminding us that we transgressed and still transgress all God's commandments, and have kept none of them. Well may we agree with him on that score; yet, in Christ, we claim that it is God that justifieth, that justifieth the ungodly, and send the tempter away with the victorious challenge: who is he that condemns us? (Rom. 8:33, 34).

O, glorious blessing of a purged conscience!

O, blessed power of the cross.

For the power so to blot out the damning handwriting of our dead works, and of God's verdict against them, in our conscience, is in the blood of our Lord Jesus Christ.

It is in His death and perfect sacrifice on the cross of Calvary.

It is in nothing else!

In that blood it is surely! It never fails. When that blood is sprinkled upon your conscience, it surely purges it from the guilt of sin. The text emphasizes this. If the sacrifices of the old dispensation made one typically and ceremonially clean, *how much more* will the blood of Christ purge our conscience from dead works!

But why is there that cleansing power in that blood? The blood of Christ is the life He poured out on the cross in perfect obedience to the Father, and that, too, in our stead, as our Representative, and in our behalf. And the text emphasizes a few things about this act of self-sacrifice on the part of Christ, in order to make plain why His blood has this power to purge our conscience from dead works. First of all, let us notice that it is the blood of a self-sacrifice. By shedding His blood, Christ offered Himself to God. And this means that His act of dying on the cross was of His own free choice and determination. He laid down His life: no one took it from Him by force. He willingly shed His blood: no one drew it from His body. His death was an act of obedient love to the Father in behalf of sin. Hence, it was a sacrifice. Secondly, and in close connection with the first point, He could offer Himself *without spot* to God. He had no sin. No dead works were inscribed in His conscience. There was no judgment against Him. Of Him the Father testified: "This is my beloved Son, in whom I am well pleased." Hence, He did not have to die for Himself. And He was able to offer the perfect sacrifice, to express the perfect Yes over against the No of our sin. Thirdly, He offered Himself up "through the eternal Spirit." This may simply refer to His Godhead, or it may refer to the Holy Spirit. It is best to understand the term as referring to both. He is the Son of God. And as the eternal Son, very God of God, and Light of Light, He suffered all the wrath and judgment of God against sin, the Holy Spirit preparing and sanctifying Him to the task, in His human nature. Hence, His sacrifice was not only without spot, and acceptable to God, but as the death of the Son of God it is also of infinite value, abundantly powerful to atone for all the sins of all His own. By that blood of the cross, the guilt of our sins was completely blotted out, and an eternal righteousness was obtained for us, on the basis of which we are declared worthy of life everlasting.

That blood is sprinkled upon our conscience, by His own Spirit, through His own gospel, the Word of the cross, and by means of the faith He gives us. It is all of Him, and none of self.

And through the sprinkling of that blood upon our consciences, they are purged. When the Spirit begins to apply that blood of the Lamb to our consciences, we begin by seeing our sins in a new light: we are filled with a true sorrow after God, and repent in dust and ashes. We cry out with the publican: "God, be merciful to me, a sinner!" And in that blood we find the answer. In the blood of the Lamb we experience the power of redemption, of forgiveness, of the purging of our conscience, of perfect justification, so we have peace with God. We have experienced and do experience the truth of the Word of God: the blood of Jesus Christ our Lord cleanseth us from all sin! That is the power of the cross!

Yet, this is not the end. Having thus been redeemed, and our conscience having been purged from dead works, we also experience a new freedom: the liberty to serve the living God! As long as we are under guilt and condemnation we have no right to this blessed service. We cannot, we will not, we cannot will to serve God, nor do we have the right to be delivered from this spiritual bondage. But in the blood of Christ there is the power to cleanse our conscience from the guilt of sin, and, therefore, also the right to be delivered from the bondage of corruption. Justified, we are also sanctified. Redeemed, we are also delivered. And standing in that new freedom, we fight the good fight against sin and the devil, and with a new delight in His precepts we serve the living God, till He shall deliver us perfectly, and take us with Him in His blessed tabernacle! There we shall serve Him day and night!

That is the power of the cross!

CHAPTER 6

The Power of Death to Sin

How shall we, that are dead to sin, live any longer therein? — ROM. 6:2.

What shall we say then?

Shall we continue in sin that grace may abound?

With this very serious question, that really implies an indictment against freely justifying grace, the sixth chapter of the epistle to the Romans begins.

There was reason for the question.

The truth of God's gracious act of justifying the ungodly had been set forth in the preceding chapters of the epistle. The glorious gospel that in the blood of the cross there is the power of justification for sinners that are, in themselves, damnable, had been explained. It is the truth that a man is lost in himself, and that, as far as his works are concerned, there is no way out, no hope of obtaining righteousness.

The wrath of God is revealed from heaven upon all unrighteousness and ungodliness of men that hold the truth in unrighteousness. There is, in this respect, no difference between the Jew and the Greek: all have sinned, and come short of the glory of God. Nor is there any hope in the works of the law. By the works of the law no man shall be justified before God, for only the knowledge of sin is by the law. Man's case, therefore, is hopeless.

327

Whatever he may do, he remains a damnable sinner before the tribunal of God.

But God revealed another, an altogether new righteousness, possessing which the sinner is justified, so that his sins are blotted out, he is declared worthy of life, and has peace with God. This righteousness is not of man, but of God; it is not of works, but of grace; it is not through the law, but by faith in Jesus Christ. In Him this righteousness is revealed. He obtained it for all His own, by His perfect obedience even unto death, yea, the death of the cross. He bore our sin. He took our place in judgment. He suffered the wrath of God in our stead. He died our death. And so He blotted out the guilt of all our transgressions, and merited for us a righteousness that makes us worthy of eternal life and glory.

This righteousness is imputed to us, freely, by grace; and we receive it by faith only, and even this is of grace, for it is the gift of God. Our works have no part in this righteousness. Our good works cannot add to it, or render us more perfectly righteous: it is perfect in itself. Nor can our sins render us unworthy of this righteousness: no matter how great or how many our sins may be, in Christ we are unchangeably and perfectly righteous before God. For "as by the offence of one judgment came upon all men to condemnation, even so by the righteousness of one the free gift came upon all men unto justification of life." And again: "as by one man's disobedience many were made sinners, so by the obedience of one shall many be made righteous" (Rom. 5:18, 19).

Such is the power of the cross.

On this aspect of the power of the cross we concentrated our attention in the preceding chapters of the book. The Word of the cross is the power of God unto salvation; by its power we are redeemed from the curse of the law, reconciled to God, delivered from the dominion and fear of death, and our conscience is purged from dead works. Sinners though we be in ourselves, we are righteous before God; damnable though our state may be, in Christ we are justified; the handwriting of God through the blood of Christ, inscribed in our conscience, declares us as righteous as if we never had committed any sin, yea, as if we personally had paid the penalty for our sins, and kept all God's commandments ever since!

But does not this doctrine make men careless and profane?

Is there no room, then, for the question: "What shall we say then? Shall we continue in sin, that grace may abound?"

The question, it would seem, follows very normally, and, what is more, it would appear as if the answer suggested is the only possible and logical conclusion from the doctrine of free justification: let us continue in sin, that grace may abound. The more we sin, the more we create the situation in which grace may truly shine forth in all its glory. By continuing in sin, it would seem, we serve the cause of grace. Let us, then, fathom the depth of sin, that we may taste the fulness of grace.

The opponents of the truth of sovereign grace, and of free justification through grace in Christ, without works, often claim that this is the only possible inference that follows logically from this doctrine. It makes men careless and profane. It offers them an indulgence to sin. Nay, what is worse, it changes sin into a virtue, since it becomes a means to extol the grace of God. You teach, they say, that we are justified before God without works. No matter how deeply and grossly we sin, we are righteous before God. Righteousness is simply imputed to us. Good works are not its ground: they cannot add to our righteousness. Sin cannot change it: though our sins are as scarlet, though they cry to heaven, in the judgment of God we are declared righteous. Well, then, say they, let us continue in sin: that is the only possible conclusion you can draw from such a doctrine. If it does not make a particle of difference in the judgment of God whether we sin or do good works, by all means let us sin, for this has, at least the advantage that it brings into bright relief the glory of God's forgiving mercy.

Thus the opponents of Paul's day, and the enemies of the so-called "blood theology" of modern times argue against the Scriptural truth of free justification through the blood of the cross, in order to demonstrate the absurdity and pernicious nature of this doctrine. Nor need we deny that, if their argument were correct, and their conclusion true, if it were the tendency of the cross of Christ to render men secure in their sin, to make men careless and profane, the truth of free justification could no longer

be a cause for glorying. In that case, it would indeed be a dangerous doctrine. Then the cross of Christ would be made of none effect.

But they that thus oppose the truth only speak in their ignorance.
They have not experienced, neither do they understand the marvellous power of the cross.

For rather than causing men to rest secure in their sin, seeing
they are justified without words, so that they become careless and
profane in their walk and conversation, the power of the cross
has the effect that it causes men deeply to abhor sin, to repent
in dust and ashes, and to walk as children of light in the midst of
the world. To verify this, just ask, not the enemies of the cross of
Christ, but those that have experienced the power of the blood of
Jesus unto their justification, and that know what it means to
be justified freely by His grace. Ask them, if they have any confidence in their own works as a ground of their righteousness
before God, and they will assure you that all their boasting is
in the cross of Christ, and in the atoning power of His blood.
To them, all other ground is sinking sand. They utterly repudiate
it. But again, ask them whether this exclusive confidence in the
cross as the ground of their righteousness, does not have the
effect upon them that now they become careless and profane, in-
duces them to draw the conclusion that it is profitable to continue in sin that grace may abound, and they will reply with holy
indignation and abhorrence: God forbid! They will assure you
that the power of the cross, as they experienced it, bore the very
opposite fruit: it caused them to abhor sin, to eschew it, to flee
from it, to fight it with all their might. Through the cross they have
become the enemies of sin. And for nothing they long more fer-
vently than to be delivered from the defilement of sin finally and
completely. "Live in sin?" they will say, rather amazed that you
could approach them with such a proposition, "continue in sin?
How could we, that have tasted the power of redemption in the
cross of Jesus, consider such a possibility, or do such a thing?
God forbid!"

This is also the answer of the Scriptures, by the apostle Paul,
in the sixth chapter of the Romans. Shall we continue in sin, that
grace may abound? God forbid! Such a proposition cannot be
entertained seriously, even for a moment.

But the apostle does more than merely express the spiritual impossibility of such an attitude on the part of believers. He also sets forth the reason for this impossibility. For he declares that believers are dead to sin. How shall we, *that are dead to sin,* live any longer therein? And he continues to explain that the justified believer is one that is baptized into Christ, and that, by being so baptized, he is baptized into His death. In fact, our old man is crucified with Him, and by this crucifixion the body of sin was destroyed, that we should no longer serve sin. We are, therefore, dead with Christ, and he that is so dead, is freed from sin. Christ died unto sin, we died with Him, and, therefore, we must reckon ourselves to be dead unto sin, and alive unto righteousness. Sin, therefore, must not reign in our mortal bodies that we should obey it in the lusts thereof; nor must we yield our members as instruments of unrighteousness unto sin. In a word, quite in opposition to the evil slogan: "Let us sin, that grace may abound," the truth is that sin shall have no dominion over us, exactly because we are not under the law, but under grace! (Rom. 6:2-14).

Thus the apostle explains the believer's being dead to sin in the sixth chapter of the Romans.

And the same truth is taught by him in other passages of his epistles. Thus, for instance, he writes in II Cor. 5:14, 15: "For the love of Christ constraineth us; because we thus judge, that if one died for all, then were all dead. And that he died for all, that they which live should not henceforth live unto themselves, but unto him which died for them, and rose again."

It is plain, therefore, that, according to Scripture, the redeemed in Christ have died with Him, and that now they are dead unto sin, so that sin no longer has the power to reign over them.

It belongs to the power of the cross to render men dead unto sin.

Two questions arise in this connection: 1. What does it mean to be dead unto sin? and: 2. How is this spiritual state effected by the cross?

In answer to the first question, we should carefully observe that the Bible does not say that sin is dead in the believer, but, on the contrary, that he is dead to sin. The difference is evident. It would be a grievous error to change this expression, or to understand it as meaning the same as the statement that, as long as the believer is in this world, sin is dead in him. For this error would certainly create confusion in the mind and heart of the sincere Christian. Fact is, that when we are engrafted into Christ, and the power of the cross is realized in us, sin is not dead, but remains very much alive. In this life, we never have more than a small beginning of the new obedience. Even the very holiest of the saints, he that is farthest advanced on the way of grace and sanctification, still has only a principle of the new life in Christ. Our old nature, earthly and carnal, remains with us till the grave. Not until we breathe our last are we delivered from it. And in that old nature are the motions of sin. And they are very active. In fact, it often seems that, according as we grow in grace and in the knowledge of Christ Jesus, the motions of sin in our members also increase their activity, always attempting to bring us again into bondage. We must, therefore, till the day of our death, heed the exhortation of the Word of God to put off the old man, and to put on the new.

Yet, although sin is not dead in the believer, he is surely dead to sin.

The natural man, the sinner apart from Christ, is *alive* unto sin. Sin is his lord. The power of sin is enthroned in his heart. It is his *rightful* lord, it has the right to exercise dominion over him, and he is its legal slave. God's sentence is that the sinner shall die. To this death belongs the spiritual darkness of mind, the perversion of will, the pollution of the desires and inclinations, that make the sinner a slave of sin. From this slavery of sin he does not even have the right to be delivered unless atonement be made for his sin. Sin, therefore, has dominion over him. This dominion of sin, however, is not contrary to the will and desire of the sinner, so that he ever longs to be delivered from its bondage. On the contrary, he agrees with it. He is well pleased with the reign of sin. He delights in the service of his evil lord. He is a willing servant. He loves the darkness rather than the light. He yields his members to the service of unrighteousness. He is in bondage, yet, because the service of sin is sweet unto his corrupt taste, he does not feel the oppression of his slavery. He takes sin to his bosom. Quite willingly he follows it. To the service of sin he willingly devotes his body and his soul, his mind and will, all his desires and inclinations.

For sin he lives. With sin he agrees. The paths of sin are his delight. He is alive unto sin.

To be dead unto sin is the direct opposite of this.

It is the state in which we are no longer under the legal dominion of sin. Sin is no longer our lord. It has no longer the right to reign over us. Just as a slave for whom the price is paid, or that has been declared free by law, is no longer legally bound to serve his former master, so he that is dead to sin is liberated from the legal dominion of sin by God's own verdict of liberation. Sin shall not have dominion over him, because he is not under the law but under grace.

Moreover, this sentence of liberation is also realized in him. He is actually, spiritually, liberated from the bondage of sin. His fetters are broken. Grace instead of sin, the law of the Spirit of life, rather than the law of sin and death, is enthroned in his heart and has dominion over him. His mind is enlightened, his will is turned about, his heart is renewed, and from that renewed heart all the issues of his life move in a direction opposite to that of sin. The result is that he beholds and judges sin in a new light, the light of the love of God. Formerly, he agreed with the dominion of sin, now he radically disagrees with it. Formerly, he always said "yes" when sin said "yes," and "no" when sin said "no"; now he opposes sin's "no" with his own "yes," and sin's "yes" with his own "no." When he was alive unto sin he loved the works of darkness, now he is dead unto sin he hates them with all his heart. While in his bondage to sin he yielded his members to the service of unrighteousness, he now strenuously opposes that service. He is dead unto sin.

O, sin is still present with him. And it operates in his members. Ever it attempts to regain its former lordship over him. But all that is within him, according to his inner man, hates and abhors the service of iniquity. Sin is not dead, but he is dead to sin. His entire attitude over against his former lord has radically changed. He is *converted*. And for the sin that still operates in his members, and ever attempts to divert the vehicle of his life and walk into the old ruts of unrighteousness, he humbles himself before God daily, repents in dust and ashes, and confessing his sins before God, he has no rest till he has found forgiveness in the blood of the Lamb.

He that is in Christ is a new creature: old things have passed away, behold, all things have become new! (II Cor. 5:17)

How, then, would it be possible that the believer in Christ should live according to the slogan: "Let us continue in sin, that grace may abound"?

God forbid!

How shall we, that are dead unto sin, live any longer therein?

Now, the source of this tremendous and radical change is in the cross of Christ. That this is the teaching of Scripture we have already seen. Into the death of Christ we are baptized, and we become one plant with Him in His death, and are crucified with Him. And it is because of this fellowship with the death of Christ, that we are dead to sin.

To understand this power of the cross we must consider, in the first place, that the death of Christ is the crucifixion of the old man, the destruction of the body of sin, the dethronement of sin as lord over the human nature. By the "old man" we mean the human nature as it is legally in bondage to sin, so that it has no right to be liberated unless the price for its deliverance is paid. In Christ that "old man" was crucified, killed, and buried. For by His perfect obedience, Christ paid the price for our redemption. His death is perfect satisfaction of God's justice in respect to sin. The result is that all that are in Christ are free from the law of sin and death. Sin has been deprived of the right to exercise dominion over them. Through the death of Christ they have been purchased free from its lordship. Legally, they are free from, and dead to, sin.

For, secondly, we must remember that Christ did not pay the price for His own redemption, but for ours, for all those whom the Father had given Him. He was never in bondage to sin. For He is the Son of God, the only begotten of the Father, and even in the human nature He was perfectly free. Always it was His meat to do the Father's will. He knew no sin. But He was made sin for His own. He was, so to speak, the Head of a corporation, of which all the elect are members. He represented them in the hour of judgment before God. They were all in Him. Legally, they were one with Him. When He, now more than nineteen centuries ago, was crucified, they were all crucified; when He died, they all died; when He was buried, they were all buried; when He arose from the dead, they all were raised with Him. Hence, their old man was crucified, dead, and buried. When Christ died, they all died unto sin. There and then, the price of their redemption was paid, and sin lost its right and power to have dominion over them.

That is the power of the cross.

Lastly, when this power of the cross is applied unto us personally, so that we are ingrafted into Christ by a true faith, and become one plant with Him, we at once appropriate, by faith, the atoning death of Christ, as if we ourselves had actually paid for all our sins, and experience this fellowship with His death as a power of liberation from the dominion of sin. When the Spirit of Christ enters into our hearts, and establishes the living fellowship of faith between us and the Christ that died and rose again, and calls us through the gospel, we know that we are free, that we are not under the law but under grace, and that sin shall have no dominion over us. Then we reckon ourselves dead unto sin, and alive unto righteousness. Then we reveal our having died unto sin by a hearty repentance and sorrow after God, by our eschewing and abhorring sin and fleeing from its lusts, and by a positive delight in righteousness to serve the living God.

That is the power of the cross.

What shall we say then? Shall we continue in sin that grace may abound?

How absurd!

The power of the cross is our death unto sin.

The power of His resurrection is our quickening unto a new life of righteousness.

With Him we died; with Him we are raised; that unto Him we might live!

O, glorious power of Calvary's tree!

CHAPTER 7

The Power of Universal Reconcilation

And having made peace through the blood of his
cross, by him to reconcile all things to himself; by
him, I say, whether they be things in earth, or things
in heaven. — COL. 1:20.

One of the grandest passages of all Scripture, in my opinion, is that marvelous eulogy on the preeminent and universally significant Christ which is found in Col. 1:15-20: "Who is the image of the invisible God, the first-born of every creature: For by him were all things created, that are in heaven and that are in earth, visible and invisible, whether they be thrones, or dominions, or principalities, or powers: all things were created by him, and for him: and he is before all things, and by him all things consist. And he is the head of the body, the Church: who is the beginning, the first-born from the dead; that in all things he might have the preeminence. For it pleased the Father that in him should all the fulness dwell; And having made peace through the blood of his cross, by him to reconcile all things to himself; by him, I say, whether they be things in earth, or things in heaven."

Although the profound mystery of this passage becomes more amazing according as one attempts to penetrate it more deeply, its general significance is quite plain. Christ, and that, too, as the head of His Church, and as the first-begotten from the dead, is the first-born of every creature. He is the first, and, therefore, also the last of all the works of God. He is the Alpha and, therefore, also the Omega. All things in heaven and on earth, in time and in eternity, concentrate in Him, have their subsistence and their meaning in Him. When God, if I may speak so humanly about the eternal counsel of the Most High, made His plan of all things, He conceived of the glorified Christ, crucified and raised from the dead, first of all; and all the rest of His works He so planned that they are adapted to this glorified Christ. He, the risen Lord, has the preeminence in the counsel of God. He is the head of all things. In Him dwells all the fulness. And He is the image of the invisible God, so that He is the supreme revelation of the Most High. And when this glorious counsel of God shall be fully revealed, and the works of God shall be finished in the new creation, our risen and glorified Lord will be the central and highest possible revelation of the invisible God, and the whole new creation will be a radiation of His glory.

Such, in general, is the meaning of that exalted passage in the first chapter of Colossians.

It is in that universal scheme of salvation that the text presents to us the cross of Christ as the power of the reconciliation of all things: "And having made peace through the blood of his cross, by him to reconcile all things to himself; by him, I say, whether they be things in earth, or things in heaven."

There can be no doubt that the phrase "all things" must be taken in the widest possible sense, that is, as including the entire universe and all it contains, as one organic whole. It is God's purpose to save the world, all the works of His hands, and not merely a number of men. And the text teaches us that, in the blood of Christ, God reconciled this entire world unto Himself, not only the world we know, but also the things that are in heaven. This does not imply that all individual creatures will be saved. Scripture teaches too plainly that there is no salvation for the devil and his evil angels, and also that many of the human race will be lost forever. There is no second chance, nor a final salvation of every individual creature. But it does signify that the scope of salvation is universal in the sense that it embraces the entire world, and that, in the new creation, all things in heaven and on earth will be united into one glorious whole in Christ as the Head. Hence, when the text declares that, in the blood of Christ, God reconciled all things unto Himself, the reference is to all creation. This is evident from the phrase itself: "all things" includes all the universe. Besides, lest we should limit the phrase to men, or to things on earth, it is specifically said to include both things in earth and things in heaven. Moreover, the entire context of this beautiful passage leads us to the same conclusion. It tells us that Christ is the first-born of every creature, that all things in heaven and earth were created by Him and for Him, things visible and invisible, and that in all things He must have the preeminence. All things, the whole universe, therefore, were reconciled to God in the blood of the cross.

Nor dare it be said that, in itself, this is a notion that is foreign to Scripture. On the contrary, this universal conception of salvation is thoroughly Biblical. Did not God so love the *world* that He gave His only begotten Son (John 3:16)? Is it not the mystery of God's everlasting good pleasure that "he might gather together in one all things in Christ, both which are in heaven and which are on the earth" (Eph. 1:10)? Is not even now Christ exalted far above all principality, and power, and might, and dominion, and every name that is named, not only in this world, but also in that which is to come (Eph. 1:21)? And do we not expect a new heaven and a new earth, in which righteousness shall dwell (II Pet. 3:13)? Does not the whole creation groan, travailing in pain, as it is made subject to vanity, and does it not eagerly look forward to the revelation of the glorious liberty of the children of God, in which also the brute creature shall participate (Rom. 8:19-22)? Or why, as we sing the glorious psalms of David, incomparable' in their spiritual beauty and riches of contents, should we address the heavens to rejoice, the earth to be glad, the field, and all that is therein, to be joyful, the sea to roar, and the floods to clap their hands, with a view to the coming of the Lord to judge the world, if creation had no part in the salvation of our God? Or again, why should the angels be so profoundly interested in the things concerning salvation, and so eager to look into them, if they were not personally concerned in them? And finally, does not the last part of the book of Revelation picture to us the redeemed universe, as a new heaven and a new earth, of which the new Jerusalem shall be the capital, and in which the tabernacle of God shall be with men? Why then should we hesitate, even for a moment, to give the text its full and widest possible application, when it teaches us that God reconciled all things unto Himself in the blood of the cross?

It may be objected that "all things" understood in this all-comprehensive sense can hardly be said to be the proper object of reconciliation to God. Does not reconciliation imply that the relation between God and us is one of enmity because of sin? And does not the act of reconciliation consist in the removal of sin by satisfaction? How, then, can this be applied to all things? The good angels never sin and, therefore, have no need of reconciliation to God through the blood of Christ. And the same is true of other creatures, outside of man, concerning whom you cannot even speak of sin and satisfaction.

All this may readily be admitted. As long as you look at the creatures individualistically, as merely a number of separate beings, it is impossible to understand how the Scriptures can speak of the reconciliation of all things, both in heaven and in earth, to God. But the moment you understand the Biblical viewpoint, according to which we must contemplate the world as one whole, it is quite different. For then you will understand, first of all, that sin did indeed, have the effect of alienating the entire universe from God; secondly, that it is surely God's purpose of salvation to bring back that whole world, and unite it in a higher and more glorious union with Himself than before; and, thirdly, that this was accomplished, principally, through the blood of Christ.

The cross of Christ is the power of universal reconciliation.

To understand this somewhat more fully, let us consider, in the first place, that in the beginning God created our world, the world of man, an organic whole. In this whole, there was an ascending scale of creatures. There is the inorganic world; the world of vegetation: trees and herbs, grass and flowers; the brute creation: fish and fowl, creeping things and four-footed beasts; and, finally, at the top of the scale, man, an intelligent and volitional being, a rational and moral creature, formed after the image of God. Man stood at the pinnacle of the earthly creation. In man, so to speak, all the lines of our world converged as in a center. He stood in covenant relation to God, and he was the king of the earthly creation. In his heart, the whole creation was united to the heart of God. His calling it was to gather and interpret the glory and praise of God reflected in all the world about him, and to bring it to his Creator. All things must serve him as their king, that he might, with all things serve his God as the priest of the Most High. All the earthly creation was a beautiful cosmos, one organic whole, in man, the servant of the Lord, as its lord and king.

That head of the earthly creation fell into sin and death. He became a rebel. He rejected the Word of God, and accepted the word of the devil. No longer did he function in the world as the servant of the Lord. However, his relation to the world about him, though spoiled, was not essentially changed. Though he lost much of his original power, he was still the lord of creation, now functioning as the enemy of God and as the friend of the devil. No longer did he gather the praises of God from all creation about him. When he fell, therefore, the whole creation became alienated, separated from the living God, and, accordingly, it was placed under the burden of the curse, in the bondage of vanity. Death and confusion reign everywhere. The whole creation groans, and is travailing in pain.

Secondly, let us turn our attention to the heavenly world, the region of angels. Naturally, we know much less about this than about our own world. Yet, in the light of Scripture, we may consider some facts as fairly well established. First of all, we learn from the Bible that also in the angel world there is gradation. The heavenly spirits are not all alike. They do not all occupy the same position. Scripture speaks of powers, and principalities, and mights, and dominions, of seraphim and cherubim, of angels and archangels; and it even mentions some of the princes among the angels, such as Michael and Gabriel, by name. Secondly, even from this it is but natural to infer that all these different classes of angels, these different degrees of power and dominion, originally culminated in one glorious angel, who was the prince of the heavenly world, the head and lord of all the heavenly host. Nor is the conclusion unwarranted that he, who is now the prince of darkness, Satan, originally occupied that exalted position. That he was a great one among the angels, there can be no doubt. That he is the chief of the multitude of angels that with him rebelled and left their own position, apostatizing from the living God, is also established. And when we consider that Michael, himself a great prince among the heavenly spirits, did not presume to bring a railing accusation against Satan, even in his fallen state, it seems rather sure that none other than he who is now the prince of darkness was that glorious king that was placed at the head of all the angels, as they were originally created.

Now, when Satan fell, only part of the angels apostatized with him; the rest remained faithful. Yet, it is quite evident that by this apostasy a terrible breach was struck in the world of heavenly spirits. Just as through the fall of man the earthly creation lost its representative head, so the angels lost their chief, in whom the entire angelic world culminated. And that breach was never healed.

Thus both, the earthly and the heavenly world, in their respective chief representative creatures, had apostatized from the living God, and presumed to rise in rebellion against Him.

Moreover, they had established a spiritual alliance, whereby the chief of the fallen spirits became the prince of this world.

All this, however, was strictly subservient to the counsel of the Most High.

For, in the third place, Scripture teaches that it was the good pleasure of God to unite all things, the earthly and the heavenly world, into one, under one head, and to bring the whole creation, in that new head, as one glorious organic whole, forever into the most intimate fellowship with Himself. And this new head and lord over all things in heaven and on earth was not to be a great angel, but Man. Man was, indeed, made a little lower than the angels, but he was destined to be crowned with glory and honor, and to have dominion over all things (Ps. 8; cf. Heb. 2:5-8). However, this supreme position of man in the entire universe is to be attained only in the Man Jesus Christ, the Son of God in the flesh. Him God had anointed to be the heir of all things, the Lord of all, and the head of His people, the Church. And the way to this exalted position led through the incarnation, and over the cross. The Son of God must unite the human nature inseparably with Himself: He must become man. Like unto His brethren He must become in all things, sin excepted. He must become earthy as they are earthy, weak as they are weak, subject to hunger and thirst, to sorrow and suffering, to misery and death, even as His brethren are subject to these evils because of sin. And He must take their place in judgment. Voluntarily He must take all their sins upon Himself, pay in full for all their transgressions, and thus reconcile them, and in them the world, unto God. Thus, as the Servant of the Lord, the Son of God would obtain for Himself and for all His own the right to that glorious Messianic kingdom that is called the kingdom of heaven, and in which He shall stand at the pinnacle of all created things, and all the world in heaven and in earth shall be subject unto Him, while He shall subject Himself to God.

Thus all things shall be reconciled to God.

Even now this is already accomplished. For "we see not yet all things put under him. But we see Jesus, who was made a little lower than the angels, for the suffering of death crowned with glory and honor" (Heb. 2:8, 9). He came in the flesh, He suffered and died, He was raised to glory, and is now exalted at the right hand of God, all the world being subject to Him.

This reconciliation of all things was accomplished through the blood of Christ.

Through the blood of His cross, He is become the new Head of the whole universe, and the two worlds, the earthly and the heavenly, are united under Him, and in Him to God.

In the heart of Jesus, the Son of God in the flesh, the entire universe is united to the heart of God, and that, too, in a higher and more intimate fellowship than ever before.

That is the power of the cross.

Universal peace has been principally established through His blood, and will be fully revealed when He shall appear in glory. Of this peace the text speaks: "having made peace through the blood of his cross, by him to reconcile all things unto himself."

God is the God of peace. In Him is harmony, perfect agreement with Himself. There is no conflict, no strife, no contention, no unrest, no war in God. For He is the triune God. One in essence is He, yet three in Persons. And on the basis of their essential oneness, the three Persons of the Holy Trinity, live a covenant life of friendship in the sphere of perfect harmony and peace, the harmony of pure love.

Hence, apart from Him, or in opposition to Him, there is no peace for the creature. Peace for the creature is essentially harmony with God. It is, therefore, inseparable from perfect righteousness. For righteousness is to be right with God, and to be right with God is to live in harmony with Him, in perfect knowledge of Him, righteousness, and holiness, so that our mind is in accord with His mind, our will with His will, and our whole nature is consecrated to Him. Thus to be in harmony with God, in our inmost being, and to be taken up in that fellowship in which we taste that the Lord is good, and that His lovingkindness is better than life — that is the state of peace. And in that state of peace with God, we also have peace with one another, and with all things.

It follows that there is no peace in the state of sin. Sin is unrighteousness, rebellion against God, war. In that state, God is against us. He leaves us no peace. He strikes us down in His holy wrath. And as long as we are in that state, there is confusion and strife, hatred and envy, war and destruction everywhere. War there is between God and us, for we stand in enmity against Him. War there is in the angel world: the good angels rise up against Satan and his hosts. War prevails in the world of man: always the powers of darkness set themselves against God's Anointed, and the righteous must suffer affliction in this world; but also the world is divided against itself, nation rises against nation, group against group, and there is strife and confusion all about us. War and destruction there is between man and the animals, and between the animals mutually. Wherever we look in the world that has no peace with the living God, strife and war predominate. And all the efforts of man to establish peace, apart from God, are hopeless.

"Destruction and misery are in their ways. And the way of peace have they not known" (Rom. 3:16, 17).

"There is no peace, saith my God, to the wicked" (Isa. 57:21).

But God made peace!

Peace He made, not by compromising with unrighteousness, or by denying His justice, which is impossible, but by establishing a basis of righteousness through the blood of the cross. For through the blood of the Son of God He removed the cause of all unrest and war, namely sin. He blotted out all our iniquities, and obtained for us eternal righteousness. Thus He removed the cause of our estrangement from Him, and reconciled us unto Himself. Moreover, through the blood of the cross, He destroyed the power of the prince of darkness, justified the heavenly spirits that had remained faithful, and united them under a new Head, the Lord of lords. The whole world He reconciled unto Himself. And in that new world in Christ, peace, universal, everlasting peace reigns supreme, peace with God, and peace in all the relationships of the various creatures.

All this must still be revealed in its final realization.

But revealed it shall surely be, when the Son of man shall come into the glory of His everlasting kingdom.

Then shall be fully realized the beautiful picture of the world to come that is presented in the well-known passage of the prophecy of Isaiah:

"And righteousness shall be the girdle of his loins, and faithfulness the girdle of his reins. The wolf also shall dwell with the lamb, and the leopard shall lie down with the kid; and the calf and the young lion and the fatling together; and a little child shall lead them. And the cow and the bear shall feed; their young ones shall lie down together: and the lion shall eat straw like the ox. And the suckling child shall play on the hole of the asp, and the weaned child shall put his hand on the cockatrice' den. They shall not hurt nor destroy in all my holy mountain: for the earth shall be full of the knowledge of the Lord, as the waters cover the sea."

Peace everywhere!

Peace in the sphere of universal reconciliation!

That is the power of the cross!

CHAPTER 8

The Power of His Resurrection

That I may know him, and the power of his resurrection. — PHIL. 3:10.

In the third chapter of the epistle to the Philippians, the apostle Paul gives a personal testimony of his profound appreciation of the knowledge of Christ. Christ is his only boast. In Christ alone he would glory. The knowledge of Christ is above all things excellent to him. Although he could mention many things in which he might boast according to the flesh, he counts them all but loss, and considers them as so much dung, in comparison with the excellency of the knowledge of Jesus Christ his Lord. All the distinctions of the flesh, his circumcision, his being a real Hebrew of the tribe of Benjamin, his great zeal for the law, his strict righteousness according to the law — all these he utterly repudiates, in order that he may gain Christ, and the righteousness which is of God by faith, and that thus he may know Him, and the power of His resurrection.

What is this power of the resurrection of Christ, and what does it mean to know Christ and the power of His resurrection?

It means, in brief, that Christ Who died on Calvary rose from corruption into incorruption, from mortality into immortality, from the lowliness of His earthly appearance into the glory of His heavenly form, that thus He overcame the very power of death,

347

so that death had no more dominion over Him, and that He is the living Lord of His Church, mighty to bestow upon her all the glorious blessings of salvation which He merited for her by His suffering and death and perfect obedience.

Christ is risen!

He is the living Lord!

Without the resurrection on the third day, the cross of Christ has neither power nor meaning. If Christ is not raised, all is still dark. Then there is no answer to Christ's question of amazement on the accursed tree: "My God, my God, why hast thou forsaken me?" Then there is no corroboration from heaven of the confident statement made by the dying Christ: "It is finished." If Christ is not raised, His death is no atoning sacrifice, He did not satisfy the justice of God with respect to our sins, nor did He merit for us eternal righteousness and life. If Christ is not raised on the third day, there is no living Lord that can quicken us, and make us partakers of the blessings of salvation.

But He is risen!

And by His resurrection we know that He who died on the accursed tree of Calvary is the true Son of God, God of God, Light of Light, and that He is the resurrection and the life. By His resurrection we know that He represented us in all His suffering, took our place in the judgment of God voluntarily, and by His perfect obedience, even unto the death of the cross, blotted out the guilt of our sin, and obtained for us everlasting righteousness and life. By His resurrection we know that the cross is, indeed, a power of God unto salvation.

That is the significance of the resurrection of Christ.

Moreover, Christ now lives, and as the living Lord He ascended up on high, leading captivity captive. And He received the promise of the Holy Spirit, that in Him He might return to His Church, and make all His own partakers of the blessings of salvation He purchased for them by His death. Hence, we may say that the power of Christ's resurrection is the power of the risen Lord Himself. To know the power of His resurrection we must know Him. And if we truly know Him by a living faith, we also have experiential knowledge of the power of His resurrection.

Knowing Christ, the living Lord, we experience His resurrection as a power of righteousness and justification. This is first and most fundamental. Righteousness before God is our great need. Without righteousness we cannot expect a single blessing of grace. For God loves the righteous, but His face is against them that do evil. It is essential, therefore, that we be made righteous. For in ourselves, and by nature, we are corrupt and guilty, worthy of damnation and eternal death, objects of the wrath of God. In our state of guilt, we have no right to be delivered from the bondage of sin and from the dominion of death. Our legal status, our position before the tribunal of the Judge of heaven and earth, must be changed from one of guilt and damnation into that of righteousness and justification. This righteousness Christ purchased for us. By His perfect obedience on the cross He merited for us the forgiveness of sins and perfect justification before the bar of heaven. By His humiliation even unto death He is become our righteousness.

And let us note the excellency of this righteousness of God in Christ. It is far more excellent than the righteousness with which the first man Adam was endowed in the state of rectitude in Paradise. The righteousness of Adam was his own, it rested in him, in the choice and determination of his own will; the righteousness which is bestowed upon us in Christ is never our own, it is always Christ's righteousness. It is imputed to us, reckoned as ours by grace, and for that very reason can be appropriated by us only through faith. It does not have its ground in our obedience, but in the perfect satisfaction of Christ alone. The righteousness of Adam was amissible: it could be forfeited and utterly lost by disobedience; the righteousness we have in Christ is established forever, and can never be lost, because it has its ground and source only in the Son of God in the flesh, in His death and resurrection. The righteousness which Adam possessed in the state of rectitude was sufficient to sustain and continue him in his earthly position and life, as long as he remained faithful to God's covenant; but the righteousness of Christ is light out of darkness, justification of the ungodly, life out of death, and it makes us worthy of that higher glory and blessedness which Scripture calls eternal life. For it is a righteousness which the Son of God merited for us by descending into deepest death and utter desolation, thus offering the perfect sacrifice for sin in free and loving obedience to the Father, a sacrifice of infinite power and value.

Of this everlasting righteousness the resurrection of Jesus Christ from the dead is the divine revelation. It is the Word of God concerning our complete justification, the divine answer to Christ's word on the cross: "It is finished."

That is the power of the resurrection of Christ.

To understand this truth, we must remember that God raised Jesus from the dead, and that justifying faith clings to God exactly as the One that raised up Christ.

Christ is, indeed, *risen,* but He is also *raised.* The Scriptures teach both, yet more often they present the resurrection of Christ as an act of God. When they speak of Christ as having risen, they refer to His resurrection as an act of His own, of the divine Son Himself, Who by the resurrection from the dead is powerfully set forth to be the Son of God, the resurrection and the life. However, when the Bible speaks of Christ's being raised, it would have us consider that resurrection as an act of the Triune God. And as such it is the Word of God concerning our justification, our everlasting righteousness in Christ. For "he was delivered for our offences, and was raised again for our justification" (Rom. 4:25).

Let us try to understand this blessed mystery of the Gospel a little more fully.

Christ died for our sins. Our place He took in God's judgment. For our sins He assumed full responsibility although He was, personally, without sin and guilt, perfectly righteous. In that position, as our Mediator, who represented us and appeared before the judgment seat of God in our stead, and who had assumed complete responsibility for all our transgressions, He was worthy of death, even though, personally, He was worthy of God's favor and was ever the object of God's delight and lovingkindness. With the load of responsibility for our sins upon His mighty shoulders, He appeared before the tribunal of God in the hour of judgment, and voluntarily He descended into the darkest depth of death and hell, where He suffered the wrath of God against the workers of iniquity, and all the pain and agony and sorrow in body and soul that is implied in the curse.

Out of that depth of hell there was only one way: the way of perfect obedience. Had Christ, by His suffering and death, failed to pay the last farthing, and to satisfy the justice of God against sin, had the sacrifice He offered to God not been without spot or blemish, had He not removed the burden of sin that was upon Him as our Mediator and representative, He must needs have perished, never could He have been raised from the dead. For just as, in the righteous judgment of God, sin and death are inseparably connected, so righteousness and life are inseparable. When, therefore, God raised Christ from the dead to resurrection glory, He thereby declared that the sins He had borne were no more, were completely blotted out, and that He, the Christ of God, was worthy of eternal life and glory. By raising Him from the dead, the Judge of heaven and earth set His seal of divine approval and acceptance on His perfect sacrifice.

But remember now that the sins He bore and which by His death He removed and blotted out were not His own, but ours, and you will understand that the resurrection of Christ is the Word of God to us that our sins are obliterated, and that we have obtained everlasting righteousness and life through the death of God's Son. He was delivered for our offences, and was raised again for our justification. The resurrection of Jesus Christ from the dead is the gospel of God concerning our everlasting righteousness and worthiness of eternal life.

Such is the power of His resurrection!

Nor is this all.

For the question arises: How do we come to know Him, and to know the power of His resurrection? It is of this knowledge that the apostle Paul speaks in Philippians three, the tenth verse. It is this knowledge of Christ, and of the power of His resurrection, and that, too, as a power unto righteousness, that is most precious to him. For he writes: "Yea, doubtless, and I count all things but loss for the excellency of the knowledge of Christ Jesus my Lord: for whom I have suffered the loss of all things, and do count them but dung, that I may win Christ, And be found in him, not having mine own righteousness, which is of the law, but that which is through the faith of Christ, the righteousness which is of God by faith: That I may know him, and the power of his resurrection."

But what is this knowledge of Christ that is so exceedingly excellent, and above all things precious? Is it the mere theoretical knowledge of theology? Suppose you knew all about Christ, would this be the same as knowing *Him?* Suppose you were even a professor of theology, able to instruct others in the knowledge of Christ as contained in the Scriptures; and suppose that you could explain, clearly and in detail, the idea and the meaning of the death and resurrection of Jesus Christ, would this be the knowledge of the power of His resurrection of which the apostle speaks?

No, indeed, it would not!

O, do not misunderstand my meaning. It is not my purpose to depreciate the great value of true and full and correct theoretical knowledge of our Saviour, and of all the Bible reveals of Him, and of the God of our salvation in Him. Such knowledge is indispensable. You cannot know Him without knowing about Him. And the more you know about Him, the better you can know Him. But the two are not identical. Mere intellectual knowledge about Christ, precious and indispensable though it be, is not sufficient unto salvation.

We must know *Him.*

It is necessary to distinguish between two kinds of knowledge. The one is intellectual, the other is experiential. The one is a matter of the head, the other of the heart. Two men may sit at a table laden with delicious food, the one a doctor of chemistry with cancer of the stomach, the other an ignorant laborer with a healthy appetite. The chemical expert may take the food into the laboratory, analyze it, and give a minute description of its ingredients and their nutritional value, but he cannot eat of it; the hungry laborer knows very little about the chemical composition of the meal, but he tastes its deliciousness, eats and digests it, and thus knows its power of nutrition by experience. Thus the mere theologian, without faith, may be able to analyze and explain theoretically the knowledge about Christ, without being acquainted with the power thereof; while the simplest child of God who would surely fail in an examination on Christology, appropriates Him by faith, tastes His goodness and mercy, and thus knows Him, and the power of His resurrection.

It is this knowledge which the apostle has in mind, and for the excellency of which he counts all things but dung.

But how is this spiritual, this experiential knowledge of the risen Lord acquired? The answer to this question is that it is not at all acquired by man himself: it is given to him, and that, too, by the living Lord that is risen from the dead. It is He Himself that causes us to know Him, and the power of His resurrection, and that makes us partakers of the righteousness He purchased for us by His obedience unto death on the cross.

For He is risen! He lives!

The Church does not believe in a dead Christ, but in a living Lord. He arose from the dead, is exalted at the right hand of God, and is become the quickening Spirit. And thus He is able to touch us in our inmost heart by the power of His grace, to make us experience His power of life, to impart Himself and all the benefits of His death and resurrection unto us. The power of His resurrection is the power of the living Lord. And the true, spiritual knowledge of that power is wrought within us by that living Lord Himself. And thus we taste the power of His resurrection as a power unto righteousness.

By nature, we are not partakers of the righteousness of Christ, nor could we of ourselves ever lay hold upon that righteousness or even desire it. For we are dead through trespasses and sins, darkened in our understanding so that we love the lie, perverse of will so that we are inclined unto iniquity, rebellious in heart, polluted in all our desires and inclinations. We do not care for righteousness. We love the darkness rather than the light. Righteousness we do not want, even though it be freely offered us, and we can obtain it for nothing. We prefer to pursue the way of unrighteousness that leads to destruction. And even though the gospel of a free righteousness were preached to us by men, and though a thousand preachers would warn us of our imminent peril of perdition, and earnestly urge us to accept the righteousness of Christ, we would only despise and reject it.

So foolish we are by nature.

Such is our state of death.

But Christ has overcome death, and He lives. And as the living Lord He is able to make us partakers of His righteousness, to quicken us, and to establish the living bond between Himself and our soul. This living bond is established by that marvelous gift of grace that is called faith, and which unites our soul to Christ, so that we become one plant with Him. It is the power of a saving knowledge whereby we know not merely about Him, but Himself in all the riches of His grace and in the power of His resurrection. It is the power, too, of a hearty confidence whereby we surrender ourselves unconditionally to Him, and rely completely on Him, in life and in death, as the revelation of the God of our salvation. Faith is the power wrought in our hearts when the living Lord touches us by the quickening power of His resurrection. It is that spiritual gift of grace whereby our whole soul, with mind and will and all our desires, become conscious of a profound need of Christ, yearns for Him and for His righteousness, hungers and thirsts after Him, seeks and finds Him, cleaves to Him, knows Him as no faithless soul is capable of knowing Him, wants Him as above all things precious, and appropriates Him and all His spiritual benefits. And through that faith, which the living Lord works in us, and constantly maintains in our soul, we know Him and the power of His resurrection as the power unto everlasting righteousness.

That is the knowledge of Him, and of the power of His resurrection!

O, blessed resurrection of the Son of God! Blessed Lord, crucified on Calvary, and raised from the dead on the third day! Blessed Word of God, through the resurrection of Jesus Christ from the dead, justifying the ungodly! Blessed power of His resurrection whereby we who lie in the midst of death are quickened unto a new life, and filled with the spiritual knowledge that our sins are forgiven, that we are clothed with an everlasting righteousness, and that we are heirs of eternal life! Well may we count all things but dung for the excellency of the knowledge of Jesus Christ our Lord!

BOOK FIVE

"...AND JESUS IN THE MIDST"

CHAPTER 1

The Crucifixion

Where they crucified Him .... —JOHN 19:18.

"And sitting down they watched him there."

Thus we read in the twenty-second chapter of the gospel according to Matthew, the thirty-sixth verse, of the soldiers that had executed the crucifixion of our Lord.

In these Lenten series we propose to follow the example of these soldiers, except that, by the grace of God, we hope to do so from different motives than they, and in a different attitude.

Just what is the import of these words: "they watched him there," is not quite clear.

Was there, deep in the hearts of these cruel men of the sword, a certain undefined and vague fear and wonder whether this strange Prophet of Galilee would still show some sign of His power, and come down from the cross? Hardly could they have failed being impressed by the mysterious power of this King of the Jews, whose weakness was His strength, whose suffering was a mighty battle, whose meekness surpassed all human conception, and whose defeat was His victory. And yet, these somewhat vague emotions must have been mingled with a profound contempt for this King without an army, whose servants would not fight for Him, and Who had made no attempt to defend His own cause; with a certain complacent glee, too, that

He, whom they had scourged, crowned with a wreath of thorns, and made the victim of their rebel mockery, was now, finally, made a spectacle to all the world of shame and reproach. And so, there was neither fear nor reverence in their attitude as they sat down and watched Him there.

We, too, will watch Him.

However, we hope to contemplate this Sufferer, not in order to add to His reproach, but to behold, in His shame, our own; not to heap more contempt upon His head, but to despise ourselves in our sin and shame; not to exalt ourselves in our imaginary righteousness and religiousness above those that nailed Him to the accursed tree, but to confess that we rejected Him; not to clamor with the multitude that He is worthy of death, but to sign our own condemnation; not to challenge Him to come down from the cross, but to acknowledge that the Christ must suffer thus in order to enter into His glory; to confess that He was wounded for our transgressions, bruised for our iniquities, and thus to behold in the crucified Jesus of Nazareth the God of our salvation, our Reconciler and Redeemer!

Thus contemplating Him by faith and the light of revelation, we cannot possibly "sit down" on Calvary. Rather will we *stand* there, with bowed heads and bared, remove our shoes from off our feet, realizing that the ground on which we stand is holy ground, and worship this crucified Lord, whose condemnation is our justification, whose shame is unto our glory, whose death is for us the way into the blessed life of God's heavenly tabernacle.

How utterly simple is the Gospel record of the moment of the crucifixion of our Savior! Writes John: "Where they crucified him." And he adds: "and two others with him, on either side one, and Jesus in the midst." John 19:18. Similarly, Luke: "And when they were come to the place, which is called Calvary, there they crucified him, and the malefactors, one on the right hand, and the other on the left." Luke 23:33. Mark mentions the crucifixion almost in passing: "And when they crucified him, they parted his raiments." Mark 15:24. And so in the Gospel according to Matthew: "And they crucified him, and parted his garments, casting lots." Matthew 27:35. Completely stripped is the narrative of all sensational details, of all that might make headlines in the daily papers, of anything that might arouse mere human emotions. No description here of how they stretched His emaciated form upon the cross-beam of the tree, hammered the cruel spikes through His hands, in order then to hoist the body to the perpendicular beam that had been planted on Calvary, and spike His feet to the foot-rest that must support the body on the cross. No word-pictures here about the human reaction of the Savior. It seems as if the Gospel writers realized that the mystery of the cross could not possibly be expressed in human language, and that the simplest words, recording the barest fact, would best serve the purpose. The cross of Christ must not be made vain by human description and imagination. And so, we had better follow their example and make no attempt to supply the element of human sensation, lest we render the cross of Christ of none effect.

"Where they crucified him!"

Were ever four words written, burdened with a heavier load of momentous significance than these?

Each one of them carries its own load of human shame and divine glory, of human enmity of God and divine love, of human hopelessness and divine redemption.

They crucified Him; that means that we sealed our own and the whole world's condemnation. They *crucified* Him: that signifies that we utterly put Him to naught, despised, and rejected Him; but also that He bore the curse for us, in order that we might never be accursed. *Him* they crucified: and that reveals that we were filled with a deeply rooted enmity against the living God; but also that God loved us, and that, too, at the very moment when we were yet sinners and hated Him. And it was *there,* on Calvary, outside of the gate, that this drama of furious hatred on the part of man and of amazing, unquenchable divine love, was enacted: and that means that Christ offered Himself a sacrifice for our sins, sprinkling His blood upon the mercy seat in the inner sanctuary, but also, that we must go out to Him outside of the camp, bearing His reproach.

Let us contemplate these various aspects of the crucifixion somewhat in detail, as we stand on Calvary and "watch him there."

They crucified Him!

Two questions clamor for an answer. Why did they commit this
deed? And who were they that crucified Him?

As to the first question, there can be but one answer: they
nailed Him to the tree because of what He is. He is the Son
of God, the only Begotten of the Father, God of God and Light
of Light. And this Son of God, by whom also the worlds were
made, came as near to us as possible when He assumed our flesh
and blood, and appeared in the form of a man. He entered into
our world, walked among us in the likeness of sinful flesh, lived
our life, spoke our language, and became like unto us in all
things, sin excepted. All the thirty-three years of His earthly
sojourn, but especially during the three years of His public ministry, He revealed the Father, in the words He spoke, in the works
He performed, yea, in His entire person. Always He stood for
the cause of God's righteousness, of His glory, and of His everlasting covenant. In the midst of a world of sin and darkness He
never drew back. With the unfruitful works of darkness He
never compromised. Always He revealed Himself as the light, and
there was no darkness in Him at all. In Him God was manifested
in the flesh.

This is the deep reason why the world hated Him.

For men were and are by nature enemies of God. They love
the darkness and hate the light.

Oh, do not object that they knew not that He was the Son of
God, that His glory was hid completely behind the form of a
mere man, and that, if He had only been manifest in His divine
glory, they would never have laid hands on Him. For this does not
alter the case whatever. For although it stands to reason that
they would never have ventured or been able to lay their vile
hands on Him and to nail Him to the cross had He been revealed
in the naked glory and majesty of His divinity, the fact remains
that His entire sojourn among us was one clear and glorious
revelation of God in His righteousness and holiness, His justice
and truth, His love and mercy, and His power to save. God's
representative He was. As the Son of God in the flesh, He was
manifest to all, through His words of eternal life and through His
mighty works. The sinless among sinners He was, and the sinners
hated Him. The light shining in the darkness He was, and the

darkness would have none of Him. The Son of God tabernacling among men He was, and men, although they did not express it in those very words, said, in effect: "This is the Son, let us kill Him!"

They *crucified* Him. And that means that their hatred knew no bounds. Oh, always they had despised and rejected Him! The more clearly He became manifest as the revelation of the Father, as the light of the world that would never condone the darkness, as the Son of God that absolutely refused to compromise with the cause of mere Man, the more they found Him intolerable, and hated Him with a bitter hatred. Always they opposed Him, contradicted Him, reviled Him, accused Him of standing in alliance with Beelzebub, marked Him as a deceiver and blasphemer. And frequently they sought to lay hands on Him and cast Him out of their world. But the cross was the climax, the ultimate revelation of their insatiable hatred. By the crucifixion they expressed that they considered Him a worthless fellow, to be numbered with the worst of criminals, accursed of men, utterly unfit to occupy a place in human society. Thus they revealed that the carnal mind is enmity against God, implacable, incurable, furious, bent upon the obliteration of His very name from the face of the earth.

But who were these men that so crucified Him?

Were they, perhaps, bloodthirsty savages, uneducated cannibals, uncivilized heathen? Were they men from the lowest ranks of society, unscrupulous criminals, the scum of mankind, upon whom we may well look with disdain?

On the contrary, they were men that represented the world at its best. Literally every conceivable class of men was represented. Oh, when the Gospel record has it that "they crucified him," the reference is, perhaps literally to the soldiers that spiked Him to the tree. But after all, these were only the agents. Behind them stood the representative of the Roman world-power, proud of its culture and civilization, famous for its knowledge and development of human jurisprudence, represented by Pontius Pilate. And back of this world-power stood the religious world, that is, mere men, natural men, as they had come into contact with the outward revelation of the word of God, the law and the prophets. There were the scribes and the lawyers, the theologians of that time, who made it their business to discover what is the will of God; the Pharisees, who were renowned as men that walked in all the external righteousness of the law; and the priests, headed by the high priest, who functioned in the sanctuary made with hands. And there was even one of the inner circle of Jesus' closest associates, who had heard His words, and been witness of His mighty works for three years, who even had been sent out to preach the Gospel of the Kingdom, to heal the sick and to cast out devils in His name, but who assumed the despicable role of betraying the Master into the hands of the enemy.

What does it mean?

It signifies that you cannot explain this most atrocious sin of the crucifixion from lack of culture, civilization, education, religious influence; or from a difference in social standing, or in character.

It means that the crucifixion of our Lord is the revelation of something that is universal, that is common to all men, as mere men, apart from grace. And that is sin, enmity against God. It means that you and I, as mere men, crucified Him. It means that all our modern praise of the man Jesus, all our pretended goodness, and willingness to follow His example, all our religiousness, as long as it is nothing else than *our* religiousness and goodness, is pure sham, camouflage, deceit, hypocrisy. It means that if the Lord sojourned among us today, and walked the streets of our civilized world, we, mere men, no matter what our station may be in life, no matter how beautiful may be the polish and glamor of our culture, would no more give Him a place, and tolerate Him, than did the mere men of His day. We certainly would crucify Him! *They* crucified Him. That means: mere men crucified Him. And that means: mere men always crucify the Son of God in the flesh. Let us bow our heads in shame as we stand on Calvary and watch Him there. And let us confess that the cross of the Son of God is our greatest condemnation! But even this confession would be impossible for us to make, were it not for the power of that very cross. And that cross would not have that power, if it were nothing more than the expression of man's implacable hatred of God; if it were not also, at the same time, and above all, the highest revelation of God's all-enduring, sovereign, victorious love, through which He gave His Son to be the propitiation for our sins.

Thanks be to God, however, the cross is not only man's cross but also the cross of God!

For consider now that it is *He,* the Son of God, whom they crucified!

But how could they? How could they possibly lay hands on the Son of God, even as He appeared in the likeness of sinful flesh? The answer is: only because, in perfect obedience of love to the Father, and in love to His brethren, He voluntarily surrendered Himself into the hands of sinners, willingly suffered all the reproach and shame that was heaped upon Him, gave His blessed body to be nailed to the cross, and by His own will remained on the accursed tree even to the bitter end. And what else does this mean than that the Father sent His Son into the world that He might bear our sins, satisfy the justice of God with respect to our iniquities, atone for our transgressions, and obtain for us righteousness and eternal life? O, indeed, it was *they* that crucified Him! Yes, but only because He was delivered by the determinate counsel and foreknowledge of God could they lay their wicked hands on Him. They crucified Him! Indeed, but they could accomplish this most heinous sin only because God gave His Son, the Son gave Himself, the Spirit sanctified Him to bring the perfect sacrifice for our transgressions. They crucified Him! O, but considered in the light of God's revelation this means that He took the cross upon Himself, and with the cross the curse of God's wrath against our sins, the curse under which we must needs perish everlastingly, and that He, by bearing that curse in perfect obedience of love to the Father, removed the guilt of our sins. Through the darkest night of our corruption and enmity against Him, it pleased God to penetrate with the most glorious light of His wondrous love.

That is the paradox of the cross, and at the same time its power of salvation!

Let us put all our imaginary righteousness away, in order to put all our confidence in the righteousness of God through Jesus Christ and Him crucified!

There they crucified Him.

Our attention is called to the place. The name of that place was Calvary, the place of the skull. Various explanations have been offered of that name with which we are not concerned. The most probable explanation seems to be that which has it that there was a little hill outside of Jerusalem that resembled in shape a human skull. The important point, however, is that Calvary was outside of the city. And this, according to the Epistle to the Hebrews, signifies that on Calvary, we behold the atonement of the Great Day. "For the bodies of those beasts, whose blood is brought into the sanctuary by the high priest for sin, are burnt without the camp. Wherefore Jesus also, that he might sanctify the people with his own blood, suffered without the gate." Heb. 13:11, 12.

A three-fold significance, therefore, there is in the place of the skull. First, it signifies that there on the cross of Calvary hangs the body of our sins. The bodies of the beasts that were sacrificed on the Great Day of Atonement were laden with the sins of the people, and as such they were burnt without the camp. Christ is made sin for us. "For he hath made him to be sin for us, who knew no sin: that we might be made the righteousness of God in him." II Cor. 5:21. He, the Lamb of God, contracted all our iniquities, as they were loaded upon Him by God Himself. In His body, the body of sin is forever destroyed. Secondly, it signifies that there on Golgotha, hangs our High Priest, who carries the blood of His perfect sacrifice into the inner sanctuary, not made with hands, and sprinkles it upon the mercy-seat before the face of God, a propitiation and perfect covering for our transgressions. For thus it was done by the high priest on the Great Day of Atonement. Thirdly, Calvary reminds us once more that Jerusalem, that the world considered Him a reproach, and as such casts Him out as a thing to be abhorred. For that was the meaning of the sacrificial bodies without the camp. And that is the significance of Christ's suffering without the gate.

Let us go out, therefore, to Him without the camp.

Go out to Him, indeed, in order to find forgiveness and everlasting righteousness in that sacrificial blood of atonement.

But go out, too, to separate ourselves from that wicked Jerusalem and the wicked world to confess Him as our Lord.

Then we shall have to bear His reproach, for always the cross is a thing of reproach. But if we suffer with Him, we shall also be glorified with Him. If we die with Him we shall also live with Him forevermore!

CHAPTER 2

The Three Crosses

*Where they crucified Him, and two others with
Him, on either side one, and Jesus in the midst.*
— JOHN 19:18.

Rich is the Word of God that proceeds from Calvary. For, to
be sure, also the Place of the Skull is a Word of God to us.

"The heavens declare the glory of God; and the firmament
showeth his handiwork." But Calvary no less.

"Day unto day uttereth speech, and night unto night showeth
knowledge." But also from Golgotha the eternal Wisdom directs His
speech unto us.

By the Word of God all things were made in heaven and on
earth. By that same Word they are being preserved continually,
even as the breath of God's wrath causes them to bear the heavy
burden of His curse. Hence, the invisible things of Him from
the creation of the world are clearly seen, being understood by
the things that are made, even His eternal power and Godhead.

But it is also by the same Word of God, by which the heavens
and the earth and all things they contain are made, even though
that Word speaks to us and operates through ungodly hearts and
evil hands, that Calvary is called into existence, that the "Place
of a Skull" and all the details that belong to the divine drama
of the cross of His Son, were ordered and arranged. That cross

is God's cross. The "Hour" is God's hour. The place "without the gate" is God's place. Also the two others, that were crucified with Him, were ordained and put there by the hand of God. God is giving His Son over into death; the Son puts down His life in voluntary obedience to the command which He received from the Father; and the Spirit supports, prepares, and sanctifies Him, in order there, on the accursed tree, to bear the burden of God's wrath against sin, and with one sacrifice to perfect forever those that through Him are sanctified.

And therefore also from the "Place of a Skull" the Word of God proceeds to us: Golgotha is revelation of God!

Only it must be remembered that there is a profound difference between the speech of God in and through creation and His Self-revelation on Calvary.

There, in creation, He is indeed known in His eternal power and Godhead, as the Lord, who calls the things that are not as if they were, who must be glorified and thanked. There, in creation, He speaks also of His terrible wrath which is revealed from heaven against all ungodliness and unrighteousness of men, who hold the truth in unrighteousness. Here, however, on the cross of Calvary, He reveals Himself as the reconciler of the world, as the one who overcomes and destroys sin, who blots out all our iniquities, and who through death reveals life everlasting. For, indeed, Golgotha also testifies of His burning and righteous wrath, but of that wrath as He Himself bears it, in order that we, being redeemed from sin and death, might dwell eternally with Him in His glorious tabernacle as His covenant friends.

On Golgotha God reveals Himself as the One who keeps His covenant and maintains it forever.

He reveals Himself as the God whose love is ever first, and completely sovereign, a fire that can never be quenched.

Calvary is the revelation of God who doeth wondrous things, whose path is ever in the sea.

Rich indeed is the Word of God speaking through the cross.

––––––

Three crosses were planted on Golgotha.

All of the four gospel narratives make mention of two others that were crucified with our Lord. In Matthew we read: "Then were the two thieves crucified with him, one on the right hand, and another on the left." Likewise in Mark: "And with him they crucified two thieves; the one on his right hand and the other on his left." And in the gospel according to Luke we read: "And when they were come to the place, which is called Calvary, there they crucified him, and the malefactors, one on the right hand, and the other on the left." And, finally, in the gospel according to John it is stated: "Where they crucified him, and two others with him, on either side one, and Jesus in the midst."

Three crosses, therefore, not one, or two, but three crosses must serve the symbolism of the speech of God to us from Calvary. And to this speech of God we will now listen for a moment.

Surely, we know that it was according to the will of God and in His providential care that His Son in the flesh should die the death of the cross. He may not simply die of a disease. Nor may He be stabbed to death, or stoned by the enemy. He must die the death of the cross. This had not been the intention of evil men. The "hour" of the cross was not their hour but that of the Father. Men would rather have killed Him by subtilty, aided by the traitor. They did not desire to make His death a public spectacle. For the same reason it was not their intention to kill the Son of Man on the feast day, lest there should be an uproar among the people. Yet, God's counsel always stands, and it was according to His determinate counsel that His Son should die as a public spectacle on the accursed tree, and that, too, on the Feast of the Passover.

We also know what is the speech of God that proceeds from the cross. For according to Scripture, the death of the cross symbolizes the curse of God upon the sinner. Thus we read in Deut. 21: 22, 23: "And if any man have committed a sin worthy of death, and he be put to death, and thou hang him on a tree: His body shall not remain all night upon the tree, but thou shalt in any wise bury him that day; (for he that is hanged is accursed of God;) that the land be not defiled, which the Lord thy God giveth thee." It is plain that the reference here is not to capital punishment by hanging, but to the hanging and public exposure of the bodies of those that had been put to death either by the sword or by stoning. Such a public hanging was considered an intensification of capital punishment. It was, therefore, the hanging itself, and not the death by hanging, that was an abomination, and that caused the hanged one to be accursed of God. And this passage in Deuteronomy is referred to in the Epistle of Paul to the Galatians as follows: "For as many as are of the works of the law are under the curse: for it is written, Cursed is everyone that continueth not in all things which are written in the book of the law to do them. But that no man is justified by the law in the sight of God, it is evident: for the just shall live by faith. And the law is not of faith: but the man that doeth them shall live in them. Christ hath redeemed us from the curse of the law, being made a curse for us: for it is written, Cursed is everyone that hangeth on a tree." Gal. 3: 10-13.

The curse of God is His word of wrath upon us.

It is the opposite of His blessing and His favor. Both, blessing and cursing, are words which God speaks. The former is the word of His favor, His grace and lovingkindness, drawing us into His fellowship and causing us to taste that the Lord is good. When God blesses us, He receives us in His tabernacle, and causes us to taste the sweetness of His fellowship, so that we live. The latter, the word of His curse, is the expression of His wrath and hot anger, expelling us from His home, causing us to experience Him as a consuming fire, casting us away from His presence and fellowship, forsaking us in utter terror of darkness and desolation, and making us unspeakably wretched. The word of His blessing is life; that of His curse is everlasting death.

That curse-word of God is the speech that proceeds from the cross.

And do not say that this speech would have been clearer if on Calvary there would have been planted only one cross instead of three, seeing that He, the Son of God, must bear the curse of God alone. For through the crosses of the other two the Word of God also speaks to us, the Word, namely, "Cursed is *everyone* that continueth not in all things which are written in the book of the law to do them." Or as we read in the Epistle to the Galatians, "For *as many* as are of the works of the law are under the curse."

Those two malefactors represent "the world"; they represent us, you and me, as in ourselves we are transgressors of the law and lie under the curse.

O, in the eyes of men, these two malefactors that had been condemned to death together with Christ were special criminals, men that were not worthy to occupy a place in human society. Before God, however, they were simply transgressors of the law, of His law, and, therefore, they were but representatives of us all. For we all are under the law. And we all are also transgressors of the law. Without distinction, therefore, we lie under the curse of God.

The three crosses together, therefore, speak of the common curse of God upon the whole world.

O, it is true, the Christ, the Son of God in the flesh, hangs on that cross not because He was personally a transgressor of the law. The curse which rests upon the two others, the curse of the entire "world" is upon Him simply because He voluntarily took it upon Himself.

But He was reckoned with the transgressors. Reckoned He was as such, indeed, by men that reproached Him, covered Him with shame and cast Him out, outside of the gate.

But reckoned He is as such also by God, for it is He that causes the curse of the transgressors to be upon Him.

The common curse was upon Him.

That is the language of the three crosses.

———

And with Him two others!

On either side one, and Jesus in the midst!

Such is the picture on Calvary: three crosses, Jesus and two others. But there is a plain distinction between that central cross and those on the right and on the left side.

It is true that from all three of them proceeds the Word of the curse of God, the Word that everyone is cursed who doth not continue in all that is written in the book of the law to do it. Yet, from the cross of Christ proceeds plainly the Word of the God of our salvation, who took our condemnation, our sin, and our curse upon His own mighty shoulders.

For the revelation of this distinction God had taken special care. Just read the superscription attached to each of the crosses.

That also above the heads of the two malefactors a super-scription was nailed, cannot be doubted. It was simply the custom that, when a criminal had been condemned to the death of the cross, his crime as the ground of his condemnation was written on a little board, and so was published before the eyes of all the spectators. Sometimes that superscription was prepared at the place of judgment, hung around the neck of the criminal, and thus by himself through the streets of the city carried to the place of execution, in order then to be nailed to his cross. In other instances, as was most probably the case with the crucifixion of the Lord, the superscription was prepared at the place of execution. It may therefore well be accepted as an established fact that also above the heads of the two thieves such a superscription was attached.

But on their superscriptions one could only read their crimes, the ground of their condemnation, together with their names.

Cursed were they as transgressors of the law!

But, behold, that cross in the midst of the two malefactors bears an entirely different superscription. God Himself had directed Pilate's heart and hand to write: "Jesus, the Nazarene, the King of the Jews." And however strenuously the hostile Jews, as was to be expected, protested against this indication of the ground of His condemnation; and however they insisted that there should be added to this superscription that He only had claimed to be the King of the Jews, Pilate maintained his own super-scription: "What I have written I have written."

But, how marvelous!

What an entirely different speech of God proceeds from that cross now!

Jesus! That name means Jehovah-Salvation. That was the name whereby He was called by the angel before He came into the world. And the same angel had explained this name in the words: "He shall save his people from their sins." Jesus, Jehovah-Salvation, the God of our complete salvation, who shall redeem His people from their sins, here is exposed on the accursed tree as under the common curse of the world, our curse! That is the speech of the three crosses with Jesus in the midst! It is the Word of God that comes to us from Calvary.

The Nazarene!

O, from a human point of view this name was meant to be a name of reproach. Can anything good come out of Nazareth? But interpreted as the speech of God this name signifies something entirely different. Does not Scripture teach us in Matthew 2, verse 23, that it was under God's direction that "He came and dwelt in a city called Nazareth: that it might be fulfilled which was spoken by the prophets, He shall be called a Nazarene." But where was this ever spoken by the prophets? We can understand this when we note that the name *Nazareth* is derived from the Hebrew NAZAR, which means *rod* or *branch,* and which literally occurs in Isaiah 11:1, "And there shall come forth a rod out of the stem of Jesse, and a branch shall grow out of his roots."

The Nazarene!

The Rod, the Branch out of the stem of Jesse, a Root out of a dry ground, the Promised One, the long-expected One, the Servant of Jehovah, of whom it was predicted that He would have no form or comeliness, no beauty that we should desire Him, who was long ago described to the people of God as the despised and rejected one, the man of sorrows, from whom we hid our faces, who should bear our griefs and carry our sorrows, who would be wounded for our transgressions, and bruised for our iniquities, who was oppressed and afflicted, yet He opened not His mouth –– He it is that stands here on the place of God's judgment and wrath, under the curse which is upon us as transgressors of the law! The suffering Servant of Jehovah! Such is the speech of God proceeding from the three crosses, and Jesus in the midst!

The King of the Jews! Thus the superscription above the cross of Jesus ends.

But who else is the King of the Jews than the Messiah, the Christ of God, the One that was anointed, appointed of God and qualified by His Spirit to overcome the powers of darkness and destroy them forever; who, in the way of His suffering and death, should approach the Ancient of Days, and inherit His kingdom; and who should lead the children of the kingdom, given Him of the Father from before the foundation of the world, into the everlasting glory of God's eternal covenant?

Jesus, Jehovah-Salvation, Immanuel, God in the flesh, the revelation of the God of our salvation, who shall redeem His people
from their sins; the Nazarene, the long promised Stem out of
the root of David; the King of the Jews, the anointed of the
Lord — He it is that hangs on the accursed tree on the Place
of a Skull.

What is the meaning of it all?

What else does it mean than this that, while the two other malefactors are *by nature* under the wrath of God, He, the Christ of
God, *came* under the law, and by doing so *submitted* Himself
voluntarily under the curse? What else does it signify than this
that, while the two others bear the curse of God *as transgressors,*
He bears that curse because He was *reckoned* with the transgressors, He, the sinless servant of the Lord? What else does it
mean than this that, while the two evil-doers must sink away
under the burden of God's wrath in everlasting desolation, He is
capable to *bear* that curse on His mighty shoulders, and bear it
away forever?

Indeed, a marvelous speech of God proceeds from the three
crosses.

————

And Jesus in the midst!

This, too, is mentioned with emphasis by all the writers of
the gospel.

And it is but proper that, according to the symbolism of Calvary,
it should be thus. Jesus must not be crucified either to the right
or to the left but in the very center of the two malefactors. Not only
does the speech of God thus proclaim loudly that He was reckoned
with the transgressors, and that He bears the curse of the world
before the face of God, but also does this position plainly indicate that the cross of Christ makes separation in the world of sin
and death.

Indeed, does the Christ of God bear the curse of the world, yet
not for all in that world.

The cross also speaks of divine, sovereign good pleasure, of
gracious election, but also of righteous reprobation: on either
side one, and Jesus in the midst.

The cross of Christ is also the cause that the thoughts of many hearts shall be revealed, thoughts manifesting grace and sin, faith and unbelief. "For the preaching of the cross is to them that perish foolishness; but unto us which are saved it is the power of God." Always the Jews require a sign, and the Greeks seek after wisdom. But the cross of Christ, while it is a stumbling block unto the Jews, and foolishness unto the Greeks, is unto them which are called, both Jews and Greeks, the power and the wisdom of God. Even on Calvary this separation is at once manifest in the attitude of the two malefactors to that central cross: the one is received and accepts, the other is reprobated and rejects.

And thus it will continue according to the sovereign counsel of the Most High even unto the end of the world: the cross is a power of God and foolishness!

And thus the speech of God on Calvary is complete: "And Jesus in the midst."

CHAPTER 3

Intercession

Then said Jesus, Father, forgive them; for they know not what they do. — LUKE 23:34.

As we stand at the Place of a Skull, and humbly confessing our sin and corruption, and enmity against God, reverently "watch Him there," and "survey the wondrous cross," we cannot but be amazed at the forbearance and longsuffering of God in permitting this most dreadful of sins to be committed to the very end.

His longsuffering over the Son of His love, hanging on the accursed tree, and crying to Him from the depths.

And His forbearance in not striking down in His wrath the wicked world that here pours out its vials of anger and wrath upon the Son of God, the Servant of the Lord, in whom He is well-pleased.

Here men lay hold upon the Son of God in the flesh. Here they put their wicked hands on the faithful Servant of the Lord, who came to do the Father's will. All the vials of their mad hatred and fury they pour out upon Him. They put Him to nought, beat and maltreat Him, spit upon and scourge Him, and finally lead Him to Calvary and strike Him to the tree. And even then their insatiable hatred they express in jeers and mockeries. In all this they, mere men, sinners, the whole world, you and I as we are by nature in sin and iniquity, fill the measure of our transgression.

377

There on Calvary is the judgment of the world. There we stand exposed in all our enmity against God. There the mask of our sham goodness and religiousness is torn from our faces. The hour of the cross is the hour of the judgment of the world.

But why is it, then, that this judgment is not executed there and then?

How is it to be explained that the wicked world is left to finish this greatest of all crimes: the crucifixion of the Son of God?

Would we not expect, as wicked men lay their hands on Jesus, stretch His form upon the cross, and cruelly hammer the spikes through hands and feet, that the heavens will open, and God will come from Teman, and the Holy One from Mount Paran, to execute vengeance upon His enemies? Is not this the day "that shall burn as an oven; and all the proud, yea, and all that do wickedly, shall be stubble"? Shall not, here on Calvary, judgment be executed, and all the wicked be burnt up and consumed?

Yet, nothing happens!

The enemies perform and finish their wicked work; the Son of God suffers, cries to the Father in His agony, and gives up the ghost; but the heavens remain closed, and no judgment is executed upon that wicked world that now has clearly revealed its enmity against God, and filled the measure of its iniquity.

How must this be explained?

The key to the answer to this question may be found in the intercessory prayer of our Lord, uttered on Calvary, perhaps, at the very moment when they nailed Him to the tree. For we read: "And when they were come to the place, which is called Calvary, there they crucified him, and the malefactors, one on the right hand and the other on the left. *Then* said Jesus, Father, forgive them for they know not what they do." Luke 23:33, 34. As long as our Lord can utter this prayer, judgment cannot be executed, the time for the final destruction of the world has not yet come. For this prayer means that even in that wicked world there are still of God's elect, for whom at this very moment Christ sheds His lifeblood, and that must be redeemed and delivered from the power of sin and death, and transformed into glorious children of the living God. There will come a time, when the last of these shall be gathered in, and when the Son of God will no longer pray for those that crucify Him. Then judgment may come. But as long as this is not the case, as long as this prayer for those that maltreat and kill Him rises from the lips of the Savior, God is longsuffering, and the pouring out of His wrath upon the world of iniquity must wait. And the blood of Christ, which, by wicked hands, they shed, the sovereign love of God for His chosen church, that is still in the loins of that fallen world, turns into the blood of atonement, on the ground of which the Son in the flesh, by the Spirit, is able to intercede for the transgressors: "Father, forgive them; for they know not what they do."

That is the paradox of the cross; but also its possibility and saving efficacy.

For remember that it was at the moment of the crucifixion, that our Lord and Savior, as our great High Priest, uttered this prayer for the transgressors. Luke informs us: *"Then* said Jesus, Father, forgive them." And that little word "then" is of profound meaning. Just what was the precise moment of the intercessory prayer, whether it was when Jesus lay still on the ground and they nailed His hands to the crossbeam of the accursed tree, or after the crucifixion was finished, is of little moment, though we prefer to think that the former supposition is correct. The point, however, is that the Lord interceded for the transgressors. And what else does this mean than this, that He already is busy as our great High Priest? As they draw the blood from His hands, He sheds it voluntarily, seeks and finds entrance with it in the sanctuary above, and sprinkles it before the face of the Father upon the mercy-seat, a propitiation for sin. And on the basis of His blood He pleads for forgiveness. He says, as it were: "Father, they shed my life-blood, but I give it willingly and freely for those whom Thou hast given Me out of the world. From the very first drop of my life-blood, to the very last, I will offer Myself a sacrifice for their sins: forgive them, for they know not what they do!"

What may be the meaning of this intercession?

Already you must have understood that we interpret this prayer of the suffering Savior as a prayer for forgiveness in the full and final sense of the word.

There are those who would understand this word "forgive" in this petition in the sense of postponement of judgment, and apply it particularly and exclusively to the Jewish nation. It was the nation of Israel that here rejected the promised Messiah, say they, and that, by doing so, filled the measure of iniquity, and became worthy of being cast away. Final judgment might have, yea, must have come upon the nation of Israel at this very moment, had it not been for this prayer of the Messiah they rejected. But the Lord prays for them. He implores the Father that this last sin, that fills the measure of their iniquity, may not be imputed to them at this moment, that the execution of judgment may be postponed, that a period of respite may be given to the Jews, in order that they may have time and opportunity to be saved. According to this interpretation, the answer to the Lord's prayer must be found in the fact that the final judgment upon Israel and Jerusalem was postponed forty years: it was not until the year 70 that Jerusalem was destroyed, and that the nation of Israel as such ceased to exist.

But numerous are the objections that may be raised against this view.

Not the least of these is the meaning of the word "forgive". The original word used here means "to dismiss, to remit, to send away or dismiss from one's mind, to talk no more about it," and thus "to forgive". It simply never means "to postpone". It is always used in the Bible for the forgiveness of sins. It is, therefore, the only meaning that may be allowed here as the correct interpretation of Jesus' prayer.

Besides, the crucifixion of the Messiah marked the end of Israel as a nation irrevocably. For it was God's inscrutable purpose that through their fall salvation might come unto the Gentiles (Rom. 11:11); the middle wall of partition might be broken down (Eph. 2:14); and the same Lord might become rich over all that call upon Him, whether he be Jew or Greek (Rom. 10:12). No postponement of judgment could possibly restore the nation of Israel to its former peculiar position. It is true, indeed, that there is salvation also for the Jews that rejected their Messiah; but for this, postponement of judgment upon Jerusalem and the nation as such is neither necessary nor sufficient: they need forgiveness. In the way of repentance they will be grafted in again upon their own olive tree, together with the Gentiles, and they shall be one flock under one shepherd.

Hence, it must be maintained that the Lord here strictly prays for forgiveness.

He implores the Father, first of all, that the sin of the moment, which they committed in crucifying the Son of God, may be remitted unto them.

But you understand, that this implies a petition for the forgiveness of all sins!

For, first of all, it is true, in general, that sin is not and cannot be forgiven piecemeal, so that some sins are forgiven us, while others are held against us. Before God we are either forgiven or not forgiven, we are either righteous or unrighteous. We either have complete forgiveness of all our sins, or we have no forgiveness at all. But, secondly, in the forgiveness of this one sin, this greatest of all sins, this principal sin, in which all the corruption of our depraved nature manifests itself, the forgiveness of all sin is implied. If this one sin of the crucifixion of the Son of God can be forgiven, all sin is forever blotted out; if not, there is no forgiveness of any sin. And so the Lord prays at this important and crucial moment: "Father, forgive them; impute not this sin, nor any sin unto them; let them go free, and talk no more about it; acquit them in thy righteous judgment as if they had never committed this or any other iniquity. Declare them righteous, O Father, that they may also come where I go, and be with me forever! I will love them unto the end, and bear all their iniquity away through the very blood they are shedding!"

The intercessory prayer of our merciful High Priest!

———

But the question is, for whom is the Lord here interceding?

The answer to this question may, on the one hand, be as universal as you can conceive of it; yet, on the other hand, it must strictly be limited and understood as particular.

Let me explain.

If you ask this question with reference to the class of people, or kind of sinners for which Jesus interceded on the cross, the answer must be: for all, without distinction.

You need not ask: "Did our Lord pray for the soldiers that spiked Him to the tree? Did He pray for the Roman governor that delivered Him over to the will of the Jews? Did He intercede for the Sanhedrin that condemned Him to death? Did He implore the Father in behalf of the Jews that clamored for His blood?" That would be quite irrelevant, nor would it bring assurance of forgiveness to your penitent heart. Rather put the question in this form: "If I had stood there personally, and with my own hands had nailed Him to the tree, would that prayer of my Lord concern me, and could I find forgiveness in that blood I shed, if I humble myself before God in repentance?"

To that question the answer is most surely affirmative.

O, most certainly, there is forgiveness for you who nailed Him to the tree. If you had been that member of the Sanhedrin that blindfolded Him in that darkest of nights, or that struck Him in the face, or that spit upon Him in disdain; if you with your hands had plaited that cruel crown of thorns and pressed it upon His sacred brow, or struck Him wantonly with the reed, or plowed His back with the bloody scourge; if you had been among that mob that stood before the judgment hall, and had, personally, clamored for His blood, and insisted that He should be crucified; or if you had stood before the tree on Calvary, and jeered at Him, and with devilish glee challenged Him to save Himself, and come down from the cross — if you had done any part or all of this wickedness to the Son of God yourself, in person, there would indeed be comfort for your penitent soul in that intercession of the Lord.

All your sins are included in this intercession of our Savior, and His prayer is always heard.

You may hear the Word of God, through this intercession of the Lord: "Thy sins are forgiven thee!"

And this is strictly necessary.

For mark you well, although you were not personally present on Calvary, in the flesh, you did all this to Him, as really as if you had been present there in the body. For your name is sinner. And that means that you are an enemy of God, by nature, and that you always reject the Son of God. What the Jews, the Romans, the soldiers did is but a clear and horrible manifestation and expression of what you and I always do. The "world" crucified Him. And to that "world" you and I belong as we are in ourselves, apart from Christ. But that intercession of our Lord, uttered at the moment of the crucifixion, means that there is no sin so great, so terrible and dreadful, that is not covered by His blood, and for the which there is no forgiveness in the way of repentance. In this sense, the intercession of the Man of Sorrows is all-comprehensive. Never does any penitent sinner, no matter in what foul mire of sin he has been wallowing, approach the throne of grace in vain.

On the other hand, however, the scope of this intercession is strictly limited to those that repent and believe, and, therefore, to the elect.

For, first of all, the Lord Himself tells us that He prays not for the world but for those whom the Father has given Him. And surely, to that limitation this prayer can be no exception.

Secondly, the scope of this intercessory prayer cannot be wider than that of His atoning blood. And He gave His life for His sheep, and they are those that were chosen in Him before the foundation of the world

Thirdly, the prayer of Christ is always heard; those for whom He interceded on the cross have forgiveness of their sins, and they are surely saved.

And, finally, this petition of our Lord covers all penitent sinners, that are truly sorry for their sins, and seek forgiveness and right-eousness in His blood. But it covers none other. And true repentance and sorrow after God, in which you confess your sins, and seek refuge in the atoning blood of the Lamb, is not of yourselves, it is the gift of God's free and sovereign grace, the out-flow of His gracious election.

As high as the highest heavens, as deep as deepest hell, but also as free and sovereign as God's elective grace, and, for this reason, as sure as the faithfulness and immutability of God Himself to all that repent, is the mercy of our High Priest expressed in the intercession on Calvary.

Repent, therefore, and believe!

And so repenting, be assured that you are one of those whom God in everlasting mercy has chosen unto salvation!

And when you do repent, and are truly sorry after God, you will not plead ignorance of your iniquities as the ground upon which you may be forgiven, but confess your sin wholeheartedly, and plead only on His atoning blood.

For let us not misunderstand this intercession of our Savior.

It is true, He adds to His intercessory prayer: "for they know not what they do." But, first of all, it is to be carefully determined just what it was that they did not know. It is evident that they cannot have been ignorant of the fact that they committed a heinous sin. Had not the Jews been witness of His mighty works, and had He not openly taught, in their synagogues, in the temple, and on the streets of their cities, the things of the kingdom of heaven? Had He not been revealed in all His teaching and mighty works as the manifestation of the Father? Did not the Sanhedrin know that they were motivated by hatred of the light, when they condemned Him to death? Had they not delivered Him for envy? Had not the Roman governor repeatedly and most emphatically declared that he had found no guilt in Him at all, and yet had he not delivered Him over to their will?

O, one and all they were conscious of their guilt of shedding innocent blood!

But there was, indeed, an element of ignorance in what they committed. They did not understand that He, whom they crucified, was shedding the blood of atonement. They did not discern the blood of the Lamb that carries away the sin of the world. Hence, they did not knowingly commit the sin of counting the blood of the new covenant an ungodly thing, and of doing despite unto the Spirit of grace. If that had been the case, there would have remained no sacrifice for their sins, but only a certain and fearful looking for judgment. Heb. 10:26, 27.

And so, the words in Jesus' prayer "for they know not what they do," are not added as a *ground for forgiveness,* for this can only be found in His perfect sacrifice: but rather as the ground of the *forgivableness* of their sin.

And so we may paraphrase the prayer of the Lord as follows: "Father, forgive them, on the ground of my perfect atonement; for their sin is still forgivable, seeing that they do not knowingly despise the blood of the new covenant!"

If, therefore, we respond to this intercession of our Lord in true repentance, we will not plead ignorance, but rather confess the iniquity of our sin, admit that we are worthy of damnation, in order to believe that Jesus' prayer for us is heard, and that we have forgiveness and righteousness in the blood of the Lamb.

In that way we will hear the answer: "Thy sins are forgiven thee, go in peace!"

CHAPTER 4

The Response

Lord, remember me, when thou comest into thy kingdom. — LUKE 23:42.

Father, forgive them; for they know not what they do." Thus our Lord interceded for the transgressors at the very moment when they nailed His blessed body to the tree.

And a few moments later came the response from the Father in heaven that His prayer was even then heard, and would be heard in the forgiveness of sins of thousands upon thousands afterward, in the confession and prayer of the penitent thief: "Lord, remember me, when thou comest into thy kingdom."

Three crosses there were planted on the hill of a skull. For two malefactors were crucified with the Savior, one on the right hand, and the other on the left. Nor may we overlook this fact, as we stand on Calvary and "watch Him there." For the entire scene of the crucifixion was arranged by the hand of the divine Artist, and according to His determinate counsel, so arranged that every detail has its meaning, and that, through it all, the Word of the cross is addressed to us. It was, as we know from the gospel narrative, by divine direction that Jesus died the death of the cross. The Jews had not intended a public trial, still less the crucifixion. They meant to take Him by subtilty and secretly kill Him. But God's plan was different, and His counsel must stand. And so it was, without any doubt, according to the same counsel, and by the direction of the same divine hand, that, simultaneously with Jesus, two malefactors were led to Calvary to receive the penalty for their misdeed. And so, Calvary presents a triple spectacle of human misery and suffering.

These three crosses have, as we have seen, a profound meaning. They bring to us the Word of God that everyone that continueth not in all that is written in the book of the law is accursed, for it is our flesh and blood that is crucified on Calvary, and the cross is God's Word of the curse. We all have transgressed, and are worthy of God's terrible wrath, and of the punishment of death.

Such is the message of the three crosses.

And yet, there is a difference, and we must make a distinction between that cross in the center and the two others. The two malefactors represent all mankind, as they are by nature children of wrath, under the curse of God, because they have sinned and are enemies of the Most High. But Jesus is the God of our salvation, the Son of God in the flesh. He is not by nature a child of wrath, but He came under the law and under the curse voluntarily, in order that He might deliver us, and redeem us from the curse of the law by His atoning death. He was without sin, but He was reckoned with the transgressors. He knew no sin, but He was made sin for us. And so it was but proper that He should not die alone, but that the world for whom He died, and out of whom His own must be redeemed and saved, should also be represented.

Two others they crucified with Him, one on each side, and Jesus in the midst.

It was out of that world, lost in sin, and under the curse, as it was represented by the two malefactors that were crucified with our Savior, that the response came to the intercessory prayer of Jesus. The Savior had prayed: "Father, forgive them; for they know not what they do." The response came in the form of another prayer, this time from one of the thieves: "Lord, remember me, when thou comest into thy kingdom."

When in this connection we speak of the response to Jesus' intercessory prayer, we are not thinking of the reaction of the thief, but of the answer of the Father from heaven to the plea of His Son on the cross. Christ had prayed to the Father in His intercession, and even now the Father answers Him. The Savior had prayed for forgiveness, for the remission of this sin of the crucifixion, and therefore, of all sin; the Father answered, through the repentance and confession of this malefactor. And the response was clear: "I heard thy intercession, and accept it; Thy blood is sufficient to redeem the greatest sinner."

That the confession and prayer of the malefactor were the Father's answer to the Savior's prayer could never be maintained, of course, if the penitence of the thief were not the work of God from beginning to end. If it were simply the better choice of his own free will that distinguished the one malefactor from the other, there was no sign here from heaven that the Father had heard the petition of His faithful Servant. Now, however, it is different. Sovereign grace only caused the thief to repent, to humble himself, and to plead for mercy. Hence, his repentance is the Father's answer to Christ's intercessory prayer. Christ had prayed for His own. Here the Father brought one of them to Him, even before He had finished the sacrifice of atonement, and thus comforted the heart of His Son and suffering Servant on the cross.

The prayer of the dying thief is the Father's response to the intercession of our merciful High Priest on the accursed tree.

To recognize this truth we must compare, for a moment, the different attitudes of the two thieves; understand that of themselves, by nature, they were both alike, even as we all are; and then answer the question what power it was that distinguished them in their attitude toward the Christ with whom they were crucified.

By nature, we are all like that impenitent thief.

In the same position we are, as he. For we are all transgressors, and are under the wrath of God, and under the curse of the law. We have sinned, are born in sin, and are guilty before God, and worthy of eternal death. And we lie in the midst of death; nor is there a way out, as far as we are concerned. We have been exiled from the house and fellowship of God. Dying we die, and we cannot, nor will we, redeem our souls and deliver ourselves from death. And we are corrupt, dead through trespasses and sins. We have lost the image of God with which we were created. Our mind is darkened, so that we cannot know and acknowledge God as the only good. Our will is perverse, so that we cannot and will not perform the righteousness of God. Our heart is motivated by enmity against the living God, so that in all our walk and conversation we rebel against the Most High, turn our necks upon Him, and follow after the vanity of our own evil imagination.

Such is our state and condition by nature.

Now, in that state, what is our attitude with respect to the cross of Christ?

Is it possible that we take the initiative, and of our own free will decide to come to Him?

The attitude of the impenitent thief, is the only answer to this question.

We read: "And one of the malefactors which was hanged railed on him, saying, If thou be the Christ, save thyself and us." Now, in these few words, the thoughts of his heart concerning all the fundamental questions of sin and righteousness, of suffering and death, of God and His Christ, were plainly revealed. For notice first of all, that he is not concerned about his sin at all. He does not repent, and is not filled with sorrow after God. In the blindness of his mind, and the bitterness of his soul, he rebels against his sufferings, although, according to the testimony and confession of his fellow thief, his suffering is but the just punishment for his crime. From his suffering and misery he desires to be delivered, not from his sin. This is the implication of his words: "Save thyself and us."

And in this respect we are, by nature, all like that impenitent thief. Oh, we hate the wages of sin. We dread suffering, and we do not want death. We try to avoid the results of sin, to escape the heavy hand of God. We fight against the misery of the world, and propose to make a better world, a world of peace and prosperity. But we do not, and never will repent, seek redemption from the guilt of sin, and long after true righteousness.

It follows that in our conception of salvation there is no room for a suffering and dying Christ. Since we do not seek deliverance from sin, we have no need of, and no room for the blood of atonement.

This, too, is plain from the words of the impenitent thief. He wants a Christ that is able and ready to save Himself, to leave that cross, and to overcome His enemies that nailed Him to it.

He wants a Christ of power, not of patient suffering and obedience. His Christ is really a mighty anti-Christ! And so, he can only despise this suffering and dying Servant of the Lord. He rails on Him. He must have nothing of this "blood theology." He crucified Him again. One that silently and patiently suffers himself to be nailed to the cross, and even prays for his enemies, can not be the Christ, surely is not the Christ he seeks and wants!

There you have it. That is the picture of the natural man, of you and me. We will not come to Christ. Even though we are perishing, we must have nothing of Him and of His cross.

Do not object that modernism and the modern world assume a much different, much more appreciative, or at least tolerant attitude over against Him, that they are willing to recognize in Him a good man, a profound teacher, a great religious leader, a worthy example. For all this has nothing to do with the Christ of the Scriptures. And the crucified Christ they despise and reject. Like the impenitent thief they rail on Him, and fill Him with reproach. They take the part of those that nailed Him to the cross, and crucify Him again.

It is exactly for such sinners that Christ interceded. His prayer was not uttered for sinners that are partly depraved, but for those that are wholly corrupt; not for men who are willing to receive Him if He is only offered to them, but for those that must have none of Him; not for sinners that are willing and able to come to Him, but for those that can only reject Him and crucify Him again.

How, then, can this prayer of Christ for the forgiveness of such sinners be answered?

Certainly not through any effort on the part of the sinners themselves, nor on the basis of any goodness or merit on their part. This possibility is excluded, wholly ruled out. The answer can only come from above, and that, too, through sovereign and efficacious grace. And what happens when the God of grace responds to the intercessory prayer of our great High Priest? What changes are wrought in that wholly depraved and hostile sinner, when God answers this prayer of His suffering Servant?

The answer to this question you may find in the attitude of the penitent thief.

Remember, by nature, and apart from the operation of God's sovereign grace, this second malefactor is just like the first. He, too, would have despised the crucified Christ, and railed on Him.

But notice now the effect of the Father's answer to Christ's prayer upon and in this man. We read: "But the other answering rebuked him, saying, Dost not thou fear God, seeing thou art in the same condemnation? And we indeed justly; for we receive the due reward of our deeds: but this man has done nothing amiss. And he said unto Jesus, Lord, remember me, when thou comest into thy kingdom." Luke 23:40-42.

Principally, these words contain all the real elements of a true conversion, as the fruit of God's saving grace and of His efficacious calling. It is true, this penitent thief did not have the light that we have. We must be careful lest we ascribe a meaning to his words they could not possibly have had for his own consciousness. Yet, there is nothing wanting in this confession and prayer, nothing that is necessary for a sinner to come to Christ and be saved.

First of all, there is in these words a confession of sin. When God responds to the prayer of our Saviour in behalf of sinners that are dead through trespasses and sins, and performs the wonder of His grace in their hearts, the very first manifestation of this marvelous work of God is conviction of sin, the unconditional acknowledgment on the part of the sinner that he is worthy of God's righteous condemnation. God's grace causes us to see our sin as never before in the light of God's righteousness, and to acknowledge the justice of our eternal condemnation. This acknowledgment and confession of our sin and of the justice of God in condemning us, is already rooted in true sorrow after God. We hate our sins. We are sorry because of our iniquities. We repent. We confess our sins before God and before men. Unless this element is present, not just once, but constantly, daily, as long as we are in the "body of this death," we know not what it means to come to Christ, and we cannot enjoy the glad experience of the forgiveness of sins. Hence, when God hears Christ's prayer for forgiveness of the sinner, His response to it reveals itself in this conviction of sin, and the whole-hearted acknowledgment of the righteousness of God. We may find this element in the words of the penitent thief: "Dost not thou fear God, seeing thou art in the same condemnation? And we indeed justly, for we receive the due reward of our deeds."

Secondly, the words of the repenting malefactor are the expression of a new, marvelous knowledge of Christ. This, too, belongs to true conversion. When God, by the power of His grace, hears the intercession of His Son, our merciful High Priest, He works in the heart of the sinner a new, spiritual knowledge of Christ, as the revelation of the God of our salvation. That sinner must have forgiveness. For this Christ prayed. In order to obtain this blessing of grace he must see and acknowledge his sin and the righteousness of God. But he must also behold the Christ in all the preciousness of His perfect atonement and satisfaction for sin, of His complete and finished redemption. This knowledge, too, God works in him by the power of His wondrous grace. He causes the sinner to behold the Christ of God as the Sinless One that was made sin, that we might be made the righteousness of God in Him, as the living One that was dead, as the fulness of righteousness and redemption for all that believe on His name, as the God of our salvation. And also in this respect, the prayer of Christ was heard in the conversion of the penitent thief. He knows and confesses that Christ is the Sinless One: "This man hath done nothing amiss." Yet, far more marvelous is the knowledge of Christ he reveals in his prayer. He believes that Jesus is the Christ! Somehow, he knows that the cross is not the end of this Man of Sorrows, but that, through suffering and death, He will enter into the glory of His kingdom. God will justify Him and give Him glory. He will raise Him from the dead! That is evident from the prayer: "Lord, remember me, when thou comest into thy kingdom."

Thirdly, note, too, that this penitent thief casts himself unconditionally upon the mercy of Christ. He prays. He wants to be remembered by this Christ, when He shall have come into His kingdom. But how does he desire that this Christ shall remember him in the kingdom of heaven? What is there about him that is worthy to be remembered, or on the ground of which he may hope to have a place in that kingdom of glory? Is he not a criminal? Is not his condemnation just? Or does he, perhaps, have a glimmer of hope that this last defense of Christ will earn him a place in glory? By no means! When God hears the intercessory prayer of Christ in behalf of sinners, He works in them a profound need of forgiveness, a true knowledge of the righteousness of Christ, and the grace of unconditional surrender to Him. This is the attitude of the thief. Had he not heard Christ's prayer in behalf of sinners? And when he prays that the Lord may remember him when He shall have come into His kingdom, does he not mean: "Lord, before the face of Thy Father, in the kingdom of glory, please, utter Thy intercessory prayer in my behalf, in order that I may have the forgiveness of sins"?

Thus the repentance of the thief is the response of the Father to the intercession of Christ.

And the Saviour recognizes the Father's answer to His prayer. For He assures the penitent thief: "Today thou shalt be with me in paradise."

All that the Father giveth Him shall surely come to Him, even though it must be in the very hour of their death; and they that come to Him, He will in no wise cast out.

Salvation, as God's response to Christ's intercession is sure and immutable!

CHAPTER 5

The Challenge

If thou be the Christ, save thyself and us.
— LUKE 23:39.

Jesus is the Christ, the only begotten Son of God.

This may be called the very heart of the Christian faith.

In this confession, the name Jesus does indeed signify Jehovah-Saves, the God of our salvation.

But it also denotes the historical Jesus, the One that is and was well-known. In His own day, He was known in all the land of Canaan as Jesus the Nazarene. In our day, His fame is world-wide. He is a man among men. He is the One that was born in Bethlehem in the year one of our era, that grew up in the home of His parents in Nazareth, that lived among us, taught the people, is reported to have performed many wonderful works, was hated by His own people, and killed by crucifixion on Calvary in the year thirty-three.

Such is the implication of the name Jesus.

And as such a historical person He is universally known. In this sense, it requires no faith to speak of Jesus of Nazareth.

But of this Jesus the Christian faith asserts that He is the Christ, the only begotten Son of God.

This assertion cannot be made except by faith, and through

the Spirit of God. For that He is the Christ signifies that He is the One that was ordained by God from before the foundation of the world to represent the cause of God's covenant, to overcome the powers of darkness, of the devil, sin and death, to bring salvation to His people, and to be their Lord and the Lord of all for ever. To confess by faith that Jesus is the Christ implies that we belong to Him, in life and in death, with body and soul, and that He is responsible for us in time and eternity, that we put all our confidence in Him, have salvation by faith in His name, and acknowledge Him, and no other, as our Lord, whose will we obey and whose word we keep. And again, when the Christian calls Him the Son of God, he signifies thereby, not that He was a creature of high honor and exalted position, or that He was a person that was deeply God-conscious, but that the historical Jesus is none less than very God, the same that created the world, God of God, Light of Light, the revelation of the God of our salvation.

That the historical Jesus, whom everyone knew, and still may know, is that divinely ordained Christ, God of God, the only begotten Son, the Lord of all — that is exactly the faith of the Church.

This confession is so essential and fundamental that whatever departs from it, denies it, distorts and corrupts it, thereby reveals the spirit of anti-Christ.

When in reply to the Lord's question: "But whom say ye that I am?" Peter answered: "Thou art the Christ, the Son of the living God," the Saviour set His seal upon that confession, by saying: "Blessed art thou, Simon-Barjonah, for flesh and blood hath not revealed it unto thee, but my Father which is in heaven. And I say also unto thee, That thou art Peter, and upon this rock will I build my church; and the gates of hell shall not prevail against it." Matt. 16:15-18. And the apostle John writes: "Who is a liar but he that denieth that Jesus is the Christ? He is the anti-Christ that denieth the Father and the Son." I John 2:22. And again, "Every spirit that confesseth that Jesus Christ is come into the flesh is of God. And every spirit that confesseth not that Jesus Christ is come into the flesh is not of God: and this is that spirit of anti-Christ, whereof ye have heard that it should come; and even now is already in the world." I John 4:2, 3.

It matters not how highly one may speak of the historical Jesus, whether he exalts Him as a wonderful man, as a great teacher, as a worthy example to follow, or as one who taught us to know God as the Father — if he does not confess that He is the Christ, the only begotten Son of God, he is not a Christian: he is of the anti-Christ!

Nor is it difficult to understand the central and fundamental importance of this confession for the Christian faith. If Jesus is not the Christ, He did not come with divine authority to do the will of the Father, and His Word and work have no special significance for us. If He is not the Son of God, He is worse than a deceiver and imposter, for He certainly claimed to be just this. Then His suffering and death have no power. In that case, He that died on the cross of Calvary in the year thirty-three, was a mere man. His death may have been a mistake; or He may have died for His principle; but His blood surely has not the power of atonement for sin. Moreover, if He is not the Christ, the Son of God, you may, perhaps, attempt to write a "Life of Jesus," but you certainly must close His biography with His death on the cross: you certainly cannot proceed to His resurrection. Then we still lie in the midst of death, and there is no way out. But now, Jesus is the Christ, the only begotten Son of God! His death is the death of the Son of God, who laid down His life for His own in obedience to the Father. His blood cleanseth us from all sin, and in His resurrection we have the victory over death by faith!

That the historical Jesus, who died on Calvary, is the Christ, the Son of God — that is the heart of the Christian faith!

Do you wonder that the devil-inspired spirit of anti-Christ is always near, and ever active, wherever there is the revelation of Jesus Christ, the Son of God?

That Jesus is the Christ was the great issue between Him and His hostile opponents during the three years of His public ministry. Oh, that a Christ should come was not in debate. All Israel looked for the Messiah that had been promised by the prophets. But that *this* Jesus, who appeared without form or comeliness, this son of Joseph, whose father and mother they knew, who had no beauty or glory according to the world; this prophet, who ever spoke of God and His cause, His righteousness and glory, and who uncompromisingly condemned the unfruitful works of darkness, and those who committed them; who announced Himself as the bread and the water of life, and who refused all power of the flesh — that He should be the Christ that was expected they could not tolerate, they would not believe. They wanted another. They looked for a Christ that would give honor to those that sought the honor of men, whose credentials would be earthly glory and power to establish the kingdom of this world. And so, they despised and rejected Jesus of Nazareth. The more, during His public ministry, it became evident that He was, indeed, the Christ according to the Scriptures, because His word and work testified of Him, the more furious became their hatred, the more insistent their denial and contradiction. They called Him a deceiver and a blasphemer, contemptuously named Him Jesus the Nazarene, said He was in alliance with Beelzebub, and more than once would have killed Him, had it not been that His "hour" was not yet come.

The spirit of anti-Christ, that denies that Jesus is the Christ, was very active during the Saviour's sojourn on earth.

Vehement in its furious hatred that same spirit became, when the "hour" was finally come.

For it was, indeed, the same spirit of anti-Christ, denying that Jesus is the Christ, the Son of God, that motivated the enemies in plotting Jesus' death. At the trial before the Jewish council this was clearly revealed. All their attempts to find some other pretended reason, to concoct some plausible indictment on the ground of which they might pronounce the death sentence upon Him, with a show of justice, utterly failed. He was condemned on the ground of His own testimony, given under oath, and never proved to be false, that He, Jesus, is the Christ, the Son of God.

Before the Roman governor, the same indictment was brought against Him. His whole trial concentrated around the accusation that He was the King of the Jews, the Christ of prophecy, to which was added that He made Himself the Son of God. Nor was His claim ever proved to be false.

And when, finally, He is suspended on the cross and made a universal spectacle on Calvary. the accusation written above His head is still the same: Jesus of Nazareth, the King of the Jews, that is, the Christ.

It is only when we consider the matter in this light, from this most fundamental aspect of the antithesis of Christ and anti-Christ, that we can understand the otherwise strange and inhuman spectacle of the mocking and railing spectators that watch the dying Christ on Calvary.

Usually there is some sympathy for the criminal when he is finally led to the place of execution. But for Jesus of Nazareth there is nothing but bitter hatred to the very last. The cruel hatred and malevolence of the enemy is insatiable. One and all, the chief priests, the scribes, and the elders, the people, the passers-by, the soldiers, and even one of the thieves that were crucified with Him, they rail on Him, and continue to heap reproach and shame upon His silent head.

And notice that is still the same spirit of anti-Christ that moves them, and comes to manifestation in the challenge they fling at Him.

For they challenge Him to come down from the cross.

And that challenge implies the denial of the truth that Jesus is the Christ, the Son of God.

From every one of the three-fold aspects of His Christ-ship, that of prophet, priest, and king, His claim to be the Messiah is challenged and attacked.

The passers-by shout at Him: "Thou that destroyest the temple, and buildest it in three days, save thyself," thus challenging His priesthood, and, by exposing Him as a liar at the same time deny His prophetic office.

The leaders of the Jews mocked Him in these words: "He saved others, himself he cannot save. If he be the king of Israel, let him now come down from the cross, and we will believe him. He trusted in God; let him deliver him now, if he will have him, for he said, I am the Son of God." Matt. 27:39-43. They denied and challenged His royal as well as His prophetic office. At another time they said, in conjunction with the people: "He saveth others, let him save himself, if he be the Christ, the chosen of God." Luke 23:35.

The soldiers, as might be expected, attacked and derided Him especially in His kingship: "If thou be the king of the Jews, save thyself." Luke 23:36.

And even one of the malefactors casts the same anti-Christian challenge in his teeth: "If thou be the Christ, save thyself and us." Luke 23:39.

Besides, all, except the soldiers and the thief, challenged His divine Sonship.

That this Jesus of Nazareth is not the Christ, the Son of God, is the emphatic testimony of all. And the cross is adduced and appealed to as sufficient evidence of the truth of this denial.

We must pay special attention to this last named element: a Christ that is crucified is to them an absurdity, a contradiction in terms, an abomination.

This is the deepest ground of their denial. It is the major premise of their argument. It is taken for granted. They consider it an axiom, that may be accepted *a priori,* a self-evident truth, something that needs no proof, that is universally admitted. For notice that, as always, so on Calvary, there is logical argumentation in the challenge of the anti-Christian spirit. The argument plainly runs as follows: (1) A crucified Jesus that is incapable of delivering Himself is evidently not the Christ. (2) Jesus is crucified and He cannot save Himself. (3) Hence, Jesus cannot be the Christ. The first, or major, premise of this syllogism they take for granted. Of the second they are sure, and, besides, they demonstrate the truth of it by challenging Him to come down from the cross. If He does not answer that challenge, they think, it indubitably proves His incapability to save Himself. And so, the third statement, or conclusion, follows: Jesus is not the Christ. How can a Christ that is incapable of saving Himself be the Saviour of others? The cross proves beyond a doubt that He never did save others, that all the stories about His marvelous works are pure myths, that He never did heal the sick and raise the dead, that He is a liar and impostor.

The spirit of anti-Christ on Calvary takes the cross as proof that Jesus is not the Christ, the Son of the living God!

How could it be different?

Is not the cross always a stumbling-block of unbelief?

Is not exactly the crucified Christ foolishness, utter folly and absurdity, without power to save, to them that perish?

Oh, the natural man can readily see that there is something wrong with the world. There is sin and death, there is greed, covetousness, envy, maliciousness, hatred and enmity among men. There is confusion and unrest, war and destruction on every side. He realizes that there is room for improvement. The world must be saved. He looks for a Christ, or for many Christs. He looks for a wise man, a philosopher that can find a solution for all of the world's problems. He wants a mighty man that is able to overcome the evils of war and destruction, and can give us unity and peace. Man must be educated into a better man: knowledge is virtue. He must be given a good example and a better environment: there is power in reformation. But he does not, and will not acknowledge that he is a sinner, wholly and helplessly depraved, blind in his mind, corrupt in heart, perverse of will, guilty and damnable before God. He refuses to confess that his perverse relation to God is the deepest cause of all his misery, and that God is against him. He will not humble himself under the heavy hand of God that pursues him and oppresses him in all his sinful way, that makes futile all his self-willed attempts to make a better world, and leads him and all the world to destruction.

Small wonder, then, that there is in his conception of the world's salvation no need of atonement, no room for the cross, no place for the Christ of the Scriptures. The cross is foolishness to him. He is motivated by the spirit of anti-Christ, and denies that the crucified Jesus is the Christ, the Son of God.

Let Him come down from the cross, and we will believe Him!

For the same reason, no human argumentation, persuasion, pleading, sentimentality, begging, or threatening with fire and brimstone, will ever induce the natural man to retract his anti-Christian denial.

The chasm between faith and unbelief cannot be bridged by human logic or sentiment.

Only the heart-changing grace of God can make the sinner see the folly of his denial of the truth that Jesus, the crucified One, is the Christ, the Son of God. When the God of our salvation regenerates our hearts, and calls us by His spirit through the Word of the gospel, we are radically turned about with respect to our relation to the living God, and we see all things, God, the

Christ, His cross, ourselves, in a new and radically different light. Then we know the righteousness and justice of God, that cannot be compromised, that must either be perfectly satisfied or damn us into everlasting desolation. Then we behold ourselves in our sin, and repent in dust and ashes, in true sorrow after God, and long for forgiveness and righteousness. Then we behold the folly of what in our spiritual blindness, we consider a self-evident and universally valid truth: that a crucified Jesus cannot be the Christ, the Son of God; and we recognize that the exact opposite is true: only a crucified Jesus can possibly be the Christ of God! Then we acknowledge, with terror in our hearts, that we were utterly in error when we argued that our challenge of Him to come down from the cross was sufficient evidence of His impotency to save Himself; and we realize that He remained on that accursed tree, to which we had nailed Him, by the power and choice of His own will, and by the great love of His own, whom the Father had given Him. We know, then, that He voluntarily took all the sins of His own upon Himself, and that He bore them before the face of God upon the cross. We understand, then, that by His voluntary suffering and death, He brought the price of perfect obedience and satisfaction that could and did atone for our sins.

And then we thank Him that He did not respond to our blind and mad challenge to come down from the cross, but was obedient even unto death.

Then we find redemption in His blood, even the forgiveness of sins.

And so we learn to confess with the whole church, of all ages, that Jesus, the crucified Nazarene, is the Christ, the Son of God!

No, He did not come down!

There was, in this anti-Christian challenge that He come down from the cross, no doubt, also a final attempt of the devil to persuade Him to leave the way of obedience.

But He loved us even unto the end!

And by faith we now adore Him for His wondrous love, and amazed at so all-enduring patience, we fall down in worship before His feet, and cry out in adoration: "My Lord, and my God!"

CHAPTER 6

The Descension

My God, my God, why hast thou forsaken me?
— MATT. 27:46.

How radically different from the hero worship of the world is what the church confesses concerning her Lord!

When the world commemorates its great men, it lauds their wonderful life, and exalts them for the mighty deeds they perform, for the good they did in the world. A hero is someone that left some impression upon the world, whose name is worthy of remembrance because his life and work served some good purpose, were conducive to the benefit of mankind.

But in this respect the church has nothing to say about her Lord. For the improvement of this world He really accomplished nothing. It would seem that the most important part of His work on earth is that He died. And so, in her most general confession the church declares: "I believe in Jesus Christ, born of the virgin Mary, suffered under Pontius Pilate, was crucified, dead, and buried. He descended into hell." The church's account of the earthly career of her Lord closes with the statement that He went down into hell!

And this is quite in harmony with the gospel narrative.

Whoever would be interested to write a biography of Jesus would find little or no material for this purpose in Scripture. The

403

gospel stories are chiefly interested in His birth and death, that is, as far as His earthly life and work are concerned. Of His early childhood we know very little; of His adolescent years practically nothing. The gospel narratives do record His words, and many of His wonderful works, but even these are not such as would be of interest to the world. But it elaborates upon and emphasizes His death as the important event. In fact, He came to die! He was born to descend into hell! He deliberately walked the way of the cross. Freely He assumed our nature, and our life, and that, too, for the very purpose that He might of His own will lay it down again. He was born, He suffered, He died — such is the brief account of the life and work of Jesus Christ, the only begotten Son, our Lord.

In a sense, therefore, we may say that all of Jesus' earthly sojourn was a descension into hell.

When we confess this descension, we do not mean that our Lord at any time personally went into the place of the damned, but that, during His whole life, but especially on the cross, He suffered the sorrows and fears, the astonishment and perplexity, the pains and agony of hell. In that sense, He descended into hell when He came into our world in the likeness of sinful flesh. For thereby He came under the law, and under the curse, though He was personally without sin. All His life He suffered. He bore the sins of His people before the face of the Father, and in their stead was burdened with the load of the wrath of God. And He was contradicted and hated by men. His way was a gradual descent. It became deeper, darker, more difficult to travel as He proceeded. He travelled, so to speak, in the terrible storm of God's fierce wrath, the center of which was on Calvary. And toward that center He deliberately directed His way. Its distant thunder He heard all His life: "Cursed is everyone that is under the law!" As He proceeded the awful and threatening rumble of that thunder became more distinct. He spoke of it to His disciples. At the sound of it His soul was troubled, yet He deliberately set His face toward Jerusalem and Calvary. In Gethsemane the terror of it gripped Him, so that His soul became exceedingly sorrowful, even unto death; yet He did not draw back. And finally He stood in the very center of it, when, on the cross, He became a curse for us. All His life, but especially on the cross, He descended into hell.

Yet, even during that six hours of suffering on the accursed tree, there is a difference between the first half of that period and the last.

Even on the cross, His way descends into the depths, declines steeply, until He has tasted death to the full, the vials of God's wrath had been emptied over His head, and He had suffered all the terror and anguish of hell itself. That anguish was conveyed into His body and soul through the means of the cross. For to Him that cross was the Word of God: "Cursed is everyone that hangeth on a tree." And He understood its language. But that terror of God's cursing wrath gripped His soul in all its agonizing horror and astonishment through the darkness that descended upon the scene at noonday. For to Him that darkness spoke of the day of the Lord, who had come to execute judgment, and to visit the iniquities of His people. Then, especially, His way led steeply down into that awful gloom whence we hear Him utter the agonizing cry of utter astonishment: "My God, my God, why hast thou forsaken me?"

Sharply the six hour period of the crucifixion is divided into two equal periods by the falling of the darkness at noonday.

Before noon, the cross appears rather emphatically the work of man. For all the enemies that behold the spectacle on Calvary loudly rail on Him, challenge Him to come down from the cross, and seek to demonstrate to all the world that He is not the Christ, the Son of God, and that He is rejected, not only by men, but also by God Himself. The powers of darkness celebrate their victory.

Then, too, during that first three hours, the Lord Himself is not exclusively occupied with, engulfed in His own suffering. He pays attention to others, to His own. Three times He speaks a word of comfort and salvation: interceding for them, promising to them the glory of paradise, taking final leave from His mother, and entrusting her to the care of His beloved disciple.

But at noon, when the darkness descends upon Calvary, all this changes. The enemies realize that, by this darkness, God has come upon the scene, and the judgment of the cross is taken out of

their hands. They are filled with terror, no doubt. They blaspheme
no more. In silence they wonder what will be the end of this. And
the Lord, too, is silent. He is completely occupied with His own
suffering. He speaks not again until the ninth hour, when the
darkness is dispelled, and the light of the sun once more floods
Calvary with its blessed joy.

For we must understand that this darkness that enveloped
Calvary at high noon was directly and plainly a special Word
of God.

It was not a phenomenon that could be explained from natural
causes by the wise men of this world. No sun eclipse could possibly
account for it. In the case of a sun eclipse, it is never completely
dark: there is a gradual dimming of the light, followed by a gradual
brightening into full light of day. But the darkness on Calvary
descended suddenly and completely, at noon, remained for three
hours, and was lifted exactly at three o'clock in the afternoon.
Moreover, it was neither limited to Calvary, nor did it extend
beyond the limits of the land of Canaan; it was over the whole
land. And from the text of the account of this darkness in the
gospel according to Luke that is followed by the authorized version,
we receive the impression that the darkness was first, the eclipse
of the sun followed: "And it was about the sixth hour, and there
was a darkness over all the earth (*land* is the proper translation, as
in Matthew and Mark) until the ninth hour. And the sun was
darkened." Luke 23:44, 45. It was not the eclipse of the sun that
caused the darkness, but on the contrary, the darkness that hung
an impenetrable veil before the sun. When the darkness descended
the sun could, perhaps, still be seen, for a moment, appearing
through the gloom like a pale disc; then also that faded away, and
it was completely dark on Calvary, and night over the whole
land of Canaan. The darkness reminded of that judgment of God
which for three days spread its terror over the land of Egypt, when
God was delivering His people from the house of bondage with a
mighty arm.

What is the meaning?

It signified that God Himself had come down upon the land
to judge His people, that He was present there on Calvary, and
in the whole land, in His fierce anger, to visit our iniquities upon

our heads, to execute judgment in righteousness, to destroy all the workers of iniquity.

The great day of the Lord has come!

This is the plain language of Holy Writ. When the Lord appears for judgment, "clouds and darkness are round about Him: righteousness and judgment are the habitation of his throne." Ps. 97: 2. When He visits the land of Pharaoh in His wrath, He covers the heaven, and makes the stars thereof dark; He covers the sun with a cloud, and the moon shall not give her light. The bright lights of heaven He makes dark over Him, and He sets darkness upon His land. Ezek. 32: 7, 8. Always the day of the Lord is described as a day of darkness. "The earth shall quake before them: the heavens shall tremble: the sun and the moon shall be dark, and the stars shall withdraw their shining." Joel 2: 10. "For the day of the Lord cometh, for it is nigh at hand; a day of darkness, and of gloominess, a day of clouds and of thick darkness, as the morning spread upon the mountains." Joel 2: 1, 2. "The sun shall be turned into darkness, and the moon into blood, before the great and terrible day of the Lord come." Joel 2: 31. "Multitudes, multitudes in the valley of decision: for the day of the Lord is near in the valley of decision. The sun and the moon shall be darkened, and the stars shall withdraw their shining." Joel 3:15.

That day of the Lord is a day of judgment, of judgment, to be sure, upon the whole world, but centrally upon His people.

For always judgment must needs begin at the house of God.

God shall judge His people, His church, Zion, in righteousness.

Thus the prophets had spoken of that day of the Lord. "The end is come upon my people of Israel; I will not again pass by them any more . . . The Lord hath sworn by the excellency of Jacob, Surely, I will never forget any of their works. Shall not the land tremble for this, and everyone mourn that dwelleth therein? and it shall rise up wholly as a flood; and it shall be cast out and drowned, as by the flood of Egypt. And it shall come to pass in that day, saith the Lord God, that I will cause the sun to go down at noon, and I will darken the earth in the clear day." Amos 8: 2-9. "Woe unto you that desire the day of the Lord! to what end is it for you? the day of the Lord is darkness, and not light . . .

Shall not the day of the Lord be darkness, and not light? even very dark, and no brightness in it?" Amos 5: 18, 20. It is the day of wrath, and of vengeance, when the Lord smites us with madness, and blindness, and astonishment of heart; when we shall grope at noonday, as the blind gropeth in darkness. Deut. 28: 29.

That is the significance of the darkness on Calvary, and over the whole land of Canaan, from noon until three o'clock, on the day of the crucifixion of our Lord.

God is come for judgment upon His people.

For, mark you well, the darkness is not a mere symbol of what the Lord *might* do, or *will* do, in some future day: it means that there and then He is present in His fierce wrath.

The period of darkness is very really the day of the Lord. From the sixth to the ninth hour of the fifteenth of Nisan of the year thirty-three of our era, the Judge of heaven and earth was very really visiting our sins upon us, executing righteous judgment, emptying all the vials of His terrible anger against sin over our heads.

As we stand here in the darkness of those three dreadful hours, we stand before the tribunal of the Judge of heaven and earth.

He is remembering all our iniquities. The verdict has already been expressed.

Righteous judgment is executed upon us.

―――――

But how is this possible?

How can we stand in that judgment?

If God is come to judge His church, to visit our sins upon our heads, to pour out all the vials of His wrath upon us, how can we stand?

Must we not rather expect, as we stand on Calvary, that the end of the world is come upon us, and that we will all be swallowed up in the outer darkness of hell? Is not God here to judge His church, and all the world with her? Are we not standing here at the cross of the Son of God, whom we rejected and filled with reproach, nailed to the accursed tree? Have we not been exposed in all the horrible nakedness of our sin as enmity against God? Did we not fill up the measure of our iniquity? What else, then, can we expect than that this judgment of God will surely deliver Him, the Son, the Only Righteous, from that cross, and damn us into everlasting desolation?

Yet, nothing happens!

For three long hours God is pouring out His wrath over us.

The darkness passes.

And we are not consumed.

How to account for this astonishing mystery?

The answer to this question is found in the center of the three crosses that are planted on the Hill of a Skull. For He that is suspended on that cross is the Son of God, Immanuel, God with us. God is with us in the darkness, under the darkness. That is why we are not consumed in this dark hour. What you behold here on Calvary is the highest realization of that marvelous revelation of Jehovah that Moses beheld in the bush that constantly burned, and was never consumed.

Let us remember that God loves His church, His chosen Zion, with an everlasting love. He loved her freely, sovereignly, from before the foundation of the world, for His own name's sake. In His unfathomable love, He ordained her unto everlasting life and glory in the heavenly realization of His covenant of friendship. Unto that end, He appointed over them a Captain, His own, only begotten Son, that He might represent them in the hour of judgment, and lead them on to the glory of eternal life. And when that beloved church falls, together with the whole human race, into sin and death, He is, to be sure, angry with them in His just judgment, but He still loves them in His wrath. He will execute judgment upon them, for Zion must be redeemed with justice, but so that in His judgment He will reach out for them in His love, and redeem them unto Himself. For this purpose He sent His only begotten Son into the world in the fullness of time. And He came, as the Captain of their salvation, to take their place in the hour of judgment. To that hour and place of judgment He travelled all His life upon earth. And in due time, that is, exactly at the time when God poured out the vials of His wrath, He reached it: "In due time Christ died for the ungodly." And so we behold the amazing spectacle, the paradox of paradoxes, that God from heaven is pouring out His wrath upon His people, and that God in the flesh, suspended on the accursed tree of Calvary, receives all the wrath of God in our stead and in our behalf.

God is pouring out His fierce wrath upon God in the flesh!

God is with us in the darkness, Immanuel is descending into lowest hell for us!

It is the mercy of the Lord that we are not consumed in that hour of darkness!

O, that is why He is so silent in this hour of judgment. He cannot speak now. He must be left utterly alone, wrestling with God. He must hear the Word of God, the Word that speaks to Him through the cross: "Cursed is everyone that continueth not in all that is written in the book of the law to do it." That Word addresses His inmost being through the darkness: "The day of the Lord is come! The end is come upon my people Israel; I will not again pass by them anymore." He listens. Through His deepest soul, and through every fiber of His body that Word vibrates. It curses Him. It fills Him with fear and terror. Yet, He does not rebel. Willingly, out of love to the Father, He descends into deepest hell. He bears it all even unto the end. And so dreadful is His agony that, when finally He has reached the depth of His descension, His outcry can only be a question of astonishment: "My God, my God, why hast thou forsaken me?"

Blessed hour of redemption!

Darkness covered the land until the ninth hour, then the light returns, the light of God's everlasting love and favor.

The last bitter drop of the wrath of God the Servant of the Lord had drunk. He had borne all and atoned. No longer was there any reason or ground left for the darkness. And in the light that dispelled the darkness, the Son of God, hearing the Word of God's justification, responds in the victorious: "It is finished."

And because, in the dark hour of the day of the Lord on Calvary, the Servant of the Lord descended into the depth of hell, and there sprinkled His life-blood in perfect obedience on the mercy-seat, before the face of the Father, His brethren, all that believe on His name, may be assured, even in their greatest temptations, that for them the judgment of condemnation is past.

They are redeemed forever.

Christ hath redeemed us from the curse of the law, having been made a curse for us.

There is no condemnation for them that are in Christ Jesus, and in the day of the revelation of the righteous judgment of God they shall be justified forever.

Hallelujah!

CHAPTER 7

Justification

Certainly, this was a righteous man.—LUKE 23:47.

The final events of the drama on Calvary followed one another in quick succession.

It can have been only a few moments from the end of the darkness till the moment that our Lord commended His Spirit into the hands of the Father.

Immediately upon the agonizing outcry of the Savior expressing His astonishment at being forsaken of God, one of them "that stood there" said: "This man calleth for Elias." Another "ran and took a sponge, and filled it with vinegar, and put it on a reed, and gave him to drink." Matt. 27:47, 48. According to John, this drink was offered Him in answer to His fifth cross utterance: "I thirst," from which we infer that this utterance followed immediately upon the fourth. In the meantime, the veil of the temple was rent in twain, for the gospel according to Luke mentions this important sign in connection with the darkness. Soon after this, the Lord triumphantly announces that "it is finished," and in the clear consciousness that all is performed, He finally addresses the Father, and commends His Spirit into His hands. An earthquake accompanies His death, rocks are rent, and many graves in the vicinity are opened. The Roman centurion and "those that were with him" gave Him testimony that He was truly the Son of God,

413

Matt. 27:54. And, according to Luke, "he glorified God, saying, Certainly this was a righteous man." Luke 23:47. "And all the people that came together to that sight, beholding the things that were done, smote their breasts, and returned." Luke 23:48.

What does it all mean?

What is the Word of God that speaks to us through all these events, utterances, signs, and testimonies of men?

One and all they clearly witness of one central truth: God justified His righteous Servant, His Son in the flesh, before His own consciousness and before men, even before He finally laid down His life.

He had been reckoned with the transgressors by God and men, but He died as a righteous man. He had descended into the depths of hell, but in hell He did not die. He had been forsaken of God, but He died in the consciousness of perfect fellowship with the Father. He had borne the curse, and was made a curse for us, but when He died He rejoiced in the consciousness of God's blessed favor. He had been reviled, mocked at, filled with reproach, cast out as the most unworthy criminal by men, even by all that stood and watched Him on Calvary, but they left with the sentence of self-condemnation in their conscience, and the testimony that He was righteous.

God gave His Servant witness that He was justified, and He died in perfect peace.

Of this, that God would help Him and justify Him, He had been confident even before He entered into the deep and dark vale of His suffering and shame.

Long before the fulness of time, He had expressed this confidence in the word of the prophet: "The Lord God hath opened mine ear, and I was not rebellious, neither turned away back. I gave my back to the smiters, and my cheeks to them that plucked off the hair: I hid not my face from shame and spitting. For the Lord God will help me; therefore shall I never be confounded: therefore have I set my face like a flint, and I know that I shall not be ashamed. He is near that justifieth me; who will contend with me? let us stand together: who is mine adversary? let him come near to me. Behold, the Lord God will help me; who is he that shall condemn me? lo, they all shall wax old as a garment; the moth shall eat them up." Isaiah 50:5-9.

And on the eve of His crucifixion and death, He had said to His disciples: "Behold, the hour cometh, yea, is now come, that ye shall be scattered every man to his own, and shall leave me alone: and yet I am not alone, because the Father is with me." John 16:32.

In this hope He was not ashamed. Already on the cross, before He gave up the ghost, it was realized. For a moment, the moment of His deepest anguish, it had seemed as if God had utterly cast Him away. But from the depth of desolation He ascended, even on the cross, into the blessed consciousness of God's approval and favor. O, He must still lay down His life, and descend into Hades. The final and perfect justification can only be revealed in the resurrection. Yet, we may be sure that, while facing death and the grave, the song of Psalm 16, His own song, was in His heart: "I have set the Lord always before me: because He is at my right hand, I shall not be moved. Therefore my heart is glad, and my glory rejoiceth: my flesh also shall rest in hope. For thou wilt not leave my soul in hell; neither wilt thou suffer thine Holy One to see corruption. Thou wilt show me the path of life: in thy presence is fulness of joy; at thy right hand there are pleasures forevermore." 8-11.

The dying Christ is justified; He died in peace.

You may remark, perhaps, that our Savior needed no justification, seeing that He was perfectly righteous, and no sin was ever committed by Him.

This, of course, is true. Personally, and in the sense that His sins must be blotted out, the Christ was in no need of justification. He was without sin. In the likeness of sinful flesh He had come, but without sin itself. The guilt of the whole human race did not involve Him, for He was the Son of God. And the corruption of the human flesh did not defile Him, for He was conceived by the Holy Ghost. He was "holy, undefiled, separate from sinners." Nor did He commit sin in all His life and sojourn on earth. No guile was in His mouth. His way was one of most perfect obedience, even unto death and hell. Never did He rebel, hesitate, or draw back. Willingly, in love of the Father, He descended into the depth of His suffering and death. Every step of His way He was perfectly righteous. Personally, therefore, He was in no need of special justification.

Yet, in another sense, Christ, too, was justified.

The Word of God even employs this very term with application to Him, for the apostle Paul writes: "And without controversy great is the mystery of godliness: God was manifest in the flesh, justified in the Spirit." I Tim. 3:16. We must remember that Christ did not suffer and die for Himself as an individual. He was the Head of the church. From before the foundation of the world, He had been appointed the Head of all the elect, and they had been chosen in Him. This implies that He represented them before God. On Him the Lord laid the iniquity of all His people. He bore them. In the hour of judgment He was held responsible for them. For them He must atone. And so, "He was wounded for our transgressions, He was bruised for our iniquities: the chastisement of our peace was upon him." Isaiah 53:5. No, personally, He had no sin, but: "He hath made him to be sin for us, who knew no sin, that we might be made the righteousness of God in him." II Cor. 5:21.

Not as an individual, but as the Mediator, He needed justification.

Not from His own sin, but from ours He must be justified.

From God He must receive the testimony that His work is finished, that the atonement is made, that the sins He bore had been blotted out, and that, as the Mediator of His people, He had obtained eternal righteousness.

Besides, must not He and His cause be justified before men?

Must not the whole world be condemned?

He had tabernacled among us as the Son of God in the flesh, and as such He had become manifest in His Word and in His work. He had represented the cause of God's holy covenant, and revealed the Father. And the world had condemned Him, and trampled God's cause under foot. They had contradicted Him, reviled and reproached Him, called Him a liar and deceiver, and blasphemed His name. They had finally made Him an open spectacle, emphatically denied that He was the Christ, the King of the Jews, the Son of God, and by their jeers and mockery on Calvary they had attempted to seal their testimony that He was an imposter.

Must not the cause of the Son of God, then, be justified before men, before all the world, and must not that world be condemned?

Now, the final events on Calvary proclaim clearly that Christ was justified before God and men, even before He gave up the ghost.

That is the significance of the signs, the last cross utterances, and the testimonies of those that came together "to that sight."

Let us briefly consider them from this view-point.

First of all, let us fix our attention for a moment on the lifting of the heavy veil of darkness, and the return of the clear light of day.

Especially two facts deserve our particular notice in this connection.

First of all, we must understand that the darkness was dispelled, not very gradually, but rather quickly and suddenly. All at once, at the sixth hour, at high noon exactly, the darkness had enveloped the spectacle on Calvary and covered the whole land; with equal suddenness, at the ninth hour, at three o'clock in the afternoon, it was driven away, and the bright sun once more flooded the scene with it blessed light.

Secondly, it seems quite evident that the light returned, not after, but before our Lord gave up the ghost, to be exact, immediately after He had cried out: "My God, my God, why hast thou forsaken me?" It was about the ninth hour that Jesus uttered this cry of His deepest anguish and desolation; and it was at the ninth hour that the darkness was dispelled. Moreover, in the gospel according to Matthew, and also in that according to Mark, an incident is mentioned that points in the same direction. We read that, following this outcry, one of them that stood by *ran,* took a sponge, filled it with vinegar, put it on a reed, and gave Him to drink. I take it that the nature of the darkness was such that one would hardly be *running* in it, and do all these things in a moment. The darkness had suddenly been lifted, and the golden sunlight had returned.

And what else was this return of the light than a Word of God to our Lord, lifting Him out of the depth of His desolation, assuring Him that the judgment was past, and that He was justified.

Christ died, not in the darkness of condemnation, but in the bright sunlight of justification!

The same meaning the rending of the veil must have had for Him.

We have already called attention to the fact that in the gospel according to Luke this sign is mentioned in immediate connection with the darkness. And as a sign of judgment upon the house of Israel, proclaiming that the house of God in Jerusalem was destroyed, and that the dispensation of the law had reached its end, it belonged to the darkness.

Yet, on the other hand, as a sign that the true temple of God had been built, and that the way into the inner sanctuary and fellowship with God had been opened, the rending of the veil also belonged to the return of the light. There can be no doubt that the sign of the rending of the veil was certainly meant for Christ on the cross, and that He in whose flesh the real veil of the temple was presently to be rent, had knowledge of this sign. It must be understood, therefore, that the veil of the temple was rent in twain, immediately upon Jesus' outcry of anguish and desolation, and simultaneously with the return of the light, that is, therefore, before our Lord finally laid down His life.

Now, what is the significance of the rending of the veil?

It is the veil of separation, symbol of the flesh that bars our entrance into the fellowship of God's covenant. In the tabernacle and temple that veil hung between the holy place and the holy of holies: it closed the inner sanctuary, the dwelling place of God. No one could enter there, except the high priest, and he only for a moment, once a year, on the great day of atonement. All the blood of bulls and goats had not been efficient to tear that veil, and to open the way into the sanctuary of God. Now, at the ninth hour, upon the outcry of Jesus marking His descent into deepest hell, and at the end of the darkness, the veil was rent, the way into the most holy place was wide open.

What does it mean?

What had happened, that God with His own hand rent the veil in twain?

It means that at that moment the real veil had been rent on Calvary!

The temple and its veil in Jerusalem were but shadows, the real temple and veil were at that moment suspended on the cross. God had come into the flesh! He that dwells in the real sanctuary, beyond the veil, had come on this side of the veil, by assuming our flesh. That flesh, our flesh, His flesh, is our sin, our iniquity, our guilt and corruption, that separate us from God, that make us exiles from His house. With them we can never enter into the blessed fellowship of His friendship. That flesh Christ, the Son of God, assumed. That is the mystery of the incarnation: God also became man, the Creator became creature, the Lord of all appeared as a servant, the Sinless One was made sin, He that eternally dwells within the veil, in the bosom of the Father, in the days of His flesh also sojourned outside of the veil.

But He came as the High Priest.

His mission and purpose was to rend that veil of His flesh, and through the rent veil to enter into the inner sanctuary, the eternal tabernacle of God's friendship. To accomplish this, He must bear our iniquities, atone for our sin, offer Himself a willing sacrifice to Him that dwells in the most holy place. By fulfilling all righteousness He must tear the veil of the flesh, and open the way into God's communion.

This has now been accomplished.

When He cried out: "My God, my God, why hast thou forsaken me?" He descended into hell and atoned for sin. He tore the veil of the flesh wide open. And God opened unto Him the way into the sanctuary. He gave His testimony, there on the cross, that He had finished all, that His sacrifice had been accepted, and for Him and His people the way into the fellowship of God was manifest.

God justified Him!

That is the meaning of the rent veil.

All this does not mean that the Lord could at that moment have come down from the cross, that He did not have to lay down His life. The signs rather imply His death. They assume that He, who was obedient unto the descension into hell, now certainly will be faithful unto death. He cannot return into the flesh. His way lies through death and the grave into the glory of the resurrection. But they surely are a Word of God to Him, that all that must be accomplished in the flesh has been finished, that His work, His death included, is accepted by the Father, that He, therefore, may now give up the ghost, and that He may be assured that His spirit will be with the Father in paradise, and that He may look forward in hope to the glorious resurrection.

Thus the Lord, no doubt, understood the Word of God to Him by these signs.

This is evident from the last three cross utterances, which were spoken in quick succession.

That He spoke of His thirst is evidence of the fact that His deepest anguish and agony were past, and that His attention was now concentrated upon His physical want and suffering. The next to the last cross utterance, "It is finished," reveals beyond all doubt that He is conscious of the Father's approval of His accomplished work, and that, therefore, God justified Him. All that the Father gave Him to do had been performed in perfect obedience. He was now ready to leave the flesh, and lay down His life. And the last cross word: "Father, into thy hands do I commend my spirit," shows that He died in the perfect consciousness of God's favor and fellowship, and in the confidence that the Father would receive Him into the glory of paradise.

The Savior lays down His life in the consciousness of His perfect justification!

And thus men bore witness that He is the Son of God, a righteous man. The centurion and those that were with him openly gave testimony to this effect: the others on Calvary beat their breasts in self-condemnation, and departed.

By the cross of Christ the world had been judged and condemned!

Let us, too, beat our breasts as we behold this sight, in true repentance, because of our sin.

But let us, by faith, also hear the Word of God that speaks from Calvary even now: "The judgment is past. Zion is redeemed by justice. God has reconciled us unto Himself. The way into the inner sanctuary is open. There is no condemnation for them that are in Christ Jesus."

Come unto Him!

Draw near with boldness of faith.

He will receive you, and give you rest.

CHAPTER 8

Victory

. . . and the earth did quake, and the rocks rent;
and many bodies of the saints which slept arose, and
came out of the graves after his resurrection.

— MATT. 27:51-53.

Marvelous sign!

At the moment of Jesus' death everything shook and split.

With the latter part of the passage from Matthew 27, that which speaks of the resurrection of many saints, we are not now directly concerned. Suffice it to say that the text conveys the idea that, while the earthquake and the opening of the graves occurred at the occasion of Jesus' death, the resurrection of the saints accompanied the resurrection of the Savior. These saints, that appeared to many in Jerusalem, no doubt entered into glory with the Lord.

But we are particularly interested in that part of this sign that occurred at the occasion, and as an interpretation of the significance of the death of our Lord: the earthquake, the rending of the rocks, and the opening of the graves.

What does it mean?

Why does the earth tremble on its foundations, and do all things split and rend the moment when the Lord lays down His life on Calvary?

421

In general, it proclaims that the death of Christ is victory, final, decisive, and universal victory. It spells the victory of the kingdom of God over the dominion of darkness. It means that, with the death of Christ, old things have passed away, all things have become new. It is a prophecy of the moment when the Word of God shall be realized: "Yet once more I shake not the earth only, but also heaven. And this word, Yet once more, signifieth the removing of those things that are shaken, as of things that are made, that those things which cannot be shaken may remain." Heb. 12:26, 27.

In order to understand this, we must consider for a moment the significance of the earthquake in the Word of God.

Frequently Scripture mentions earthquakes, and always they signify the victory of God's cause, and the redemption of His people, accompanied by the destruction of the powers of darkness, and the passing away of the present fashion of the world. They look forward to the end of all things, and the revelation of the Lord in glory. The Old Testament psalmist, celebrating the mighty deliverance of God's people from the house of bondage in Egypt, sings: "O God, when thou wentest forth before thy people, when thou didst march through the wilderness; The earth shook, the heavens also dropped at the presence of God" Ps. 68:7, 8. And again: "When Israel went out of Egypt . . . the sea saw it and fled: Jordan was driven back. The mountains skipped like rams, and the little hills like lambs . . . Tremble, thou earth, at the presence of the Lord, at the presence of the God of Jacob" Ps. 114:1, 3, 4, 7. In Haggai 2:6, 7, we read: "For thus saith the Lord of hosts: Yet once, it is a little while, and I will shake the heavens, and the earth, and the sea, and the dry land; And I will shake all nations, and the desire of the nations shall come: and I will fill this house with glory, saith the Lord of hosts." And although this word entered upon its fulfillment with the first advent of the Lord, His death, resurrection, and the outpouring of the Spirit, the Epistle to the Hebrews teaches us that its final fulfillment must still be expected, in the words we already quoted above: "Whose voice then shook the earth: but now he hath promised saying, Yet once more I shake not the earth only, but also heaven. And this word, Yet once more, signifieth the removing of those things that are shaken, as of things that are made, that those things which cannot be shaken may remain. Wherefore we receiving a kingdom which cannot be moved, let us have grace, whereby we may serve God with reverence and holy fear." 12:26-28.

The Saviour, too, speaks of earthquakes, and of the shaking of all things, as signs that accompany the last things.

"For nation shall rise against nation, and kingdom against kingdom: and there shall be famines, and pestilences, and earthquakes, in divers places. All these shall be the beginnings of sorrows." Matt. 24:7. cf. Mark 13:8; Luke 21:11. Besides, there will be a universal upheaval: "Immediately after the tribulation of those days shall the sun be darkened, and the moon shall not give her light, and the stars shall fall from heaven, and the powers of the heavens shall be shaken: And then shall appear the sign of the Son of Man in heaven." Matt. 24:29, 30. cf. Mark 13:25; Luke 21:27.

Accordingly, the book of Revelation, in apocalyptic vision, pictures for us the approach of the end and the breaking through of the unmoveable kingdom, in colors of universal catastrophe: "And I beheld when he had opened the sixth seal, and, lo, there was a great earthquake; and the sun became black as sack-cloth of hair, and the moon became as blood; and the stars of heaven fell unto the earth, even as a fig tree casteth her untimely figs, when she is shaken of a mighty wind. And the heaven departed as a scroll when it is rolled together; and every mountain and island were removed out of their places. And the kings of the earth, and the great men, and the rich men, and the chief captains, and the mighty men, and every free man, hid themselves in the dens and in the rocks of the mountains; And said to the mountains, Fall on us, and hide us from the face of him that sitteth on the throne, and from the wrath of the Lamb: For the great day of his wrath is come; and who shall be able to stand?" Rev. 6: 12-17. And again, at the occasion of the pouring out of the seventh vial: "There were voices, and thunderings, and lightnings; and there was a great earthquake, such as was not since men were upon the earth, so mighty an earthquake, and so great." Rev. 16:18. The earthquake is the Word of God proclaiming that the present order of things is movable and shall pass away, to make room for that new economy of things which John introduces in the words of Revelation 21:1: "And I saw a new heaven and a new earth: for the first heaven and the first earth were passed away; and there was no more sea."

In this light, therefore, we must interpret the earthquake, the rending of the rocks, and the opening of the graves, at the occasion of the death of our Lord.

These signs are a revelation of Jesus Christ. They mean to interpret to us the significance of His death. They proclaim that, principally, the death of Christ is the victory, the end of the present world, and the beginning of the new.

Old things have passed away, behold, all things have become new!

What, then, are these old things that pass away? And what are the new things that are breaking through the old to replace them? What is the connection of this tremendous and universal change with the death of Jesus? Who, then, is this Christ that laid down His life on Calvary?

To answer these questions we must, briefly, draw the historical line, from the beginning, in the light of God's revealed counsel.

In the beginning God created our world a kingdom. The world is not an aggregate of individual creatures, but an organic whole. Out of the chaos it arose, by the mighty hand of the Creator, in an ascending scale of creatures that reached its apex in man. It was a kingdom with man as its king. And man was the friend-servant of God. He was so formed that he might bear the very image of God, and with that image he was endowed, in order that he might know his Creator in love, have his delight in the doing of His will, and consecrate himself and all things in true obedience of love to the living God. In the heart of man the whole creation was united to the heart of God, in perfect fellowship of friendship. All things must serve man, that man might serve his God.

However, this state of original perfection did not continue.

A breach was struck. And it was struck in the heart of man. Man became a rebel. The king of our world rose in insurrection against his Sovereign. He rejected the Word of God, and preferred the word of the devil, who had instigated a similar rebellion in heavenly places. The covenant with his God man violated, and he made an alliance, a spiritual-ethical alliance, with the prince of darkness. He served notice that he would no longer consecrate himself and all things to the living God, and proposed, henceforth, to be his own lord and master, to do the will of the devil, and to press all things into the service of sin. Man, the friend of God, became a rebel, and stood in enmity against Him.

We must remember, that, essentially, man's relation to the earthly creation had not changed. He is still king. True, God deprived him of his original glory and powers. He was subjected to death and corruption. And all creation was made to bear the curse. The creature was made subject to vanity, and the earth was cursed to bring forth thorns and thistles. But even so, man was king in the cursed world, and he still performs many wonderful and mighty things, as is especially evident in our modern times. That world and all it contains, the world of sinful man, in which all things are subjected to the service of sin and the devil; the world with all its vaunted glory and culture, with its science and invention, its industry and commerce, its pleasures and treasures, its lust of the flesh, and lust of the eyes, and pride of life; the world, too, in its present earthly form, as it bears the curse, and is subject to vanity, in a word, the entire present economy of things constitutes the old things, that are moveable, and shall pass away.

But God had provided some better thing for us.

He will give His glory to no other, nor leave His world, the work of His hands, in the clutches of Satan, in the power of rebellious man, and under the curse of vanity, sin, and death.

He loved His world.

His purpose, His eternal good pleasure it is to raise that world, even through the deep way of sin and death, by the wonder of His grace, to the higher level of His heavenly kingdom, the new heaven and the new earth, in which righteousness shall dwell, and in which the tabernacle of God shall be with men.

That is the marvellous work of God's grace!

Of that new world, Christ, the only begotten Son of God, in the flesh, crucified and raised from the dead, is the everlasting head. He is the heir of all things. In that new world He has the preeminence. All things are united under Him. They reflect His glory, the glory as of the only begotten Son of God. In Him that whole new creation, as it is conceived and purposed in the counsel of God, is united with the heart of God forever. And He is the Head of the church, the millions upon millions of the elect that are chosen in Him, ordained to reign with Him, to be priest-kings with Him, under God, forever, in that new and eternal kingdom. They are redeemed of God, purchased by the blood of the only begotten Son of God in the flesh, the blood of the Lamb. All things are theirs, and they are Christ's, and Christ is God's, that He may be all in all.

That, in general outline, is the new order of things, according to Scripture, as they are conceived in the counsel of God, and as they will break through the present old order, to be revealed in the day of the Lord.

That this all-embracing conception of God's counsel of redemption is the plain teaching of Scripture there can be no doubt.

God has "made known unto us the mystery of his will, according to his good-pleasure which he hath purposed in himself: That in the dispensation of the fulness of times he might gather together in one all things in Christ, both which are in heaven, and which are in earth." Eph. 1:9, 10. And of Christ it is said that He is "the image of the invisible God, the firstborn of every creature: for by him were all things created, that are in heaven, and that are in earth, visible and invisible, whether they be thrones, or dominions, or principalities, or powers: all things were created by him, and for him: And he is before all things, and by him all things consist. And he is the head of the body, the church: who is the beginning, the firstborn from the dead; that in all things he might have the preeminence. For it pleased the Father that in him should all the fulness dwell; And having made peace through the blood of his cross, by him to reconcile all things unto himself; by him, I say, whether they be things in earth, or things in heaven." Col. 1:15-20. "And when all things shall be subdued unto him, then shall the Son also himself be subject unto him that put all things under him, that God may be all in all." I Cor. 15:28.

That this old order of things, the earthly economy, with its curse and vanity, its sin and death, shall pass away, to make room for the unmoveable order of God's eternal and heavenly kingdom in Christ — that is the Word of God to us through the earthquake.

This explains, too, why it is at the moment of the death of

Christ, and again at the occasion of His resurrection that an earth-quake occurred.

The new kingdom is not a creation in the sense that it will be established next to the old. On the contrary, it will be gathered out of, and overcome the present order of things.

The powers of sin and corruption, of death and the curse, of Satan and hell, must be vanquished, and the fashion of this present world must be changed.

To do this is the work of Christ.

He must fight the battle of Jehovah against all the forces of darkness, overcome them, destroy them, redeem His church from the guilt of sin, deliver them from its dominion, make them priest-kings of God, establish His own kingdom, and make all things new.

Unto this He was ordained from before the foundation of the world. As such He was announced from the very dawn of history as the seed of the woman that would crush the serpent's head, and His coming was promised throughout the ages of the old dispensation, revealed to patriarchs and prophets, and foreshadowed in all the types and ceremonies of the law. Unto this purpose He came in the fulness of time, the Son of God in human flesh, as the babe of Bethlehem, and tabernacled among us in the form of a servant. With a view to this He was delivered into the hands of sinners, suffered, and died on the accursed tree. For only in the way of God's justice and perfect righteousness could the powers of darkness be overcome. Sin must be atoned. Perfect satisfaction of the righteousness of God must be provided. Only in this way could the brethren of Christ be redeemed, and His everlasting kingdom be established.

The Christ must suffer in order to enter into His glory.

There was no other way than the way of the cross. On the cross He grapples with the powers of darkness. There He crushes the head of the serpent. There He holds death in a strangle-hold.

And He overcame!

In perfect obedience He drank the cup which the Father gave Him to drink. He fully satisfied for all our sins, and merited for us eternal righteousness. The dominion of sin is broken. Satan is cast down. The old world is condemned. By His voluntary and perfect sacrifice He has laid the foundation of His everlasting kingdom in righteousness.

The old things have principally passed away; behold all things have become new!

That is the meaning of the earthquake, and of the splitting of the rocks, at the moment of Jesus' death.

The present order of things is shaking on its foundations. All things rend and split. Very death is forced to open its jaw, that the redeemed of God may come forth, and be clothed with the glory of His resurrection!

And so, as we stand on Calvary, and hear the Word of God through the earthquake and its accompanying signs, we know that all is finished indeed. We know, by faith, that He that gave His life on the accursed tree is the Son of God, the firstborn of every creature, the heir of all things, and that He vanquished the powers of darkness.

He has the victory.

We may now depart from Calvary without fear, trusting in His blood. Even though all things are shaken, the world trembles on its foundations, the mountains are cast into the midst of the sea, we shall not be afraid. Rather shall we, looking on Him that died, and was raised from the dead, look forward in hope to the time when God shall shake, not only the earth, but also heaven, knowing that in that day we shall inherit the kingdom unmoveable.

And in the meantime, we shall not seek the things that are below, still less love the world and its lust; but we shall seek the things which are above, where Christ sitteth at the right hand of God, and keep our garments unspotted from and in the world.

Presently, He shall make all things new!

Then the tabernacle of God shall be with men!

CHAPTER 9

The Resurrection of the Crucified One

Ought not Christ to have suffered these things, and
to enter into his glory? — LUKE 24:26.

In general, three distinct factors enter into the revelation of
the Risen Lord, that is, in the revelation of the reality of Jesus'
bodily resurrection, and of its wonder.

First, there is the empty tomb, opened for inspection by the
angel that rolled away the stone, and "sat on it," in which could
be seen the place where the Lord had lain in the position of the
linen clothes. It was visited, very early in the morning of that
marvelous and glorious first day of the week by several of the
women that had followed and served the Lord in His earthly
sojourn; and, later in the day, by Peter and John. It bore the
silent but very clear testimony both of the fact that Jesus had
left the grave, and that His resurrection was no return to His
former state, but an advance into the glory of immortality.

Secondly, there is the first resurrection-gospel, preached by the
heavenly ambassador to the women that had come to mourn and
to perform the last service of love upon the body of their departed
Master, but that left in amazement, yet rejoicing, because they
had found the living Lord.

And thirdly, there are the recorded manifestations of the Risen
Lord to His disciples, ten in number, five of which took place on

the very day of the resurrection, viz., to the Magdalene, to the women returning from the grave, to Peter alone, to the two disciples on the way to Emmaus, and, in the evening, to the disciples without Thomas.

These manifestations are not all the same, but differ according to the different attitude and spiritual mentality and disposition of the subjects to whom the Lord revealed Himself. Thus, in the manifestation to which we now wish to pay particular attention, that to the two travellers to Emmaus, He reveals Himself as the Christ that must needs suffer in order to enter into His glory. Once more, then, we are invited to look upon Calvary, now, however, in the blessed light of the resurrection, in order that we may understand that, for Him, there could be no glory without the cross.

It was late in the afternoon of the seventeenth of Nisan, the day of our Lord's resurrection.

Jerusalem was full of rumors, often conflicting, about Jesus of Nazareth that had been crucified on the Hill of the Skull. Not at once had the joy of His resurrection filled the hearts and minds of the disciples. The terrible cross had been too real. Its dark shadow still cast its gloom over their souls. And they did not expect His resurrection on the third day. The clear and repeated instruction of their Lord, that He must suffer and die, and on the third day rise again, had not penetrated their minds. They were but ill prepared for the glorious gospel that would be revealed to them on this first day of the week. In the meantime, strange reports reached their ears. There was the story about the vacated tomb, of the place where the Lord had lain, and of the linen clothes, that lay in the grave in the very shape in which they had been wrapped about the body of the Lord. Some reported that they had seen a vision of angels that had preached to them about the Living One that had risen. There was even the report that He, the Lord Himself, had appeared to some of them. And then, finally, there was also the rumor, spread by the bribed soldiers, that the disciples had come, and while they, the soldiers, had been sleeping, had removed the body of their Lord from the sepulchre.

Such was the situation when, in the latter part of the afternoon, two disciples left the Holy City to make their way to Emmaus, a distance of about six or seven miles.

In Jerusalem, they had heard the different rumors concerning Jesus. And they were profoundly interested. Perhaps, they had waited until this advanced hour of the day for further developments, but had finally given up hope. Still, however, as they are in the way together, they talk of the subject that fills their hearts: Jesus, and Him crucified! For we read: "And they talked together of all these things which had happened."

What a subject!

There was no end of material for their conversation. Well had they known Him. His wonderful words of eternal life they had often heard. Of many of His mighty works they had been witnesses. No doubt, they had stood afar off when His enemies had crucified Him on Calvary. Indeed, there was abundant reason to talk. And the subject captivates them. It has the love of their heart, and demands all their attention. And so they had not noticed whence came the stranger that joined their company, and seemed to be interested in the subject of their lively discussion. Nor do they recognize that it is He of whom they are speaking that now walks with them in the direction of Emmaus. For "their eyes were holden that they should not know him." Luke 24:16.

Nor do they notice that this Stranger purposely draws them out and invites them to tell Him all about their problems and troubles. "What manner of communications are these," thus He asks, "that ye have one to another, as ye walk, and are sad?"

The answer He receives is half a rebuke. "Art thou only a stranger in Jerusalem," is their retort, "and hast not known the things which are come to pass there in these days?" They cannot understand that anyone could ask such a question. What would anyone talk about in these days, except about the one subject of exclusive interest and importance?

This Stranger, however, will not be rebuffed. Gently He persists that they rehearse the matter for Him by the question: "What things?"

Why does the Lord so persist that they rehearse the matter of their conversation before Him? Certainly not because He had need of this. But these men had a problem. They were not simply rehearsing things. They were reasoning about the things concerning Jesus of Nazareth. They wanted to understand. The knowledge of

Christ was very precious to them. And they were trying to see the things concerning Him in their proper light and divinely logical connection. But they had serious difficulty. They had reasoned and argued, and looked at the matter from every angle, but they had found no solution to their problem. The things concerning Jesus of Nazareth seemed to them like a jig-saw puzzle, which they had almost solved. But always there was just one part that did not seem to fit. And so our Lord, as the most perfect of teachers, knowing how essential it is that they clearly see their own problem, invites them to state it once more, and urges them to tell Him: "What things?"

And talk they do!

We can well imagine that their heart was overflowing, and that, in the text in Luke, we have but a brief resume of all they told the Lord. Yet, in this brief account, we clearly understand what was their problem: in their conception of Jesus the Christ they could not find a proper place for that dreadful cross.

Listen to what they say. They tell the Lord all about Jesus of Nazareth, that He was "a prophet mighty in deed and word before God and all the people." Was He not the Christ? But then they mention the fact that does not seem to fit into the whole of things concerning the Christ: "the chief priests and our leaders delivered him to be condemned to death, and have crucified him." vs. 20. "You see," we can hear them say, "there is our great difficulty. The thing is not simply that he died or sacrificed himself, but our leaders did it! And they are men that are supposed to know! The Church condemned him! He was crucified as an evil-doer! How could they do it, and how could he permit them to do it, if he were really the Christ?" Yet, so they continue, that was our hope; "we trusted that it had been he which should have redeemed Israel." Notice the language. They *trusted* that it *had been* he which *should have redeemed* Israel. They speak of it as a forlorn hope, all because of that horrible cross! It made the whole thing a confused puzzle. Even the resurrection had no sense in connection with that cross. O, of it, too, they talked: "and besides all this, today is the third day since these things were done. Yea, and certain women also of our company made us astonished, which were at the sepulchre: And when they found not his body, they came, saying, that they had also seen a vision of angels, which said that he was alive. And certain of them which were with us went to the sepulchre, and found it even as the women had said; but him they saw not."

So they talked, Cleopas being the speaker, and the other, we may well imagine, nodding his lively consent.

And always it was the cross that was the great stumbling block.

That the Christ should have been delivered, condemned to death by their leaders, and crucified — that they did not understand!

But now they receive a surprise.

For this Stranger, who had appeared to be ignorant of the things everybody talked about, the things concerning Jesus of Nazareth, suddenly reveals Himself in a radically different light. He now takes the lead in the conversation. He will instruct them in those very things concerning which they had thought to inform Him. He now acts as if He knows all about them, as if, indeed, He is an authority on those matters. He even begins by rebuking them: "O fools (or better, as in the Revised Version, "O foolish men"), and slow of heart to believe all that the prophets have spoken. . . ."

Why does the Lord address them thus?

Usually, it may be considered rather unpedagogical and impractical for a teacher to impress his pupils from the outset with a sense of their stupidity and their slowness to absorb instruction. It might discourage and even antagonize them.

But in this case, we must remember, first of all, that there was sufficient reason for this rebuke, considering that these men were not only acquainted, evidently, with the prophets, but had also been instructed by the Lord Himself. Secondly, He that administered the rebuke had the more right to do so, because He had the power and was about to solve their problem, and to remove their difficulty. And, thirdly, these men did not mind. They were not unbelievers. Nor did they have just a mere theological argument. They were sincerely after the knowledge of Christ. Nor were they rationalists that would only believe what they could reach and comprehend with their own mind. But they were believers that could only see a flat contradiction between the true knowledge of Christ and the dark and horrible cross. And they knew that contradictions could not be accepted, even by faith. Earnestly, with all their heart they sought for a solution. And the sudden and sharp rebuke of this Stranger left the impression upon them, and aroused the hope in them that He would solve their problem, and that presently the light would break through the darkness, so that they might still believe that Jesus of Nazareth was He that would redeem Israel. Besides, was there not some remotely familiar note of authority in this rebuke?

Already their hearts began to be burning within them!

And so, the Lord instructed them.

Perhaps, you remark that it would have been much more simple if, instead of hiding His identity, the Lord had at once manifested Himself to them, and showed them His hands and His side, as He did later to Thomas.

But this is not true. Thomas' problem was altogether different. He wanted, or thought he needed to see and touch the Risen Lord. These men, however, had a problem: the cross. They must understand. Had the Lord only manifested Himself to them, in order then to vanish again from their sight, they would not have been benefited thereby. Their problem would still have remained, and would presently trouble and confuse their minds again. They might actually wonder whether they had seen the Risen Lord, or had been subject to hallucinations. Hence, even before they receive a glimpse of the Risen Lord, they needed instruction.

The subject of this instruction is the divine necessity of the suffering of Christ with a view to His entering into glory.

Without the cross no resurrection!

Without death and resurrection no glory for the Christ of God!

That was the theme of the discourse Jesus now delivered to them. "Ought not the Christ to have suffered these things, and to enter into his glory?" Was there, then, another way? Through the deep way of sin and death, God had ordained to lead His people into the heavenly glory of His everlasting covenant, a glory that far transcends the glory of Adam in the first paradise, or that he could ever have attained. And, at the head of that people, leading them as the Captain of their salvation, representing them as their Head, stood the Christ, by divine ordination, from before the foundation of the world. He must redeem them.

But redemption can be accomplished only in the way of atonement, of perfect satisfaction, of bearing the curse, of death and
hell, and therefore of the accursed tree.

Must not the Christ have suffered these things?

Another glory than that in which He should appear as the glorious
Head of the church there was not for Him. Another way than
that of the cross could never lead into that glory. Without the
cross no glory for the Christ!

And, as to the method of this instruction, the Lord "beginning
at Moses and all the prophets, expounded unto them in all the
scriptures the things concerning himself." vs. 27. Those Old
Testament Scriptures contained the divine program of the things
concerning Jesus, and they revealed from the beginning to end, in
Moses, in the Protevangel of Genesis 3:15, in all the types and
shadows, in temple and altar and sacrifices, and in all the prophets,
that the Christ must enter into His glory in the way of the cross.

What a sermon that must have been!

An expository sermon it was, as all sermons should be: not a
philosophical discourse, neither a wild appeal to the emotions.
He expounded unto them the things concerning Himself. It was,
moreover, a sermon with a single theme, the only proper theme
of every good sermon: Christ, and the necessity of the cross with
a view to the resurrection! And there was a line in that sermon:
"beginning from Moses and all the prophets," removing every
obstacle, and solving every problem, it led up to the grand and
glorious climax: "the Lord is risen indeed!"

And the two travellers to Emmaus understood and believed.

And as they listened their hearts rejoiced, and were burning
within them.

And now, for a moment, their eyes may behold Him!

For as they constrained Him, "He went in to tarry with them.
And it came to pass, as he sat at meat with them, he took bread,
and blessed it, and broke it, and gave it to them. And their eyes
were opened, and they knew him; and he vanished out of their
sight." They had believed the Scriptures, they had seen the revelation of the risen Lord, they rejoiced with great joy.

And now they must impart their joyous knowledge to the rest
of the disciples. They cannot wait. To Jerusalem they return that

same night, only to be met with the glad shout of joy from the lips of the disciples: "The Lord is risen indeed, and hath appeared to Simon!"

For us the truth is still the same as it was for the sojourners to Emmaus: without the cross of Jesus, no glory for the Christ of God, and without the glory of Christ, no redemption and resurrection for us. If we do not want to take our way over Calvary, we cannot reach the wonder of the empty tomb. If we will have nothing of the atoning blood of the Crucified One, we cannot share in the joy of His glory. At the cross we must confess our sin, in order to be glorified with Him in His resurrection. The cross is the way to the resurrection, also for us.

Perhaps, we are inclined to say that we could wish to have been present with those travellers to Emmaus, and to have listened to that marvelous sermon that caused their hearts to burn. And a marvelous experience it must have been, indeed. But let us not overlook the fact that we do have that sermon, and much more. For Christ, the Risen Lord, returned in the Spirit, expounded through the apostles and prophets, all the things concerning Himself, and still speaks His word unto us through the preaching of the gospel.

Let us believe and rejoice!

The Lord is risen indeed, and is become our eternal justification, the resurrection and the life for all that believe on His Name.

More than conquerors we are through Him that loved us! And nothing can ever separate us from His marvelous love!

BOOK SIX

MAN

OF SORROWS

CHAPTER 1

The Tongue of the Learned

The Lord God hath given me, the tongue of the learned . . . . — ISAIAH 50:4.

The following pages are designed as meditations during the lent season. It is customary for the church during lent season to pay special attention to those portions of the Word of God that speak of the sufferings of our Lord Jesus Christ. This I consider a very good custom, because the sufferings of our Savior, together with His resurrection, constitute the heart of the gospel of our salvation.

This time we wish to call your attention to certain passages of the prophecy of Isaiah that speak of the Suffering Servant of Jehovah. In the present chapter we wish to discuss the passage that is found in Isaiah 50:4: "The Lord God hath given me the tongue of the learned, that I shall know how to speak a word in season to him that is weary: he wakeneth morning by morning, he wakeneth mine ear to hear as the learned."

The question is, first of all: who is the speaker in the words of this passage? According to his own testimony, he is evidently a learned man. Shall we give him an appointment in one of our wordly universities, perhaps to occupy a chair of philosophy or science? But the trouble is that he speaks of himself, and no one appears to support his testimony. In fact, the following context indicates that almost everyone contradicts him. His contemporaries seem to despise him and hate him, for they smite him on the back, and pluck out the hair, and cover him with shame and spitting. This would appear to be a poor recommendation for a chair in one of our universities or colleges.

Besides, we may well ask the question whether this man has received sufficient education. He testifies of himself that the Lord his God has given him the tongue of the learned, and that he knows how to speak a word in due season. He does not seem to appeal to the background of his education, but he depends upon the momentary inspiration by the Lord God. It is God that awakens him morning by morning. It is He that opens his ear, so that he can speak as the learned. It is not very probable that on the basis of this particular testimony concerning himself he will be received in one of our worldly institutions of learning.

Moreover, he apparently seeks a very strange audience. For he addresses only those who are weary, and not those who are strong in body and mind. And weary students are certainly not fit to attend our institutions of learning. And therefore it seems to be very appropriate to ask the question: who is the man who speaks in this present passage of the fiftieth chapter of Isaiah?

The man assures us that he has the tongue of the learned. This implies, of course, in the first place, that he is a learned man. But in the second place, it means also that he can speak as such. Now a learned man is certainly one that is well instructed and thoroughly educated. His mind is enlightened and trained. He therefore is a man who knows whereof he speaks, a man of true knowledge, who understands his subject and has thoroughly investigated it. He knows the nature of the things whereof he speaks, as well as the manner of their existence. Moreover, he has investigated the source and origin, as well as the character, of the things whereof he speaks. Hence, he is also able to tell you the reason and the purpose of their existence, the "why" and the "wherefore" of them. Then too, he is able to speak of things he knows. Sometimes those that are learned have no ability to express themselves. They are learned, but they have not the tongue of the learned. But this particular person is very able in that respect. He has the ability to speak of those things which he knows. And besides, he declares that he is able to speak a word in due season.

This man, therefore, according to his own testimony, must be a very able and educated man.

Besides, he also tells us about the audience he prefers to address and to whom he speaks a word in due season. He addresses those that are weary. The weary are those who have toiled hard in the sweat of their brow, and with all their labor have accomplished exactly nothing. They are like a person who attempts to roll a heavy stone up a steep slope to the top of a mountain. He strenuously exerts himself. But all his efforts are vain. For long before he has reached the top, he is exhausted, and the stone rolls down again. The weary are those who have carried heavy burdens, under which they have succumbed. They have labored very hard, until their strength is utterly exhausted, so that they finally sit by the wayside wearily and utterly disappointed, and give up the struggle.

We may note at the outset that this term does not refer to any natural weariness, to men who are exhausted and tired in soul and body in the natural sense of the word. Scripture is not interested in such natural weariness. On the contrary, these weary of whom the text speaks are the same as those to whom reference is made in Matthew 11:28, and whom the Lord Jesus addresses in the well-known words: "Come unto me, all ye that labour and are heavy laden, and I will give you rest." They are the spiritually weary. They are those who are burdened under a load of guilt, of the guilt of sin, that makes them worthy of condemnation and death. They are burdened under a load of guilt which they must constantly bear, of which they can never rid themselves: for they can never pay. Perhaps they have attempted to pay their debt by their own good works, by works of penitence; but their conscience found no rest, and they abandoned the attempt. Moreover, they are burdened under a load of corruption and defilement. They feel that they are totally depraved, that they hate God and their neighbor, that they are incapable of doing any good and inclined to all evil. They are oppressed by a burden of suffering and death. For they lie in the midst of death, and they know that they go from death to death until they arrive in eternal desolation. They are in the midst of the world, and they are oppressed by the burden of corruption in that world. They long for righteousness, and they cannot find it. They long for God, but they feel that He has forsaken them because of their iniquities. They long for life, for life in the true sense of the word, for life in fellowship with the living God; but there is nothing but death. And so they are weary, burdened, heavy laden. And they perish under their heavy burden of sin and death.

To them the man who is mentioned in the words of the passage we are now discussing addresses himself. He has a word for them, a word in due season, a word that fits their miserable condition, a word they need and for which they long.

How wonderful!

What sort of learning does this man have, that can appeal to the spiritually weary? Does he, perhaps, have a word of natural knowledge, a word of science? Does he know all about the science of astronomy, and can this comfort those that are under the burden of sin and death? Has he made a thorough study of nature, and will he perhaps explain to them that all their troubles, all their sicknesses and pains, all their miseries and death are after all perfectly natural? Is he learned in the science of mathematics, so that he can mathematically demonstrate that they have nothing to worry about? Can they perhaps put their trust in him because he is learned in all the languages of the world? We know better. Not all the science and philosophy of the world can help the spiritually weary, the sinner who lies dead in sin and misery. But when all the learned philosophy of the world falls short, and utterly fails, the one who has the tongue of the learned, according to the text, begins to speak. He alone speaks a word in due season to the weary, that is, at the right time — a word that can help and comfort them, that affords strength and courage to the weary.

We ask: why? What is there, then, in the word of this learned man which all the knowledge of the world cannot bring?

The answer in brief is: it is a word of redemption and deliverance. This all the science and philosophy of the world does not and cannot have. It has no word of comfort for those who are spiritually weary. In fact, it despises the weary. It cannot do anything with them or for them. The weary are miserable, and long for redemption from sin and death. They sigh, perhaps, that the Lord has forsaken them. But the Lord answers: "Not I have forsaken you, but your iniquities make separation between Me and you. These must first be put out of the way. Then, and then only, even death and desolation will flee away." They need redemption and deliverance. And this no earthly science and philosophy can ever offer them. It can probably explain to a certain extent how things are; but it can never overcome them. It can investigate the causes of death and all kinds of diseases and sufferings. It can also bring a measure of relief, a partial and temporary removal of the evil. But sin and death remain. It can tell you all about the causes of upheavals and catastrophes in the world. But it can offer no cure or remedy for them. Over against them all they stand entirely powerless. The word of redemption and deliverance, the one word for which the weary long and wait, the tongue of worldly science can never speak. But this is exactly what the man who is mentioned in the passage of Isaiah speaks to the weary, to us, who are dead in sin and misery. When they cannot see through the darkness, then he speaks the word of light. When they cannot see through the night of sin and suffering and death, of all the misery of the world, then he speaks to them the word of redemption and deliverance. For he opens for the weary pilgrim in the midst of the world the hope of a new world, and he says to them: "There will be no night there: no sin, no death, no misery, but eternal life and joy in the presence of God."

Who then is this man who has the tongue of the learned?

You know the answer. He is the Christ of God.

He is the one who, in the prophecy of Isaiah, is repeatedly referred to as the Servant of Jehovah.

It is true, the concept *servant of Jehovah* in the prophecy of Isaiah has different connotations. But principally they all concentrate around the Christ of God, Jesus, Jehovah-Salvation.

Sometimes the term refers to Israel of the old dispensation, to the entire nation. Thus, perhaps, we may interpret Isaiah 44:21: "Remember these, O Jacob and Israel; for thou art my servant: I have formed thee; thou art my servant: O Israel, thou shalt not be forgotten of me." Sometimes the reference is to the elect remnant in Israel, as undoubtedly is the case in Isaiah 44:1-3: "Yet now hear, O Jacob my servant; and Israel, whom I have chosen: Thus saith the Lord that made thee, and formed thee from the womb, which will help thee; Fear not, O Jacob, my

servant; and thou, Jeshurun, whom I have chosen. For I will
pour water upon him that is thirsty, and floods upon the dry
ground: I will pour my spirit upon thy seed, and my blessing
upon thine offspring." This is also the case in Isaiah 45:4: "For
Jacob my servant's sake, and Israel mine elect, I have even called
thee by thy name: I have surnamed thee, though thou hast not
known me." The one who is addressed here, and of whom it is
said that the Lord has surnamed him, even though he did not know
Him, is Cyrus, the king of Persia, through whose hand Jehovah
would deliver Israel from the bondage of captivity. But sometimes
the concept *servant of Jehovah* refers to the prophet as he represents Christ, the Servant of Jehovah *par excellence*. This is evident
from Isaiah 42:1-4: "Behold, my servant, whom I uphold; mine
elect, in whom my soul delighteth; I have put my spirit upon him:
he shall bring forth judgment to the Gentiles. He shall not cry,
nor lift up, nor cause his voice to be heard in the street. A bruised
reed shall he not break, and the smoking flax shall he not quench.
He shall bring forth judgment unto truth. He shall not fail nor be
discouraged, till he have set judgment in the earth: and the isles
shall wait for his law." It is evident, therefore, that centrally the
concept *servant of Jehovah* refers to none other than the Lord
Jesus Christ. For Christ, according to the testimony of all Scripture, is our Chief Prophet. He is the true subject in all the old
dispensation, the one who declares the name of God unto His
brethren, and reveals unto us the full counsel of redemption. He
is the same as that Wisdom that is speaking in Proverbs 8, Who
was "set up from everlasting, from the beginning, or ever the earth
was." And as He functioned in the old dispensation, speaking
through and in the prophets, so He came personally in the fulness
of time, to dwell among us and to speak to us face to face and
mouth to mouth. For "the Word was made flesh, and dwelt among
us. And we beheld his glory, the glory as of the only begotten of
the Father, full of grace and truth" (John 1:14). And, "No man
hath seen God at any time; the only begotten Son, which is in the
bosom of the Father, he hath declared him" (John 1:18). He
speaks, and is able to speak, of heavenly things. For He is the
one that "came down from heaven, even the Son of man which is
in heaven." He is the light of the world, that shines in the dark-

ness. And they that follow Him shall not walk in darkness, but shall have the light of life (John 3:19. 8:12; 12:35, 36, 46). He is the true and faithful witness, Who receives not testimony from men, but Whom the Father Himself bears witness as being sent from Him (John 5:33 ff). He speaks the words of eternal life, and His words are spirit and are life (John 6:63, 68). His doctrine is not His own, but the Father's Who sent Him. And if any man will do the will of God, he will surely acknowledge that Christ's doctrine is of God. For "he that speaketh of himself seeketh his own glory, but he that seeketh his glory that sent him, the same is true, and no unrighteousness is in him" (John 7:16-18). He speaks the things which He has seen with the Father (John 8:38). And He always glorifies not Himself, but the Father (John 17:4). Or, as the words of this particular passage in Isaiah have it, this Man, Jesus Christ, the Son of God, Who has the tongue of the learned, speaks only as He hears from the Father. God wakeneth Him morning by morning, and He wakens His ear to hear as the learned.

That this Servant of Jehovah has the tongue of the learned, so that He knows the things heavenly and eternal, and so that He can speak a word to the weary in due season, He explains from the fact that it is the Lord His God Himself Who teaches Him. For this is evidently the meaning when He says: "He wakeneth morning by morning, he wakeneth mine ear to hear as the learned." And again, in verse 5 of the same chapter: "The Lord God hath opened mine ear, and I was not rebellious, neither turned away back." We understand, of course, that when this Servant of the Lord tells us that the Lord wakeneth Him morning by morning, and that He openeth His ear, He speaks in His human nature. And this wakening and opening of the ear of the Servant of the Lord is done directly and immediately. We must remember that this Servant is the Person of the Son of God, Who is eternally in the bosom of the Father. He is the eternal Word, the express image of the Father's substance, the effulgence of His glory. He is God of God, Immanuel, Who knows the Father with an infinitely perfect knowledge. It is this Person of the Son of God, Who from eternity to eternity is essentially and truly God, Who also assumed the flesh and blood of the children, Who took upon Himself our nature and united that human nature with the divine in His own Person. In Him, therefore, there is the closest possible union of God and man, the most intimate fellowship between the divine and the human natures. In Him the Person of the Son, very God, lived with us, walked with us and talked with us, thought in our mind, willed in our will, had human desires and human passions, human love and human sympathies, human joy and human sorrow. He spoke to us by a human mouth and in human language. He had the tongue of the learned. He is the most perfect Servant of the Lord, the most perfect Prophet conceivable. Who could be more excellently equipped to be our Prophet and Teacher than He, Who knows the Father by the inseparable union of the divine and human natures? Who could be more able than He, Who with the Father and the Holy Spirit Himself is the co-author of the divine counsel, to make known unto us the secret counsel and will of God concerning our redemption? He knows the Father as none other could possibly know Him. His human consciousness is constantly and perfectly enlightened and filled with the knowledge of God from within. He perfectly knows and understands the revelation of the Father in the Holy Scriptures. For He is not only the chief subject of all that is revealed in Holy Writ, but also with the Father and the Holy Spirit He is Himself its author. Because of the union of the divine and human natures, the knowledge of God in Christ is direct and immediate. It is complete and perfect in the highest conceivable sense of the word. In the darkness of the world He is the light. Over against the lie of the false prophet He is the truth. Always He is the faithful witness. God wakeneth Him morning by morning, and He openeth His ear. Therefore, when He speaks, He indeed speaks with the tongue of the learned.

And of what does this Servant of the Lord speak?

He speaks of eternal and heavenly things.

O, indeed, He also speaks of things earthly and things temporal. But when He does speak of them, He always brings them into relationship with, and views them in the light of things eternal and heavenly.

He speaks to us of redemption, which He Himself accomplished as the Suffering Servant of Jehovah when He died on the accursed tree, and rose again on the third day. On the basis of His own atoning work, He speaks to us of perfect righteousness and justification in the forgiveness of sins. To the weary, to those who are burdened under the load of guilt and sin and corruption, He speaks of perfect deliverance and eternal glory. He speaks of the wonder of God's eternal love and of His eternal counsel, according to which He has chosen His own from before the foundation of the world, in order that they should be holy and without blame before Him in love. He speaks of God as the unchangeable and faithful One, Who will certainly preserve His own unto salvation, even unto the end, so that they can never finally fall back into sin and corruption and death. And He speaks of Himself as the Servant of Jehovah, as Him that is sent of the Father in order to accomplish the Father's will. And that will of the Father is that He must become the Suffering Servant, that He must die and shed His lifeblood for His sheep on the accursed tree, that thus He might redeem the sheep whom the Father hath given Him; that He must be raised from the dead, and exalted in the highest heaven, clothed with all authority and power in heaven and on earth, and that thus, as the mighty Lord, He must deliver His people from sin and death unto everlasting life and glory. And He assures us that He has and shall have the complete victory over sin and death and corruption, that He shall surely justify and sanctify us, raise us from the dead, and glorify us with the glory which He had before the world was. For He speaks of the new heavens and the new earth, in which righteousness shall dwell and in which the tabernacle of God shall forever be with men.

In one word, this Servant of Jehovah speaks of the unchangeable and faithful and unconditional promise of God to His people.

This Word He spoke to the weary from the very beginning of the world. He spoke this Word throughout the old dispensation, directly, as in the protevangel in paradise, through the angels that are desirous to look into these things, and through the prophets of the Old Testament. He spoke this Word when He dwelt with us in the flesh, through the mouth of Immanuel, God with us. He Himself spoke this Word to the weary through the apostles in the new dispensation. And this same Word is still being proclaimed by the church, even to the utmost ends of the earth.

But remember that it is always His Word, the Word which He speaks to those that are weary and heavy laden, even when it is proclaimed by the church. Never must it be presented as a mere word of man. For man's word has no power. Even though a man proclaim the gospel, unless the Servant of Jehovah, Christ Himself, speaks through that word that is proclaimed to the hearts of the weary, his word is powerless. Nor may it ever be presented as a sort of mere offer, which man can either accept or reject by his own free will. For man is in darkness. He is corrupt, and can never understand the things of the Spirit of God. He will not, and cannot, and cannot will to hear the Word of the Servant of Jehovah. All he can do is despise and reject it. But when He Himself speaks His own Word to the weary and heavy laden, when He Himself calls them through the gospel out of darkness into His marvelous light, when by His Word of power He Himself calls them, "Come unto me, all ye that labour and are heavy laden, and I will give you rest," then those who are heavy laden realize how really weary they are. Then they repent and become truly sorry for their sins. Then they long to be delivered and take hold of the promise of God's covenant. And then, and then only, they come to Him, are redeemed and delivered from all the burden of their sin and death, and are filled with the glad hope of glory in the eternal tabernacle of God with men.

CHAPTER 2

Meek in His Suffering

I gave my back to the smiters . . . . — ISAIAH 50:6.

That the Suffering Servant of Jehovah, Who is the general subject of our discussion in all our lent meditations, was indeed truly meek in all His suffering is very evident from the passage that constitutes the basis of our meditation in the present chapter. Our text is taken from Isaiah 50:5, 6: "The Lord God hath opened mine ear, and I was not rebellious, neither turned away back. I gave my back to the smiters, and my cheeks to them that pluck off the hair: I hid not my face from shame and spitting."

That the Servant of Jehovah was meek in His suffering is also emphatically expressed elsewhere in the prophecy of Isaiah. In chapter 53, for instance, we read that this Servant had no form or comeliness: when men looked at Him, there was no beauty that they should desire Him. "He was oppressed, and he was afflicted, yet he opened not his mouth: he is brought as a lamb to the slaughter, and as a sheep before her shearers is dumb, so he openeth not his mouth" (Isaiah 53:7).

In the beginning of our previous meditation we asked the question whether, perhaps, the Man of Whom mention is made in this passage would not be considered capable of occupying a chair in some university of the world. According to His own testimony, He is a very learned man. Besides, He is a capable speaker, for

He says Himself that He has the tongue of the learned, and that
He is able to speak a word in due season. But from the words that
form the present meditation it is very evident that He will never
be appointed to a chair in any institution of learning. He may
testify of Himself what He will, but in the world He has but a bad
reputation. Men evidently hate Him and despise His very appearance. For they smite Him on the cheek, they scourge His back,
they pluck out the beard. He has a very contemptible appearance
and opprobrious name. And such a man will undoubtedly never
receive a recommendation and be considered worthy to occupy a
position in one of the worldly institutions of learning.

Nevertheless, we must not be too hasty in our judgment, and
base our opinion on the reputation He may have among the men
of the world. The fact is that He is a truly learned Man. He is
learned in the highest sense of the word. For He is taught of God.
He is undoubtedly a very able speaker, who is able not only to
speak a word in due season, but to appeal to those that are weary
in the world, weary with sin and misery, that are oppressed by a
load of guilt and corruption, and that lie in the midst of death.
For His name is Jesus, Jehovah-Salvation! He is the Christ of
God, Immanuel, the Son of God in human nature. His speech is
always of redemption and deliverance from sin and death, and
points beyond the mountains that surround this vale of tears to
everlasting life and glory, and to the tabernacle of God with men.

The question therefore is quite proper: why is this Man so
ill-treated by and in the midst of the world? Why is He so despised
and rejected of men? Moreover, why, as is evident from the words
of the passage we are now discussing, does He allow Himself to
be so ill-treated? Why does He give His back to the smiters and
His cheeks to those who pluck out the beard? Why does He not
revenge Himself upon the enemies, or at least defend Himself or
hide His face from shame and spitting?

It is these questions that must be answered in our present meditation, when we consider that the Suffering Servant of Jehovah is
meek in all His suffering.

We may note that in the words of Isaiah 50:5, 6, the suffering
of the Servant of Jehovah, Who is centrally the Christ of God,
is presented as assuming a three-fold form. In the first place, the

text refers to a juridical punishment inflicted upon Him in the way of a legal process by the judges of the world. It is evident that they have found Him guilty of some crime, have legally condemned Him. And now they chastise Him and scourge His back. For as He Himself testifies, "I gave my back to the smiters." In the second place, the text speaks of the fact that they pluck off the hair, that is, they pull out His beard. This is evidently a manifestation of bitter passion, of extreme anger and wrath, and of a deadly hatred. For some reason or other men cannot tolerate Him. They hate His very public appearance in the streets of their cities. In the third place, they smite Him on the cheek and cover His face with shame and spitting, which is evidently an expression of bitter reproach and utter contempt. They therefore hate Him and despise Him, fill Him with shame and contempt, and finally execute judgment upon Him through the worldly court.

The text, therefore, refers to the suffering of Christ, the Servant of Jehovah. And the text emphasizes that this suffering was inflicted upon Him through the instrumentality of wicked men.

All His life He suffered, ever since He lay as a babe in the manger of Bethlehem, when He was persecuted by Herod, who attempted to kill the babe in His very infancy, up to the time when He laid down His life on the accursed tree.

It is very evident from the Scriptures that Christ suffered all His life. No, this does not mean that He was subject to special sicknesses and diseases, or even to the common ailments of mankind. If we consider the life of Jesus in as far as we become acquainted with it from the gospel narratives, we can find no special suffering of pain or sorrow that distinguishes Him in any respect from other men. It is according to the gospel of Matthew, that He took all our sicknesses upon Himself: "When the even was come, they brought unto him many that were possessed with devils: and he cast out the spirits with his word, and healed all that were sick: That it might be fulfilled which was spoken by Esaias the prophet, saying, Himself took our infirmities and bare our sicknesses." Nevertheless, not once do the gospel narratives mention that He was ever sick. Yet He suffered all His life. To understand this, we must remember that He, the Son of God in the flesh, the Sinless One, assumed the likeness of sinful flesh. This implies that

He took upon Himself the corruptible human nature, in which
life is nothing but a continual death. This death He tasted more
than any man during His entire life. He tasted it in its true meaning and nature, namely, as the heavy hand of the wrath of God
against sin. Moreover, in the likeness of sinful flesh He also came
into a world that was sinful and under the curse of God. The
creature itself was made subject to vanity, and was subjected to
the bondage of corruption. And the Person of the Son of God in
the sinless human nature tasted and suffered through it all the just
wrath of God. And do not forget, as is evident from the passage
we are now discussing, that He suffered the contradiction of sinners against Himself, that He dwelt among men that loved the
darkness rather than the light, with whose enmity against God
and against one another He came into daily contact, and in the
corruption of whose nature He apprehended the wrath of God
revealed from heaven. In the light of all this we need not try to
discover some special suffering, sicknesses, or calamities in the
life of Jesus on earth, in order to understand that in the corruptible and mortal flesh and in the midst of the world filled with enmity against God and of a creation that bore the curse of God,
Christ's life was nothing but a continual death, and that in this
death He experienced the wrath of God during His entire sojourn
in the world.

Besides, we should never forget that all His life Christ lived
in the shadow of the cross, and that with increasing consciousness
He moved deliberately in the direction of that cross. He had come
under the law, not only under the moral law, but under the entire
Mosaic institution of ordinances and shadows. That meant that
He came under the curse, and that it was His task to remove that
curse. He knew the program of His suffering, as is evident from
the repeated and rather detailed announcement of it to His disciples. He had come to lay down His life. And He was aware of
it all His lifetime! In a sense all His life was a Gethsemane, an
anticipation of the hour of the righteous judgment of God, when all
the vials of God's wrath would be poured out over His head.

But the text in Isaiah 50:5, 6 speaks especially of the suffering
of this Servant of Jehovah as it was inflicted upon Him by men.

He was despised and hated. They smote His cheeks. They

plucked off the hair. They pulled out His beard. They spit in His face!

Evidently He was a very public character. He appeared among men. That He was despised does not mean that He belonged to those lowly and simple men who occupy a forgotten place in society, who live without being noticed and die without being missed, to whom no one pays any attention. The very contrary is true. Christ came into contact with men. And they all expressed an opinion about Him, and treated Him accordingly. In the days of His flesh the Savior was well-known, as He is universally known in the world of today. Who did not know Jesus of Nazareth? Throughout the land His fame was spread abroad. His name was on the lips of high and low, of rich and poor, of the common people and those who sat in high places. His fame was spread abroad in Judea as well as in Galilee and in the Trans-Jordanic regions.

But although His teachings and His mighty works were famous and known by all, and although there was a time when multitudes followed Him, He was nevertheless despised of men. He was considered a worthless fellow, a good-for-nothing, who was not fit to live in decent and civilized society. This became true in an increasing measure as men began to understand the meaning of His instruction and the purpose of His coming. No one offered Him a place in the world, or furnished Him with a recommendation. This contempt of men for Him was so profound that they spit in His face and plucked off the beard. They would pull up their noses in utter contempt. They must have nothing of Him. It is true that He appeared with a certain definite claim, that He said that He was a learned man, and that He could speak a word in due season to the weary. But they did not want His doctrine. They hated Him with a deadly hatred, as is evidenced from the words of our text. Men of all classes hated and rejected Him: men of position and of authority, the leaders of the people, those who were supposed to know what they were about, princes, kings, governors, theologians, scribes and Pharisees, men that were honored for their wisdom and discretion, their piety and religion, all were filled with hatred and contempt concerning Him. Yet it is not only they, the leaders of the people, who expressed their contempt. He finally was literally hated of all men. O, it was not only the rabble of men, those who were of no-account, who despised and rejected this Servant of Jehovah. But men, mere men, as they are found everywhere in this world, men exactly in their capacity and character of men, filled Him with contempt and hid their faces from Him and smote Him on the cheek. Men of all classes and of all ages are included in this. Respectable men and men of disreputable character, honorable men and men in dishonor, religious men and men without religion, men of high moral standard and immoral men, professors of theology and ethics and the common people, educated and uneducated men; kings, governors, theologians, scribes, pharisees, business men, fishermen, soldiers — all condemned, despised, and hated this Servant of Jehovah.

Sometimes, indeed, it seemed that He was very popular. Multitudes appeared to be enthusiastic about His works and instruction. When they had witnessed the astounding miracle of the feeding of the five thousand, they recognized that "this is of a truth that prophet that should come into the world" (John 6:14). They wanted to make Him king. But when on the following day Jesus said unto them: "Verily, verily, I say unto you, Ye seek me, not because ye saw the miracles, but because ye did eat of the loaves and were filled. Labour not for the meat which perisheth, but for the meat which endureth unto everlasting life, which the Son of man shall give unto you: for him hath God the Father sealed," their enthusiasm was quickly subdued. And when the Lord had further explained to them that He Himself is the bread of life, and that no one could possibly come to Him except the Father draw him, the end of it all was that the multitude left Him, and walked no more with Him (John 6:26 ff.).

One of His own intimate followers betrayed Him and sold Him for thirty pieces of silver. Another of His disciples swore and cursed himself, rather than have anything to do with Him in the hour of His extreme suffering. All His own disciples were offended in Him and forsook Him.

O, how men despised Him! They called Him a liar, a deceiver, a blasphemer, an ally of Beelzebub, a glutton and winebibber, a companion of publicans and sinners. They contradicted Him, cast Him out of their synagogue, buffeted Him, spit upon Him, taunted and mocked Him, filled Him with reproach and contempt, scourged

Him and pressed a crown of thorns upon His brow, and finally nailed Him to the accursed tree and set Him up between two malefactors. And even then they still railed on Him and poured the vials of their inexpressible fury and contempt upon His head.

We may ask the question: why must this Servant of Jehovah thus suffer all His life long, and especially on the cross? Why do men hate and despise Him?

Certainly, the reason for this cannot be found in Himself as the Servant of Jehovah. He was indeed a learned Man, Who could and did speak well, men even testifying to the fact that gracious words proceeded out of His mouth. Besides, He did nothing but good, to the benefit of men. He spoke to the weary, and comforted them with words of redemption and deliverance and eternal life. He went throughout the land doing good. He fed the hungry, He cleansed the lepers, He cured the sick, He healed the lame, He opened the eyes of the blind and the ears of the deaf. He cast out devils, and even raised the dead. Always He corroborated His doctrine, His Word in due season to the weary, by His acts, His signs and wonders. What then is the reason that they hated Him with such a deadly hatred, and despised and reviled Him, plucked out the beard, smote His cheeks, and covered His face with shame and spitting?

There is only one reason, and that is that in the midst of a world of sin and death and darkness and enmity against God, He always spoke the Word of the Lord, and never anything else. He was indeed a man of learning, but His learning was not of men, but of God. Of this He had already spoken in the preceding verse: the Lord wakened Him every morning. And this He once more speaks in the words of our text: "The Lord God hath opened mine ear." The human ear in itself is closed to the Word of God. It cannot hear, and will not receive the Word of God. But in Christ the human ear is opened in a wholly marvelous and unique sense of the word. For He is the Person of the Son of God in human flesh, God and man most intimately united in the Person of the Son. Hence, He is taught of God, and His ear is always open unto the Word of God. He is filled with knowledge and wisdom, with knowledge of God and of all divine things. Hence, He never speaks anything else than that which He has learned of God, and His

Word is always the Word of God. As He is taught of God, thus He speaks. Never does He speak the word of mere man, the word of human philosophy. Always He speaks the Word of Jehovah.

This is the reason why in the midst of the world He must suffer, and why men must hate Him. For through this suffering of the Servant of Jehovah, Who always spoke the Word of God, the world which inflicts this suffering upon Him reveals itself in its enmity against God, and is condemned. By this suffering the whole world of sinful humanity, as it reveals itself and develops in the present world, the world in its ethically evil sense, with its lust of the flesh and its lust of the eyes and the pride of life, was tried, weighed in the balance of God's justice, exposed as corrupt, and found wanting. It was judged and condemned when it passed judgment and inflicted suffering and death upon the Lord Jesus Christ, the Son of God in the flesh. This the Lord Himself had already expressed a few days before He was delivered unto death, when He said: "Now is the condemnation of the world, now shall the prince of this world be cast out" (John 12:31). By the very suffering of the perfect Servant of Jehovah, the Son of God in human nature, the world was called before the bar of divine justice, examined and exposed in its corruption and hypocrisy, its worthiness of damnation. It was forced to cast off its mask of goodness and nobility, of justice and love of the truth, of piety and religion, in order to become manifest in its inner wickedness and rottenness, its love of the darkness rather than of the light, its constant suppression of the truth in unrighteousness, its enmity against the living God. It was the condemnation of the world!

We know, of course, that there was a positive purpose in all His suffering. And that positive purpose is this, that the Son of God in human nature, the perfect Servant of Jehovah, in all His suffering, and especially on the cross, bore the sins of all those whom the Father had given Him, and removed that sin forever. The Son of God tasted the depth of death and hell. He bore the full burden of the wrath of God, and sustained it to the end. He finished death in dying. And He only had the right and power to take the place of the elect, to satisfy the justice of God in respect to their sins. And His death, the death of the Son of God Himself in human nature, was so deep, so precious, in the sight of God that by His obedience many could be made righteous. Our sins are forever blotted out, and in Christ we have the righteousness of God by faith.

But this aspect of His suffering does not have the emphasis in the text in Isaiah 50:5 and 6. It stresses the fact that His suffering was inflicted upon Him by the wicked world in the midst of which He lived.

The passage we are discussing at the present emphasizes that this Servant of Jehovah was truly meek in all His afflictions. The text tells us that when the Lord opened His ear, He was not rebellious, neither turned back. In all His life and suffering over against men He never retreats. They indeed desperately attempt to bar His way and to close His mouth; but He does not take flight, and He never keeps silence. Always He is the Servant of Jehovah. He is very patient and meek. For the text tells us not that they smite His back, but that He gave His back to the smiters; not simply that the enemy plucked off the beard, but that He gave His cheek to them that plucked off the hair. And never did He hide His face from shame and spitting.

We readily understand that this is literally true.

As the Son of God in human nature, He could easily have consumed His enemies. How powerless they were to capture Him except by His own permission, as became evident in Gethsemane, when He caused the band of men conducted by Judas into the garden to prostrate themselves before Him on the ground (John 18:6). And could He not have hid Himself and made Himself invisible and passed through the midst of the enemies that came to take Him? Or could He not have called upon twelve legions of angels to defend Him? But He did not. Voluntarily He gave His back to the smiters, and His face to those that plucked off the beard. He gave Himself in obedience to the Father and for the salvation of His people.

This indeed is true meekness and patience. For these are powerful spiritual virtues. Meekness and patience must not be confused with a certain weakness of character. Nor are they natural gifts. On the contrary, they are those spiritual virtues and powers according to which one is able to suffer for God's sake and for the sake of His cause in the world. And this was, according to the words of our text, and according to all Scripture, certainly true of the Suffering Servant of Jehovah. He could say indeed: "Learn of me, that I am meek and lowly of heart."

In this particular aspect of the suffering of Christ His people, the believers, the saints of all ages, must needs participate. They too suffer in the world. No, they do not partake of the atoning suffering of the Lord: this is vicarious, and He alone suffered it for all whom the Father had given Him. In it we can never share. But we do partake of the suffering of Christ as it was inflicted upon Him by the hatred of a wicked world. In a measure all the saints partake of what the apostle Paul calls "the remnants of his suffering." And the reason is evident. The sufferings of the saints in the world are principally still the sufferings of the Servant of Jehovah. He is in them, and dwells in them by His Spirit. He becomes manifest in them, in their word and work. And the world hates them for Christ's sake. Literally we may say that Christ still suffers in His people in the world. And those sufferings of the saints, both of the old dispensation and of the new, are often severe. We read in Hebrews 11: "And others had trial of cruel mockings and scourgings, yea, moreover of bonds and imprisonment: They were stoned, they were sawn asunder, were tempted, were slain with the sword: they wandered about in sheepskins and goatskins; being destitute, afflicted, tormented; (Of whom the world was not worthy:) they wandered in deserts and in mountains, and in dens and caves of the earth" (verses 36-38). That suffering will once more be inflicted upon the people of God in all its cruelty and severity in the days of Antichrist, when they shall not be able to buy or sell unless they bear the mark of the Beast.

Nevertheless, we may be of good cheer. For, according to the Scriptures, "if so be that we suffer with him, that we may also be glorified together. For I reckon that the sufferings of this present time are not worthy to be compared with the glory which shall be revealed in us" (Rom. 8:17, 18).

To that glory we may look forward in hope.

CHAPTER 3

The Immovable Confidence of the Servant of Jehovah

. . . I set my face like a flint. — ISAIAH 50:7.

We have been discussing the theme of the Suffering Servant of Jehovah as He is pictured in Isaiah 50.

Of Him we learned, first of all, that as the Son of God in human nature He has a most intimate knowledge of God and divine things. The Lord God had given Him the tongue of the learned. He knows how to speak a word in due season. And He addresses Himself to those who are weary, that is, to those who are burdened under the load of guilt and sin and corruption.

However, we found that this learned Servant of the Lord finds no acceptance in the world. They hate Him, they despise and reject Him, and cast Him out. They smote and scourge Him and plucked off the beard, and covered His face with shame and spitting. He was utterly despised and reviled.

Finally, we found that in all His suffering and maltreatment He was very meek and humble. He was not rebellious. He did not turn away when they heaped suffering and contempt on Him. But on the contrary, He gave His back to the smiters, and His cheeks to them that plucked off the hair, and He did not hide His face from shame and spitting.

We may well ask the question: how is all this humanly possible?

How can the Suffering Servant of the Lord, Christ Jesus, the Son
of God, so willingly and meekly and patiently endure all His
suffering? He is indeed very meek and patient. But what is the
secret of this power?

The answer is found in the words of Isaiah 50:7-9, to which we
wish to call attention in the present chapter: "For the Lord God
will help me; therefore shall I not be confounded: therefore have
I set my face like a flint, and I know that I shall not be ashamed.
He is near that justifieth me; who will contend with me? let us
stand together: who is mine adversary? let him come near to me.
Behold, the Lord God will help me; who is he that shall condemn
me? lo, they all shall wax old as a garment; the moth shall eat
them up."

This, therefore, is the reason why the Suffering Servant of the
Lord can be so truly meek and patient. This is the secret of His
power. He is the Servant of Jehovah. And His power is an immovable confidence in the Lord His God. In Him, and in Him
alone, does He put His trust.

In the face of all opposition the Suffering Servant of Jehovah
here challenges all His enemies with an emphatically triumphant
question: Who will contend with Me? Who is Mine adversary?
Who is he that shall condemn Me? The implication is, of course,
that no one can successfully contend, strive, in opposition to the
Servant of the Lord. When they attempt to do so, they shall surely
be defeated. Hence, He challenges His enemies: "Let us stand
together." He looks about Him at all that try to oppose Him, and
asks: "Who is mine adversary?" And the implication is that no
one even dares to come forth, knowing that he shall be worsted in
the fight. Hence, He challenges: "Let him come near me." He
even asks the question: "Who is he that shall condemn me?"
conscious of the fact that He represents an absolutely just cause,
which no one can possibly condemn. And if for the cause which He
represents they shall nevertheless condemn Him, it will only be
their own condemnation. The reason why the Servant of Jehovah
thus approaches and confronts His enemies with such a triumphant challenge is that He has unshakeable confidence that His
cause is the cause of God. Therefore He is absolutely certain
that God will help Him, and that He in the end will justify Him,

while all His enemies shall wax old like a rotten garment, in which the moth already operates with its process of corruption. For God shall surely justify His own cause. It is the cause of His eternal covenant and kingdom that shall surely stand, and be realized, and have the victory. It is the cause of His own glorious name, the cause of His justice and faithfulness, of His own righteousness and everlasting mercy. And therefore, let the world rage and rave: He, the Servant of the Lord, stands unmoved and unmovable. He sets His face like a flint. Let all the powers of darkness rise up against Him, falsely condemn Him, reveal their hatred of him, and even execute the sentence of death upon Him: God will help Him, take His side, and justify Him. Therefore He is perfectly confident that He shall never be confounded, and that the cause for which He stands is God's cause and shall surely have the victory. Such is the perfect and immovable confidence of the Servant of Jehovah, our Lord Jesus Christ, in all His suffering and agony and sorrow.

What a marvelous spectacle this Servant of Jehovah presents as He is pictured to us in the Scriptures, particularly in the gospel narratives!

Literally He stands all alone in the whole world.

Yet He stands steadfast and absolutely immovable.

He stands over against all the powers of darkness as the Servant of the Lord. He knows that He is taught of the Lord, for the Lord openeth His ear and awakeneth Him morning by morning. He is perfectly confident that when He speaks a word to the weary, His speech is always of God, Who to them is the God of their salvation. In this confidence He is able to stand entirely alone.

Nowhere in the entire world does this Suffering Servant of Jehovah find any support. There is no one among the children of men who defends Him, who pleads for His cause, who takes it up for Him. Even His kinsmen are afraid of Him, afraid that He will suffer defeat because of His enemies, afraid that He is mad and that in His madness He will hurt Himself. That is the reason why, on a certain occasion, they attempt to draw Him away from the crowd and take Him home with them. For thus we read in Mark 3:31, 32: "There came then his brethren and his mother, and, standing without, sent unto him, calling him. And the multitude

sat about him, and they said unto Him, Behold, thy mother and
thy brethren without seek for thee." But when it is a question of
the cause of God, this Servant of Jehovah even disowns His
mother and His brethren. "And he answered them, saying, Who
is my mother, or my brethren? And he looked round about on
them which sat about him, and said, Behold my mother and my
brethren! For whosoever shall do the will of God, the same is
my brother, and my sister, and mother" (Mk. 3:33-35). The
same is evident, though from a slightly different point of view,
from the passage in John 7:2-9. His brethren evidently did not
believe on Him, but nevertheless wanted Him to show His power
and His glory, which they doubted, in the very center of Jewish
life, in Jerusalem, and on the feast day. For thus we read: "Now
the Jews' feast of tabernacles was at hand. His brethren therefore
said unto him, Depart hence and go to Judea, that thy disciples
also may see the works that thou doest. For there is no man that
doeth anything in secret, and he himself seeketh to be known
openly. If thou do these things, shew thyself to the world. For
neither did his brethren believe in him." But the Suffering Servant
of Jehovah did not seek this carnal popularity, but always stood
for the cause of God. And therefore He answered His brethren:
"Then said Jesus unto them, My time is not yet come: but your
time is always ready. The world cannot hate you; but me it hateth,
because I testify of it, that the works thereof are evil. Go ye up
unto this feast: I go not up yet unto this feast; for my time is not
yet full come. When he said these words unto them, he abode still
in Galilee." Also from this it is evident that His brethren also
did not approve of His attitude and did not believe in Him. Alone
He stood for the cause of God, and for its sake He repudiated
even the ties of blood.

The same is true in regard to His relationship to His disciples,
the narrow circle of men who forsook all and followed Him. For
when the Lord revealed unto them that He is the Suffering Servant
of Jehovah, and "that he must go unto Jerusalem, and suffer
many things of the elders and chief priests and scribes, and be
killed, and be raised again the third day," Peter, who had just
confessed that He is the Christ, the Son of the living God, "began
to rebuke him, saying, Be it far from thee, Lord: this shall not be

unto thee." And in saying this, he evidently represented the opinion of all the disciples. But the Servant of the Lord remained immovable, standing alone for the cause of God. And therefore He answered Peter: "Get thee behind me, Satan: thou art an offence unto me: for thou savourest not the things that be of God, but those that be of men." All alone He stood when the climax of His suffering drew nigh, and the accursed tree was in sight. For on the way to the garden of Gethsemane He said to His disciples: "All ye shall be offended because of me this night: for it is written, I will smite the shepherd, and the sheep of the flock shall be scattered abroad." It is true, they were willing to defend Him with the power of the sword. But when they understood that the Lord determined to go in the way of the Suffering Servant of Jehovah and trusted absolutely in Him alone, "then all the disciples forsook him and fled" (Matt. 26:31, 56).

He stood alone, therefore, for the cause of God over against His kinsmen and His disciples. And always He stood for the cause of God.

Thus He also stands over against the whole wicked world. They all utterly despise Him, great and small, rulers and people, high priests, Pharisees, and scribes, as well as the rabble of the nation. They will have nothing of Him. They pull up their noses at Him in utter contempt. In the streets of their cities they shun Him and do not meet Him with a friendly greeting. On the contrary, they attack Him. In bitter and fierce anger they pull out His beard. They cover His face with spittle. They scourge His back. They condemn Him, and reckon Him with the most abominable criminals. They judge Him worthy of death, even of the death of the cross. They think no punishment too severe for Him. And all this has its reason in the cause for which He stands, which is the cause of God. His friends forsake Him. His kinsmen are afraid of Him. He becomes a stranger to His brethren. Even the quiet woman that usually keeps all things, hiding them in her heart, appears to be afraid sometimes that He stands for the wrong cause. And His enemies round about Him loudly proclaim that His cause is out of Beelzebub, the prince of the devils. Therefore they proclaim, in word as well as in deed, that He will be confounded, that His cause will suffer defeat, and that it will presently become evident that even God does not want Him.

Yet, under all these circumstances, when all have forsaken Him and He stands utterly alone, His trust is evidently still in the Lord His God and looking about at His enemies He sends forth the challenge: "Who shall condemn me? Or who shall contend with me?"

Marvelous challenge, indeed!

How must this utterly strange and unique attitude of the Servant of Jehovah be explained?

Was there, then, not every reason for Him to lose all confidence in His cause, and all courage to proceed on His way? Does, then, the question never arise in His mind and heart whether, perhaps, the whole world after all was right and He alone was wrong? Is He never shaken in His conviction that His cause is the cause of God and that, therefore, it must be right and that, too, over against the judgment of all men, as expressed by rich and poor, learned and unlearned, Pharisee, priest, and scribe?

But no, He stands immovable.

He claims that no one can possibly contend with Him, that no one can condemn Him and His cause, that no one can successfully be His adversary, because it is God that will justify Him and that justifies Him even now while all men rise up against Him. With this bold challenge He stands in the midst of the condemning, reviling, and cursing enemies. Even in the very hour when everyone apparently contends with Him, and when all, in this contention, appear to be stronger than He, He nevertheless maintains that to contend with Him is impossible and inconceivable, is utter folly. He is absolutely confident that all who rise against Him in judgment will surely be defeated. Even to the very last, when all the world executes its sentence of condemnation upon Him; when it appears that the sentence of the Lord from heaven corroborates that of the whole world, when all men curse Him and God forsakes Him, He still claims that no man can possibly bring anything against Him. He challenges His judges and all the powers that be: "Let us stand together: who is mine adversary? Let him come near to me." With those that revile and condemn Him He places Himself and His cause before the Judge of heaven and earth

Who judges righteously, and Who is the only one that can finally decide. Standing there with them, He is confident that He will be justified and that His cause will never be condemned. He is thoroughly convinced that His enemies and their cause will be put to shame. They all shall wax old as a garment, and the moth shall consume them. And when they all shall have perished, He and His cause will still stand, because it is the cause of God. Therefore, He knows that He shall never be put to shame.

Of two things He is absolutely convinced, and they constitute the ground of His confidence.

First of all, He lives in the immovable conviction that His cause is the cause of God and His righteousness. And, second, He is also perfectly assured, all appearances of things to the contrary, that the righteousness of God will triumph, because God alone is God and the powers of darkness cannot prevail against Him. In Him is the confidence of the suffering Servant of Jehovah.

Therefore, He tells His enemies that He shall never be confounded.

Confounded is one who is put to shame because something of which he was confident, and of which he spoke to others, after all proves to be nothing but a daydream, a product of his own imagination. He represents a certain cause and proclaims to all who come into contact with him that he shall have the victory. He boasts about it. He is wholly confident of it. And now he must finally experience that the cause of which he boasted is nothing but an illusion, that it has come to nothing. Bitterly disappointed is he. He stands shamefaced before those to whom he boasted of the certainty of his cause. The more important, the greater the cause which he represents, and the more confidently he boasted that it surely should be realized, the more deeply he shall be confounded. And he who thus is confounded because his cause, about which he boasted that it should have the victory, suffers defeat is also being put to shame. In profound disappointment he shall have to be ashamed. And the more he boasted of his cause, the more bitter his shame shall be.

But thus it will never be with the Servant of Jehovah and with the cause which He represents. Of this the Servant of Jehovah is absolutely confident. Everything, absolutely everything, He puts

at stake for His cause, the cause of God. His own name and honor,
His reputation and life He voluntarily surrenders. They finally
even tear His garment from His body and draw His blood drop
by drop out of His veins. Mockingly they tell Him that even God,
in Whom He trusted, does not want Him, and that He to Whom
He entrusted His cause has utterly forsaken Him. Thus they deliver to Him the tangible proof that His cause is before God and
men a lost cause, and that it is utterly hopeless. Yet, even in that
hour of utter shame and desolation He proclaims: "I will never
be confounded; I will never be put to shame. It is God that justifies Me." He proclaims: "Although it seems as if the world has
overcome Me, I nevertheless maintain that I overcome the world.
Although the things that are seen seem to proclaim that the world
condemns Me, yet I maintain that My condemnation by the world
is essentially the condemnation of the world itself. Although the
prince of this world seems to celebrate his triumphs, nevertheless
he is now being cast out. Even in the hour of utter confusion I know
that I shall never be confounded. I still say to the weary, even in
My hour of shame and desolation: 'Come unto Me, and I will give
you rest.' Out of this hour of shame and desolation comes eternal
glory for you and for Me. For out of this condemnation comes My
and your justification forevermore. I, not they, have the victory.
Therefore I set My face like a flint. I will never compromise. I
will never deny the cause of God's eternal covenant."

O, what an immovable confidence does this Servant of Jehovah,
this Christ of God, reveal in all His suffering and desolation!

What, then, is the ground of His confidence?

What is the secret of His power and trust?

The answer is in one word: it is Jehovah God. He is confident
that Jehovah God, or the Lord Jehovah, is ever on His side and
will surely help Him. He is perfectly confident that Jehovah God
will justify Him. That is the secret of His power. He, Adonai
Jehovah, for the sake of His eternal covenant and for the eternal
glory of His great name, which He never gives to another, had
drawn Him out of the womb of His mother — Him, the Son of
God in human nature. He, Adonai Jehovah, had from the very
dawn of awakening consciousness as a little child caused Him to
trust in Him even on His mother's breast. He, Jehovah God, had

taught Him to say in the very first words which His stammering baby-lips could utter: "Thou art my God." In that unshakable confidence the Servant of Jehovah never wavered. Thus it remained in all His life on earth. Thus it still was in the hour of darkness, when the waves of desolation roll over His anxious soul, even when all that see Him on the accursed tree mock at Him and put out the lip at Him and jeer, "He trusted in God; let him deliver him now, if he will have him: for he said, I am the Son of God" (Matt. 27:43); even when He may well complain in the words of Psalm 42, "With anguish as from piercing sword reproach of bitter foes I hear, while day by day, with taunting word, where is thy God, the scoffers sneer." Even then, in His darkest hour, He still sings:

> O why art thou cast down, my soul,
> And why so troubled shouldst thou be?
> Hope thou in God, and Him extol,
> Who gives His saving help to me.

Or, in the words of our text, He still challenges: "For the Lord God will help me; therefore shall I not be confounded. He is near that justifieth me. Behold, the Lord God will help me; who is he that shall condemn me?"

In that confidence He knows that He shall be justified.

He knows that He is the Servant of the Lord. And on Him alone is His confidence. He knows that as the Servant of the Lord He was taught by Him. For God opened His ear, and He awakened Him morning by morning. Therefore He knows that He must always be and always is in the things of the Father. He was deeply and clearly conscious of the fact that He stood for the cause of God's covenant in the midst of the world. For that reason He can put His face as a flint. His cause is the cause of God, the cause of Adonai Jehovah. If He should go under, God would go under. And that is forever impossible. If He should be confounded, the Lord God Himself would be confounded. And that is utterly inconceivable. If He should be defeated, the cause of God's covenant would be defeated. And that is eternally impossible. For God is the Lord, Adonai, the Lord of all. He is Jehovah, the eternal *I Am*. He is the One that eternally is. He is the eternally unchangeable One, the Rock, in Whom there is no changeableness or shadow of turning. His faithfulness is sure. He can never deny Himself. And because He cannot deny Himself, He cannot possibly deny His Servant. Besides, He is the only Lord, the Lord over all, the Sovereign of heaven and earth. And the only Lord, the Almighty God, is also the only judge. His counsel shall stand, and He shall do all His good pleasure. No one can or ever will resist His will. And therefore, He will surely justify His Servant, Who stands for His cause, in order that He may be praised and glorified by all His creatures. He is near to His Servant. He helps Him. He surrounds Him. He gives Him power and strength. He protects Him. And of that nearness of the Lord His God, the Servant of the Lord is perfectly conscious. For even in the depth of His suffering He still cries out: "My God, my God. . ."

In this confidence He was never put to shame.

Justified He surely was.

O, in His deepest hour of suffering all the bulls of Bashan come upon Him to condemn Him. They take up His challenge and loudly shout: "We shall contend with thee; we shall bring thee into judgment and condemn thee. We shall so confound thee that no one ever dares to mention thy cause in the world again."

And apparently they succeed for a while.

Nevertheless, He that justified Him is near, near even in the hour of His darkest agony, near to the very cross. Already in the judgment before Pilate it becomes evident that He is the One that was justified. For the process of judgment after all really condemned those that meant to condemn Him. They may indeed loudly shout and cry for His condemnation and crucifixion. But in the midst of all this tumult the worldly judge nevertheless expresses the sentence, "I find no guilt in him." Justified He is already at the time when He hangs on the accursed tree. For a while the enemies may still rage and rave at the cross, and shout that He is now utterly lost, and that God does not want Him. Nevertheless, presently, about noon, the entire scene changes. A mysterious and fearful darkness descends upon the cross. Terror is struck in the hearts of the enemies. And henceforth they are silent. In that darkness both the Servant of the Lord and His accusers and murderers stand in the judgment of God. And in that judgment the Servant is justified.

Presently the earth quakes and the rocks rend and the graves are opened.

And before many hours God raises Him from the dead, justifying Him and His cause, and at the same time justifying all His people. And presently He comes again to judge the quick and the dead. And then it shall appear forever that His cause is the cause of God's covenant.

Blessed are they that put their trust in Him!

CHAPTER 4

No Form Nor Comeliness

. . . There is no beauty that we should desire Him.
— ISAIAH 53:2

The theme, we remember, of all these lent mediations is the Suffering Servant of Jehovah.

First of all we called your attention to some passages in Isaiah 50. This time we will turn to the 53rd chapter of the same prophecy of Isaiah.

This 53rd chapter no doubt contains the very heart of the series in the prophecy of Isaiah concerning the Suffering Servant of the Lord, or the sufferings of Christ.

What a marvelous chapter this is!

Although it was written centuries before the appearing of our Lord Jesus Christ in the flesh, it might have been written in the very shadow of the cross. In the searchlight of his prophecy Isaiah beholds Him there, standing all alone, forsaken of men, despised and rejected, and subjected to untold sufferings. And as the prophet beholds Him thus, standing in the distance, viewing Him from the mountain tops of prophecy, he feels at once that no natural man will ever believe his report concerning Him. For according to that report, this Servant of the Lord is the Messiah, He that should redeem and deliver Israel, the mighty arm of Jehovah, the King of kings and Lord of lords. But He certainly does not look like a mighty deliverer. There is nothing in His appearance that can possibly appeal to the eyes of the flesh. Unbelief finds nothing attractive in Him. And therefore the prophet cries out in the very first verse of chapter 53: "Who hath believed our report? and to whom is the arm of the Lord revealed? For he shall grow up before him as a tender plant, and as a root out of a dry ground: he hath no form nor comeliness; and when we shall see him, there is no beauty that we should desire him."

It is to this particular passage that we wish to call your attention in the present meditation.

We must remember that the prophet is speaking here of the Servant of Jehovah, and of that Servant as He suffers in the world.

As we already remarked before, the concept "Servant of Jehovah" has a wider and a narrower connotation. If we would have a proper conception of this notion, we might imagine a wide circle. The circumference of that circle represents Israel as a nation in the widest sense, with its carnal and spiritual seed. Within that circumference there is a narrow circle, representing the spiritual seed, or Israel according to the election of grace. Again, within the circumference of that second circle there is a third, still narrower, representing the prophets, and particularly Isaiah. And the very center of that circle is *the* Servant of Jehovah, our Lord Jesus Christ. Always that Servant of Jehovah, even in its widest conception, suffers in the world. But all its suffering is related to and because of the sufferings of Christ. And it is evident that in the fifty-third chapter of this prophecy Isaiah speaks particularly of Him.

The prophet begins by asking the question: "Who hath believed our report? and to whom is the arm of the Lord revealed?" He evidently intends to say that no man of himself will ever believe the preaching of Isaiah concerning this particular Servant of Jehovah. To the flesh it is inconceivable and absurd to maintain that this Man, Whom Isaiah describes in this chapter, is the arm of the Lord.

O, to be sure, He is exactly this. This Servant of Jehovah is the true representative of God's power and might. He is mighty, and He is the only one that is mighty to redeem and to deliver God's people. His, and His alone, is the power to maintain and establish forever God's eternal covenant of friendship, and to re-establish the mighty throne of David, and thus to reveal the kingdom of God in everlasting glory. Such is the calling of the Servant of the Lord. To this He was appointed and anointed in the eternal counsel of God at the head of His elect. And to realize this calling He came into the world in the fulness of time. This idea is most beautifully expressed in the figure "the arm of the Lord." This Servant is the very arm of Jehovah. By this arm God Himself reaches out to save His people. This figure emphasizes the fact that this Servant of the Lord is inseparably connected and united with God Himself. In the most literal sense of the word Christ *is* the arm of the Lord, through Whom God redeems and delivers His people, and establishes His eternal Kingdom and covenant.

But surely, this particular Man, Whom the prophet describes in the fifty-third chapter of his prophecy, does not appear like the mighty arm of Jehovah. His appearance is not such that you can have any expectation of Him with a view to the deliverance of Israel and the establishment of God's eternal kingdom and covenant. For, first of all, the prophet describes Him here as comparable to a tender plant, that grows up before the face of God. In connection with what follows we might interpret that this means that He grows up as one of those shoots, or suckers, that appear among the lower branches of a plant or tree, and that one cuts out of the organism of a plant as being superfluous, never bearing any fruit and sucking the life out of the plant proper. As one looks at this Servant of Jehovah, He appears as a parasite, a sponger, that always does more harm than good in the life of society. He seems to have no proper place there, and it is far better that He be cast out. This is emphasized in the next figure, that of a root out of a dry ground. This figure makes us think of a tree that is hewn down to the very ground. Besides, that tree was planted in dry ground, in the midst of the desert, in bare sand. For a while, perhaps, that root may continue to live and reveal its life by shooting forth little branches. But everyone knows very well that it will never develop into a full-grown tree again, strong and majestic, and that it is bound presently to die.

Thus, then, as such a parasite, as such a tender branch, as a sucker that one cuts out from the organism of the plant, as a root in sandy soil, in the barren desert, from which there is no longer any expectation, this Servant of the Lord grows up before the face of Jehovah. Thus men see Him. Thus He appears to His contemporaries in the midst of the world. How then is it possible that this Man be the strong and mighty arm of the Lord to redeem and deliver His people? On the very face of it this seems to be absurd. Men can never receive Him as such.

This is the meaning of the question whereby the prophet introduces this chapter: "Who hath believed our report? and to whom is the arm of the Lord revealed?"

That this was true, that this was actually the reputation of this Servant of the Lord among the men of His own time, is evident from all that we read of Him in the gospel narratives, and especially from John 12:37-41: "But though he had done so many miracles before them, yet they believed not on him: That the saying of Esaias the prophet might be fulfilled, which he spake, Lord, who hath believed our report? and to whom hath the arm of the Lord been revealed? Therefore they could not believe, because that Esaias said again, He hath blinded their eyes, and hardened their heart; that they should not see with their eyes, nor understand with their heart, and be converted, and I should heal them. These things said Esaias, when he saw his glory, and spake of him."

You understand, of course, that in this figure of the tender plant and the root out of a dry ground there is a certain history. For that root is the remnant of a tree.

This history, therefore, we must briefly review.

And then we must begin in paradise, in the state of righteousness. Adam, our first father and head of the entire human race, was created after the image of God, in true knowledge, righteousness, and holiness. As such he stood as the servant of Jehovah, prophet, priest, and king of God. And his calling was to serve and glorify Him in God's house and covenant. God lived in covenant communion with His friend-servant.

However, this first man did not remain in the state of righteousness. He fell away from God by an act of wilful disobedience. He stood no longer in covenant fellowship with his Lord, but fell into sin and death, and became hopelessly a slave of the devil.

But God appointed His own Servant from before the foundation of the world. He is the Messiah, the Anointed of the Lord.

He stands back of Adam and of the whole human race. When Adam fell, he fell on Him. If that had not been the case, Adam would have perished in paradise, and the human race would never have come into existence. But Christ becomes the new root from which the tree of God's covenant, that had been cut down in Adam, received new life, and continued to grow up in the generations of God's people in the old dispensation even until the coming of our Lord. For Christ is principally the seed of the woman that was promised in the protevangel in Gen. 3:15: "And I will put enmity between thee and the woman and between thy seed and her seed; it shall bruise thy head, and thou shalt bruise his heel." That seed appears in all the generations of the people of God. Frequently in the history of the old dispensation it almost perishes, and the seed of the devil appears to have the victory. But always it reappears. It is present and appears in the generations of Seth to Noah. And at the time of Noah the tree is once more cut down to its very root. It almost perishes. But God preserved and saved it through the flood and in the ark. The tree grows up again in the generations of Shem and Abraham. And also in those generations it was repeatedly threatened with destruction. It was so threatened in the building of the tower of Babel, by which wicked men prematurely attempted to establish the kingdom of Antichrist. But God frustrated the attempt by the confusion of tongues, separating the human race into the branches of tribes and nations, and preserving the seed of His people and the root of Christ in the generations of Abraham. Again that seed of the woman, with Christ as its root, was threatened with extinction in the land of Egypt, in which the wicked Pharaoh intended to destroy Israel. But God marvelously delivered the people through the Red Sea, and led them through the terrible desert by the hand of Moses into the rest. For a while the root of the tree, which is Christ, appeared in all its glory in the kingdom of David. But even this did not last. Again the tree is cut down. The kingdom of Israel is divided, and only two tribes remained faithful to the throne of David. Before long the ten tribes disappear and are swallowed in the captivity of Assyria. For a while the kingdom of Judah remains, and in it the seed of the woman and the root of David is preserved. But also this does not last, and Judah is led into the captivity of Babylon. From Babylon indeed the remnant is saved, and led back into the land of Canaan. But the throne of David is never re-established, and the scepter appears to have departed from Judah. The tree of David has completely lost its glory. The root has indeed become a root in a dry ground. And even then, during the four hundred years before Christ the attempt is repeatedly made even to take out that root, that it may never flourish into a tree again. The seed of the woman is threatened with extinction. This was the evident purpose of the wicked Haman. And still later it was the devilish attempt of Antiochus Epiphanes, that Old Testament type of Antichrist. And finally the only representative of this powerful and mighty and glorious kingdom of the Servant of the Lord is a poor virgin, living in oblivion in the city of Nazareth, from which nothing good can ever be expected.

That is the root out of a dry ground.

Nevertheless, Christ appears. By the wonder of the incarnation He comes forth out of that apparently dead root. He is indeed the root of David.

But that root of David seemed to be hopelessly lost. From any human point of view there is no expectation that out of that root the glorious house of David could ever be re-established and again appear in glory.

Is it any wonder, then, that the preaching of Isaiah was not believed, and that no one could see in that root out of a dry ground, in that parasite out of a plant, the mighty arm of Jehovah to deliver Israel and to re-establish the glorious kingdom of David? Did not His contemporaries ask in contempt: "Who is this man? Do we know Him? Is He not the son of Joseph? Are not His brothers and sisters with us here? How then can He possibly be the arm of Jehovah?"

Literally, therefore, the question which the prophet asks in the first verse of chapter 53 is realized: "Who hath believed our report? and to whom is the arm of the Lord revealed?"

Besides, in the searchlight of his prophecy Isaiah beholds Him as having no form nor comeliness, and as having no beauty that we should desire Him. To be sure, His contemporaries observed Him and looked at Him. Their attention was repeatedly called to Him. They could not help but inquire whether this man was indeed the arm of the Lord, mighty to deliver Israel. But they find in His appearance nothing that affords them any ground to believe it.

We must understand, of course, that Isaiah here describes the Servant of the Lord only from the carnal point of view, from the viewpoint of natural men, from the viewpoint of those who had no eyes to see, and no ears to hear. It is from this point of view that Jesus had no form nor comeliness, and no beauty that they should desire Him. From a spiritual point of view it was quite different. It certainly was impossible that Jesus' appearance was in itself ugly and contemptible. For, in the first place, although He appeared in the likeness of sinful flesh, there was no sin in Him, but He was holy and undefiled and separate from sinners. No one could help noticing this distinction in His appearance and this separation from sinners. Besides, He was the Son of God in the flesh. And although His divinity was hid, nevertheless this also must have made a difference in His appearance and caused Him to be distinctive from mere men.

Besides, from the viewpoint of faith, that is, an assurance of things unseen and a ground of the things hoped for, Christ certainly had beauty to be desired. The babes in Israel recognized in Him the Messiah, the mighty arm of Jehovah, and expected from Him redemption and deliverance. For them Jesus had form and comeliness. They recognized that Jesus had the proper descent and that He was the Son of David, the promised Servant of the Lord. They knew that He was born in Bethlehem, and not in Nazareth, and that according to prophecy it was in the little town of Bethlehem that the Messiah was expected to be born. Moreover, He certainly had form and comeliness and beauty that we should desire Him because of His mighty words and works which He performed. His wonders testified that He was the Son of God in human flesh, and that therefore He was the mighty arm of Jehovah to redeem Israel. He healed the sick and fed the hungry. He cured the lame and the lepers. He gave sight to the eyes of

the blind, and hearing to those that were deaf. He even raised the
dead, and therefore could and did testify: "I am the resurrection
and the life. He that believeth in me, though he were dead, yet
shall he live. And he that liveth and believeth on me shall never
die."

But the carnal mind, which is enmity against God, nevertheless did not recognize in Him the arm of Jehovah. When the
carnal Jews looked at Him, they saw Him with natural and blinded
eyes (John 12:39, 40). Their hearts yearned for earthly power
and worldly glory. And from that carnal point of view there certainly was no form nor comeliness in the Servant of Jehovah. There
was in Him no earthly majesty. He did not appear in purple and
scarlet and in royal array. He came in the likeness of sinful flesh.
He had no human and worldly power. He had no armies, no
soldiers, upon which He could call to help Him in the battle. He
had no earthly throne. He did not desire one. For He Himself
said that His kingdom is not of this world. Indeed, from any
worldly and carnal point of view there was in Him no form nor
comeliness.

The carnal mind and the carnal eye could find in Him no beauty
to be desired.

To be sure, they looked at Him. For they could not avoid Him.
Their attention was called to Him repeatedly, even by the shep-
herds that visited Him in Bethlehem and by the wise men that
came to the court of Herod to inquire of Him. The attention of
the wise and mighty of this world was called to the arm of Jehovah. John the Baptist pointed Him out to all that came to him in
the desert, and said: "Behold, the Lamb of God, that taketh away
the sin of the world" (John 1:29). And thus it was in all His
sojourn among His people, and especially during the three years
of His public ministry. They heard His words; they saw His signs
and wonders; they asked for Him. But they desired Him not.
Though they heard His words and were amazed at the pleasant
words that proceeded out of His mouth, and though they witnessed His mighty signs and wonders, yet they did not believe
on Him. Once during His public ministry, when the Servant of
Jehovah had taught the people, many of them "believed on him,
and said, When Christ cometh, will he do more miracles than

these which this man hath done?" And by this murmuring of the people the attention of the earthly leaders was called to this Servant of Jehovah. But they did not believe. They saw no beauty in Him that they would desire Him. For we read: "The Pharisees heard that the people murmured such things concerning him; and the Pharisees and the chief priests sent officers to take him" (John 7:31, 32). But these officers returned without the Lord. For we read: "Then came the officers to the chief priests and Pharisees: and they said unto them, Why have ye not brought him? The officers answered, Never man spake like this man" (John 7:45, 46). Again, therefore, the attention of the carnal Jews was called to this Servant of Jehovah. But did they desire Him and believe on Him? On the contrary; we read: "Then answered them the Pharisees, Are ye also deceived? Have any of the rulers of the Pharisees believed on him? But this people who knoweth not the law are accursed" (John 7:47-49).

And why did they not believe on Him?

The ultimate answer is found in John 12:39, 40: "Therefore they could not believe, because that Esaias said again, He hath blinded their eyes, and hardened their heart; that they should not see with their eyes, nor understand with their heart, and be converted, and I should heal them." In the Servant of Jehovah they only sought worldly things, and these things they could not find in Him. Hence, it was inevitable that they finally should reject Him, cut out of the tree what they considered a sucker and a parasite, or, to speak literally, kill Him and nail Him to the accursed tree.

Who hath believed our report? Who hath believed that this Man without earthly form or comeliness, appearing in the likeness of sinful flesh and without any worldly beauty that we should desire Him, is the arm of Jehovah? Who believes? Who accepts? Who through this preaching trusts in Him as the mighty Redeemer of the people of God? Such is the question of Isaiah.

The answer to this question is really in the following question: "To whom is the arm of the Lord revealed?"

Indeed, it is a question of revelation, not of human philosophy. He only believes to whom it is revealed.

Revealed how? Is this revelation accomplished only through the external preaching of the gospel?

By no means: for the natural mind does not understand the things of the Spirit of God. If there is nothing else, the gospel only blinds the eyes of the natural man, and hardens his heart. He cannot believe.

But when through the preaching of the gospel the Spirit of God powerfully reveals to the sinner the arm of Jehovah, then he believes and puts his trust in Him in life and in death, for time and eternity. Then he knows spiritually his own guilt and sin. Then the breach of his own heart is revealed to him, and he spiritually recognizes the death in which he lies by nature. Then by the preaching of that report of Isaiah concerning the Suffering Servant of the Lord, through the Spirit, he desires to be redeemed and delivered from sin and death. Then he learns to hunger and thirst after righteousness. And then this Servant of the Lord, the arm of Jehovah, does indeed receive form and comeliness. Then He indeed appears as the mighty arm of Jehovah to deliver him from sin and death. Then, indeed, he finds all that is in this Suffering Servant of Jehovah very desirable. And then only he believes in the report of Isaiah, and through that report in Him, the Servant of Jehovah, Who died on the cross for our transgressions, and was raised again for our justification.

Then this Servant of the Lord becomes to that sinner the only comfort in life and death forevermore.

CHAPTER 5

Forsaken and Rejected

He is despised and rejected of men . . . .
— ISAIAH 53:3.

Our theme in these lenten meditations is still the Suffering Servant of the Lord.

This time we wish to discuss this theme in the light of Isaiah 53:3: "He is despised and rejected of men; a man of sorrows, and acquainted with grief: and we hid as it were our faces from him; he was despised, and we esteemed him not."

Instead of the clause, "He is rejected of men," the Dutch translation has, "Hij was de onwaardigste onder de menschen," that is, "He was the most unworthy of men." This is possible as far as the meaning of the Hebrew word for "rejected" or "forsaken" is concerned. But the word for "men" in the text does not refer to the common people, but to men of rank and position and esteem among the nation. And if we would translate the clause, "He was rejected of men," by "He was the most unworthy of men," He would nevertheless still be classified with men of rank and position; and this certainly is not the meaning of the text. He was not the most unworthy of the men of importance and influence; but He was entirely outside of them. He could not be classified with them, and He had no position whatever among them. He does not take the last place among men of reputation and influ-

481

ence; but the text rather affirms that He had no place among them whatsoever. And therefore we prefer the English translation, presenting this Suffering Servant of the Lord as rejected or forsaken of men. Men of rank refused to have anything to do with Him, denied Him any assistance, left Him without help or support. The chief men of the Jewish nation, who towered far above the multitude, as well as the great men of the world, drew back from Him. None of the men of rank took His part and were on His side. Such is evidently the meaning of the text.

The text is a continuation of verses 1 and 2. There the prophet had asked the question, "Who hath believed our report? and to whom is the arm of the Lord revealed?" It was apparently so unbelievable, in fact, so humanly impossible, that the Man Whom the prophet saw in his prophetic vision could possibly be the arm of the Lord, Who was to redeem and deliver Israel. For the prophet saw Him in his prophetic vision as one who grew up before the face of God as a tender plant, as a sucker, as a parasite, and, as a root in a dry ground, from which there is no expectation whatsoever. He appeared without form or comeliness, and there was no beauty in Him that anyone could possibly desire Him. Who then could possibly believe the report concerning this Servant of Jehovah? Who of the children of men as such did ever believe it? Now in the words of verse 3 the result of this opinion of men concerning Him is expressed. Because there was no beauty, because there was no form nor comeliness in this Servant of the Lord, therefore He had no position in the world; therefore He was despised and forsaken; therefore, as well as because of the added fact that He was a man of sorrows and acquainted with grief, men hid their faces from Him, and He found no esteem among the children of men, particularly not among the men of rank.

And what is the attitude over against this Suffering Servant of the Lord today? Who believes the report of Isaiah?

Do you? If you do, this certainly cannot possibly be of yourself. No natural man will ever believe the report concerning this Suffering Servant of Jehovah. Do not be too certain that you will believe His preaching, that you will embrace Him, that you will put your trust in His name, that you will be willing to bear His cross and share with Him the suffering of this present time. Perhaps the Christ of your imagination may be entirely different from the Savior of the Scriptures. Do not weep over Him because He is the Man of Sorrows, and acquainted with grief. He certainly does not ask for and demand your sympathy. And do not be too hasty to shout your Hosannas. The tears you shed over Him may quickly dry up when you look at His real appearance. And the enthusiasm of your Hosannas soon dies away. For He is not a Jesus that is highly esteemed of men, especially not of the men of position and rank in this world, as we already said. He is not a man who readily adapts Himself to all classes of society, and becomes popular. He did not come to improve the world. He did not appear in the world as an example for all men to follow. He is not the ideal man who indeed failed to receive recognition by His contemporaries because the men of that day did not understand Him, but Who today in a more enlightened and civilized world, which aims at better things, will be acknowledged in His true worth and received with enthusiasm. That Jesus of your imagination is a mere dream. He never did exist, and certainly does not exist today.

The Servant of the Lord was in the world always despised, rejected, and forsaken; and He still is. Throughout the history of the world men always heaped contempt on Him. He was forsaken and rejected of men, One from Whom everyone hid his face, Who was a stranger even to His brethren. Wherever even a reflection of this Servant of the Lord appeared in history, there the world raved and raged, there men shook their heads in contempt, there they stuck out their tongue, there they whetted their swords and kindled the fires at the stake, there they filled the prison cells, and there they always raised the accursed tree, to annihilate, if possible, the Servant of the Lord.

He was despised and forsaken of men.

To be despised and forsaken refers to one's reputation. And without a reputation no one can have a place and influence in the world. To be sure, to gain a position in the midst of society it is of significance that one has ability and power, and that his appearance makes an impression upon men. But public opinion, one's name and honor of men, one's reputation, is almost of still greater significance. When one has not any special power and ability, but knows how to maintain a good reputation with men, one can gain and preserve one's position in the midst of the world. But in the last analysis it becomes impossible to stand over against public opinion, no matter how much ability and power, and no matter how many gifts and talents one may have. Hence, it is of the greatest significance what men say of you, and especially men of position and rank and influence in the world.

With them the Servant of the Lord was despised. Men hid their faces from Him.

And this, as was said before, and as the text indicates, was especially true of the great men in the church and in the world. The text does not refer so much to the common people. With them the Lord was not despised, at least not for a long time. As the Lord Himself expresses it in Matt. 11:25: "At that time Jesus answered and said, I thank thee, O Father, Lord of heaven and earth, because thou hast hid these things from the wise and prudent, and hast revealed them unto babes." The babes heard Him gladly, and followed Him. To the Galilean fishermen the Father revealed indeed that this Servant of the Lord was the Christ, the Son of the living God. But these babes were not men of importance and of influence in the church and the world. When they would say something about the Christ of God, the Pharisees and scribes characterized them in these words: "This people that know not the law are cursed." But the text refers to people who were leaders in church and state, people with knowledge, who understood the law and the prophets, and who could teach the common people. The text refers to men of influence, who assumed leadership, who occupied important positions in the world, men whom the common people respected highly. They were members of the Sanhedrin, Pharisees, scribes, and priests. They were men to whom the majority of the people looked for leadership, and whom they followed.

With these the Servant of the Lord was despised, and He was forsaken of them.

The text uses the strongest terms to express this. He was despised and forsaken of men. And therefore we, who belonged to the common people, esteemed Him not. He was not only refused a place in society and in the world and in the church, but He had a very evil reputation. Everyone hid his face from Him. He was so horribly bad that when people passed Him on the street, they turned away their heads and refused to speak to Him. That is the meaning of the text. And such was the case with the Servant of the Lord in reality.

This was the history of the Servant of the Lord under the old dispensation. We must remember, as I said before, that this Servant of the Lord, Whom Isaiah describes in his prophecy, is centrally indeed the Messiah, the Christ of God. But nevertheless, it is also the nation of Israel and the people of God throughout the ages. And O, how it was always despised and rejected, and hated by all men! Egypt intended to choke Him in the waters of the Nile. In the terrible desert the enemy from within and from without attempted to annihilate Him. Moab and Edom, Amalek and Midian, Philistia and Assyria wanted to obliterate Him from the face of the earth. As I said before, in Haman's time the mighty empire of Persia made plans to extinguish Him. And Antiochus Epiphanes scourged His back even unto death. A plaything of the nations was the Servant of the Lord. Even His own ungodly brethren according to the flesh despised Him utterly. Well indeed might Israel complain in the words of Psalm 129:1-3: "Many a time they afflicted me from my youth, let Israel now say: Many a time have they afflicted me from my youth: yet they have not prevailed against me. The plowers plowed upon my back: they made long their furrows." And there was indeed reason for the prayer of Psalm 123:3, 4: "Have mercy upon us, O Lord, have mercy upon us: for we are exceedingly filled with contempt. Our soul is exceedingly filled with the scorning of those that are at ease, and with the contempt of the proud."

Thus it was with the Servant of the Lord throughout the old dispensation.

Isaiah, however, now beholds Him as He appears in the fulness of time, the Servant of the Lord *par excellence,* the very heart of the seed of the woman, as He appears in the Person of Immanuel. He beholds Him as He finally appears as a sort of parasite, as a tender plant, as a root out of a dry ground. He beholds Him as the One Who is more despised than anyone, Who is rejected and forsaken by all, from Whom all hid their faces. No, do not make a mistake. As Isaiah beholds Him, He is not the forgotten one, the unknown, Whom everyone passes without taking any notice. On the contrary, He stands in the midst of the world, where everyone must take note of Him. He appears in the public marketplace of life, where all come into contact with Him, especially men of renown, of power and authority, of position and learning. These scribes, the Pharisees, the high priests, and those that serve in the sanctuary, yet also the common people and His brethren according to the flesh, yea, even the powers of heathendom, come into contact with Him and take note of Him. The whole world beholds Him and forms an opinion of Him, and is compelled to express its inmost thoughts concerning Him. And all despise and reject Him, consider Him a fool, an impossible man, who cannot adapt Himself to the life of the world, a man with whom no one can do anything, an outcast.

Thus the prophet beholds Him in his prophetic vision.

And thus it was in reality.

O, how deeply He was despised, and how universally He was made an object of contempt! Among men in the world and among those who occupied a foremost place in society and in the church. He had no name and place. If you asked the scribes, the chief priests of Israel, the Pharisees, and the leaders of the people about Him, they answered that He was a deceiver of the people, who must scrupulously be avoided as a dangerous man. They answered that He was a glutton and a winebibber, and a friend of publicans and sinners. They said that He was an ally of Beelzebub, who performed His signs and wonders through the power of the prince of darkness. They said that He was not ashamed to utter the most awful blasphemies, making Himself the Son of God, that He was a rebel, a revolutionary, a man worthy of death. And although an enthusiastic crowd for a time followed Him and shouted their Hosannas, they too finally forsook Him and left Him alone. Literally He becomes rejected and forsaken of all, despised by everyone. No one ultimately takes His side. One of His own disciples offers Him for sale for the price of a slave. Another one denies Him publicly in the face of His enemies. All the others flee away, and leave Him alone, not being able to carry the load of His shame and contempt any more. And when He finally stands alone, forsaken by all, then men heap all the contempt upon Him that could possibly arise in the minds of ungodly men. They utter false testimony against Him. They condemn Him to death. They mock Him and spit in His face. They hit Him and scourge His back. They crown Him with the mock crown of thorns, put a mock scepter in His hands, put a robe of mock royalty about His shoulders, and offer Him mock obeisance. Thus they hang Him on the accursed tree, despised and rejected by all the world, forsaken by all men. Leaders of the people and Caiaphas, soldiers and officers — the whole world despises Him. He is the reproach of all. Or, as the prophet has it, "we hid as it were our faces from him; he was despised, and we esteemed him not."

The question may be asked: why is He so despised? What may be the cause of this profound reproach? Why is all this contempt heaped upon Him? Why was He so universally the object of disdain and hatred? Was He, perhaps, a man who always stood in everyone's way? Did He always push Himself to the foreground in human life? Did He aim at greatness in the world, at glory and power and honor of men? Did He, perhaps, aspire to become king?

The very contrary is true. In the world as such He did not even attempt to take a place. He was born at the very edge of the world. His house was a stable, His cradle a manger. In His sojourn in the world He testifies Himself that foxes have holes, and birds of the air have nests, but the Son of Man has no place where to lay His head.

The cause of this contempt and hatred must undoubtedly be found in the very fact that He was the Man of Sorrows, acquainted with grief.

Such a man the world does not want. In Him they find no beauty that they should desire Him. The world looks for power and wisdom that is from below, looks for a man who is filled with majesty and glory, in whom they may put their trust instead of in the living God. But this Servant of the Lord is *the* Man of Sorrows. That is His very name. It is not that He merely suffered as every man suffers, and occasionally is steeped in sorrow as every man is. Such a man even the world does not despise. He is the object of pity and sympathy. Also in the world men shed a tear at the bed of one who is sick, mourn over the dead, and place flowers on the graves. But of such pity and such manifestation of sympathy the Servant of the Lord never was an object. Even when He is finally hanging on the accursed tree, when He is literally cursed and crushed in body and soul, when He hangs on the cross with a bloody back, and the blood slowly trickling from His hands and feet, even when the world would shed a tear over the suffering of its most bitter enemy and the most hardened criminal — even then there is no pity for the Man of Sorrows, even then they continue to mock Him and to heap contempt upon His head with a hatred that can never be satiated.

Why? Once more, because He was *the* Man of Sorrows. That was His very name. For the very purpose of suffering sorrow and grief He came into the world. To bear sorrows was the choice of His life. Intentionally, willingly He chose the way of suffering. They offered Him a scepter and a crown, but He declined the honor, and chose the cross. All the kingdoms of the world were offered Him, but instead He steadfastly set His face to Jerusalem, in order to walk the way of sorrow and suffering and death. He came into the world in order to be *the* Man of Sorrows. Despising all the honor of men and all the glory of the world, He steadfastly chose the cup of suffering and agony, in order to empty that cup even to the dregs. And as such, as the Man of Sorrows and acquainted with grief, He stood before the face of the Father, and became obedient in the way of suffering even unto death, yea, the death of the cross. And again, as such, as the Man of Sorrows, He proclaimed loudly to all that could hear: "I am the arm of Jehovah." He proclaimed and still proclaims to all the world: "In my sorrows and sufferings there is salvation and bliss eternal." To all He proclaimed and still proclaims: "Only when you eat my flesh, can your hunger be satisfied forever; only when you drink my blood, can your thirst eternally be quenched. For your misery is your sin, and the basis of your death is the guilt of sin. In my blood there is reconciliation and forgiveness. In my sorrows lies the secret of your redemption. In my death is your deliverance. Therefore I, the Man of Sorrows, am the arm of the Lord." Thus we can understand that exactly because He was the Man of Sorrows, He was despised and forsaken of men.

Who hath believed our report? And to whom is the arm of the Lord revealed?

Certainly, this Suffering Servant of the Lord, this Man of Sorrows, is not and cannot be revealed to the wise and prudent. The world does not and never will and never can believe the report of Isaiah about the Christ of God. The natural man can never recognize the arm of the Lord in the Man of Sorrows. For the Jews require a sign, and the Greeks seek after wisdom. The world wants power and glory, wisdom, and an arm of flesh. Of the Man of Sorrows, Who always stands for the cause of God in the midst of a sinful and corrupt world, they will have nothing. In One Who proclaims that the deepest misery of the world is its guilt and sin, and Who proclaims that in His blood there is redemption and remission, and therefore deliverance from sin and death, they will never confide. In such a One they will never seek their salvation. For the world does not know its sin and iniquity in the true, spiritual sense of the word. It does not know the sorrow over sin. For that reason the natural man despises this Man of Sorrows, Who came as the light of the world.

Yet, even through the means of this reproach and shame, heaped upon the Suffering Servant of the Lord, the God of heaven and earth executes His counsel of redemption. The blood of reconciliation was shed upon the altar of God's righteousness and justice. And through that blood the people of God are redeemed forever.

Who hath believed our report?

Only he who knows his sin and misery as they are revealed to him by the Spirit of God in Jesus Christ our Lord through the Word of the gospel, only he who in contrition of heart and brokenness of spirit is filled with the sorrow after God, knows and understands that this Man of Sorrows, without form or comeliness, despised and forsaken of men, and even forsaken of God, is the arm of the Lord.

It is indeed the Man of Sorrows Who always speaks of God and Who always stands for the cause of God and His covenant in the midst of the world, Who is the powerful, mighty arm of Jehovah whereby the guilt of sin was obliterated, the powers of death and hell are crushed, death is forever overcome, righteousness and life are revealed, the covenant of God is maintained and established forever.

To whom is the arm of the Lord revealed? Who hath believed the report of Isaiah?

Only the babes, to whom the Christ of God is revealed by His Spirit and Word.

Through that Spirit and by the Word of the gospel they become broken-hearted, filled with sorrow after God, and mourn over their sin. Their minds God enlightens. For them the wisdom of the world becomes foolishness, the foolishness of God. They seek the cause of God's covenant. They hunger and thirst after righteousness. They receive a place in their hearts for the Man of Sorrows. And they behold in Him His true form and comeliness. And they desire His beauty.

And in the midst of the world that still heaps contempt upon the Man of Sorrows they confess with joy of heart: "Thou art my Savior and Redeemer, my God, in Whom I trust, my only comfort in life and death."

May God give us grace to believe on His name!

CHAPTER 6

Bruised for Our Iniquities

When I survey the wondrous cross
On which the Prince of glory died,
My richest gain I count but loss,
And pour contempt on all my pride.

Only when we repeat the above stanza by Issac Watts in heart-felt humiliation of self, and really "pour contempt on all our pride," can we possibly believe the preaching, or the report, of Isaiah concerning the Suffering Servant of the Lord.

Only then can we recognize in Him the arm of Jehovah and our mighty Redeemer.

The natural man is in quest of a mighty lord according to the standard of the flesh, according to the power of man, according to the wisdom of the world. Mighty in strength of body and mind must he be, in order to be recognized as the deliverer of man. He must have all the respect of all the world.

But such is not the picture of the mighty arm of the Lord as Isaiah describes Him in chapter 53. The portrait the prophet visualizes and depicts before us in this chapter of Him Who is the arm of the Lord and Who is to deliver us is contrary to all the desires and expectations of natural men. A Redeemer Who grows up not with a display of might according to the standard of the world, but as a tender plant, as a sucker, as a parasite, Whose

491

descent is not with power and glory, but is as a root out of a dry ground, Whose appearance among men makes no impression of majesty and beauty, and in Whom there is neither form nor come- liness — such a Redeemer the world does not want. There is nothing that appeals to the human heart and mind so that we should desire Him.

Such a picture of a Redeemer is too deeply humiliating for our sinful pride and vanity.

Moreover, as we saw in our previous meditation, men certainly do not appreciate Him. They do not pour out their honor and glory upon Him. On the contrary, He is despised. They do not put their confidence in Him, follow Him, and hail Him as their Deliverer. He is rejected and forsaken of men. His proper name is Man of Sorrows. He is acquainted with grief. So marred is His visage, so burdened is He with grief and sorrow, that He becomes utterly contemptible, so that men hide their faces from Him and are astonished because of His appearance.

Is it not utterly humiliating to imagine that such a Man is the arm of the Lord Who must redeem us and deliver us from our sin and death?

Who will believe this report? Who will embrace such a gospel? In whose eyes can such a Savior find favor?

The answer is: only in the eyes of those who are spiritually acquainted with the deepest cause of all their woe and misery. Not as long as we stand with unbended knee and stiff neck, glory- ing in the righteousness of the law and in the goodness of man, boasting of the things of the flesh, refusing to humble ourselves before the living God and to acknowledge in shame and contrition of heart that we have lifted in wanton foolishness our fist rebel- liously in the face of the Most High; not as long as we walk in the vain imagination that we are well able to work out our own salvation, as long as we are spiritually ignorant of the abomina- tion of our sin, and know not that to live apart from God is death.

Then we hide our face from the Man of Sorrows. Then we turn to put our confidence in men, in the might and glory of men, in their power and wisdom. Then we look for a redeemer garbed in all the majesty and pomp the world possesses. Then the preach- ing of the cross is indeed foolishness to us because we are of those who perish. Then we can never understand that the foolishness of God is wiser than men, and that the weakness of God is stronger than men (1 Cor. 1:25).

But when our eyes are opened and enlightened to see the truth, as soon as we understand and acknowledge that the deepest cause of all our woe and misery, from which we must be redeemed, is our guilt and sin and corruption before the Lord, when by grace we have learned to acknowledge that we lie in the midst of death, from whose bonds we can only in vain attempt to deliver ourselves — then indeed this Man of Sorrows, with His visage so marred, is the Savior after my heart, the Redeemer Who satisfies my deepest needs. Then all our pride slips away, and we pray and confess with Isaac Watts:

> Forbid it, Lord, that I should boast,
> Save in the death of Christ, my God!
> All the vain things that charm me most,
> I sacrifice them to His blood.

Then we make the words of Isaiah 53:5 our personal confession: "But he was wounded for our transgressions, he was bruised for our iniquities: the chastisement of our peace was upon him; and with his stripes we are healed."

Notice that in these words the prophet first of all describes the dreadful suffering of our Lord Jesus Christ. He was wounded, He was bruised, He was chastised; stripes were laid upon His back. In the second place, Isaiah points to the real reason and causes of His suffering. That cause lay not in Himself; it was not for any personal sins that He so suffered. The cause must be found in the fact that He bore our sins and transgressions upon His mighty shoulders: "He was wounded for *our* transgressions." And in the third place, Isaiah indicates the fruit of His suffering in the words, "The chastisement of our peace was upon him; and with his stripes we are healed."

The prophet says that He was wounded, that He was bruised. By these words Isaiah expresses the suffering of the Man of Sorrows in body and soul. O, how deeply wounded, how terribly bruised He was! Was there any form of suffering inflicted by a wicked world upon the righteous which He did not bear? Was there any fire of hatred smoldering in the dark bosom of sinful humanity

that did not flare up against Him? Are there any dark desires of
wicked hatred still concealed in the deep recesses of a human soul,
filled with enmity against the living God, that did not eagerly leap
forth to seek satisfaction in His excruciating agony? Are there
still latent in the human mind powers to lay plots and to conspire
for evil that were not brought into action against Him? Is there
beyond the footsteps He left in the valley of humiliation and shame,
of suffering and agony, still a deeper descent? Are there pains
which He did not suffer, sorrows which He did not bear, agonies
that did not cause His frail frame to writhe?

Indeed, no! Centrally, all the hatred against God, all the corruption of the human heart came to clearest manifestation in the
suffering which a wicked world inflicted upon the Servant of
the Lord.

He suffered all, and He suffered for all whom the Father had
given Him. It was for their transgressions that He was wounded;
it was for their iniquities that He was bruised.

The whole burden of suffering He bore, and He bore it alone.

Consider that Man of Sorrows as His frame is suspended by
the bloody nails on the accursed tree of Calvary. Remember how
His brutal suffering is the final result of the hatred of all men.
He was forsaken by His own, betrayed by one that ate bread with
Him, persecuted and condemned by the church in its most representative body, delivered by the power of the sword, despised
as a fool by the wisdom of the world.

He is a spectacle of woe to all that behold Him.

Deep lines of past agony in His countenance still tell of His
unspeakable suffering, the suffering He endured in the night just
past, the beginning of the hour of darkness, when all the powers
of hell were sallying forth to capture and destroy Him, when His
soul had been exceedingly sorrowful, even unto death, when His
bloody sweat had mingled with the dust of the garden, when the
kiss of treachery had been pressed on His lips, when they had
led Him forth as the most dangerous criminal. In that night He,
the holy and righteous One, had met with all the manifestation
of the wicked heart of man, with all the cunning devices of hatred,
the bold hypocrisy of a priesthood long corrupt, the grievous
denial of the disciple weak according to the flesh, the fierce hatred

of an impotent darkness against the light. They had mocked Him, spit on Him, beaten Him, tantalized Him, condemned Him to death.

With the dawn of the morning the way had become still deeper. The power of the Roman sword had been summoned against Him. A murderer had been preferred above Him. Cruel stripes of a wicked scourge had plowed their furrows upon His back. Mock robes of royalty had been cast about His bloody shoulders. The mock crown of cruel thorns had been pressed on His brow. A mock scepter had been pressed into His hand. And mock obeisance and respect had been offered Him. He had been compelled to bear His own tree to the place of execution, till His enemies feared that their victim would succumb before they could satisfy their thirst for blood by gazing at His agonized frame on the cross. Mercilessly He had been spiked to the tree. And still there is no pity! Still they plot to deepen His grief, still they mock, curse, rail, shake the head, and pour out the vials of their fury upon Him.

This Man of Sorrows is indeed wounded, bruised, broken, in body and soul as He is suspended on the accursed tree.

But even so we have not penetrated into the awful darkness and depth of His suffering and grief.

We have only looked upon the outward manifestation of His agony and sorrow. If we would understand a little, at least, of the nature of His suffering, we must turn again to the words of Isaiah 53:5: "He was wounded for our transgressions, he was bruised for our iniquities." In other words, His suffering was the punishment for sin. That He was so completely broken in body and mind was because the wrath of God was upon Him, the wrath of God against the sin of the world. Was there ever a sin which He did not bear? Was there ever in God's own heart a consuming fire of wrath that did not burn against Him? Was it not God Himself Who delivered Him — Him, His only begotten Son — and Who put all the burden of our sin and transgressions upon Him?

Such indeed is the mystery of His suffering.

With these words of Isaiah in our mind let us look upon that cross once more. Watch Him as darkness covers Him and the sun begins to hide its face from Him. Watch and hear as the darkness swallows that bloody spectacle on Calvary. Listen to His profoundly mysterious, yet heart-rending cry, "My God, my God,

why hast thou forsaken me?" That is His deepest agony. He bore
the sins of many. He was made sin for all His people, as the
apostle Paul says in II Cor. 5:21: "For he hath made him to be
sin for us, who knew no sin; that we might be made the righteousness of God in him." It was God who put Him to grief. Only when
we remember this can we begin to understand a little of the agony
of the Man of Sorrows.

It was for *our* transgressions that He was wounded. It was for
our iniquities that He was bruised. That is the blessed solution
of this mystery of Calvary's Man of Sorrows and of all His suffering and grief. That is the answer, and the only answer, to the
question why the Servant of the Lord must suffer thus, and endure
all this agony of soul and body. He was smitten of God and
afflicted. We must never imagine, even for a moment, that He was
so smitten for His own, personal transgressions and His own iniquities. Nor may we explain the bloody tree of Calvary only from
the wickedness and hatred of men who were instrumental in its
realization. To be sure, those men, those representatives of the
church and of the world, were responsible for their wicked deed.
And by inflicting this terrible suffering upon the Man of Sorrows
they manifested their hatred of God. Yet, ultimately it was not
man's but God's cross. As the apostle Peter proclaimed in Jerusalem on the day of Pentecost: "Him, being delivered by the
determinate counsel and foreknowledge of God, ye have taken,
and by wicked hands have crucified and slain."

Remember: He was the Son of God in the likeness of sinful
flesh. Even in that likeness He was personally without sin. For
His own sin and iniquity He could not suffer and die. Nor could
His enemies ever have nailed Him to the accursed tree without
His own will. On the hill of the skull He could have consumed
them. His suffering was entirely voluntary. Although His enemies
were instrumental in opening His veins, He nevertheless willingly
shed His lifeblood for His people. And therefore we can understand the suffering of the Servant of the Lord in its true nature
only when we remember that He was wounded for our transgressions, and bruised for our iniquities. Let us therefore turn
away our eyes from the wicked deviltry of a world of which you
and I by nature are also a part, and whose darkness is condemned

by this onslaught on the light. Let us turn our gaze from the cruel
soldiers and the mad crowd, and close our ears to the cutting
mockery of priests and scribes. And let us contemplate the deeper
cause, the more profound reason, for all this agony of the Man
of Sorrows.

What then is that deepest source from which all this suffering
springs?

The answer is: love, divine, unfathomable love, the love of
God to His people, whom He has known from before the foundation of the world. God loved you and me, who stand gazing on
the accursed tree from the dark recesses of a broken and humiliated heart. He loved us, I know not why, before the world was.
He loved us with a love that will shrink from nothing to glorify
us with the image of His Son, with a glory that could not be attained except through that deep and awful way of sin and grace
and the death on the cross of His only begotten Son. He chose us,
I know not why — us, and no others. He gave us to His Son,
ordained to be the Christ, the head of His people, the captain of
their salvation. He imputed all our sin and guilt to Him, and He
sent Him into the world, that by His blood He might make reconciliation and prepare for us eternal life and glory. God's boundless love and our transgressions, God's boundless love in Jesus
Christ our Lord and our iniquities — there is the key to the true
explanation of this awful spectacle of suffering on Golgotha's
mount. For our transgressions, for our iniquities He was wounded
and bruised.

O, how marvelous is that love of God as it is revealed in the
cross of our Lord Jesus Christ! Well may we respond to such
amazing and profoundly mysterious love in the words of the poet
we quoted before:

>*Were the whole realm of nature mine,*
>*That were a present far too small;*
>*Love, so amazing, so divine,*
>*Demands my soul, my life, my all.*

For our transgressions, for our iniquities He suffered and died.

We were hopelessly lost in sin and death. Condemnation and
wrath were upon our heads because of our actual sins rising up
against us day by day. Hopelessly we lay under condemnation

because of the actual transgressions of our body and of our soul, transgressions of our eyes and ears and mouth, transgressions of our hands and feet, transgressions of our thoughts and our desires, our contemplations and our emotions. These actual transgressions constantly issue forth like a foul stream from our sinful heart. And these actual sins issue forth from the foul fountain of our corrupt nature, by which we are in ourselves abominable in the sight of Him Who is holy and righteous. But the case is still more hopeless. For this corruption of our nature is corruption of the whole human race, bound with chains of death because of the sin of one righteously imputed to all. Neither was there any hope of deliverance till all this foul stream of our iniquities was blotted out, and till the foul source of our transgressions was stopped. Nor could our guilt be blotted out without the most perfect satisfaction: for God cannot wink at and condone sin. Nor could this satisfaction be accomplished without the suffering of death, the bearing of the punishment inflicted by God's just wrath. This we could never do.

But this Christ did in our stead. Because in God's eternal counsel He was made our head and Redeemer, one with us, our Lord, responsible for us, representing us, covering us before God, all our sins and transgressions, the full burden of our iniquities was laid upon Him. He alone bore the great wrath of God, the holy and true, against the sin of us all. The cross is no mere empty spectacle. It is no mere vain display. Its suffering is a matter of strictest necessity. There was no other way in which the love of God could spread itself over His transgressing children. For "God was in Christ, reconciling the world unto himself, not imputing their trespasses unto them."

Love, therefore, the love of God, is the only explanation of the mystery of the cross. "For God so loved the world, that he gave his only begotten Son, that whosoever believeth in him should not perish, but have everlasting life" (John 3:16). And again: "In this was manifested the love of God toward us, because that God sent his only begotten Son into the world, that we might live through him. Herein is love, not that we loved God, but that he loved us, and sent his Son to be the propitiation for our sins" (I John 4:8, 9).

What then is the fruit of this profound suffering of the Man of Sorrows?

The answer is in the last part of the verse we are discussing: "the chastisement of our peace was upon him; and with his stripes we are healed."

The light of beauty and grace radiates marvelously from the awful spectacle of the cross of the Servant of the Lord.

We are at war with the living God. And in that state of war there is no peace anywhere. We live in rebellion against the Most High. And therefore there is no rest. We live in enmity against the Lord of heaven and earth. And the result is that unrest fills our soul and disturbs our entire life. And when the Lord opens our eyes and causes us to see ourselves in the light of His holiness and justice, that unrest overwhelms our soul with sorrow after God, and causes us to realize how true it is that our heart finds no rest till it rests in the living God. That rest is the peace that passeth all understanding. And that peace we have and find only in the cross. For it was the chastisement of our peace, the chastisement that brings us peace, that was upon Him. We, therefore, being justified by faith, have peace with God.

And by that same power of the wondrous cross of the Man of Sorrows we are healed. By nature we are sick, hopelessly sick, spiritually dead in sin and iniquity. And there is no earthly physician that can possibly help us or cure us. We are slaves of sin by nature, following after the lust of the flesh, foolish, and loving darkness rather than the light, willing servants of the devil by reason of our corrupt nature, hating God and hating one another.

Nor did we have the right to be healed. Our death is exactly the just punishment for our sins.

But in His stripes there is healing. For by His suffering and awful agony He secured for all His own the right to be delivered. And having thus merited the right, He received the power to heal us by His Holy Spirit. By His Spirit He delivers us from the power of sin and death. He completely heals us, making us children of light, and bestowing upon us the blessing of life everlasting.

Such is the wondrous power of the cross of the Man of Sorrows!

CHAPTER 7

Suffering as a Dumb Lamb

He was appressed, and he was afflicted, yet he opened not his mouth. — ISAIAH 53:7.

The suffering and death of the Servant of the Lord were expiatory.

Expiation is an act of satisfaction. And satisfaction can be made only by one who voluntarily pays the penalty for sin.

This truth is emphasized in all of Holy Writ, and it is also clearly expressed in our Reformed Confessions.

Thus, for instance, in the Heidelberg Catechism, Lord's Day XV, the question is asked: "What dost thou understand by the words, 'He suffered' ? " And the answer is: "That he, all the time he lived on earth, but especially at the end of his life, sustained in body and soul, the wrath of God against the sins of all mankind: that so by his passion, as the only propitiatory sacrifice, he might redeem our body and soul from everlasting damnation, and obtain for us the favor of God, righteousness and eternal life." And in Lord's Day XVI, Question and Answer 40, we read: "Why was it necessary for Christ to humble himself even unto death? Because with respect to the justice and truth of God, satisfaction for our sins could be made no otherwise, than by the death of the Son of God."

The same truth is emphasized in the Netherland Confession,

501

Article 20: "We believe that God, who is perfectly merciful and just, sent his Son to assume that nature, in which the disobedience was committed, to make satisfaction in the same, and to bear the punishment of sin by his most bitter passion and death. God therefore manifested his justice against his Son, when he laid our iniquities upon him; and poured forth his mercy and goodness on us, who were guilty and worthy of damnation, out of mere and perfect love, giving his Son unto death for us, and raising him for our justification, that through him we might obtain immortality and life eternal." And also in the next article of the same Confession it is said that Christ "presented himself in our behalf before the Father, to appease his wrath by his full satisfaction, by offering himself on the tree of the cross, and pouring out his precious blood to purge away our sins."

The Canons of Dordrecht, under the Second Head of Doctrine, confess the same truth. There too, in Article 1, it is emphasized that God is just, and that therefore we can never escape the punishment for sin unless satisfaction is made to the justice of God. And then in Article 2 and 3 we read: "Since therefore we are unable to make that satisfaction in our own persons, or to deliver ourselves from the wrath of God, he hath been pleased in his infinite mercy to give his only begotten Son, for our surety, who was made sin, and became a curse for us and in our stead, that he might make satisfaction to divine justice on our behalf. The death of the Son of God is the only and most perfect sacrifice and satisfaction for sin."

It is evident, therefore, that atonement for sin can be made only in the way of satisfaction, and that this satisfaction consists in the offering up of a voluntary, expiatory, and substitutionary sacrifice.

This idea was already expressed in the passage we discussed in the preceding chapter, where it was said that the Suffering Servant of the Lord was wounded for our transgressions, and bruised for our iniquities, and that the chastisement of our peace was upon Him. And this is repeated from a slightly different point of view in Isaiah 53:6, 7: "All we like sheep have gone astray; we have turned every one to his own way; and the Lord hath laid on him the iniquity of us all. He was oppressed, and he was afflicted, yet he opened not his mouth: he is brought as a lamb to the slaughter, and as a sheep before her shearers is dumb, so he openeth not his mouth."

Notice that in these words it is emphasized that we sinned, and that God laid on His Servant our iniquities. And notice especially that the text emphasizes that when the Servant of the Lord bore these iniquities, He did so voluntarily. For in His suffering He was utterly silent. He offered no protest, but willingly performed the good pleasure of God in suffering for sin.

This thought we wish to develop a little in the present chapter.

The text once more refers to the suffering of the Servant in the words, "He was oppressed, and he was afflicted," but especially emphasizes that He endured His suffering without protest: "he opened not his mouth: he is brought as a lamb to the slaughter, and as a sheep before her shearers is dumb, so he openeth not his mouth."

This does not imply that the Suffering Servant of the Lord did not speak at all when He suffered. The Scriptures teach us differently. A few days before His final suffering on the accursed tree He said: "Now is my soul troubled; and what shall I say? Father, save me from this hour: but for this cause came I unto this hour. Father, glorify thy name." In the upper room, and perhaps on the way to Gethsemane, the Lord spoke many words for the instruction and comfort of His disciples. He exposed the traitor, and told the rest of the twelve that they should all be offended in Him that very night. In the garden He declared that His soul was exceeding sorrowful, even unto death. He asked His disciples to watch with Him, and casting Himself down in the dust of the garden He prayed: "O, my Father, if it be possible, let this cup pass from me: nevertheless not as I will, but as thou wilt." More than once He emphasized His sinlessness over against those who were His enemies and who condemned Him to the cross, reckoning Him with the transgressors. He said unto them: "Are ye come out as against a thief with swords and staves for to take me? I sat daily with you teaching in the temple, and ye laid no hold on me. But all this was done, that the scriptures of the prophets might be fulfilled." When the high priest asked Him about His doctrine, He said: "I spake openly to the world;

I ever taught in the synagogue, and in the temple, whither the Jews always resort; and in secret have I said nothing. Why askest thou me? Ask them which heard me, what I have said unto them: behold, they know what I said." When the high priest challenged Him to confess that He is the Christ, the Son of God, He did not deny it, but said: "Thou hast said: nevertheless I say unto you, Hereafter shall ye see the Son of man sitting on the right hand of power, and coming in the clouds of heaven." Before Pilate He witnessed of His kingship when He said: "My kingdom is not of this world: if my kingdom were of this world, then would my servants fight, that I should not be delivered to the Jews: but now is my kingdom not from hence." And when the governor asked Him whether He really was a king, the Lord answered: "Thou sayest that I am a king. To this end was I born, and for this cause came I into the world, that I should bear witness unto the truth. Every one that is of the truth heareth my voice." And even at the cross the Lord opened His mouth seven times, and uttered His voice even to the very end of His life on earth.

This, therefore, is not the meaning of the text when it tells us that He was dumb in His suffering.

But the text emphasizes that He was dumb and that He opened not His mouth with respect to and over against His suffering. O, indeed, He suffered very deeply in body and soul. He suffered from men and from God. Men reckoned Him with the transgressors, and treated Him as such. In every possible way they caused Him to suffer, and poured out the vials of their wicked wrath upon Him by buffeting Him, and spitting in His face. They blindfolded Him and beat Him; they mocked Him and heaped their scorn upon Him; they scourged His back and pressed a crown of thorns upon His head; they nailed Him to the accursed tree. And even when He was suspended on the cross, their fury knew no bounds, and mockingly they challenged Him to come down from the cross if God would have Him. But this was by no means the depth of His suffering. He suffered the wrath of God against sin that was upon Him in all its awful weight, so that He finally cried out: "My God, my God, why hast thou forsaken me?" Truly, He was oppressed and He was afflicted. But He never opened His mouth in protest. He did not complain to God about the way He must travel. Even in Gethsemane, when His soul was exceedingly sorrowful, even unto death, so that He asked the Father whether there would be no other way than the way of the cross, He nevertheless ended His prayer by saying, "Not my will, but thy will be done." Willingly He lets Himself be captured in the garden, and meekly He goes along with His enemies to the place of the high priest, and to the Roman governor. He does not defend Himself over against any false accusation, whether before the Sanhedrin or before the Roman governor. When they mal-treat Him and scourge His back and press the crown of thorns upon Him and hang the purple mock-robe around His bloody shoulders, He does not protest or cry out in indignation. And even when they nail Him to the accursed tree, He prays for the transgressors. Literally it is true that He suffered as a dumb lamb, and as a sheep that is dumb before its shearers, He opened not His mouth.

How can we explain this unbelievable spectacle?

Certainly not by any consciousness of guilt. For He had no sin, and there was no guile found in His mouth. He was the Person of the Son of God, come in the likeness of sinful flesh, but Himself without sin. He was holy, undefiled, and separate from sinners. Nor can we explain the fact that He was utterly dumb in His suffering, and that He opened not His mouth in protest, from any lack of power. He could have consumed His enemies at any moment. He manifested His power when in Gethsemane He prostrated His enemies before Him in the dust of the garden. And He told His disciples in the hearing of those who came to capture Him that He could call upon twelve legions of angels to prevent His being taken captive. There is only one answer to the question why He opened not His mouth in protest. And that answer is found in the text: "The Lord hath laid on him the iniquity of us all."

We all went astray like sheep. We turned every one to his own way. Thus the text has it. And note that this is a confession which the prophet places upon the lips of all the people of God. This is evidently the reference of the personal pronoun "we." This does not refer to all men, but to the people of God, those whom the Father had given to Christ. O, it is true: all men without

distinction sinned against the Holy One. They all went astray
from the path of righteousness and truth. Every man turns to
his own way, that is, to his own particular way of sin and corruption. But in the first place, the text speaks in the first person.
It is a confession. And all men will never confess their sin and
transgression before the Lord. Only those whom the Lord has
enlightened by His Word and Spirit are filled with sorrow after
God, confess their sins before His face, and acknowledge that
as far as they are concerned they are walking the way to eternal
desolation. And in the second place, the same is true of the words,
"The Lord hath laid on him the iniquity of us all." This also is
a glad confession on the part of the people of God. They know
the Suffering Servant of the Lord. They know that He was
wounded and bruised not for His own sin, but for their iniquities
and transgressions. And they rejoice in their salvation. It is
evident, therefore, that the text does not speak of all men, but only
of the people of God. They erred. They went astray as sheep.
And they confess it. They turned each in his own way of sin
and corruption. And they know and acknowledge it. They are as
sheep inclined to err by nature. For their going astray is not
only a question of the act, but is something that is rooted in
their very nature: they are dead in sin and misery. And they know
it and confess it before the Lord.

But — and this is the reason why the Servant of the Lord
opened not His mouth in protest against His suffering — "the
Lord hath laid on him the iniquity of us all."

Such is the mystery of the cross.

This implies, in the first place, that all His life, but especially
on the accursed tree, God caused all the sins of all His people to
concentrate upon the head of His Servant, Whom He loved with
an everlasting love. It means, in the second place, that God
caused His Servant during His entire life, but especially on the
cross, to experience His wrath as the expression of His justice
against sin. No, He did not hate His Servant, even on the cross.
He loved Him, for His Servant was obedient even unto death.
Nevertheless, He heaped all His wrath upon Him even while
He loved Him, by causing Him to descend into the depth of
hell and desolation. In the third place, it implies that God thus

laid the iniquity of all His people upon His Suffering Servant in order to save His elect. For this salvation of the elect could be accomplished only in the way of the satisfaction of God's justice. And His justice could be satisfied only by a payment of the full penalty for sin. God reconciled us to Himself by the atonement of His Suffering Servant, by causing Him to feel all the burden of His awful wrath against sin and sinners, by laying on Him the iniquity of us all. In the fourth place, it means that the Suffering Servant of Jehovah during all His life, but especially on the cross, consciously bore the wrath of God against sin.

And this is the reason why He opened not His mouth.

He bore that wrath of God obediently, as the Servant of Jehovah. That bearing of the wrath of God was not mere passive suffering, but it was an act on the part of Christ, the Son of the living God. For, as we said, satisfaction must be an act, an act of perfect obedience in the love of God. Just as sin is an act, a willful act of disobedience against the God of heaven and earth, so atonement must be an act. Just as sin is an act of rebellion, of willful rebellion against the living God, so atonement must be an act of self-subjection, of voluntary self-subjection and obedience. And just as sin is an act of enmity against God, a manifestation of hatred against the Holy One, so atonement must be an act motivated by perfect love for God. Only then is atonement an expiation and satisfaction for sin. For we must remember that the fundamental demand of the law of God upon man is expressed in the one commandment: "Thou shalt love the Lord thy God with all thy heart, with all thy soul, with all thy mind, with all thy strength." This demand is unchangeable. God never relinquishes it, not even when He subjects fallen man to His wrath, to the suffering of the curse. Even then God's demand is: Love Me! Even in His wrath God is holy and just, and must be loved by man. That demand is of force even in hell. That is why hell is so utterly hopeless and why the suffering of hell can never atone for sin even to all eternity. The wrath of God is an expression and revelation of His goodness and perfection. Hence, — the guilt of sin can be removed only by an act of love under the curse, and under the wrath of God. He who would atone for sin must willingly, voluntarily, motivated by the pure love of God, seek to fulfill all the justice and righteousness of God against sin. He must will to suffer all the agonies of the expression of that wrath in death and hell, for God's sake.

Only such an act is a sacrifice.

Only such a willing sacrifice is satisfaction of God's justice, and therefore, atonement.

This act of obedience of love under the wrath of God, Christ performed all His life, but especially on the accursed tree. In His suffering Christ was never purely passive. He was active also in His passion and death. He willed to fulfill all righteousness. He was determined to satisfy the justice of God against sin. Therefore, He voluntarily assumed the obligation to suffer the wrath of God. When God laid on Him the iniquity of all His people, He bore that wrath of God willingly, actively, voluntarily, in the love of God. Only thus was His suffering the perfect *Yes* over against the rebellious *No* of sin.

That He was allowed to suffer for the sins of all His people, must be traced to the counsel of God. In God's counsel the inseparable bond was established between Him and His people, so that in time He might appear as their representative-head. Thus He was made sin for us, that we might become the righteousness of God in Him.

O, what abundant grace and love of God!

What boundless love of God toward those whom the Father had given Him is manifested in that dumbness of the Servant of the Lord in all His suffering!

In this is our complete salvation. God caused on the cross all our iniquities to concentrate upon the head of His Servant.

The Servant bore our iniquities, and bore them away forever. The Lamb of God took away the sin of the world. It can never be imputed to us anymore.

We are saved by the dumb suffering of the Servant of Jehovah. In His suffering we have righteousness and life forevermore.

CHAPTER 8

With the Rich in His Death

And he made his grave with the wicked and with the rich in his death. — ISAIAH 53:9.

The Suffering Servant of the Lord had reached the end of His earthly life.

Whatever may be the correct translation of verse 8 of chapter 53 of Isaiah's prophecy, this is certain: He was taken away from the land of the living.

It is not easy to translate that eighth verse, and we shall not enter into detail concerning it here because we wish to call special attention in this chapter to verse 9. The Authorized Version translates verse 8 as follows: "He was taken from prison and from judgment: and who shall declare his generation? for he was cut off out of the land of the living: for the transgression of my people was he stricken." The Revised Version has a considerably different translation: "By oppression and judgment he was taken away: and as for his generation, who among them considered that he was cut off out of the land of the living for the transgression of my people to whom the stroke was due?" We prefer the rendering: "He had been taken away from prison and from judgment: and as for his generation, no one considered that he was snatched away out of the land of the living for the wickedness of his people, whose punishment fell upon him."

509

But whatever may be the proper translation of this verse, this much is certain: it emphasizes the end of the Suffering Servant of Jehovah as far as His earthly life was concerned. He was snatched away out of the land of the living.

It is finished, as the Lord Himself declared from the cross. The plague had been upon Him. He had been stricken with the punishment of His people. Not until He had perfectly borne the iniquities of those whom the Father had given Him, and had voluntarily sacrificed Himself in the love of God for the sins of His people, could He be snatched away. But now His earthly work was finished, and He was taken away from the land of the living.

Since He had finished all at the moment when He gave up the ghost, He could suffer shame and contempt no more. Already the Servant of the Lord is justified before God. Hence we read in verse 9: "And he made his grave with the wicked, and with the rich in his death; because he had done no violence, neither was any deceit in his mouth."

We cannot agree with the interpretation of this passage that is implied in the Revised Version: "And they made his grave with the wicked, and with the rich man in his death; although he had done no violence, neither was any deceit in his mouth." This interpretation presupposes that the rich man who is mentioned in this verse is the same as the wicked who are referred to in the first part of this text. The meaning then is that His grave was indeed assigned with the wicked, and that the enemies also succeeded in giving Him in His death a place among the ungodly. This is erroneous. In the first place, it is an error to identify the rich man in the text with the wicked. In the second place, it is then necessary to introduce the second part of the text by the conjunction "although," which is impossible according to the Hebrew original. And in the third place, this is in conflict with the history of Jesus' burial according to the gospel narratives. Therefore we prefer to circumscribe the meaning of the text in this way: "Although the enemies indeed assigned his grave with the wicked, yet he was given an honorable burial with the rich, and that too, because he had done no violence, neither was any deceit found in his mouth."

Jesus was buried.

He died the physical death, and His spirit separated from His earthly frame, as with dying lips He Himself announced from the cross in His last prayer: "Father, into thy hands do I commend my spirit." And it was necessary that He too should die the physical death, the death of the body. He might not simply suffer the agonies of death on the cross, in order then to be revived or glorified in the sight of the enemies, and ascend up to heaven. He must bear the wrath of God to the end. Physical death is God's declaration that the sinner has absolutely forfeited every right to his existence in the world. And this sentence was executed upon Christ also. God takes away His entire earthly house. His very name perishes. His body, too, collapses. And He gives up the ghost. Upon Him also the sentence is pronounced that He is unworthy to exist on earth. Death belongs to the wages of sin, also physical death. It is the expression of the wrath of God, the revelation of His justice against the sinner. Only, in the case of the Suffering Servant of the Lord, He made also of physical death an act, an act of love to God. He lays down His life willingly, even at the moment when God takes it away. His spirit He commends to the Father; His body He delivers over into the place of corruption. His name and position He freely offers up to the righteousness of God. And in delivering up His soul unto death He confesses that God is just when He judges that the sinner must be utterly destroyed from the earth. Christ therefore willingly performed the act of dying.

And so He descended into the grave, the place of physical corruption.

In Question and Answer 41 the Heidelberg Catechism explains that He was buried in order to prove that He was really dead. However, even apart from the fact that a man is not buried to prove that he is dead, such proof on the part of Christ was hardly necessary. That He had died before He was taken down from the cross was evident in His own outcry, commending His spirit to the Father. Besides, it is also evident from the spearthrust in His side by one of the soldiers while He was still hanging on the cross. We read in John 19:31 ff.: "The Jews therefore, because it was the preparation, that the bodies should not remain upon the cross on the sabbath day, (for that sabbath day was a high day), besought Pilate that their legs might be broken, and that they might be taken away. Then came the soldiers, and brake the legs of the first, and of the other which was crucified with him. But when they came to Jesus, and saw that he was dead already, they brake not his legs: But one of the soldiers with a spear pierced his side, and forthwith came there out blood and water." And the apostle John explains this incident as a fulfillment of Scripture: "A bone of him shall not be broken. And again another scripture saith, They shall look on him whom they pierced." But Christ must die to the very end. He too must be buried. And although, according to Scripture, He did not see corruption, He must enter the place of corruption nevertheless. He must deliver His body to the humiliation of the grave, to the place where the sinner returns to the dust. In perfect obedience to the Father He enters into Hades, and commits His body to the grave. And this too was a voluntary act on the part of the Suffering Servant of Jehovah. Just as He entered into the womb of the virgin, to assume the likeness of sinful flesh, so He obediently submitted to the sentence of God, "Dust thou art, and to dust thou shalt return." That He could do so, and that even His entering into the grave was a voluntary act of His own, may be explained from the fact that He was the Son of God, and the Person of the Son was never separated from His human nature, even in His death and in the grave.

So He accomplished all of death, and fulfilled all righteousness.

Now although the Jews had assigned His grave with the wicked, He nevertheless was with the rich in His death. There is, therefore, a significant symbolism in the burial of Jesus.

In the grave we see *our* aspect of temporal death. Temporal death is the final earthly separation of spirit and body in man. It has, therefore, two aspects: an aspect that refers to the earthy and material, and an aspect that refers to the spiritual and eternal side of man's existence. The grave is our aspect, that which we see of temporal death. We keep the dead body, and the spirit proceeds to God. Again, temporal death is twofold, as we know from Holy Writ. For the ungodly it is a passage into eternal desolation. This is true immediately after death of the soul, or spirit. We read of the rich man in the parable: "The rich man also died and was buried; And in hell he lifted up his eyes, being in torments, and seeth Abraham afar off, and Lazarus in his bosom. And he cried and said, Father Abraham, have mercy on me, and send Lazarus, that he may dip the tip of his finger in water, and cool my tongue; for I am tormented in this flame" (Lu. 16:22-24). And as to the body of the ungodly, it is simply waiting in the grave for its eternal desolation, beginning in the morning of the resurrection. For thus we read in John 5:28, 29: "Marvel not at this: for the hour is coming in the which all that are in the graves shall hear his voice. And shall come forth; they that have done good, unto the resurrection of life; and they that have done evil, unto the resurrection of damnation." But for the godly, in distinction from the wicked, physical death is a passage into everlasting glory. That this is true is evident from what the Lord said to the one malefactor who was crucified with Him: "Today thou shalt be with me in paradise." And in II Cor. 5:1 we read: "For we know that if our earthly house of this tabernacle were dissolved, we have a building of God, an house not made with hands, eternal in the heavens." The soul of the godly, therefore, immediately passes on to heavenly glory. And as to his body, it is simply sown in the earth, that presently it may appear in the glory of the resurrection: "It is sown in corruption; it is raised in incorruption: It is sown in dishonor; it is raised in glory: it is sown in weakness; it is raised in power: it is sown a natural body; it is raised a spiritual body" (I Cor. 15:42-44). For this reason we said that in the burial and in the grave there is a significant symbolism.

In several places of Scripture we find that the wicked are not entitled to an honorable burial together with the righteous. This is no doubt the idea of the separate grave-yards of the Roman Catholics. But in Scripture the separation of the righteous and the wicked in burial is emphasized more than once. When carnal Israel rebels against Jehovah in the desert, the Lord threatens through Moses and Aaron: "Your carcases shall fall in this wilderness" (Nu. 14:29; Cf. Heb. 3:17). Isaiah prophesies of wicked Babylon: "But thou art cast out of thy grave like an abominable branch, and as the raiment of those that are slain, thrust through with the sword, that go down to the stones of the pit; as a carcase trodden under feet. Thou shalt not be joined with them in burial" (Isa. 14:19, 20). And of the carnal and ungodly children of Judah Jeremiah prophesies: "And the carcases of this people shall be meat for the fowls of the heaven, and for the beasts of the earth; and none shall fray them away" (Jer. 7:33). And of king Jehoiakim we read: "They shall not lament for him, saying, Ah my brother! or, Ah sister! they shall not lament for him, saying, Ah Lord! or, Ah his glory! He shall be buried with the burial of an ass, drawn and cast forth beyond the gates of Jerusalem" (Jer. 22:19). And again, of the wicked children of Judah we read: "I will even give them into the hand of their enemies, and into the hand of them that seek their life: and their dead bodies shall be for meat unto the fowls of the heaven, and to the beasts of the earth" (Jer. 34:20). On the other hand, it is a lamentable thing when the righteous and the saints of God suffer the same lot with the wicked, and are not honorably buried. About this the psalmist complains in Psalm 79:1, 2: "O God, the heathen are come into thine inheritance; thy holy temple have they defiled; they have laid Jerusalem on heaps. The dead bodies of thy servants have they given to be meat unto the fowls of the heaven, the flesh of thy saints unto the beasts of the earth." In the symbolism of the grave, therefore, it is made plain that although the righteous and the wicked live promiscuously on the earth in this present life, in physical and temporal death they separate forever. For the soul of the righteous passes into glory, that of the wicked into desolation. And the body of the righteous awaits in the grave the morning of the glorious resurrection, that of the wicked the morning of the resurrection of damnation.

Now according to the passage of Isaiah we are discussing at present, the enemies of the Lord had assigned His grave with the wicked. During His life they had reckoned Him with the transgressors. As a transgressor they had captured Him in Gethsemane, had led Him to the Sanhedrin and to Pilate. They had accused Him and condemned Him to death. He had been killed as the worst malefactor, between two murderers, as one that is accursed of God. And the intention of the hostile Jews was that He also should be buried as such. They assigned His grave with the wicked. That is the meaning of the text. And this is evident also from the history recorded in the gospel narratives. For according to John 19:31, the Jews came to Pilate and besought him that the legs of all the three malefactors might be broken, in order that the bodies might not remain on the cross on the sabbath day. And if this had been done, the bodies would simply have been put into the ground in the neighborhood of the cross without any formal or honorable burial. They would have done this also to the body of Jesus. Then He would not have been buried at all, but simply, perhaps with His cross, been put under the ground. And the Jews would have expressed by this act that Jesus had passed on into eternal desolation, accursed of God, forever separated from the righteous, and that also His body should not share the resurrection of the just. When they assigned His grave with the wicked, they designated that His proper place was with the eternally damned.

But in this the Jews did not succeed.

According to the text, He was with the rich in His death. And although being rich is not a proper antithesis to being wicked, neither does it stand in direct contrast to being righteous. Besides, the rich usually see that their loved ones are buried honorably. This, moreover, is the only interpretation of the text in Isaiah that is possible in the light of the gospel narratives concerning Jesus' burial. The rich man was Joseph of Arimathea, who together with Nicodemus was a disciple of Jesus, though secretly for fear of the Jews. And he waited for the kingdom of God (Matt. 27:57; Mk. 15:43; Lu. 23:50, 51; John 19:38). He approached Pilate and begged for the body of Jesus. He evidently feared the worst, and understood that the hostile Jews would assign His grave with the wicked. And this he was anxious to prevent. Pilate apparently was at first reluctant to give his consent. But when he marveled once more at Jesus because he heard from the centurion that He had already died, he gave the body to Joseph (Mk. 15:44, 45). Thus Jesus received a very honorable burial. For the body was wrapped in fine linen, together with spices, a mixture of myrrh and aloes, about an hundred pound weight, which Nicodemus had brought. And Jesus' body was laid in a new rock-hewn sepulchre, wherein never man was yet laid

(John 19:39-41). And a heavy stone was rolled in front of the sepulchre.

Thus, although the Jews had assigned His grave with the wicked, He was nevertheless with the rich in His death.

In this burial of the righteous which was given to Jesus God already showed that His Suffering Servant was justified.

O, it is true, His glorious resurrection was the special proof that God justified Him, and that we are justified with Him. For He "was delivered for our offences, and was raised again for our justification." Nevertheless, His burial also was the beginning of His glorification, and therefore of His justification. That is why the reason for this honorable burial is expressed in the last part of Isaiah 53:9, "because he had done no violence, neither was any deceit in his mouth."

Personally Christ was the Sinless One. The sin of the race in Adam could not be imputed to Him. He had no original guilt, for personally He was the Son of God. Nor did He have original defilement and corruption, for the chain of corruption was broken in His case by the conception of the Holy Spirit. Nor did He personally have any actual sin. Always He was motivated by the love of God, and walked in perfect obedience even in the midst of a wicked world. He did no wrong. An evil word never proceeded out of His mouth. He always did the will of the Father. Moreover, even when He bore the sins of His people, and God laid on Him the iniquity of us all, He committed no sin whatsoever. On the contrary, He was always obedient. Every moment of His life in the world the Father in heaven could say to Him: "This is my beloved Son, in whom I am well-pleased." Even when He was counted with the transgressors, He nevertheless was the Sinless One. Even then He did no injustice, nor was any deceit ever found in His mouth.

Therefore, now that all was finished and the Lamb of God had completely taken away the sin of the world, it was the Father's will that in His burial He should be reckoned with the transgressors no more, but counted with the righteous. His spirit was already with the Father in heavenly glory, and His body waited in the sepulchre of Joseph of Arimathea for the morning of the glorious resurrection. Hence, although His enemies assigned

His grave with the wicked, the Lord so directed the affairs of men that He received a place with the rich in His death.

The burial of Jesus, therefore, was the beginning of His justification.

Thus the burial of Jesus is our comfort. For it teaches us what the Lord God judges about the grave of the righteous. When they die, they shall go with Him into paradise, while their body rests in the grave.

And presently the corruptible body shall put on incorruption, and the mortal body shall put on immortality. And death shall be swallowed up in victory.

With their eye on the place of corruption in the light of the burial of the Suffering Servant of the Lord, the people of God may well shout: "O death, where is thy sting? O grave, where is thy victory? The sting of death is sin; and the strength of sin is the law. But thanks be to God which giveth us the victory through our Lord Jesus Christ."

CHAPTER 9

Bruised According to the Good Pleasure of the Lord

Yet it pleased the Lord to bruise him; he hath put him to grief. — ISAIAH 53:10.

The cross of our Lord Jesus Christ from any human point of view, looked at from the aspect of its being the work and accomplishment of men and of the world, is a terribly dark spectacle.

There is nothing in all the history of the world that so reveals the corruption and the darkness that rules in the hearts of men as the cross of Jesus Christ our Lord. It is indeed the condemnation of the world of men. From a human point of view there is absolutely no hope in the cross.

From this point of view the cross appears to be nothing else than the fulfillment of the will and the good pleasure of ungodly men, the triumph of an ungodly world, the final victory of the darkness over the light, of death over life. For as we have seen in all our former discussions on this theme of the Suffering Servant of Jehovah, He was thoroughly despised and rejected of men. He Who came to reveal the light, and Who was the revelation of the God of our salvation, stood entirely alone, was forsaken by all. His name was Man of Sorrows. Everyone hid his face from Him, stuck out the lip and mocked Him in evil hatred. Nowhere

519

did He find a place among the children of men even though He had the tongue of the learned, and knew how to speak a word to the weary in due season. The judges among His own people found Him worthy of death, guilty of being a deceiver of the people and of speaking blasphemy against the living God. And although the judge of the world did not find Him guilty, and attempted to deny all responsibility on his part, yet he surrendered Him to be nailed to the accursed tree and to be cast out as a criminal. Indeed, "He was oppressed, and he was afflicted, yet he opened not his mouth: he is brought as a lamb to the slaughter, and as a sheep before her shearers is dumb, so he openeth not his mouth."

O indeed, the cross is the darkest moment in the history of the world.

Bearing the hatred of men without murmuring or protest, He hangs there, completely powerless apparently, and despised by all men. Exposed in His nakedness to the eyes of all, He is covered with His own blood. He is alone, completely forsaken. And He finds no pity. For even at the cross His enemies still mock Him, and cast in His teeth the challenge that He had better prove to them now that He is the Christ, the Son of the living God. But He remains dumb. More deeply and deeply He sinks away. Presently the awful darkness covers the fearful spectacle, and the Servant of the Lord calls from the depths of misery and death to Him who can send salvation. But it is a cry of anguish, pressed out of a soul that is completely overwhelmed, rejected by men and forsaken of God. And it also appears in vain that this Servant of the Lord cries unto God in the anguish of His soul.

Presently He sinks into the depths of death.

It has become quiet on Golgotha. No more mocking and jibes are heard around the accursed tree.

And presently, at the end of three hours of darkness, the most awful cry that is ever pressed from the human heart is sounded forth by the Suffering Servant of Jehovah, "My God, my God, why hast thou forsaken me?"

Then it is finished.

Presently Joseph of Arimathea carries the soulless remains to the grave, followed only by some Galilean women.

It is the end of the Servant of the Lord. He went under. He

must succumb to the hatred and power of men. The pride of the Pharisees, the mocking unbelief of the Sadducees, the long provoked hatred of the Sanhedrin, and the overpowering sword of an evil world were too much for the Servant of the Lord. He suffered defeat.

Horribly dark is the cross from this human point of view.

Was He after all not the light of the world? Was He not the One Who had come down from heaven to speak in the midst of a world that lay in darkness and that was oppressed by the burden of sin and death, to speak of heavenly things and to prepare a way through this vale of tears to eternal life and glory? Was He not the Son of God, a last ray of hope in the pitch dark night of human misery? And now the light of the world was extinguished, it seems. The victor was overcome. The truth had become dumb. The life was murdered on Golgotha. The Savior of the world was condemned. Where, then, is there any hope if the light itself is being extinguished by the darkness of this world? Where, then, is the hope of those who wait for the morning if He Who is the life and the resurrection is murdered by ungodly men? If He on Whom all our hope was fixed as the Redeemer of Israel must suffer defeat at the hands of the powers of this world and its prince, how can we still look for the dawn of redemption?

Calvary indeed is hopeless, as long as we view the cross as the work of men.

But blessed be God! There is a higher viewpoint.

After all, in the deepest sense of the word the accursed tree on Calvary's mount is not men's cross, but God's. And in the present chapter we wish to turn our eyes away from the wicked power of the world which crucified our Lord Jesus Christ, and gaze at the cross in the light of eternity and from the viewpoint of the good pleasure of the Lord Who bruised Him. This we do on the basis of Isaiah 53:10: "Yet it pleased the Lord to bruise him; he hath put him to grief: when thou shalt make his soul an offering for sin, he shall see his seed, he shall prolong his days, and the pleasure of the Lord shall prosper in his hand." It is evident that in these words of the prophecy of Isaiah a ray of light from eternity illumines the cross of our Lord. For it pleased the Lord to bruise Him, His servant Who had come to build the house of God and to deliver His people. The most High Himself had put His Anointed to grief. His Servant, Whose meat it was to do the Father's will, God Himself had bruised. Here, therefore, we behold the accursed tree in the light of the good pleasure of the Lord, in the light of eternity. All of a sudden in this passage of Isaiah's prophecy the light of God's eternal counsel and good pleasure is shed upon the cross. It pleased the Lord to bruise Him. He hath put Him to grief, not men. It is true, according to Acts 2:23, that ungodly men took Him and by wicked hands crucified and slew Him. But nevertheless, He was delivered by the determinate counsel and foreknowledge of God. Behind the Sanhedrin and the wicked high priest, behind the Roman judge and governor, behind the raving and raging powers of darkness that turn themselves against this Servant of the Lord, stands the Almighty, the eternal God. And through all the hatred and iniquity of men He executes His own good pleasure. When in this light we see the suffering and death of this Servant of the Lord, our soul finds rest. When not the pleasure of the ungodly, but the good pleasure of Jehovah triumphs at the cross, we know that all things are well, and that all things work together for good to them that love Him. It pleased the Lord to bruise Him; He hath put Him to grief. There is light, the light of eternity, in the horrible darkness of the cross.

When we read in the text that it pleased the Lord to bruise Him, it is evident that this refers to the eternal good pleasure of the Most High. That good pleasure was indeed realized in time. It was manifested in the suffering and death of the Servant of Jehovah. Nevertheless, what pleases God in time is rooted in His eternal good pleasure. The light of eternity here falls upon the fearful suffering of our Lord Jesus Christ. For that reason we may rest assured, as we stand by the cross and contemplate the mystery of the suffering of this Servant, even when apparently we see Him defeated and swallowed up by the ungodly powers of darkness, that the cross is nevertheless not a victory by the world, but its complete condemnation, and the triumph of God.

God's good pleasure has its deepest motive and it highest purpose in God Himself. Always its purpose is His own glory and honor, the highest revelation of His divine goodness, the proclamation of His own eternal virtues. For God is God! And there is no God beside Him. He is the only good, Whom to know is eternal life, and Whom to despise and reject is eternal damnation and death. Around Himself concentrates the eternal good pleasure of God, in order that all the creatures may finally glorify Him and boast in His absolute goodness. It is by that good pleasure of Jehovah that the Servant of the Lord is anointed from before the foundation of the world. In that pleasure it was decreed that He should be the head of all His people, their prophet, priest, and king. It is by the same good pleasure of Jehovah that the brethren of Christ, His elect church, were given unto Him from all eternity, that He might redeem them from sin and death and exalt them into the highest heavenly glory of God's eternal tabernacle. For the highest revelation of God's infinite virtues, and especially for the revelation of His own divine covenant life, this Servant of the Lord must be bruised and put to grief. Around this good pleasure of Jehovah concentrates even all the hatred and wickedness of an ungodly world which nails the Suffering Servant of the Lord to the cross. It is true, when that world cooperates with the Most High to execute His own good pleasure, they, on their part, have an entirely different purpose. They plan to extinguish the light, to kill the life, to silence the voice of truth, to trample under foot the glory of God's name. And by doing so, they sign their own condemnation. Yet in the meantime, every thought of the heart, every contemplation of the mind, every evil plan and secret counsel, every word of accusation and of false testimony, every stripe of the scourge, the weaving of the crown of thorns, the blows of the hammer that strike the cruel nails through hands and feet, and the darkness that presently covers the spectacle on Golgotha — everything concentrates around the good pleasure of Him Who sitteth upon the throne.

It pleased the Lord to bruise Him; He hath put Him to grief.

The cross is God's cross, not man's.

For it was the eternal good pleasure to lead His own to the heavenly height of His eternal covenant life, and to do so from the depths of misery and death. For this reason the Servant of the Lord must stand at the head of His brethren, according to the good pleasure of Jehovah. They were hopelessly lost in sin and death. They had no right to live in the blessed fellowship of God's covenant because of the guilt of their sin. Moreover, because of their sinful condition they would never will or desire to enter into that fellowship of the Most High. They were corrupt, and in the darkness of desolation and death. They could not, they would not, and they could not possibly will to live in God's blessed communion. Nor could they ever obliterate the guilt of their sin. On the contrary, they daily increase their guilt. They could never conquer death, and they could never attain to life. They could never find the way out of darkness to the light of eternal life. But He, the Son of God, Immanuel, is the Servant of the Lord, to represent and to stand at the head of His people. In the volume of the book it was written of Him. He represents all His brethren. He is appointed and anointed to suffer for them and to die for them, to enter into the very depth of their misery, in order in that depth to taste death for them and to be obedient unto God even unto the death of the cross. All this was the eternal good pleasure of Jehovah concerning His Servant. And this good pleasure was finally realized in the cross.

It pleased the Lord to bruise Him.

This good pleasure of Jehovah was known to His Servant. For of this we read in Psalm 40:6-8: "Sacrifice and offering thou didst not desire; mine ears hast thou opened: burnt offering and sin offering hast thou not required. Then said I, Lo, I come: in the volume of the book it is written of me, I delight to do thy will, O my God: yea, thy law is written in my heart." He Himself made His soul an offering for sin. Only in the way of such an offering, of such a perfect sacrifice by the Son of God in the flesh, could there be redemption from sin and death. For God is righteous: He cannot deny Himself. God's justice must be perfectly satisfied. And that justice could never be satisfied unless the guilt of sin were completely obliterated. That guilt of sin could never be removed, except by bearing the terrible wrath of God in the willing obedience of love. Only in such an act of love, only in laying the sacrifice of love upon the altar of God, and that too, as that altar stands in the very depth of hell, lies the obliteration of sin, the satisfaction of God's justice, and therefore the redemption of the brethren.

It is this offering of love which the Servant of the Lord brings upon the cross of Golgotha.

The text refers to this when it declares: "When thou shalt make his soul an offering for sin, he shall see his seed." The "thou" in these words refers to God. And the rest refers to the Servant of Jehovah. God, and not men, made the soul of His Servant a trespass offering. For He laid on Christ the iniquity of us all. Nevertheless, Christ was not merely passive. He was active in this entire transaction. He was not merely the object, but also the subject of this offering. When God made His soul an offering for sin, He Himself sacrificed and offered up His soul to God in willing obedience. It is true, Jehovah bruised Him according to His good pleasure, and the Lord put His Servant to grief. Nevertheless, on the part of the Servant of the Lord, He bore our iniquities; and this bearing of our sins was an act of love in perfect obedience to the Father. Always, even in His deepest suffering, even when the sweat of agony was pressed from His brow and His bloody sweat dropped in the dust of the garden, He still continued to say: "I come to do Thy will, O God. Not my will, but Thy will be done." And although His blood was pressed out of wounds inflicted by ungodly hands, yet every drop of that blood was willingly, in obedience of love, poured on the altar of God's righteousness and justice. He Who was without sin took the guilt of sin of all His people and the punishment of that sin willingly upon Himself. He, the Person of the Son of God, God of God, Immanuel, Who was powerful to enter into the depth of our suffering as we could never have entered into it, with one offering satisfied perfectly and forever. God indeed made His soul an offering for sin. But when God did so, His Servant willingly sacrificed Himself. He sacrificed His soul. He sacrificed a life that was holy and pure, without sin, and free from corruption. Therefore He could bring the offering that was well-pleasing to the Lord, the trespass offering that was the satisfaction for the sin of all His people.

God bruised Him. He, and not men, ultimately put Him to grief.

At the cross of the Servant of the Lord we behold the manifestation of the eternal good pleasure of Jehovah. That good pleasure shall certainly prosper in the hand of His Servant.

If the cross were only the good pleasure of ungodly men, the accursed tree would be nothing but awful and horrible darkness. Then there would be no positive fruit in the suffering of Christ Jesus our Lord. Then nothing could ever prosper in the hand of the Servant, and all would still be hopeless.

But now it is different. His death is not the end. That it should be the end was indeed the purpose and also the expectation of His enemies. And it would inevitably have been the end, had the cross been the realization of the good pleasure of men. But the good pleasure of God prevails. He prolongs the days of His Servant. He sets the seal of His divine approval upon the trespass offering that was brought on the cross. He hears His prayer. He delivers Him out of the power of the world. He exalts Him out of the depth of death. He causes Him to rise in the glorious, eternal life of the resurrection. Delivered for our transgressions, He is raised for our justification. He is exalted to the highest pinnacle of glory and power and honor. He is exalted as highly as He humiliated Himself deeply. He ascends up on high, taking captivity captive. He receives a name which is above every name, and is clothed with all power and majesty in heaven and on earth at the right hand of the Father. Indeed, His death is not the end. He prolongs His days into ages of ages. And on the basis of His trespass offering He is glorified forever.

Moreover, He shall see His seed. That seed is the same as the seed of the woman which was mentioned in the protevangel in paradise. That seed is the spiritual seed of the elect, His brethren, who were given Him from before the foundation of the world. It is indeed the spiritual seed of the remnant of Israel, but it is also the spiritual seed of the elect from all the nations of the world. Them He draws unto Himself, calling them efficaciously out of sin and death into the fellowship of God's eternal tabernacle. Them He gathers into a church, the house of the living God, by His Spirit and Word. That seed He already beheld as the realization of God's promise to Him in the malefactor on the cross. And that seed He shall gather out of every nation and tribe and tongue, until the last of the elect shall have been called, and the church shall stand in everlasting perfection before the throne of God and the Lamb.

Such is the promise of God to His Suffering Servant when Jehovah makes His soul an offering for sin. Therefore, the pleasure of the Lord shall prosper in the hand of His Servant.

That pleasure of the Lord is the realization of His eternal covenant, the revelation of His divine, triune covenant life, the establishment of His eternal house and tabernacle. And to this purpose the Son of God was ordained in the good pleasure of the Lord to be the Servant of Jehovah, in order, as the Firstborn among many brethren, to dwell in God's house forever. For that reason He must at the head of His brethren, pour out His soul unto death, in order that the foundations of God's eternal house may be established in His own righteousness and justice. For that reason the Servant of the Lord must go under in death, in order out of that death to receive His life, the life of the resurrection in eternal glory. And in that resurrection the Servant of Jehovah hears the answer of the Most High from heaven to what He finally said on the cross, "It is finished." For that reason He is exalted, even at the head of all creation, far above all might and power and dominion and every name that is named in this world and in the world to come. For this purpose the Servant of the Lord receives the promise of the Holy Ghost, in order that He may realize and execute the entire good pleasure of Jehovah and perfect the house and tabernacle of God.

Looking at the accursed tree as the work of man, it presents the darkest moment in all the history of the world.

But viewing that same cross in the light, in the eternal and blessed light of God's eternal good pleasure, we rejoice in it as the revelation of the God of our salvation in Jesus Christ our Lord.

CHAPTER 10

"... and Peter"

Tell his disciples and Peter that he goeth before you
into Galilee: there ye shall see him .... — MARK 16:7.

On the third day Jesus rose again from the dead.

Of the fact of the resurrection as such there were at the time
no witnesses at all. No one was at the grave when the Lord issued
forth from death into the glory of the resurrection. And if there
had been witnesses, they would have seen nothing special. For
Jesus arose in His spiritual, immortal body of glory, which is
invisible to the earthly eye.

But although there were no eyewitnesses of the moment of the
resurrection, yet after the resurrection the risen Lord appeared
to many of His disciples, so that there are indeed many reliable
witnesses that the Lord had risen indeed.

Such witnesses were the women who in the early morning of
that first day of the week went to the sepulchre to finish the
embalming of their Lord's body. They found the grave open.
They saw "the place where the Lord lay." And they heard the
message of the angels that the Lord had risen indeed. And as they
returned from the grave, the Lord appeared unto them. There was
Mary Magdalene, to whom the Lord appeared separately at the
sepulchre, though at first she did not recognize Him. There were
Peter and John, who upon the first report of Mary went to the

grave and carefully inspected it, marveling especially at the linen
clothes and at the place where the Lord lay. Late in the afternoon
of that same third day the Lord appeared to the sojourners
to Emmaus, and they recognized Him by the Word which He
spoke and by the breaking of bread. In the evening of that same
day the Lord manifested Himself to the disciples, except Thomas,
as they were gathered with closed doors for fear of the Jews. A
week later He appeared again unto them, now particularly to
Thomas, who was with them. Then there was the manifestation
to seven disciples at the Sea of Galilee. There were the appearances to Peter alone and to James the brother of the Lord. There
was the manifestation of the risen Lord on a mount in Galilee to
more than five hundred brethren at once. And at the end of those
marvelous forty days He appeared unto them for the last time
when He was taken up from the Mount of Olives. And Paul records in I Cor. 15:8 that He was seen of him also, as of one born
out of due time.

Very early in the morning, as it began to dawn, the women
who had followed Him to Galilee and had been witnesses of Jesus'
burial by Joseph and Nicodemus left their homes and went to the
grave with the purpose of anointing the body of Jesus. It is evident that on the evening of Jesus' burial they had not noticed
that within the sepulchre Joseph and Nicodemus had rather
thoroughly prepared the body of the Lord for His burial, wrapping
it limb by limb in linen clothes, together with sweet spices and
ointments. For the women evidently thought that they had to
complete the task which Joseph and Nicodemus had only begun.
As these women approached the sepulchre of the Lord, they were
affrighted and struck with amazement. For even when they
were still far off, they noticed that the stone was rolled away
from the door of the sepulchre. And when they had arrived at
the grave, they found it empty as far as the body of the Lord
was concerned, although the linen clothes were still there in the
very shape in which they had been wrapped around the body of the
Lord. Then too, there were two angels who addressed them and
informed them that the Lord was not in the sepulchre, but that
He had risen from the dead, and that He would go before them
to Galilee.

We need not be surprised that these women were amazed. They had followed Jesus all the way from Galilee to Jerusalem, and they had been witnesses of His suffering and crucifixion. They had watched the cross unto the very end. And not knowing the Word of the Lord concerning His resurrection, they had conceived of that cross as the end of their Lord. They had been witnesses, too, of the burial, and had seen that the body of the Lord had been hastily prepared by Joseph of Arimathea and Nicodemus for the funeral as far as time before the approaching sabbath had permitted. They had followed in the funeral procession, and had watched where they had laid the Lord. They had returned from the sepulchre sad of heart, overcome with grief, but with the purpose in their hearts of returning to the grave as soon as possible to perform the last service of love on the body of Jesus. The resurrection was far from their mind. They did not think of it. They could not conceive of it. They did not understand the real purpose of the suffering and death of their Master: far less could they conceive of His resurrection.

We can understand, therefore, that they were amazed.

And as their amazement was revealed in their faces, the young man in white, the angel of the Lord whom they saw sitting in the sepulchre, addressed them, and said: "Be not affrighted: ye seek Jesus of Nazareth, which was crucified: he is risen; he is not here: behold the place where they laid him" (Mk. 16:6). And then he addresses them in the words of the text to a small part of which we wish to call your attention in the present chapter: "But go your way, tell his disciples and Peter that he goeth before you into Galilee: there shall ye see him, as he said unto you."

From these words we wish to take only the last two, ". . . and Peter," as the basis for our meditation.

You may perhaps think that this is indeed a very short text to constitute a basis for a discussion in an entire chapter. And brief it is indeed. Nevertheless, I find in these words an ocean of thoughts and a profound comfort for the contrite soul of the people of God in connection with the death and resurrection of our Lord Jesus Christ. For these words certainly assure us, if nothing else, that our sin can never be so dark and horrible, and our condemnation of self can never be so profound and complete, that the risen Lord has no comfort for us and that He is not mindful of His people. As soon as the women had recovered somewhat from their amazement, they must have reported these words especially to Peter. At first they were so filled with consternation that they fled from the grave and said nothing. But soon they must have reported that in the empty grave they found a young man who enjoined them to tell what they saw and heard at the sepulchre to His disciples, and Peter. Perhaps when they meditated on these words, they themselves had been struck by the distinction they made between the disciples and Peter. But when Peter heard these words, he must have been cut to the heart. Mark is the only gospel writer who reports this saying. And Mark undoubtedly received the gospel narrative from the apostle Peter. Peter therefore never forgot the thrill it gave his soul when he heard these words, "Tell his disciples . . . and Peter."

I find in these words of the Lord — for it is evident that they were of Him, and not only of the angel — a three-fold distinction. In the first place, they contain a reminding distinction, reminding the apostle of his great sin of denying the Lord. In the second place, they speak of a loving distinction, assuring the apostle that the Lord still loves him in spite of his denial. And finally, and for that very reason, it is a very comforting distinction that is implied in these words.

It is evident from these words of the angel that the very first thought of the Lord Jesus as He awoke from the sleep of death and issued forth from the rock-hewn sepulchre in the garden of Joseph had been of His disciples. Then too, it is evident from these words that the memory of His disciples had fixed His mind with special attention upon Peter. Hence, He had so enjoined the angel, "When the first visitors approach my vacated sepulchre, let them tell my disciples, and Peter, that I have risen from the dead."

Tell my disciples . . . and Peter.

What a distinction there is in this brief sentence! How simple these words are, yet how pregnant with significance! How it must first of all have cut Peter to the quick to be thus distinquished from the rest of the disciples! Did this message not really imply that he was considered outside of the circle of those who were still worthy to be called the disciples of Jesus Christ? And had Peter not shown himself to be worthy of such distinction? O, how, immediately before the suffering and death of the Master, he had distinguished himself even from the rest of the disciples by his insolent boasting! By that proud and self-confident boasting he had plainly separated himself from the rest of the apostles. At the time the Lord had warned him very seriously, "Simon, Simon, Satan hath desired to sift you as wheat, but I have prayed for thee, that thy faith fail not." But Peter had paid no attention to these words. And again, the Lord had said to all of His disciples: "All ye shall be offended because of me this night: for it is written, I will smite the shepherd, and the sheep of the flock shall be scattered abroad." Again Peter had given no heed to these words of the Lord. He had contradicted the Suffering Servant of Jehovah, and boasted: "Though all men shall be offended because of thee, yet will I never be offended" (Matt. 26:31-33). And when, thereupon, the Lord distinctly addressed Peter and said unto him, "Verily I say unto thee, That this night before the cock crow, thou shalt deny me thrice," the apostle had more emphatically contradicted the Lord and said: "Though I should die with thee, yet will I not deny thee" (Matt. 26:34, 35). It is is true that the rest of the disciples took the same attitude. Nevertheless he had exalted himself openly above all the rest of the disciples when he had maintained, "Though all shall be offended, I shall never be offended." He had cast the last warning to the wind by the boastful exclamation, "I am ready to go with thee into prison and into death." Thus Peter had distinguished himself by his boasting on the eve of the cross.

But as high as had been the imaginary rock of his self-confidence, so awfully deep had become the precipice into which he had cast himself. For also by a most shameful and cowardly denial of the Lord Peter had distinguished himself from the rest of the disciples. In the dark hour of his Master's humiliating trial he had forsaken Him, denied that he ever knew Him, sworn with an oath that he would have nothing to do with Jesus of Nazareth. This denial of the Lord had been avowed not before overwhelming forces of the enemy, not under the pressure of fear and tor-

ment and bodily torture, not after a desperate attempt to remain
faithful to the end, but first of all before a simple maid and upon
the very first inquiry as to his relationship to Jesus of Nazareth.
Thus Peter had denied his Lord in the hour of His bitterest agony
and shame, and had abjured his part with the Lord of glory.

How Peter had distinguished himself!

And now he hears the message of the angel, the message of
the Lord Jesus Himself, delivered by the women, "Tell my
disciples . . . and Peter."

That message must have brought anew before the consciousness
of the disciple the dark night of his unfaithfulness. Indeed Peter
had never forgotten his sin. His heart was deeply wounded because of his shameful denial. Even in that dark night of his fall
the Lord had not forsaken him. He had continued to pray for
His disciple, that his faith fail not. That prayer, the single look
of wounded love the Savior cast upon him in the court of the
palace of the high priest, the crowing of the cock according to
the word of the Master — these all had worked together to save
the disciple from the abyss of destruction into which he would
cast himself. And he had gone out of the court of the high
priest's palace to weep bitterly, in heartfelt sorrow and true
penitence. And we can readily understand that the two or three
days following had brought him no rest. He had been miserable,
and his sin was continually before him. He had certainly not
forgotten. Yet that first message of the risen Lord must have
cut into that heart-wound still more deeply, "Tell my disciples . . .
and Peter."

Is not this always the first distinction which the gospel brings
to us? Does it not always first of all remind us of our sins and
iniquities? And does it not always emphatically single us out
personally? Surely the gospel is not afraid to emphasize our sin,
in order that we may be filled with true sorrow. The gospel does
not hesitate to emphasize our sin again and again, even after we
have beheld our own corruption. It always discovers more hidden
darknesses. The gospel always cuts before it heals.

Thus it was with Peter.

"Tell my disciples . . . and Peter."

What a distinction — a distinction not only reminding the

wretched disciple of his fall and miserable faithlessness, but also carrying a message of infinite love. God's love is always first. It is not only first in time, seeing He loved us from before the foundation of the world. Surely, that too is true. He loved us in His everlasting good pleasure. But it is always first in nature. It is always first in relation to our love to Him. The root, the infinite source of our love is the love of God. He does not love us because we loved Him. Neither did He choose to love us because He foresaw that we would love Him. But freely, sovereignly, for His own name's sake He loved us. We love because He loves first. Our love is rooted in His love. Our love is never more than a reflection of His infinite love, a return of the beam of light it pleases Him to send forth into our hearts. It is never our love, but His, that is first in character, in nature, in principle. And this is the reason why His love remains immutable. This is the reason why the love of God can stand alone. As the apostle John has it in I John 4:10: "Herein is love, not that we loved God, but that he loved us, and sent his Son to be the propitiation for our sins."

O, how marvelous is the love of God!

When His children, chosen by Him from before the foundation of the world, fall into sin and iniquity, become violators of His covenant, enemies of God, and friends of the devil, hateful and hating one another, His love never fails, but remains and conquers, brings the sacrifice of the only begotten, redeems us from the power of darkness into which we have willingly cast ourselves, seeks till it finds, works in irresistible grace till it reaches our hearts and makes us beloved children once more.

And thus it remains.

Even as His love is principally first, so that Christ died for us while we were yet sinners, so His love abides unchangeable in the midst of all our backslidings and unfaithfulnesses, even after we have been made partakers of saving fellowship with Him. O, how many are these weaknesses! We need not, we may not look down upon Peter from the lofty heights of self-conceit as his courage fails him to confess the Lord in the court of the high priest's palace. For in far brighter circumstances than those of the disciple's we often deny Him Who loved us unto death. A thousand times we forfeit His love. And where would we be were His love a response to ours? But always His love stands immovable. Always it is first. Always it seeks till it finds us again. Always the message comes from Him when, as Peter, we exclude ourselves from the circle of His people: "Tell my disciples . . . and Peter." It was of that message that Peter had need.

It was the message of immutable, living, seeking, saving, forgiving love.

As far as Peter's manifestation was concerned, the relation between the Savior and himself had been broken forever. He had severed all bonds of fellowship, and emphatically expressed and declared under oath, till the third time, that he was none of Christ's disciples. There was shame, self-condemnation, darkness, and unspeakable sorrow in his heart. Perhaps he remembered the words of the Lord, "He that denieth me shall be denied by me." What if that Word of the Lord is to be applied to him, who in strongest terms had repeatedly denied Him in the dark night of His suffering and sorrow? Therefore he needs the message of the women. It carries to him the love of Jesus. To the disciples indeed, but also and distinctly to Peter it must be reported that the Lord had risen indeed. Had the message been merely for the disciples the wretched Peter might have concluded still that it was not for him, seeing that he had excluded himself from their fellowship. But now there could be no doubt: the Lord remembered him, the Lord had thought of him as soon as He opened His eyes from the sleep of death, remembered him distinctly, remembered him in love. And realizing the need of His wretched disciple, He had emphasized: "my disciples . . . and Peter. Do not forget to bring him my love!"

Do we not hear the gospel of grace in this message of the risen Lord to Peter? Is it not the gospel of absolutely sovereign grace that is expressed in these words?

Is not that gospel of sovereign grace our only comfort in life and in death?

Who does not know the times when one's sins seem so numerous, one's unfaithfulness so great, one's transgressions so deliberate that he would be inclined to exclude himself from the communion of those who love the Lord Jesus Christ, that he dare not deem himself worthy to be called a disciple anymore, that the rich promises of the gospel he dare not apply to himself? Who does not experience the times when he would have the Lord single him out, call him by name, assure him individually, personally, directly, that He still loves him?

That distinctive message of the gospel is here. It is not only for the heart-broken disciple in his wretchedness, but certainly for every contrite heart, borne down by the load of his sin, that this communication of the Lord to Peter is true: "Tell my disciples . . . and Peter."

What a comfort there was in this message of the Lord to Peter!

How the Lord took special care to convey His love to His wandering sheep in the few words of this message!

Mark you well, He calls him "Peter," not Simon. What a comfort for the disciple even in the choice of that name. He knew that the Lord chose His words carefully, so that each syllable carried its own meaning. He felt that the Lord had intentionally mentioned his new name, the name that denoted what he was not of himself, in his own strength, but what he had become and could only be through the grace of his Lord: the Rock. Just as carefully as the Lord had called him by his old name not many hours before this morning of the resurrection, when all that was of Peter had been hid behind his empty boast, and all that was of the old Simon had revealed itself, so the Lord now calls him in His eternal love and His absolutely sovereign grace by his new name, Peter. Then the Lord had addressed him in the words, "Simon, Simon, Satan hath desired to sift thee as wheat." And Simon had fallen into the abyss of shame and sin. Would that earlier word of Christ now still be true, "Thou art Peter, and upon this rock will I build my church"? Yes: it still is true. The message of the angel assures him of it: "Tell . . . Peter." Those were the words of the Savior. And they carried into the heart of the sorrowful disciple a world full of comfort and cheer. The Lord still considered him the rock, though all that he was by nature had sunken into the mire of sin and faithlessness, though sinful Simon had openly and emphatically belied the gloroius confession that once graced his lips, "Thou art the Christ, the Son of the living God." Though according to his old name he was not worthy to be called a disciple any more, though he had broken

all the bonds of fellowship with his Master, yet he was still the
rock. Still he stood. Still the powerful grace of the Savior up-
held him.

Tell my disciples . . . and Peter.

What is the message which these women must bring to the
disciples and Peter?

That the Lord is risen indeed!

Tell my disciples and Peter that I live, and all that is implied
in the blessed message of the resurrection is wholly for them, for
them all, also for Peter. No, even now on this beautiful morning
of eternal gladness and joy of salvation, the disciples would not
and could not fully understand and fathom what oceans of heavenly joy were opened before them in that glorious message, "The
Lord is risen. He is not in the grave. He is not dead. But He
liveth." It is the message that spells the victory of the cross, the
righteousness of Zion and her redemption, the swallowing up of
all the dark night of sin and transgression. It is the message of our
justification, of complete forgiveness and adoption. It is the beginning of eternal joy, the firstfruits of an entire harvest of redeemed of God in Christ Jesus our Lord.

O, tell my disciples!

And tell Peter!

And tell all that are in darkness because of sin! A great light
has arisen, a light of righteousness and holiness and wisdom and
complete redemption!

Tell them all that their sins are forgiven, however great, however numerous, however shameful they be. The accursed tree and
its blood blotted out Peter's denial, swallowed up all the dark sin
of those whom the Father loved before the foundation of the
world.

Let therefore the message go forth. Let it gladden the hearts
of all who are bowed down. The Lord is risen! Zion, thy righteousness shines forth as the morning. The glory of the risen Lord
is thine, and thine forever.

Such is the glorious comfort of the gospel concerning the Suffering Servant of Jehovah!

And such is the joy of His resurrection!